DOUBLE-EDGED SWORD

DOUBLE-EDGED SWORD

Nuclear Diplomacy in Unequal Conflicts: The United States and China, 1950–1958

APPU K. SOMAN

Praeger Studies in Diplomacy and Strategic Thought

PRAEGER

Westport, Connecticut
London

Library of Congress Cataloging-in-Publication Data

Soman, Appu Kuttan, 1951–
    Double-edged sword : nuclear diplomacy in unequal conflicts : the United States and
China, 1950–1958 / Appu K. Soman.
        p.   cm.—(Praeger studies in diplomacy and strategic thought, ISSN 1076–1543)
    Includes bibliographical references (p.   ) and index.
    ISBN 0–275–96623–2 (alk. paper)
    1. Nuclear weapons—United States.   2. Nuclear weapons—China.   3. United
States—Foreign relations—China.   4. China—Foreign relations—United States.
5. United States—Foreign relations—1945–1989.   6. China—Foreign relations—1949–
1976.   I. Title.   II. Series.
UA23.S527   2000
355.02'17'0973—dc21   99–027719

British Library Cataloguing in Publication Data is available.

Library of Congress Catalog Card Number: 99–027719
ISBN: 0–275–96623–2
ISSN: 1076–1543

First published in 2000

Praeger Publishers, 88 Post Road West, Westport, CT 06881
An imprint of Greenwood Publishing Group, Inc.
www.praeger.com

Printed in the United States of America

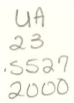

Contents

Preface

This is a study of the role of nuclear weapons in the American policy toward China in the 1950s. I have followed a traditionalist approach, focusing exclusively on power as the determining factor in inter-state relations. Factors such as gender, race, and culture may well have played a significant role in the Sino-US confrontations I analyze. However, apart from the odd comment, I did not find very persuasive evidence of their role. Nor, I must confess, did I look for evidence of such influences with very great diligence.

This study draws on the works of other scholars who have studied the Korean War and the Taiwan Strait crises of the 1950s. To a significant degree, it also benefitted from the release of new US documents. It must, however, be kept in mind that major gaps remain in archival sources. The lack of access to substantial volumes of documentation has all along made the task of historians of American foreign relations difficult. The problem is particularly acute when the topic relates to nuclear weapons.

This manuscript was at the copy editing stage when Robert Norris, William Arkin, and William Burr disclosed in an article in the November/December 1999 issue of *The Bulletin of the Atomic Scientists* that the United States had stored nuclear weapons in several countries in the 1950s. Appendix B of a partially declassified US government document, titled "History of the Custody and Deployment of Nuclear Weapons: July 1945 through September 1977," on which the article was based, listed the US overseas bases and countries in which, starting in 1950, the United States had prepositioned complete nuclear weapons and non-nuclear components of such weapons. While releasing the document, Pentagon officials had deleted the names of several countries from the list. However, the authors correctly deduced the identity of 25 out of the 27 locations of US overseas nuclear stockpiles.[1] It turns out that the United States had moved complete nuclear weapons to Okinawa and non-nuclear components to Japan during December 1954–February 1955, only weeks before the Eisenhower administration held out nuclear threats against China. Nuclear weapons were also carried by several US naval vessels stationed in the Pacific.

The new evidence called for some hasty revisions of the manuscript, but obviously the last word has not been said on the topic of US nuclear diplomacy toward China. Already, the new documentation calls into question significant areas of nuclear history relating to Japan and Europe. The claims in this study on the Sino-American crises are made with the full understanding that the release of even a single new document can substantially challenge them.

Generous assistance by many individuals and institutions made this study possible. At Vanderbilt University, I can never thank Thomas Schwartz enough for all he did to help me. His guidance was valuable in planning this study, conducting research for it, writing it, and revising it. Without his encouragement and unfailing support, I honestly do not know how I could have completed it. He patiently read more drafts of this manuscript than I can remember and offered insightful comments and suggestions. To Peter Zarrow, too, I owe a great deal. He also read several drafts and offered very valuable comments and advice. Sam McSeveney, Michael Bess, Paul Conkin, and David Bartlett also offered helpful advice. Lewis Perry and James Epstein, in their capacity as director of graduate studies, went out of their way to make things easy for me. Ernest May, Akira Iriye, Bruce Cumings, and Ode Arne Westad read an earlier draft and gave me useful comments on it. At the Institute for Defense and Disarmament Studies, Randall Forsberg was a source of great encouragement. She too read drafts of the manuscript and gave me extremely insightful comments. She also generously allowed me full use of the institute's facilities.

Vanderbilt University, the Harry S. Truman Library Foundation, the Eisenhower Institute of World Affairs, and the Institute for the Study of World Politics offered generous financial help that made the research on this project possible. I must also thank the staff of the Jean and Alexander Heard Library at Vanderbilt, the Harry S. Truman Presidential Library, the Dwight D. Eisenhower Presidential Library, the National Archives and Records Administration, the Public Records Office in London, the Seeley Mudd Library at Princeton, the Butler Library at Columbia, and the Hoover Institution at Stanford for their assistance. An earlier version of Chapter 5 was published as an essay in the *Journal of American-East Asian Relations*, winter 1994. I am grateful to Imprint Publications, Inc.

for permission to reprint it. At Praeger, it has been a pleasure to work with Heather Staines and John Donohue.

My wife's unstinted support made it possible for me to devote the time necessary to complete this project. My children cheerfully refrained from making demands on my time that they had a right to. My parents, brothers, and sisters in India were always a source of support. My mother and father passed away before they could see this in print. This book is dedicated to them.

NOTE

1. Robert Norris, William Arkin, and William Burr, "Where They Were," *The Bulletin of the Atomic Scientists* (November/December 1999); Office of the Assistant to the Secretary of Defense (Atomic Energy), "History of the Custody and Deployment of Nuclear Weapons: July 1945 through September 1977," and Appendix B to this document, "Chronology Deployment by Country 1951–1977," available on the National Security Archive (NSA) web site. The "History of the Custody and Deployment of Nuclear Weapons" is available at URL www.gwu.edu/~nsarchiv/news/19991020/04–01.html and will be cited hereafter as "History of the Custody and Deployment of Nuclear Weapons," NSA web site. Appendix B is available at URL www.gwu.edu/~nsarchiv/news/19991020/04–46.html and will be cited hereafter as "Deployment by Country 1951–1977," NSA web site.

Norris et al. could not identify one of the countries in which US nuclear weapons were stored and they mistakenly identified Iceland as one of the locations. The Pentagon, breaking its long-standing policy of neither confirming nor denying the existence of US nuclear weapons in foreign countries, denied that Iceland was one of the countries in the list. The authors subsequently concluded that the two locations were the Japanese islands of Iwo Jima and Chichi Jima. Robert Norris, William Arkin, and William Burr, "How Much Did Japan Know?" *The Bulletin of the Atomic Scientists* (January/February 2000).

Abbreviations

AEC	Atomic Energy Commission
AFSWP	Armed Forces Special Weapons Project
AWF	Ann Whitman File
CCP	Chinese Communist Party
CIA	Central Intelligence Agency
CINFE	Commander-in-Chief, Far East
CINPAC	Commander-in-Chief, Pacific
CMC	Central Military Commission
CNO	Chief of Naval Operations
CPV	Chinese People's Volunteers
CWIHP	Cold War International History Project
DEPL	Dwight Eisenhower Presidential Library
DMZ	Demilitarized Zone
DOS	Department of State
FECOM	Far East Command
FMC	Fujian Military Command
FRUS	*Foreign Relations of the United States*
HSTL	Harry S. Truman Library
IAEA	International Atomic Energy Agency
ICBM	Intercontinental Ballistic Missile
JCS	Joint Chiefs of Staff
JSPC	Joint Strategic Plans Committee

JSSC	Joint Strategic Survey Committee
MAAG	Military Assistance and Advisory Group
NA	National Archives
NATO	North Atlantic Treaty Organization
NEBDA	Northeast Border Defense Army
NNRC	Neutral Nations Repatriation Commission
NPT	Nonproliferation Treaty
NSC	National Security Council
OSANSA	Office of the Special Assistant for National Security Affairs
OSS	Office of Strategic Services
PDD	Presidential Decision Directive
PLA	People's Liberation Army
POW	Prisoner of War
PPS	Policy Planning Staff
PRC	People's Republic of China
PRO	Public Records Office
PSF	President's Secretary's File
RG	Record Group
RJCS	Records of the Joint Chiefs of Staff
ROC	Republic of China
ROK	Republic of Korea
SAC	Strategic Air Command
SIOP	Single Integrated Operational Plan
SNIE	Special National Intelligence Estimate
StratCom	Strategic Command
SWPS	Strategic War Planning System
UN	United Nations
WHCF	White House Central File
WMD	Weapons of Mass Destruction

CHAPTER 1

Introduction

During his visit to China in June 1998, President William Jefferson Clinton said at a panel discussion with Chinese intellectuals in Shanghai that "we don't support independence for Taiwan, or two Chinas, or one Taiwan–one China. And we don't believe that Taiwan should be a member in any organization for which statehood is a requirement."[1] Clinton thus became the first US president to enunciate what China calls the "three no's": no support for a two-China policy, no independence for Taiwan, and no membership for Taiwan in international organizations.

Clinton's statement was the culmination of a new approach his administration adopted toward China in the aftermath of a crisis in the Taiwan Strait early in 1996. Throughout the 1950s and 1960s, the United States had an explicit policy of defending Taiwan from a possible Chinese invasion. Successive administrations had used American diplomatic resources to the fullest to keep the Republic of China (ROC) in Taiwan in international organizations and the communist-led People's Republic of China (PRC) in mainland China out of such organizations. The United States confronted China twice in the Taiwan Strait in the 1950s with the avowed aim of defending the ROC against the PRC. After the Sino-US rapprochement in 1971, ambiguity was the hallmark of official US pronouncements on Taiwan. However, the United States remained committed to preventing a forcible attempt by China to take over Taiwan. The US intervention in the Taiwan Strait in 1996 was, in many ways, reminiscent of US interventions in the area in the 1950s.

What had brought about the dramatic change in policy by the Clinton administration was a new element in Sino-US confrontations, placed in stark relief by China's resort to a tactic that had hitherto been an American monopoly in such confrontations. In the midst of the crisis in January 1996, US diplomat Charles W. Freeman, Jr. told Chinese officials in Beijing that in the event of a Chinese attack on Taiwan, "you'll get a military reaction from the United States." A senior Chinese general, later identified as the deputy chief of staff of the People's Liberation Army (PLA), Lieutenant General Xiong Guangkai, replied, "In the 1950s, you three times threatened nuclear strikes on China, and you could do that because we couldn't hit back. Now we can. So you are not going to threaten us again because, in the end, you care a lot more about Los Angeles than Taipei."[2]

The three US nuclear threats against China to which General Xiong referred took place in the Korean War and the Taiwan Strait crises of 1954–1955 and 1958. In the 1950s, communist China was the great demon for the United States. Washington enforced strict export controls on China by the Western alliance. The United States had no diplomatic relations with the PRC and for most of the decade refused even to talk to the Chinese. Instead of exerting direct military pressure on China after the Korean War, the Eisenhower administration used an "unleashed" ROC under the Nationalist leader Chiang Kai-shek in Taiwan to contain communist China. US-supported Nationalist covert actions and the prospect of an invasion by Chiang's forces kept China under a continuous military threat. If the United States did not call China a rogue state, it was only because the expression was not in vogue then.

A story in *Life* early in 1956, based on an interview with John Foster Dulles, secretary of state under then President Dwight D. Eisenhower, conveyed the essence of the US policy toward the PRC during the 1950s. The report detailed Dulles's account of how the Eisenhower administration had secured an armistice in the Korean War and forestalled communist Chinese aggression in Indochina and the Taiwan Strait by threatening the use of nuclear weapons. Dulles acknowledged that "Nobody is able to prove mathematically that it was the policy of deterrence which brought the Korean War to an end and which kept the Chinese from sending the Red armies into Indochina, or that it has finally stopped them in Formosa." However, he claimed, "it is a pretty fair inference that it has." A complacent Dulles went on to assert:

The ability to get to the verge [of war] without getting into the war is the necessary art. If you cannot master it, you inevitably get into war. If you try to run away from it, if you are scared to go to the brink, you are lost. We have had to look it square in the face. . . . We walked to the brink and we looked it in the face.[3]

With characteristic lack of subtlety, Dulles was claiming that ownership of the world's greatest nuclear arsenal enabled the United States to have its way in adversarial relations with non-nuclear opponents. For one who had strongly criticized—on moral grounds—President Harry S. Truman's decision to drop atom bombs on Japan, this was indeed a strange position to take. As the chairman of the Commission on a Just and Durable Peace, an affiliate of the Federal Council of the Churches of Christ in America, Dulles had issued a public appeal to Truman on 10 August 1945 to suspend the atomic bombing of Japan so that Japanese leaders would have time to accept the surrender terms. Dulles warned that

If we, a professedly Christian nation, feel morally free to use atomic energy in that way, men elsewhere will accept that verdict. Atomic weapons will be looked upon as a normal part of the arsenal of war and the stage will be set for the sudden and final destruction of mankind.

If the possessors of atomic technology did not exercise "self-restraint and sense of responsibility," Dulles continued, it "might make this planet uninhabitable."[4] Five months later, Dulles warned that American failure to transfer the control of atomic weapons to "the dictates of . . . world opinion" would "wholly destroy our moral influence in the world and seriously set back the possibility of developing the greater fellowship we need." The United States would then live in a world in which, when war occurs, "nations avail themselves of any weapons which they think will make the difference between victory and defeat."[5]

Only days before Eisenhower assumed the presidency, a committee chaired by physicist J. Robert Oppenheimer had submitted a report that concluded that

In a world in which atomic war could only bring general catastrophe, it cannot be anything but dangerous that American policy should have no other alternative but a recourse to the atom as a response to many possible emergencies. . . . *[F]or us it remains a first necessity that the number of atomic wars be zero.* (emphasis added)[6]

In an effort to strike a balance between US global commitments and the need to avoid excessive strains on the US economy, however, the New Look national security policy of the Eisenhower administration had come to depend more and more on atomic weapons. This policy relied on strategic nuclear weapons to deal with a general war and on local forces backed by American air and naval forces equipped with tactical nuclear weapons to deal with regional crises. The way Dulles had articulated this policy, it came to be publicly dubbed the doctrine of "massive re-taliation," creating serious public relations problems for the administration.[7]

The glorification of nuclear saber rattling by Dulles popularized the expression "brinkmanship." Journalist James Reston caustically commented that "Dulles has added something new to the art of diplomatic blundering"—"the planned mistake." Reston explained, "He [Dulles] doesn't stumble into booby traps, he digs them to size, studies them carefully, and then jumps."[8] Predictably, the interview also raised a public uproar. Sherman Adams, Eisenhower's White House chief of staff, recalled in his memoirs that the article "stirred up one of the major controversial storms of the whole Eisenhower administration." Democratic Party leader Adlai Stevenson charged that Dulles "was willing to play Russian roulette with the life of our nation." Senator Hubert Humphrey complained that what Dulles had told the interviewer was "diametrically opposed" to what he had earlier testified before the Senate Foreign Relations Committee. Vice President Richard Nixon, however, dismissed the controversy as a "tempest in a teapot."[9]

Eisenhower had, for some time, felt the need to counter what he called a widespread feeling "that we're skunks, saber-rattlers and warmongers."[10] The Dulles interview did not come as a welcome development to the president. He gamely defended Dulles at a press conference as "the best Secretary of State" he had ever seen, but added that he did not know whether Dulles or the author of the article had used the "unfortunate expressions." Eisenhower also took objection to public disclosures of discussions in the National Security Council (NSC). The press interpreted Eisenhower's remarks as a "rebuke" of his secretary of state.[11] By suggesting that *someone* had used unfortunate expressions, Adams recalled, Eisenhower was expressing his disapproval of the claims made in the article.[12] The verdict of historians was even harsher. The Dulles interview became one more example of the "dangerous tendency toward overstatement—he was the champion of 'brinkmanship' and 'massive retaliation'—that caused distrust among America's allies and bewilderment among her potential adversaries," which led historians a generation later to rank Dulles among the five worst American secretaries of state.[13] However, in his own memoirs—particularly in his accounts of the handling of the Korean War armistice negotiations and the Taiwan Strait crises—Eisenhower himself went a long way toward lending credence to the claims Dulles made.[14]

The fact that the claims Dulles made came from a serving American secretary of state, and not communist propagandists or left-wing scholars, gave them added credibility. The sweeping claims of Dulles and Eisenhower about the success of the American nuclear threats raise fundamental questions about the role of nuclear weapons in the US China policy. They also raise broader questions about the role these weapons played in American foreign policy.

After 1949, US-Soviet confrontation was circumscribed by mutual nuclear deterrence. Strategic thought in the United States has largely fo-cused on nuclear deterrence and nuclear strategy in the context of US-Soviet relations. The enormous literature spawned by works on this topic has become a major subfield of international security studies.[15] The superpower nuclear stalemate—the result of mutual assured destruc-tion—has colored the debate on the utility of nuclear weapons and given rise to a misconception that nuclear weapons confer no great diplomatic or political benefit other than to deter an all-out nuclear attack by a nuclear adversary. Setting the tone, Bernard Brodie commented, in one of the earliest analyses of the implications of the new weapon, "Thus far the chief purpose of our military establishment has been to win war. From now on its chief purpose must be to avert them. It can have almost no other useful purpose."[16] John Mueller argues that

while nuclear weapons may have substantially influenced political rhetoric, pub-lic discourse, and defense planning, it is not at all clear that they have had a significant impact on the history of world affairs since World War II. . . . The postwar world might well have turned out much the same even in the absence of nuclear weapons. . . . Nor do the weapons seem to have been the crucial de-terminants of Cold War developments, of alliance patterns, or of the way major powers have behaved in crises.[17]

The response to this stand by Robert Jervis, who argues the opposite case, also limits itself to nuclear weapons in the superpower context.[18] Michael Mandelbaum claims that "If the United States drew any political benefits from its early advantage [over the Soviet Union in nuclear weap-ons], it is hard to see what it was."[19]

Some scholars who have studied instances of nuclear threats against non-nuclear states have also discounted the utility of nuclear weapons in crises other than superpower nuclear standoffs.[20] Morton Halperin argues in a 1987 study that a "myth" has existed in the American "na-tional security bureaucracy" about the diplomatic utility of nuclear weapons. The bureaucracy's "unwarranted faith" in nuclear weapons, in Halperin's view, "is the greatest single obstacle" to reducing American dependence on nuclear weapons. Halperin lists 19 crises involving either consideration of use of nuclear weapons or threats to use them. He con-cludes that "the perception that nuclear threats have been central to their resolution is exaggerated in some cases and entirely wrong in others." The "critical variables," Halperin argues, were factors such as the bal-ance of conventional forces, diplomacy, and the stakes involved.[21]

Halperin's analysis, however, focuses rather narrowly on foreign pol-icy decision making and hence leaves out the most powerful constitu-ency that *has* benefitted from atomic weapons—the United States' top political leadership. American political leaders, whether in or out of office, seem to have attributed a great deal more weight to nuclear weapons than do political scientists. Many of them either gave some thought to using these weapons in one form or another in crisis situations while in office, or threatened adversaries with atomic weapons in crisis situations, or at least, after they left office, claimed having won diplomatic victories by threatening to use them. Halperin is right that American presidents seldom gave serious thought to using nuclear weapons to *win* battlefield victories and that their aim was "to persuade the adversary to sue for peace."[22] But it was precisely because nuclear weapons gave American presidents the power to force adversaries to sue for peace, without having to resort to any actual use of force with all of the attendant risks and problems, that these weapons played some, often critical, role in *every* postwar US administration.

In some cases, the claims of successful nuclear diplomacy were, in all likelihood, not true. In some of the episodes involving nuclear threats, such threats, it turns out, might not have been the principal factor in determining the outcome. In some cases, the outcomes were quite different from the ones desired by American leaders while making nuclear threats. Nevertheless, most American presidents resorted to nuclear diplomacy with the declared aim of advancing American interests.[23] As historian Martin Sherwin points out, "Trapped between the reality of nuclear weapons and the politics of the Cold War, our political leaders have been increasingly attracted to the nuclear option since 1945."[24]

Thus there is a clear divergence between what armchair strategists posit about the utility of nuclear weapons and the actions of leaders who had to make real-life decisions involving nuclear weapons. This dichotomy between theory and practice has arisen not so much out of preoccupation with the mutual assured destruction framework by the theorists but because of an incomplete examination of the history of nuclear threats against non-nuclear adversaries. As this study will show, the diplomatic and political costs involved in making nuclear threats in the midst of conflicts were considerable. If, nevertheless, successive US leaders resorted to nuclear threats, the fact that these leaders perceived a net political benefit from nuclear threats over and above the costs involved must have had a great deal to do with it. The possession of the world's most powerful nuclear arsenal enabled American presidents to be seen, as Eisenhower fancied himself, as "the calm silent strong man with a gun on his hip."[25] Nuclear capability enabled American leaders to project this image of themselves. In the Cold War era, this image generally translated into votes and high approval ratings.

Among the cases Halperin lists, only one—the 1969–1970 Sino-Soviet conflict—did not involve the United States.[26] Out of the remaining 18 cases, 12 pitted the United States against non-nuclear adversaries. In some of these cases, the United States considered using atomic weapons.

In some others, it made either explicit or veiled threats to use them. A few are merely what Richard Betts calls cases of "retrospective bravado of former presidents," in which [American presidents] out of office claimed that they had scored diplomatic victories by threatening non-nuclear states with atomic weapons.[27] Out of the cases involving American nuclear threats against non-nuclear states, two involved the Soviet Union before it acquired nuclear capability; three involved China; three involved North Vietnam (one each by the Eisenhower, Johnson, and Nixon administrations); two involved North Korea (after the Korean War); and one involved India.

Nuclear threats played only a marginal, if any, role in the crises other than the three involving China. Throughout the Korean War, the United States either made atomic threats against China or almost continuously kept under consideration actual use of atomic weapons in the war. [In the two Taiwan Strait crises with China, nuclear threats played a central role. The Korean War and the two Taiwan Strait crises are, therefore, in a different category from the other cases involving a nuclear power and its non-nuclear adversary.]

This study examines American nuclear diplomacy toward China in the Korean War and the two Taiwan Strait crises, with the aim of assessing the diplomatic and political utility of nuclear weapons in these confrontations. By "utility," it is not meant that the United States achieved the outcomes it desired. The focus is on how atomic capability enabled American presidents to make the choices that they desired in critical situations in these episodes, but which they would have been reluctant, or unable, to make in the absence of atomic weapons.

Focus of the Book

Scholars have used concepts such as deterrence and compellence as analytical tools to study cases of nuclear threats in crisis situations.[28] In the layman's terms used by Daniel Ellsberg, what happened in these cases was that "Again and again, generally in secret from the American public, US nuclear weapons *have* been used . . . in the precise way that a gun is used when you point it at someone's head in a direct confrontation, whether or not the trigger is pulled."[29] Richard Betts uses the concept "nuclear blackmail" in his study of cases involving threats to use nuclear weapons. He uses it to mean "coercion by the threat of punishment, a threat designed either to deter or to compel action by the opponent."[30]

[This study uses the concept of "nuclear diplomacy," already widely used by historians, to analyze the use of nuclear capability as an instrument to achieve foreign policy goals in confrontations with a non-nuclear adversary through overt or veiled threats of nuclear attacks.] Sherwin has defined nuclear diplomacy as "either the overt diplomatic or military brandishing of atomic weapons for the purpose of securing foreign policy objectives, or a covert diplomatic strategy based upon considerations related to atomic weapons."[31]

As historians of American foreign relations have long recognized, nuclear weapons have been enormously influential in American foreign policy decisions from the beginning of the atomic age. How decisive the atom bomb was in advancing American postwar interests becomes forcefully clear from a memorandum Truman received from William Donovan, Director of the Office of Strategic Services (OSS), just days after he took over the presidency. The memorandum, which does not display any knowledge of the US atomic weapons program, set out in stark terms the implications of the formidable power the Soviet Union had come to possess by the end of World War II for postwar American foreign policy. The most optimistic scenario for the United States, the OSS analysis concluded, was that:

If Russia is offered the most elaborate guarantees, with the creation of organs for their enforcement, she may content herself with a sphere of influence in Eastern Europe and in the northern borderlands of China, and with an influence roughly equal to that of the Western Powers in Germany, China, and Japan, and may choose to devote herself to internal development and improvement of the living standard.

Obtaining even this outcome would require timely American initiatives for compromising with the Soviet Union. However, if compromises failed and the USSR united the resources of Asia and Europe under its control by gaining a dominant influence over Germany and China, it could "outbuild us in every phase of military production" within a generation. "In the easily foreseeable future," therefore, "Russia may well outrank even the United States in military potential." The consequences of such an eventuality were grave: "*[I]f the military authorities in the years to come feel the western [sic] democracies cannot stand against Russia, it may become necessary to fall back upon our hemispheric defense*" (emphasis added). Western Europe would have to be written off. "This," the OSS study summed up, "is the crux of the whole problem, and it dictates the urgent necessity of taking all measures to prevent or delay the domination of Europe and/or Asia by a power already so formidable as Russia."[32]

One can only speculate how the early postwar years would have turned out in the absence of nuclear weapons in American hands. In any case, the atom bomb came in the nick of time for Truman to secure an outcome totally unrecognizable from the picture drawn by the OSS. Backed by what historian Gregg Herken calls the "winning weapon," Truman boldly set forth on the path of containment, instead of accommodation, with the Soviet Union.[33] By the late 1940s, the Cold War lines were clearly drawn in Europe. The Truman Doctrine, the Marshall Plan, and the creation of the North Atlantic Treaty Organization (NATO) made clear the American determination not to countenance any more communist advance in Europe, a theater that Washington considered vital for American national security. The Berlin crisis of 1948 further demonstrated the determination of the Western alliance to contain communism in Europe.

In the next 10 years, the focus of the Cold War shifted eastward. Between the Berlin crises of 1948 and 1958, East Asia became the principal battleground of the United States' struggle against international communism. With the establishment of a communist government in the mainland of China in 1949, China turned from a friend and wartime ally of the United States into an enemy whose expansion into areas vital to the United States had, in Washington's eyes, to be curtailed. The "loss of China" to communism became, for a time, the most bitter and divisive issue in American domestic politics. The "Red Scare" gave the Truman administration no leeway in normalizing relations with the PRC. After toying with the idea of an accommodation with the communist regime, the Truman administration decided, in the wake of the Korean War, to deny Taiwan to the communists. American intervention to defend Taiwan made the United States a direct participant in the Chinese civil war. American, and later Chinese, intervention in the Korean War led to a long, drawn-out, bitter war between the two countries. After this war ended, American opposition to China's goal of taking the Chinese civil war to its logical conclusion by "liberating" Taiwan led to Sino-American confrontations in the Taiwan Strait area.

The Sino-American confrontations began at a critical phase in the evolution of American national security policy. The advent of atomic weapons heralded a revolution in warfare. The imbalance between the global military commitments the Truman administration decided to take on and the resources available to create and maintain the level of conventional forces required to back up these commitments strengthened the Truman administration's reliance on the deterrent power of atomic weapons. By the late 1940s, US military commitments included the defense of Western Europe and Japan. American global war plans also called for the defense of the Middle East from a Soviet invasion as well as the defense of a chain of military bases spanning the globe. The country, however, did not have the conventional forces required to fulfill these tasks. For an America whose military resources were thus stretched thin, nuclear capability became the principal weapon in its policy of opposing communist China.

Other than the threat to American security perceived from the dramatic increases in Soviet nuclear capability, the confrontation with China was the most important national security problem the United States faced in this period. The Korean War was the most serious international conflict in the decade of the 1950s. The Taiwan Strait crises of 1954–1955 and 1958 became, with the exception of the Suez crisis of 1956, the most serious international crises in the period between the Korean War and the Cuban missile crisis of 1962. The Korean War and the two Taiwan Strait crises were the three most critical international crises in the 1950s in which the United States was a principal participant. Nuclear diplomacy occupied a central role in the American policy in each of these crises. American nuclear diplomacy in its confrontations with China is, therefore, an important topic in the history of the Cold War as well as the history of American foreign relations.

The Sino-US confrontations in the 1950s have all received significant scholarly attention in recent years, comprised of case studies of the individual episodes and works covering Sino-US relations in the decade as a whole. Some of these studies have drawn on declassified US government documents in American archives and the partially available Chinese and ex-Soviet archives. These studies have helped clear up many of the misconceptions about these episodes created by the claims of former administration officials.[34] However, there is no book-length study that treats American nuclear diplomacy against China in the eight years from 1950 to 1958 as a whole.

A comprehensive study of the American nuclear diplomacy would achieve three aims. In the first place, piecemeal studies of these cases raise, but fail to answer, a variety of questions with broader implications for Sino-American relations than those involved in the episodes themselves. Perhaps the most important questions are, what role did nuclear diplomacy play in the American decision making at critical junctures in these episodes, and in the American policy toward China in this period? Did threatening a non-nuclear China with nuclear attacks produce the outcomes that the world's premier nuclear power desired? In other words, did China yield on vital issues when confronted with the possibility that resistance would invite destruction of its cities and production centers through American nuclear strikes? What constrained the United States from initiating nuclear war against China? A detailed study of the American nuclear diplomacy that would focus on the stakes, costs, and outcomes involved would go a long way toward answering these questions. Second, what long-term impact did the US nuclear diplomacy in these confrontations have on US-China relations? This is particularly significant in view of the recent Chinese attempts to play the nuclear card.

Third, the lessons of the American nuclear diplomacy against China are relevant in evaluating the post–Cold War US nuclear policy that has institutionalized nuclear diplomacy toward non-nuclear states. Since Halperin's study, apart from the Chinese nuclear threat against the United States, there have been four more cases of American threats to use atomic weapons against non-nuclear states: against Iraq by the Bush administration in the Gulf War and by the Clinton administration during the 1997–1998 crisis over United Nations (UN) inspections; and against North Korea in 1993–1994 and against Libya in 1996, both by the Clinton administration. President Clinton, with three cases, thus has the dubious distinction of having practiced nuclear diplomacy toward non-nuclear adversaries more often than any other leader in history.[35]

In addition, the Clinton administration has put into place what one might call, in keeping with the times, "virtual nuclear diplomacy," in the form of a standing threat to use nuclear weapons against non-nuclear adversaries very similar to the massive retaliation doctrine of the Eisenhower administration.[36] According to a study by Hans Kristensen based on partially declassified American documents, a review of the US nuclear policy for the 1990s begun by the Bush administration culminated in a revamped American nuclear doctrine. Clinton's presidential decision directive (PDD) 60 issued in November 1997, which incorporates the new doctrine, calls for planning for the use of nuclear weapons against states possessing chemical, biological, or radiological weapons and the means for their delivery.[37] This directive goes against formal international commitments given by the United States in the context of non-proliferation. Critics of the new policy have argued that PDD 60 would undercut a primary national security goal of the administration—curbing the proliferation of weapons of mass destruction. Further, General Eugene Habiger, commander of the US Strategic Command (the successor to the Strategic Air Command), stated in a meeting with reporters that, "We now have a policy that's articulated that says nuclear weapons will be used in response to rogue states using weapons of mass destruction."[38] An understanding of the factors that had taught the Eisenhower administration the demerits of nuclear diplomacy toward non-nuclear states will help place in its historical context the revival in the post–Cold War era of this once discredited tool.

Although this study is not an international history of the Sino-American crises of the 1950s, it does draw on works based on the considerable volume of documentary material that has come out of China and Russia in recent years. While questions have cropped up about the authenticity of some of these sources, a considerable part of them composed of memoirs and oral histories of fairly junior-level officials now in very advanced age, these new materials do help in understanding some key Chinese and Soviet actions during the Korean War and the Taiwan Strait crises.[39] It should be remembered, however, that these sources fall far short of the level of American documentation on these episodes.

Chapter 2 will lay out the background of the Sino-US confrontations. It will briefly trace the role of nuclear diplomacy in the US national security policy and the domestic considerations that made it difficult for the Truman administration not to intervene in the Korean War. The next three chapters will then discuss US nuclear diplomacy during each of the three crises in which the United States confronted communist China—the Korean War and the Taiwan Strait crises of 1954–1955 and 1958. Chapter 6 will attempt to answer the broader questions raised here.

NOTES

1. Text from the White House website.

2. *Washington Post*, 21 June 1998. Freeman later asserted that the conversation was misinterpreted by the press. "It was in the context of deterrence and in retaliation for the United States's first use of nuclear weapons," he clarified. *Washington Times*, 18 December 1996.

3. James Shepley, "How Dulles Averted War," *Life* (16 January 1956).

4. Press Release, 10 August 1945, Dulles Papers, Box 26, "Re Atomic Weapons," Seeley Mudd Library, Princeton University.

5. Quoted in Fred Kaplan, *The Wizards of Armageddon* (Stanford, CA: Stanford University Press, 1991), 179. Three years later, Dulles's view on atomic weapons had undergone a remarkable transformation. In October 1948, Dulles told General George C. Marshall, then secretary of state, that the "American people would execute you if you did not use the bomb in the event of war." On 2 February 1951, Dulles assured a Japanese audience that the United States would defend Japan by threatening would-be aggressors with "a striking power, the intensity of which defies imagination." Ibid., 178.

6. US Department of State, *Foreign Relations of the United States, 1952–1954, Vol. II* (Washington, DC: US Government Printing Office, 1984), 1070–73 (hereafter cited as *FRUS*, followed by year and volume number). Eisenhower had expressed a high opinion of the report in the National Security Council (NSC) meeting on 18 February 1953 and had requested all members of the NSC to study it. Ibid., 1107.

7. See Chapter 2.

8. *New York Times*, 16 January 1956.

9. Sherman Adams, *First Hand Report: The Story of the Eisenhower Administration* (New York: Harper & Brothers, 1961), 117; *New York Times*, 15 January 1956. See also *New York Times*, 12 and 13 January 1956, for coverage of the reaction to the Dulles interview.

10. Memo of 195th NSC meeting, 6 May 1954, *FRUS 1952–54, II*, 1425–28.

11. *New York Times*, 20 January 1956.

12. Adams, *First Hand Report*, 119–20.

13. David L. Porter, "The Ten Best Secretaries of State and the Five Worst," in William D. Pederson and Ann M. MacLaurin (eds.), *The Rating Game in American Politics: An Interdisciplinary Approach* (New York: Irvington Publishers, 1987), 90.

14. Dwight D. Eisenhower, *The White House Years, Vol. I: Mandate for Change, 1953–1956* (Garden City, NY: Doubleday & Co., 1963).

15. For an insightful overview of American strategic thought dealing with nu-

clear weapons, see Marc Trachtenberg, *History and Strategy* (Princeton, NJ: Princeton University Press, 1991).

16. Bernard Brodie, "Implications for Military Policy," in Bernard Brodie (ed.), *The Absolute Weapon: Atomic Power and World Order* (New York: Harcourt, Brace and Company, 1946), 76.

17. John Mueller, "The Essential Irrelevance of Nuclear Weapons," *International Security* (Fall 1988), 56. Mueller concludes that atomic weapons had no impact on the Korean War and the two Taiwan Strait crises either. Ibid., 67–68.

18. Robert Jervis, "The Political Effects of Nuclear Weapons: A Comment," *International Security* (Fall 1988). See also Robert Jervis, *The Meaning of the Nuclear Revolution: Statecraft and the Prospect of Armageddon* (Ithaca, NY: Cornell University Press, 1989).

19. Michael Mandelbaum, "International Stability and Nuclear Order: The First Nuclear Regime," in David C. Gompert et al. (eds.), *Nuclear Weapons and World Politics: Alternatives for the Future* (New York: McGraw-Hill, 1977), 43. See also Michael Mandelbaum, *The Nuclear Revolution: International Politics before and after Hiroshima* (Cambridge: Cambridge University Press, 1981).

20. McGeorge Bundy, "The Unimpressive Record of Nuclear Diplomacy," in Gwyn Prins (ed.), *The Choice: Nuclear Weapons versus Stability* (London: Chatto Windus, 1984).

21. Morton H. Halperin, *Nuclear Fallacy: Dispelling the Myth of Nuclear Strategy* (Cambridge, MA: Ballinger Publishing Company, 1987), 23–25.

22. Ibid., 25.

23. The perception of diplomatic utility has not always been dictated by actual lessons from earlier experiences. General Maxwell Taylor points out, after listing the reasons for not using atomic weapons in the Korean War (such as unsuitable terrain, fear of atomic retaliation against UN targets, opposition of allies, fear of giving up the surprise effect of atomic weapons in a peripheral theater), that "in the US, the ultimate effect of the Korean experience, oddly enough, was not to weaken faith in atomic air power but rather to strengthen it." Maxwell D. Taylor, *Uncertain Trumpet* (New York: Harper & Brothers, 1960), 15–16.

24. Martin Sherwin, "Foreword" to Kaplan, *The Wizards of Armageddon*, 5.

25. Dulles memo of telephone call to the president, 8 September 1958, Dulles Papers, Telephone Calls Series, Box 13, "Memo of Tel Cons-WH—August 1, 1958, to December 5, 1958," Dwight Eisenhower Presidential Library (DEPL).

26. See Halperin, *Nuclear Fallacy*, 23–45, for a list of these cases.

27. Richard K. Betts, *Nuclear Blackmail and Nuclear Balance* (Washington, DC: The Brookings Institution, 1987), 7.

28. For a discussion of deterrence and compellence, see Thomas C. Schelling, *Arms and Influence* (New Haven, CT: Yale University Press, 1966), 70–72; Patrick Morgan, *Deterrence: A Conceptual Analysis* (Beverly Hills, CA: Sage Library of Social Science, 1977).

29. Daniel Ellsberg, "Introduction: Call to Mutiny," in E. P. Thompson and Dan Smith (eds.), *Survive and Protest* (New York: Monthly Review Press, 1981).

30. Betts, *Nuclear Blackmail and Nuclear Balance*, 4; Joseph Gerson, "Nuclear Blackmail," *The Bulletin of the Atomic Scientists* (May 1984).

31. Gar Alperowitz, *Atomic Diplomacy: Hiroshima and Potsdam* (New York: Simon and Schuster, 1965); Martin Sherwin, *A World Destroyed: The Atom Bomb*

and the Grand Alliance (New York: Alfred A. Knopf, 1975), 191–92. Taking a totally different line, Henry A. Kissinger defined the "real meaning" of atomic diplomacy thus: "As the Soviet nuclear stockpile grows, overt threats have become unnecessary; every calculation of risks will have to include the Soviet stockpile of atomic weapons and ballistic missiles." Kissinger, "Force and Diplomacy in the Nuclear Age," *Foreign Affairs* (April 1956), 351.

32. Donovan memo for the president, 5 May 1945, Rose Conway File, Box 15, "OSS-Donovan-Chronological File, April–May 1945," Harry S. Truman Library (HSTL).

33. The most detailed study of Truman's Cold War policy is Melvyn Leffler, *A Preponderance of Power: National Security, the Truman Administration, and the Cold War* (Stanford, CA: Stanford University Press, 1992). See also Gregg Herken, *The Winning Weapon: The Atomic Bomb in the Cold War, 1945–1950* (New York: Alfred A. Knopf, 1980).

34. The literature on each episode is discussed in the respective chapter.

35. As Chapter 3 will show, the Eisenhower administration's claim that it had used nuclear diplomacy against China to end the Korean War has no substance. Although the Eisenhower administration considered atomic strikes against North Vietnam in 1954, it did not practice overt nuclear diplomacy in this episode. The earlier record is, thus, two instances of nuclear diplomacy by the Eisenhower administration toward China.

36. Although the focus of massive retaliation was deterring the Soviet Union, the doctrine called for the use of tactical nuclear weapons in peripheral conflicts, such as those with China.

37. Hans M. Kristensen, "Nuclear Futures: Proliferation of Weapons of Mass Destruction and US Nuclear Strategy," BASIC Research Report 98.2, British American Security Information Council, March 1998.

38. *Washington Times*, 1 April 1998.

39. For a survey of the new sources, see Shu Guang Zhang, *Mao's Military Romanticism: China and the Korean War, 1950–1953* (Lawrence: University Press of Kansas, 1995), "Introduction."

CHAPTER 2

Setting the Stage

Sixteen hours after an American aircraft dropped an atomic bomb on Hiroshima, President Truman declared that "The force from which the sun draws its power has been loosed against those who brought war to the Far East."[1] The American atomic bomb program had originated with a suggestion from scientists in the United States to President Franklin D. Roosevelt toward the end of 1939. These scientists, many of whom had fled a Nazi-dominated Europe, feared that Hitler's Germany might develop an atomic bomb first and use it to win the Second World War. On 9 October 1941, two months before the Japanese attack on Pearl Harbor, Roosevelt authorized a full-fledged American research program to see whether an atomic bomb could be made. According to the original schedule, the bomb should have been ready by July 1944. By a historic coincidence, however, the atomic bomb became available for use only a year later, just when the war with Japan reached a turning point.[2] Ever since, the atomic bomb has cast its shadow over East Asia. Atomic weapons also became the dominant factor in postwar American national security considerations.

The decision of the Truman administration to use atomic bombs against Japan in August 1945 is one of the most controversial issues in the history of American foreign relations. One school of thought holds that the United States dropped atomic bombs on Hiroshima and Nagasaki primarily because the Truman administration believed that the bombs would end the war with Japan speedily and that anti-Soviet aims were only a secondary factor that helped confirm the long-held assumption that the United States would use the bomb against Japan. The other view holds that Truman knew that atom bombs were not militarily necessary to defeat Japan and used them with postwar diplomatic relations with the Soviet Union in mind.[3] An assessment of the contending schools is beyond the scope of this study. What is important from the perspective of this study is that, when American policy makers looked at the problem of dealing with the Soviet Union, especially in the Far East, the US atomic monopoly did occupy a prominent place in their considerations. Roosevelt's policy choices, as Sherwin persuasively argues, "were based on the assumption that the bomb could be used effectively to secure postwar goals; and this assumption was carried over to Truman's administration." The selection of the targets in Japan for atomic strikes, Sherwin points out, was influenced by the desire "to transmit the message in the most dramatic fashion possible."[4]

ORIGINS OF NUCLEAR RELIANCE

The diplomatic aspect of atomic energy was very much in the minds of those involved in the American atomic bomb project from the beginning. Roosevelt had gained an idea of the destructive power of the atomic bomb and its possible diplomatic utility as early as 1942 from Vannevar Bush, chairman of the newly established National Defense Research Committee, and James Conant, president of Harvard University.[5] Secretary of War Henry Stimson, in his last talk with Roosevelt on 15 March 1945, raised the issue of international control of atomic weapons. The choice, Stimson advised Roosevelt, was between "secret close-in attempted control of the project by those who control it now, and . . . the international control based upon freedom both of science and of access." He urged sorting out this issue before the first atom bomb was used.[6] Roosevelt, however, died before he could resolve any of the critical issues raised by the bomb.

The very first discussion that Truman had as president about the bomb emphasized its diplomatic aspect.[7] James Byrnes, soon to be Truman's secretary of state, told the president when the two met for Roosevelt's funeral that the bomb could potentially give the United States the leverage to have the decisive say in the settlement of peace terms. A few days later, Stimson told Truman that "the atom bomb would be certain to have decisive influence on our relations with other countries."[8] On 6 June, Stimson advised Truman to demand that the Soviet Union either cooperate in the international control of atomic energy or the "solution of our present troubles" in Eastern Europe in return for sharing atomic secrets.[9] Truman and Stimson agreed on "the settlement of the Polish, Rumanian, Yugoslavian, and Manchurian problems" as an appropriate quid pro quo.[10] Historian Barton Bernstein has pointed out that atomic diplomacy at this stage did not go beyond the expectation that the Soviet Union would offer concessions in return for sharing nuclear secrets. No one had raised the idea of threatening the Soviet Union with atomic bombs to secure concessions.[11] However, Stimson did consider it necessary "to have it out with Russia over relations to Manchuria and Port Arthur and various other parts of North China." He thought that "over any such tangled wave of problems the S-1 secret [the US atomic bomb program] would be dominant and yet we will not know until after that time probably, until after that meeting, whether this is a weapon in our hands or not." As Sherwin points out, "Stimson did not intend to threaten the Soviet Union with the new weapon, but certainly he expected that once its power was demonstrated, the Soviets would be more accommodating to the American point of view."[12]

Truman should have had no difficulty in grasping the diplomatic advantage the atomic bomb would give him in facing the Soviet Union once he read Donovan's memorandum.[13] Not surprisingly, he was eager to know the fate of the bomb before he met Stalin at Potsdam. He delayed the conference until the test of the atomic device at Alamogordo scheduled for 14 July showed whether the bomb would work. To Stimson, the situation in the Far East posed critical issues that "cut very deep and in my opinion are powerfully connected" with the atom bomb. Mistakenly thinking that the Potsdam meeting was scheduled for the first week of July, he considered it "a terrible thing to gamble with such big stakes in diplomacy without having your master card in your hand."[14] The news of the successful test electrified Truman. As British Prime Minister Winston Churchill recalled, after reading General Leslie Groves' report on the bomb test, Truman was "a changed man." Stimson concluded that the United States now possessed "a badly needed equalizer" of Russian military power.[15]

With Soviet intervention in the war against Japan no longer required, Truman and Byrnes hoped "to outmaneuver Stalin on China" and to bring the war against Japan to an end before the Soviet Union intervened.[16] The "differences of psychology which now exist since the successful test" amazed Stimson. Byrnes told Stimson and Assistant Secretary of War John McCloy that the bomb was "a great weapon" that he could use as an "implied threat" in talks with Soviet Foreign Minister Vyacheslav Molotov.[17] He hoped that if the Chinese stood firm in their negotiations with the Soviets, it would delay the latter's intervention in the war, giving time for Japanese surrender before Soviet entry. Byrnes believed that Japan would surrender after atomic bombing, and Russia "will not get in so much on the kill, thereby not being in a position to press for claims against China."[18]

If Byrnes was under any illusions about the diplomatic leverage conferred by the atomic bomb, the London conference of the Council of Foreign Ministers soon chastened him. Molotov's repeated references during the conference to the bomb in the secretary's "side pocket" disconcerted Byrnes. Molotov coupled this with an uncompromising stance in the negotiations, to practice what Herken described as "Molotov's reversal of atomic diplomacy."[19] The secretary of state returned to Washington considerably disillusioned about the bomb's diplomatic utility.

The course that Byrnes was following aroused Stimson's apprehensions.[20] Stimson realized that an American demand for internal changes in the Soviet Union as a pre-condition for access to information on atomic matters would be counterproductive. He worried that US relations with the Soviets might be "irretrievably embittered" unless the administration handled this problem correctly. He warned against continuing to negotiate with them, "having this weapon rather ostentatiously on our hip." Instead, Stimson proposed a direct American approach to the Kremlin.[21]

Truman consulted his advisers on how to raise international control of atomic energy with the Soviet Union. A proposal by Commerce Secretary Henry Wallace discussed in the cabinet for sharing of scientific information on atomic energy was misreported in the press as a proposal for sharing the secrets of the bomb. The resultant public and congressional outcry against what was represented as giving away the nation's atomic secrets complicated Truman's task.[22] Moreover, even while the Joint Chiefs of Staff (JCS) supported political initiatives for control of atomic weapons, they argued that without concrete agreement among the major powers on "fundamental international political problems . . . release of information on atomic weapons would merely accelerate the inception and magnitude of an atomic armament race." Since the United States "was particularly vulnerable to attack by atomic weapons," they argued, releasing any information on these weapons was foolish.[23]

In the end, Truman decided against any sharing of atomic know-how with other states, a decision in which the views of the JCS obviously influenced him. Members of Truman's cabinet also strongly argued against sharing atomic secrets. The secretary of agriculture questioned how the United States could trust the Soviet Union with atomic secrets when the latter had become a competitor, when it had not trusted the Soviets with the same secrets when they were allies during the war. Treasury Secretary Fred Vinson argued that if another nation initiated war with the use of the information received from the United States, America would have "contributed to that event by making it come sooner than it would otherwise have." He found the argument that sharing information on atomic matters would "promote and induce world peace" unrealistic. The historical precedent against such a possibility, he argued, was simply too strong.[24] However, other factors surely weighed equally heavily in Truman's calculations. In deciding on this course, Truman ignored warnings that the Soviet Union might be able to develop atomic weapons within three to five years, and Under Secretary Dean Acheson's forceful plea in support of Stimson. Instead, he seemed to have accepted the estimate of General Leslie Groves, head of the atom bomb project, that it would take the Soviet Union 10 to 20 years to catch up.[25] As historian Robert Messer has pointed out, "Five to ten years of superiority was equal to the length of two terms in office. The advantage conferred by that kind of incumbency was not the sort of thing politicians such as Byrnes and Truman would forfeit or ignore."[26] Given these considerations, and the worsening American relations with the Soviet Union, Truman's decision is not difficult to explain.

After rejecting a direct approach to the Soviet Union, Truman decided on pursuing international control over atomic energy through the United Nations. Here again, he had to contend with the powerful opposition of the military. The JCS argued that arms control, even with a system of reliable safeguards, would neither eliminate war nor "preclude the use of atomic weapons in a war once begun." Moreover, "the absence of fear of immediate retaliation with atomic weapons" might "make a renegade nation less hesitant to begin a war of aggression." Once war began, safeguards against production of atomic weapons would break down. Defense against atomic bombs could never be total. The United States, therefore, needed "forces capable of immediate retaliation for the purpose not only of reducing or eliminating the aggressor's capability of continuing the attack, but also as a deterrent to its initiation."[27] The results of the atomic tests conducted as part of Operation Crossroads supported these arguments. The final report of this exercise concluded that "Offensive measures will be the only generally effective means of defense, and the United States must be prepared to employ them before a potential enemy can inflict significant damage on us."[28] Nevertheless, Truman persisted with negotiations for international control through 1948.[29]

Truman, who had no qualms about ordering the use of atomic bombs against Japan, quickly developed doubts that such weapons could ever again be used. On 5 October 1945, when told by Budget Director Harold Smith that "you have an atomic bomb up your sleeve," Truman responded that "I am not sure it can ever be used."[30] The passage of years did not alter this feeling. In a meeting on 21 July 1948, at which the custody of nuclear weapons was discussed, Truman said:

I don't think we ought to use this thing unless we absolutely have to . . . this isn't a military weapon. . . . It is used to wipe out women and children and unarmed people, and not for military uses. *So we have got to treat it differently from rifles and cannons and ordinary things like that.* (emphasis added)

Truman considered it "a terrible thing to order the use of something . . . that is so terribly destructive, destructive beyond anything we have ever had."[31] He told David Lilienthal, chairman of the Atomic Energy Commission, that "when they [people] think that this is just another bomb, they are making a very serious mistake."[32]

Despite an unspoken assumption that the United States would employ atomic weapons in any major war with the Soviet Union, the JCS did not take up operational plans involving use of atomic weapons until 1947. When they finally incorporated nuclear strikes in their plan BROILER and its successors, FROLIC and HALFMOON, Truman developed misgivings. Still convinced that nuclear weapons might be outlawed and doubtful of American public support for nuclear war, Truman, in May 1948, ordered preparation of conventional war plans. On 28 July 1948, however, Secretary of Defense James Forrestal, on his own, authorized the JCS to include atomic weapons in their war plans.[33] Even before that, demands had surfaced within the Pentagon for a review of the policy on the use of atomic weapons. The resulting study by the National Security Council (NSC), NSC 30, dated 10 September 1948, concluded that "in the event of hostilities, the National Military Establishment must be ready to utilize promptly and effectively all appropriate means available, including atomic weapons, in the interest of national security and must therefore plan accordingly."

The report left the decision whether or not atomic weapons should be employed to the president, "when he considers such decision to be required." However, it cautioned that the Soviet Union

should in fact never be given the slightest reason to believe that the US would even consider not to use atomic weapons against them if necessary (emphasis added). It might take no more than a suggestion of such consideration, perhaps magnified into a doubt, were it planted in the minds of responsible Soviet officials, to provoke exactly that Soviet aggression which it is fundamentally US policy to avert.

Although Truman did not formally approve NSC 30, he told Forrestal that "he prayed that he would never have to make such a decision, but that if it became necessary, no one need have a misgiving but what he would do so."[34]

The Pentagon had never taken kindly to civilian custody of the atomic bombs. Led by Forrestal, it pushed strongly for the transfer of the stockpile of atomic bombs to the armed forces. The Atomic Energy Commission stoutly opposed this. Truman sought the views of James Webb, director of the budget, who argued that

Contrary to the opinion and attitudes of some military spokesmen, the atomic bomb is no ordinary piece of ordinance. It is destructive beyond anything known heretofore in military science. It has a symbolic value which is almost as important an instrument of international influence as the bomb itself. The slowness of the Military Establishment to grasp these distinctions is a strong reason why custody of the stockpile should not be transferred to its hands.

Webb expressed concern over the inability of the military establishment to control the "utterances of certain highly-placed officers." Once the military had custody of the stockpile of atomic weapons, other countries might be even more bothered by the belligerent talk by these officers.[35] Not wanting "some dashing lieutenant colonel decide when would be the proper time to drop one," Truman ruled against transferring custody of nuclear weapons to the military.[36]

The dispute over custody of atomic weapons had come in the midst of the first Berlin crisis set off by the closing of the Western powers' access to Berlin by the Soviet Union in June 1948. Soviet motives in precipitating matters were unclear. In the event of a major Soviet offensive, the United States did not have the conventional forces required to face it. Admiral William Leahy, chairman of the JCS, was of the opinion that although the American atomic stockpile did not amount to much, "whatever we have we could use." Already, however, Forrestal had recommended sending American bombers to Europe. On 28 June, Truman approved the movement of the Strategic Air Command's B-29 bombers to Germany.[37] On 2 July, the 301st Bomber Group arrived in Germany.[38] The B-29s practiced dropping coal from their bomb bays.[39] Ernest Bevin, the British foreign secretary, quickly agreed to stationing American B-29 bombers in Britain. Secretary of Defense General George Marshall thought that sending American bombers to Britain would demonstrate American firmness. Even more important, it would stimulate British and French "determination" and "might offset any tendency toward weakness or appeasement." The NSC recommended stationing B-29 bombers in Britain.[40] When Marshall and Forrestal briefed him on the NSC recommendation, Truman told them that he had "come independently to the same conclusion."[41] On 15 July, 60 B-29s left for Britain in what was described as a training mission. When the bomber force arrived in England, they found 150 reporters waiting to cover their arrival. Planned activities for the force included flights to British cities to show off the planes. Hints that the planes were nuclear capable, and even that they carried nuclear weapons, surfaced, and did not escape Soviet attention. The Soviet press charged that "the British Isles had now become an aircraft carrier."[42]

Truman sent the bombers to Europe not with the intention of using them in a war with the Soviet Union but to deter the Soviets from escalating the conflict. He "wanted to stay in Berlin as long as possible, but not to the point of . . . starting a war for which the US did not have enough soldiers."[43] The US atomic arsenal in the summer of 1948 was not adequate for a major war with the Soviet Union. The bombers sent across the Atlantic were, in fact, not nuclear capable.[44] The 509th Bombardment Group, the only unit in the US Air Force with atomic bombing capability, remained at home. However, as David Holloway points out, the importance of the nuclear capability of the bombers sent to Europe is debatable. Truman could have sent nuclear-capable bombers if he chose to in a matter of days. Moreover, Stalin hardly "needed to be reminded about the American atomic monopoly."[45]

For later American strategic policy, this crisis is more important for the lessons that American leaders drew from it rather than for what happened in the crisis itself. A year earlier, Acheson had told Lilienthal, in carefully chosen words in response to a question as to how to use nuclear threats against the Soviet Union, that "the way to impress the Russian political mind is to *understate* what we are doing" (emphasis in the original).[46] Marshall now came to believe that "the Soviets are beginning to realize for the first time that the United States would really use the atomic bomb against them in the event of war," and that "the main deterrent to Soviet aggression has been the possession by the United States of the atomic bomb. . . . [T]he Soviet leaders must now realize that the use of this instrument would be possible and hence the deterrent influence now was perhaps greater than heretofore."[47] In the Korean War, in which Acheson and Marshall played pivotal roles as secretary of state and secretary of defense, the Truman administration would resort to similar tactics to deter Soviet entry into the war.

The American military's own assessment of the effects of strategic atomic bombing of the Soviet Union was, however, far from reassuring. A committee of senior military officers, headed by General H. R. Harmon, came to the conclusion that although strategic atomic bombing would destroy 30 percent to 40 percent of Soviet industrial capacity and gravely affect the Soviet Union's will and capacity to wage war, the bombing "would not, *per se*, bring about capitulation, destroy the roots of Communism, or critically weaken the power of Soviet leadership to dominate the people." Nor would it significantly retard a Soviet military advance into Western Europe, the Middle East, or the Far East.[48]

By 14 July 1949, Truman conceded that international control of atomic weapons was out of the question. "Since we can't obtain international control," he concluded, "we must be strongest in atomic weapons." He followed up this decision by approving the JCS request for a large increase in production of fissionable materials. In 1950 and 1952, he authorized further such increases.[49]

The decision to increase production of atomic weapons came at a time when fiscal problems had begun to seriously undermine the level of US conventional forces. In 1948, the United States had hardly any uncommitted forces to deal with crises in vital trouble spots overseas, nor did it have the forces required to seize and hold the overseas bases on which

US war plans depended if global war erupted. Yet Truman's request for appropriations for 1949 for the armed forces envisioned a 13 percent reduction in personnel besides reductions in air strength.[50] The communist takeover of power in Czechoslovakia in 1948 led to a clamor for increased defense spending. The resulting supplementary appropriations increased the defense budget by 30 percent.[51] In the meantime, the NSC laid down ambitious goals for the United States:

(a) To reduce the power and influence of the USSR to limits which no longer constitute a threat to the peace, national independence and stability of the world family of nations.

(b) To bring about a basic change in the conduct of international relations by the government in power in Russia, to conform with the purposes and principles set forth in the UN Charter.[52]

Even while he approved such a strategic policy, Truman rejected Forrestal's requests for higher defense allocations.[53] Obviously Truman had come to place greater reliance on the deterrent power of the US atomic arsenal.

This reliance became more pronounced as an economic slide in 1949 increased unemployment from about 3.5 percent to 6 percent and decreased industrial production by about 13 percent.[54] The budget deficit was expected to rise in 1951 and 1952. Years of low spending on domestic programs made reductions in that field impossible. The end of the Berlin crisis for the moment eased international pressures. Truman, therefore, decided to place ceilings on national security expenditure.[55] For fiscal year 1950, he proposed a defense budget of $14.3 billion, going down to $13.5 billion in 1951.[56]

Truman's failure to redefine American security goals in line with the diminished conventional military assets he had available increased the American dependence on atomic weapons. Budget Director Frank Pace complained to Truman about "the tendency in some military quarters to regard the atomic bomb as 'just another military weapon.' "[57] By the end of 1949, Acheson came to the conclusion that

we are in effect, deciding now to rely upon and use such weapons . . .

(a) Because while we had atomic weapons and no other nation had, it came to be regarded as a powerful deterrent to war and guarantee of security; they [atomic weapons] came to play a large part in military planning; and Russian behavior over the past few years overcame popular aversion to the use of the weapon. Thus acceptance of and reliance upon it has grown more subtly than through any articulate major premise. . . .

(b) Because having assumed commitments relating to the defense of Western Europe, as necessary for our own defense, we do not have any other military program which seems to offer over the short run promise of military effectiveness.[58]

Policy Planning Director George Kennan bluntly stated that "We are so behind the Russians in conventional armaments, and the attraction of the atomic bomb to strategic planners has been such, that we are in danger of finding our whole policy tied to the bomb."[59] He urged immediate remedial action.[60] Charles Bohlen, the State Department counselor, complained that "too much emphasis has been given to the atomic bomb as a deterrent in the past while we held atomic monopoly," despite lack of any evidence of the effectiveness of such a policy.[61]

The course that Truman chose at this stage bears a striking similarity to the "New Look" national security policy that the Eisenhower administration adopted: ambitious foreign policy goals, inadequate conventional forces to implement them, and heavy reliance on the deterrent power of atomic weapons. The only difference was the absence of the loud rhetoric that became the hallmark of the Eisenhower administration. Truman also used the very same argument that Eisenhower would use: the economy could not sustain a higher level of defense expenditure.

The testing of an atomic weapon by the Soviet Union in late 1949 created an entirely new strategic scenario.[62] As late as July 1948, the Central Intelligence Agency (CIA) had estimated that "the earliest date by which it is remotely possible that the USSR may have completed its first atomic bomb is mid-1950, but the most probable date is believed to be mid-1953."[63] Truman responded to the changed situation by authorizing the development of the hydrogen bomb. He also ordered a review of the US national security policy. An intelligence estimate showed that with 50 atom bombs, the Soviet Union could inflict serious destruction on the US industrial capacity as well as its administration. A Soviet attack against the US Strategic Air Command installations would require 25 bombs. Analysts estimated that by 1 July 1952, the Soviet Union would have about 90 atomic bombs—enough to cripple the US government system, industries, and retaliatory forces.[64] American planners feared that once the Soviet Union achieved this capacity, the American nuclear capability would no longer deter the Kremlin from embarking on an expansionist course. Reflecting these fears, NSC 68, adopted in April 1950, called for a massive increase in defense outlays.[65]

DOMESTIC POLITICS AND US CHINA POLICY

Until the beginning of January 1950, Acheson and his predecessor, George Marshall, had followed a China policy based on a very narrow definition of American vital interests that gave primacy to Europe and Japan. China was not heavily industrialized, had no immediate prospect of becoming so, and had no ability to develop significant power projection capability. As Kennan argued, "We Americans could feel fairly secure in the presence of a truly friendly Japan and a nominally hostile China—nothing very bad could happen to us from this combination."[66] The Truman administration prepared to cut its losses in China and disengage from the civil war in that country by stopping US aid to the Nationalist regime of Chiang Kai-shek. The support for the Chiang regime mobilized by the China Lobby and the China Bloc, however, severely restricted its ability to cut off all aid to the Nationalists.[67] The administration's decision to publish a white paper to explain its decision to withdraw US support to the Nationalists only added to its problems.[68] The US policy became, as Owen Lattimore, the leading China scholar of the day, sarcastically put it, one of "letting China fall without making it appear we pushed it."[69]

[After Chiang and his supporters withdrew to Taiwan, the Pentagon and the Nationalist government, in a series of coordinated moves, strove to bring the administration around to defending the island from the communists.] As Walton Butterworth, the assistant secretary of state for the Far East, pointed out to Acheson, the JCS proposals for US military intervention and increased aid to the Nationalists paralleled "with extraordinary fidelity the request for increased assistance from the Chinese National Government received on the same date."[General Douglas MacArthur, head of the US Far East Command (FECOM), argued that the loss of Taiwan would endanger the whole US position in East Asia, eventually shifting the US defensive line back to the West Coast of the continental United States. He did not favor US bases in Taiwan, but he considered it vital to deny the island to the communists.[70]]

[Acheson, however, took a dim view of the military importance of Taiwan.]"The coaling station strategic concept" was obsolete, he argued. His opinion of the Nationalist leadership was equally low. He told Wellington Koo, the Nationalist ambassador to the United States, that "The Chinese Government had been ingenious in making so many mistakes to a point where its armed forces had refused to fight the communists." [Acheson stoutly resisted Pentagon efforts to get involved in the defense of Taiwan from a communist invasion and went to great lengths to keep the JCS to this line. By the end of 1949, he had almost succeeded in eliminating a US-dominated Taiwan as an objective of American policy.[71] [Toward the end of 1949, Acheson did appear to be moving in the direction of recognizing the communist regime.[72] However, he made no overt move to signal a US decision to establish formal diplomatic relations with the PRC.[73] On 5 January 1950, the administration formally declared that it would not intervene in the Chinese civil war.[74]]

From the middle of January 1950, however, a series of events took place that whittled away the administration's determination not to be involved further in China's civil war. Following a dispute over American consular properties in Beijing in January 1950, the United States withdrew all of its diplomats from China. In February, the Sino-Soviet friendship treaty was signed, belying Acheson's hopes of a breakdown of the Sino-Soviet negotiations.[75] Republican Senator Styles Bridges promptly called for "a vote of censure of the administration" and for the blocking of all funds until the administration reversed its decision to abandon the Nationalists. Senator William Knowland, the leading member of the China Bloc, demanded Acheson's resignation. On 25 January, former State Department official and Acheson's close friend, Alger Hiss, was convicted of perjury in a case pertaining to charges of spying for the Soviet Union. That day, a reporter's question elicited Acheson's lofty retort that "I do not intend to turn my back on Alger Hiss."[76]

In this highly charged atmosphere, Senator Joseph McCarthy alleged, in a speech on 9 February, that the State Department was harboring communists. Sections of the Republican Party endorsed McCarthy's charges. The allegations led to an investigation by the Senate's Tydings Committee, which dragged on for months and, in the weeks preceding the beginning of the Korean War, kept the spotlight on Truman's China policy.[77]

In March, Senator Bridges announced that the Republicans would "go after" Acheson. Senator Kenneth Wherry called Acheson a "bad security risk" who "must go." Other Republicans soon joined the chorus calling for Acheson's ouster.[78] Truman's belligerent response to the Republican charges and vicious Republican counterattacks kept the spotlight on the Red Scare. As journalist Robert Donovan recalled, McCarthy used the Tydings Committee "to bring the Red issue to its highest and most effective pitch. . . . He made Acheson all but an outcast in Acheson's own party." The right-wing media, led by the Hearst, McCormick, and Scripps Howard chains, played up McCarthy's charges against the administration. "[A]lmost daily, the capital reverberated to bitter exchanges between the two ends of Pennsylvania Avenue. Relations between the president and the Republican right wing were ripped to shreds."[79] Acheson's attempts to overcome the hostility of congressional Republicans made no headway in the weeks before the Korean War started.[80]

In the meantime, the China Bloc seized on the budgetary process to overcome the administration's policy on aid to the Nationalists. As part of what he called "the greatest selling job ever facing a president," Truman had embarked on a campaign to "scare [the] hell out of the American people" in order to secure congressional approval for aid for Greece.[81] The Truman administration's refusal to offer the Chinese Nationalists American aid commensurate with its overall anti-communist rhetoric gave the China Lobby and the China Bloc a credible argument for use against the administration. As *New York Times* columnist James Reston wrote,

Mr. Truman in his doctrine of 1947 did not say that the United States would do what it could, when it could, and where it could, to block communism; he asserted flatly and broadly: I believe it must be the policy of the United States to support free peoples who are resisting attempted subjugation by armed minorities or by outside pressures.[82]

The 1949 congressional debate on the Military Assistance Program appropriations for Europe had made it clear that the administration had to move substantially to accommodate the China Bloc if it wanted to secure congressional support for its European recovery program and the rearmament program called for by NSC 68.[83] On 19 January 1950, the House of Representatives rejected a bill for aid to Korea by a 192–191 vote. Knowland said the fate of the bill foreshadowed what could happen to other administration initiatives on foreign policy unless the State Department changed its stand on aid to the Nationalists. Congress finally passed the Korea aid bill (after reducing the amount from $60 million to $50 million) after the administration agreed to the extension of the China Aid Act from 15 February to 30 June 1950.[84]

The efforts of the China Lobby and the China Bloc, combined with the Red Scare, finally began to have an impact on the administration's China policy. In reaction to McCarthy's attacks, Acheson's subordinates in the State Department turned into hard-liners on policy toward communist China. Between April and June 1950, O. Edmund Clubb and John Paten Davies, former moderates, switched over to hawkish positions on Taiwan.[85] The State Department, meanwhile, underwent important changes in personnel. Paul Nitze, a hard-liner, replaced Kennan as head of the PPS and took over the drafting of NSC 68.[86] On 28 March, Butterworth, who had fallen foul of the right wing in the Congress for his forthright views about the Nationalists, made way for Dean Rusk, known for his anti-communist leanings. In a move to mobilize Republican support for the administration's foreign policy, John Foster Dulles was brought in to handle the Japanese peace treaty. It is unlikely that Dulles would have accepted the appointment if he did not anticipate some change in the administration's China policy. He admitted as much when he stated that he promised to act as a link to the Republicans in Congress only "if Truman allowed (him) to plan some 'early affirmative action' against the 'Communist menace.'"[87]

Reflecting the change in atmosphere in Washington, the JCS resumed their pressure on the administration for assistance to the Nationalists.[88] On 18 May, Dulles wrote to Rusk and Nitze on the need for the United States to take "a dramatic and strong stand" against communist expansion, for which Taiwan offered the best opportunity. On 30 May, Rusk wrote to Acheson, virtually repeating Dulles word for word, proposing the neutralization of Taiwan.[89] By the end of May, Washington decided to expedite shipment of the remaining US military aid to the Nationalists and to step up covert operations against China. In June, Clubb recommended sending military advisers or military volunteers to assist the Nationalists. Nitze also favored US military action to defend Taiwan.[90] Proposals for US assistance to anti-communist guerrillas surfaced, and American military advisers arrived on the island. Early in June, Acheson told Oliver Franks, the British ambassador in Washington, that the State Department was "wracking its brains to see whether conditions conducive to preservation of the present status (of Taiwan) could not be encouraged or possibly created." Franks concluded that the United States would try "to delay the elimination of the token anti-communist group."[91] By this time, Dulles felt that his efforts in the State Department had brought about a "better attitude" there toward the Nationalist government and improved the prospects of American arms supplies to the Nationalists.[92]

In his memoirs, Acheson asserted that the right-wing attacks had no impact on the administration's foreign policy.[93] This is not very convincing. The Korean War started (on 25 June) at a moment when any further loss of territory to communism would have proved politically suicidal for Truman and the Democrats. In a statement that made perfect strategic sense but, in retrospect, appeared to be perfect political folly, Acheson had, in a 12 January speech, excluded South Korea from the area that the United States would directly intervene to defend. Although press coverage of the speech at that time focused on the future of Taiwan, Acheson was now vulnerable to charges of having invited a communist attack on South Korea.[94] Only days before North Korea launched its invasion, Truman was reported to have used the word "peace" 29 times in a speech in St. Louis.[95]

On 25 June itself, Dulles and State Department official John Allison cabled from Tokyo that if the South Koreans could not hold off the North Korean invasion, "we believe that US forces should be used even though this risks Russian counter moves. To sit by while Korea is overrun by unprovoked armed attack would start a disastrous chain of events leading most probably to world war." This message was very much on Acheson's mind and he apprised Truman of it after the Blair House meeting on the night of 25 June.[96] CIA Director Admiral Roscoe Hillenkoetter testified before the Senate Appropriations Committee on 26 June that the CIA had received information on North Korean military preparations weeks before the North attacked. Claiming that the invasion did not take the CIA by surprise, he asserted that it was not the agency's job to evaluate intelligence information.[97]

Republican attacks on the administration declined for a few days after the Korean War started. After Truman announced his intention to use American military forces to defend South Korea, Reston wrote:

There is in Washington tonight a spirit of far greater cooperation than at any time in the last few years.

Moreover, the somber spectacle of American planes engaged against a Communist aggressor 7,000 miles away from home, long before the United States is ready for a major war, has finally overwhelmed the atmosphere of McCarthyism that has pervaded this city for months.[98]

The attacks, however, resumed after the release of the Tydings Committee's report on 20 July with enough ferocity for Acheson to ask Truman to drop him.[99] Democratic congressional leaders, among whom Acheson had never enjoyed the standing that Marshall had, were notably lukewarm in their defense of the secretary of state.

It is easy enough to imagine the consequences if the administration had stuck to the position it held in early January that South Korea was outside the US defensive line and that the Nationalist regime in Taiwan was not worth the effort to defend it. It is difficult to argue with Donovan's conclusion that "the political damage to Truman of a successful North Korean invasion was startling. . . . A Communist military victory in Korea would have furnished the very capstone for charges that the Truman administration was soft on communism."[100] Irrespective of the strategic importance of South Korea or Taiwan, the Truman administration had no choice but to intervene, not only in the Korean peninsula but in the Chinese civil war as well.

THE IMPACT OF THE KOREAN WAR

The Korean War helped validate the fears of communist expansionism contained in NSC 68 and justify the proposals for creating additional military capability. The administration immediately embarked on a massive rearmament plan. Truman approved NSC 68/4, which called for achievement of force levels originally scheduled for 1954 in 1952 itself. By then, compared to June 1950, the army's strength would rise from 655,000 to 1,353,000; the navy and the air force from 238 to 397 major combat ships and from 48 to 95 wings, respectively. National security expenditure for 1951 and 1952 would exceed $140 billion. New programs would create the capacity to produce 50,000 military aircraft and 35,000 tanks a year, far in excess of the Second World War rate of production.[101] In the autumn of 1951, the Pentagon called for a massive increase in atomic stockpiles. On 19 January 1952, Truman approved increases in fissionable materials production that would require an investment of $5 billion to $6 billion. Planned and existing capacity would increase the inventory of nuclear weapons from 650 warheads in 1951 to over 18,000 in a matter of years.[102]

The Korean War once again brought the role of atomic weapons in American war plans into sharp focus. As Chapter 3 will show, the Truman administration relied on the US strategic atomic arsenal to deter a Soviet entry in the war when American conventional forces were inadequate to undertake a war in a peripheral theater while retaining the capability to deal with crises in theaters of primary national security concern to Washington. In the first six weeks of the war, Truman ordered the movement of nuclear-capable American bombers overseas on two occasions. This period also witnessed widespread calls within the United States by highly placed individuals for use of atomic weapons against the North Koreans and the Chinese.[103] Throughout the war, the Joint Strategic Survey Committee (JSSC) and the Joint Strategic Plans Committee (JSPC) undertook repeated evaluations of the use of atomic weapons in the war. Nevertheless, the Truman administration did not find a way either to use these weapons in the battlefield or to force China to end the war by threatening atomic bombing. A State Department Policy Planning Staff (PPS) memo in April 1951 summed up the dilemma:

While the atomic weapon is in some respects just another weapon in our national arsenal, its psychological impact is so great that use of it would doubtless precipitate general war, if war were not already underway. We are unlikely to use it, therefore, unless the vital security interests of the United States compel us to enter into general war with the Soviet Union.

Even if the Chinese expanded the war by using their air power against UN forces, atomic strikes were not feasible in the absence of suitable targets.[104] Acheson opposed suggestions for atomic diplomacy on the ground that nuclear threats would alarm US allies without yielding any tangible advantages.[105]

The Psychological Strategy Board concurred with Acheson's judgment. After careful study of the effects of public statements on atomic weapons, the board expressed doubts about whether "unconsidered statements" about atomic weapons had much "deterrent effect on the Kremlin." Such statements could be used by the communists "to encourage a belief that the US might use these weapons in a reckless, irresponsible way." Within the United States itself, "ill-considered statements" might instill "a false sense of security" and erode support for a strong military force. However, "well-considered statements," the board concluded, could promote public confidence in the will and ability of the United States and its allies to stand up to their enemies. The board recommended that before making statements on atomic weapons, US officials should question, among other things, whether their statements might generate a feeling that the United States might use nuclear weapons in a reckless manner.[106]

By the fall of 1951, it became clear that the United States would soon have a variety of tactical nuclear weapons in large quantities. As the Atomic Energy Commission's (AEC) Chief of Special Weapons described it,

Tactical atomic weapons hold forth the promise of a revolution in land war which can be compared to the revolution in air war brought about by the Hiroshima and Nagasaki bombs. . . .

Atomic weapons used tactically are the natural armaments of numerically inferior but technologically superior nations. They are the natural answer to the armed hordes of the Soviet Union and its satellites. . . . [A]tomic energy used tactically may be 300 times more economical than conventional high explosives. . . . [T]actical A-weapons—even if made of $40-per-pound raw materials in contrast to the $8 price now prevailing—will still be by far the cheapest military buy. . . .

[W]e shall want tactical weapons in what can now be termed astronomical quantities.[107]

Cost considerations were prevalent at even higher levels in the administration. As Secretary of Defense Robert Lovett explained, a ton of TNT then cost $1,700. Atomic weapons could produce equivalent destruction at a cost of $23, leading to "colossal savings."[108]

AMERICAN NUCLEAR CAPABILITY

The ability of the United States to actually wage atomic war, however, lagged far behind the deterrent power of atomic weapons until almost the end of the Korean War. On 30 June 1946, the American atomic stockpile had only nine bombs. A year later, the number of atomic bombs had increased to only 13. By the next June, it had increased to 50. By June 1950, the stockpile probably had 292 bombs. This was barely adequate to meet the requirements for the strategic air offensive against the Soviet Union envisaged in the American global war plans.[109]

Until the summer of 1948, the 509th Bomb Group based in New Mexico was the only US Air Force unit equipped with the B-29 bombers specifically modified to deliver atomic bombs. Out of the 46 B-29s thus modified during World War II, only 23 remained operational in 1946. Modification of additional bombers—including the new B-36s and B-50s—was complicated by the requirement of more than 6,000 man-hours of work on each aircraft.[110] It took as many as 39 specially trained technicians over two days to assemble each early-model bomb. Loading the bombs onto the bombers was itself a very cumbersome procedure. The bombs could only remain assembled for 48 hours before the batteries powering some of their components required recharging. In the spring of 1948, the three existing assembly teams took seven to nine days to load 12 armed bombs into bombers for strike missions. Only 32 modified B-29s remained. To man them, the SAC had only 12 fully qualified and 18 partially qualified crews capable of undertaking combat atomic bomb drops, all in the 509th Bomb Group. From the fall of 1948, the capability to deliver atomic bombs rapidly expanded, coinciding with the availability of larger numbers of bombs. By the spring of 1950, the SAC had more than 250 nuclear-capable bombers. Under the command of General Curtis LeMay, the SAC drastically improved its training and readiness.[111]

The MK-4 bomb, the main atomic weapon in the American stockpile when the Korean War began, was the first mass-produced atomic bomb. Its production on a mass scale began in 1949. Between then and 1951, the United States built some 550 bombs of this type. They weighed 10,800 pounds and were as unwieldy as the earlier model bombs. These bombs could be carried only in the bomb bays of modified B-29s and other bombers of similar size. They could, however, be assembled for combat missions in one hour.[112] The successor to this, the MK-6, weighed 8,500 pounds. Between 1951 and 1955, 1,100 of these were produced.[113]

The need for a small warhead that would allow flexibility of use had been felt from the earliest days of the atomic weapons program. The resulting product, the MK-5 warhead, weighed 3,175 pounds. Most air force bombers as well as the navy's carrier attack bombers could deliver them. Fighter bombers, however, could not carry them. In fact, the MK-5 was a small strategic bomb, not quite suitable for tactical missions. Quantity production of this model began in 1952, and 140 of them were produced by April 1955.[114] The MK-7, the first truly tactical multipurpose warhead, was tested in the fall of 1951. Its different models ranged in yield from 1 to 70 kilotons. The warhead's first full-scale test took place on 1 May 1952. About 1,700 to 1,800 of these were produced, starting in July 1952. A variety of American aircraft, including fighters and fighter-bombers, could carry externally or internally these bombs weighing between 1,645 and 1,700 pounds.[115] By 1954, Mark-12 warheads weighing about 1,000 pounds had become available, making tactical atomic attacks by land-based and carrier-based fighter-bombers an easy task.[116]

The test of an MK-8 warhead on 29 November 1951 was the first American underground atomic test. These warheads, weighing between 3,230 and 3,280 pounds, were designed for post-impact and subsurface detonation. They began entering the stockpile in September 1953. Approximately 40 MK-8 bombs were produced. These warheads could penetrate from 30 feet to 100 feet, depending on the soil type, drop altitude, and impact velocity.[117] The radius of destruction accomplished by these explosions, however, was too limited for these weapons to be used against the Chinese underground installations in Korea on a scale required for a breakthrough in the Korea War.

The designing of the 280mm atomic cannon had been completed by the spring of 1950. The gun, publicly unveiled on 30 September 1952, weighed 93 tons. The gun and its transporter measured 79 feet in length and 12 feet in height. Its M-9 shell weighed 900 pounds and needed a crane truck to handle it. It took an hour to assemble the gun and ready it for combat firing. Production of the shell began in the spring of 1953. The first and only full-scale test firing of the atomic shell by the gun took place on 25 May 1953. The shell yielded 15 kilotons (almost as much as the bomb dropped on Hiroshima). The gun had a range of 14 miles. About 80 shells were produced between April 1952 and November 1953. Only 20 of the guns were built. Neither the gun nor the MK-9 shell proved to be ideal weapons. Because of its height and weight, the gun could not use most bridges in Korea. It could not drive over soft roads. It needed to fire several "registration rounds," thus giving away its position to the enemy. A study by experts from Caltech, Project VISTA, came to the conclusion that the gun's "mobility is low, the range is limited, the projectile is costly in fissionable material." In April 1957, MK-19 shells replaced the MK-9 shells. Development of the MK-33 shell for an 8-inch cannon began in 1954. The prototype was test fired in 1957. The shell weighed 243 pounds and yielded 1.25 kilotons. This weapons system was far more mobile than the 280mm gun system, and the low yield of its shell made it considerably more suitable for battlefield use. Production of this shell began in 1957.[118]

On 4 February 1951, Chief of Army Staff General Lawton Collins told a reporter that the US forces would soon have atomic guided missiles. Such missiles, however, did not become available during the Korean War. Weapon designers first attempted to mate the MK-5 warhead to the navy's Regulus Matador cruise missiles. Initial production of the Regulus/MK-5 began in April 1954 and the Matador/MK-5 in July 1954. Before production ended in 1956, 35 warheads for the Regulus and 65 for the Matador were produced. In 1950, the JCS had approved mating the MK-7 to the Corporal missile. Production of Corporal and Honest John missiles began in September 1953. The mobile Corporal missiles with a range of 75 to 100 miles entered field service in 1955.[119]

For the air force, Project VISTA recommended forming a "combat-ready tactical atomic air force."[120] The F-84G was the first single-seater fighter-bomber with atomic capability available in late 1951. In the 1952 and 1953 fiscal years, the air force acquired 789 of these aircraft. In December 1952, the Fifth Air Force in the Far East moved an F-84G squadron stationed in Korea to Japan for training in air dropping tactical atomic weapons. The development of the technique of low altitude bombing by the middle of 1953 enabled these planes to drop small atomic bombs from low altitudes. Thus it was only by the middle of 1953, well after the Truman administration had left office and peace was in sight in Korea, that US forces had acquired the full-fledged capability to use atomic weapons in tactical combat missions.[121]

The actual development of the tactical atomic weapons, even while lagging behind public expectations, had rapidly outrun the development of military thinking on how to use them. The military still had not sorted out inter-service and intra-service disputes about how these weapons would be used and who would use them. The concept of tactical nuclear weapons in fact grew out of inter-service rivalry. A JCS study in the fall of 1945 had suggested that the advent of the atom bomb would make strategic bombing the centerpiece of future American military strategy. This would give the air force the major role in the national military establishment. The army feared that its role would be undermined in a force structure that laid primary emphasis on atomic weapons. To counter this, Eisenhower, then chief of army staff, argued against "excessive reliance" on atomic weapons. He pointed out that conventional forces would have to gain control of, and defend, the bases required by strategic bombers. He opposed excluding the army from a role in the use of atomic weapons before understanding the full implications of the revolution in warfare created by atomic weapons. Some army officers thought of combining an airborne assault with an atomic bomb strike.[122] The 82nd Airborne Division tried out this concept in an exercise in 1947. The advent of nuclear weapons had made large amphibious landing operations unfeasible, as the concentrated forces offered an ideal target to an enemy possessing atomic weapons. A combined airborne assault and nuclear bombing thus appeared a promising alternative. However, the air force did not look on this idea with favor.[123]

In March 1948, Air Force Chief of Staff General Carl Spaatz, claiming "primary responsibility" for the air force for the strategic use of atomic weapons, proposed that the air force should have exclusive control over the Armed Forces Special Weapons Project (AFSWP). To forestall the exclusion of the army from atomic weapons development, General Omar Bradley, Eisenhower's successor as the chief of army staff, staked the army's claim to control over atomic weapon matters other than strategic bombing. He thus raised the concept of nuclear operations in a ground combat role. Bradley's successor, General Lawton Collins, continued to assert the army's interest in tactical atomic operations. As John Midgley observes, "Like his predecessor, General Collins had to defend battlefield nuclear operations before the concept had taken form."[124]

Early atomic tests such as Crossroads and Sandstone had ignored the tactical potential of atomic weapons. Army participation in these programs was limited to a few observers who did not possess the expertise to make the required technical analysis. Responding to a request from the Army's Command and General Staff College for data on the effects of atomic weapons, Admiral Parsons of the AFSWP advised the college to develop tactics for atomic operations that were "practically identical to those for the largest high-explosive bomb." An estimate produced by the college's Department of Analysis and Research suggested that "under existing organizations and tactics one 20 kiloton airburst [roughly equivalent to the one dropped on Hiroshima] could effectively destroy a division formed for attack while two airbursts could destroy a division deployed for defense." Although the AFSWP had conducted a series of tests on the protection afforded by foxholes against heat, blast, and radiation from nuclear weapons, it had failed to pass on the data to the army. Midgley concludes that "As late as mid-1951, the Army had no clear data base to use in constructing an image of potential nuclear battlefields."[125]

A draft study by the Command and General Staff College in February 1950, reflecting paucity of technical data, described the atom bomb as "analogous to the artillery . . . use of high explosives in the preparation, counter-preparation and interdiction." The study concluded that the army could use conventional operational tactics on the nuclear battlefield. As Midgley comments, this "conclusion that atomic weapons could be used much like conventional artillery was really an assumption, based on admittedly inadequate data. Nevertheless, this study formed the basis of the Army's first doctrinal manual on the tactical use of atomic weapons."[126] The college produced the initial doctrine for the nuclear battlefield by simply incorporating the enhanced range and firepower of atomic weapons into conventional maneuver tactics. The army would use atomic weapons in ground support roles, either through air-delivered interdiction missions or in preparation for airborne or amphibious landings. The manual cautioned that "It is necessary that atomic weapons be regarded as a gigantic preparation, but only as a preparation, and that the exploitation by maneuver be regarded as the major element of the battle plan." This manual was approved without field-testing or war-gaming because of the need for quick development of such a doctrine. This process did not resolve the question of feasibility of battlefield use of nuclear weapons. Through these tactics, the army succeeded in claiming a role for itself in the atomic force structure.[127]

The army, however, had not given adequate thought to its own vulnerability to atomic weapons. Project VISTA experts estimated that a battalion could be destroyed by a 2-kiloton atomic explosion, a regiment by a 10-kiloton weapon, and a division in a defensive perimeter or assembly point by a 50-kiloton weapon. A classified military study warned that the UN forces in Korea were "exceedingly vulnerable to atomic attacks."[128]

The ability to effectively use atomic weapons in a ground combat role thus remained beyond the army's reach in the early 1950s. Moreover, as Midgley concludes, "even the most optimistic analyses of Army capabilities were limited to situations in which only United States forces could deliver nuclear weapons. The Army's capabilities to conduct two-sided nuclear operations had not even been addressed."[129]

THE NEW LOOK

Truman left his successor in the White House a stalemated war in Korea, a costly military buildup, and armed forces that despite nearly three years of massive conventional rearmament still left the United States heavily dependent on its atomic arsenal. The legacy of the Truman administration was captured by a report of a panel of consultants to the State Department on disarmament, chaired by Oppenheimer, in January 1953:

[T]he United States not only maintains a right to use atomic bombs, but does in fact now plan to use them in the event of a major war, and this plan is not at present dependent upon the prior use of such weapons by any possible aggressor. . . . *Indeed such is the present state of American weapons and military capabilities that no other course would seem possible.* . . .

In addition to its preparation for massive and immediate strategic counterattack, the United States Government has given attention to other uses of atomic weapons in support of local campaigns. . . . Conspicuously, the defense of Europe is more and more predicated upon the employment of atomic weapons. (emphasis added)

Because of the Soviet atomic capability against Western Europe, "the American atomic bomb will be useable only at the risk of truly horrible losses in Europe." While this possibility might not deflect the United States from its reliance on atomic weapons,

in a situation of this sort the balance of feeling and action in Europe might be sensibly altered for the worse. Thus in Europe there are at one and the same time powerful factors which tend to recommend an increasing dependence upon atomic weapons, and possible future developments which make that dependence dangerous.[130]

Despite the efforts of the Eisenhower administration to camouflage its national security goals in high decibel rhetoric, it began by embracing the strategic goals that the Truman administration had laid down. The Solarium Project taught the sobering lesson that the administration would have to be satisfied with containment, not "roll back," as its basic strategy.[131] In addition to taking over the plethora of overseas defense commitments it inherited from the Truman administration, the Eisenhower administration proceeded to assume new formal defense commitments in the form of the Southeast Asia Treaty Organization, the Central Treaty Organization, and mutual defense agreements with the Republic of Korea and the Republic of China.

Very early in his first term, Eisenhower proceeded to formulate the New Look defense policy that severely limited his means to implement even containment and further increased American dependence on nuclear weapons.[132] Eisenhower believed that "the great problem before his administration" was to "figure out a preparedness program that will give us a respectable position without bankrupting the nation."[133] The time had come, he asserted, to "take conclusive account, not only of the *external* threat posed by the Soviets, but also of the *internal* threat" posed by prolonged and heavy federal spending, especially on defense. He approved a new national security policy that would deal with the Soviet threat without destroying the US economy. The new policy deemphasized the expansion of NATO and US forces to previously projected levels by the target dates.[134] Secretary of the Treasury George Humphrey argued that only the use of atomic weapons "on a broad scale could really change the program of the Defense Department and cut the costs of the military budget." Agreeing, Admiral Arthur Radford, chairman of the JCS, asserted that "unless we could use these weapons in a blanket way, no possibility existed of significantly changing the present composition of our armed forces."[135]

Eisenhower took three decisions relating to nuclear weapons that marked a fundamental departure from the policy of the Truman administration. On 20 June 1953, he reversed Truman's insistence on total civilian custody of the US atomic weapons stockpile and authorized the transfer of a part of the stockpile of complete atomic bombs to the armed forces. He also approved their deployment overseas, including to the US bases close to China.[136]

Second, NSC 162/2, adopted on 29 October 1953, laid down that "In the event of hostilities, the United States will consider nuclear weapons to be as available for use as other munitions."[137] Eisenhower later clarified that this decision was "not a decision in advance that atomic weapons will in fact be used in the event of *any* hostilities." Rather, it was taken "primarily to permit the military to make plans on the basis of the availability of nuclear weapons, and to permit transfer of the custody of such weapons, in large part, from the AEC to the Defense Department." In certain situations, such as a nuclear attack on the United States or Western Europe, the United States would retaliate with nuclear weapons from the beginning. But in other situations, he would decide on the use of atomic weapons, depending on the merits of each case.[138]

With the clarification added, NSC 162/2 did not amount to a revolutionary departure from the Truman era NSC 30. Its significance, however, was heightened by the third initiative of the Eisenhower administration in nuclear policy: a public debate on atomic weapons, with the aim of winning domestic and allied support for the use of these weapons. As the United States planned to use both tactical and strategic nuclear weapons in future conflicts, Radford called for a "public announcement" that the United States would use these weapons. In his view, the United States had invested enormous resources on the manufacture of atomic weapons, but was reluctant to use them out of fear of public opinion. The administration must publicly clarify its position on using them without further delay, if the United States planned to use them.[139] Eisenhower agreed with the necessity of informing the American people, as well as US allies, "in the fundamentals of the problem."[140] He suggested that the United States should secure allied support for the use of atomic weapons before actually using these weapons. He clarified that the JCS could be sure of using atomic weapons in a "general war," but not in "minor affairs"; he was the one "to make the ultimate decision as to the use of these weapons, and if the use of them was dictated by the interests of US security, he would certainly decide to use them." However, he warned, "nothing would so upset the world as an announcement at this time by the United States of a decision to use these weapons."[141]

In developing a defense policy firmly grounded on nuclear weapons, the Eisenhower administration benefited from the programs that its predecessor had initiated to increase production of strategic nuclear weapons as well as to develop a variety of atomic weapons for tactical use. The availability of ground-based tactical atomic weapons systems and warheads that land- and carrier-based fighter-bombers could deliver gave US forces an unprecedented degree of flexibility. The "era of plenty" in nuclear bombs meant that the United States had enough nuclear warheads for implementing its global war plans with enough left over for use in other contingencies. From approximately 1,000 in 1952, the number of warheads in the American stockpile increased to 1,350 in 1953, 1,750 in 1954, 2,250 in 1955, and 7,100 in 1958.[142] The availability of short-range guided missiles, improved atomic artillery, and air-delivered tactical atomic warheads offered the US armed forces unprecedented options in the battlefield use of atomic weapons. Compared to his predecessor, Eisenhower thus had the means to make credible nuclear threats in a greater variety of situations.

According to Robert Bowie, the State Department's director of policy planning, the New Look grew out of Eisenhower's belief that "any major war between the United States and the Soviet Union would inevitably escalate into catastrophic nuclear war, however it began. The threat of a prompt American nuclear response would ensure that Soviet leaders recognized this reality."[143] Eisenhower proclaimed this policy in his State of the Union address on 7 January 1954, calling for "a massive capacity to strike back" to deter aggression. Nuclear weapons, he added, would play a prominent part in the new strategy.[144] A rather more melodramatic articulation of the concept by others in the administration attracted the policy much greater attention. In an address to the Council on Foreign Relations on 12 January 1954, Dulles described the administration's plan to deter communist aggression by relying on "a great capacity to retaliate instantly by means and at places of our choosing." This strategy would make the huge military forces planned by the Truman administration unnecessary and lead to "more basic security at less cost." Vice President Richard Nixon explained the new policy thus:

Rather than let the Communists nibble us to death all over the world in little wars we would rely in the future primarily on our mobile retaliatory power which we could use in our discretion against the major source of aggression at times and places we chose."

This suggested, columnist James Reston explained, that "in the event of another proxy or brushfire war in Korea, Indochina, Iran, or anywhere else, the United States might retaliate instantly with atomic weapons against the USSR or Red China."[145] Critics quickly dubbed Dulles's strategy "massive retaliation."[146]

THE NEW LOOK IN PRACTICE

As 1954 progressed, however, the limitations of the new strategy from a practical standpoint became clear. The Vietminh's attack on Dien Bien Phu on 13 March 1954 produced alarm in Washington over the communist threat to Indochina. The beleaguered French requested American air strikes in support of their encircled forces. Radford argued that "the only military solution was to go to the source of Communist power in the Far East, i.e., China, and destroy that power." He did not believe that the United States would ever get as good an excuse for taking military action against China as the one offered in Indochina. The admiral argued that "if we could put one squadron of US planes over Dien Bien Phu for as little as one afternoon, it might save the situation." Unless the United States intervened promptly and forcefully, he claimed, the whole of South East Asia might fall to communism. Eisenhower looked on Vietnam as a domino, whose fall would endanger other US allies in the region. Nevertheless, he did not favor American involvement in the war, although he was not opposed to a single air strike "if it were almost certain this would produce decisive results." Eisenhower also expressed interest in the idea of air attacks by "a little group of fine adventurous pilots" flying clandestine missions from American aircraft carriers.[147]

However, he refused to move without authorization from Congress. The congressional leaders opposed American action without allied involvement. On 3 April, Dulles and Eisenhower agreed on three preconditions for American intervention: allied (especially British) support, full independence for all countries in Indochina, and a commitment from France not to withdraw French forces once American intervention began. These conditions effectively ruled out any US action to relieve Dien Bien Phu. The British had no intention of being dragged into what Foreign Secretary Anthony Eden called "Radford's war against China."[148] Churchill told Radford that "since the British people were willing to let India go, they would not be interested in holding Indochina for France."[149] If Indochina was to be granted full independence, the French obviously had no reason to continue to fight there.

The US military made contingency plans for a nuclear strike on Dien Bien Phu. Nathan Twining, then chief of staff of the air force, later revealed that there was some consideration of dropping atomic bombs on the communist forces attacking the French stronghold. He did not "think that three small A-bombs placed properly would have caused too much trouble or set a precedent, but it would have taught those Chinese a good lesson."[150] The United States, however, did not make any nuclear threats. Nor did these plans get leaked to the press or generate any public discussion.

Internal discussions on strategy after the Indochina crisis reflected a more chastened mood as well as a certain degree of confusion over nuclear weapons. While discussing NSC 5422/1, Dulles spoke against the paper incorporating "a mandate to boast of our nuclear capabilities." He feared that talk of atomic war "tended to create 'peace-at-any-price people' and might lead to an increase of appeasement sentiment in various countries." Eisenhower expressed doubts about "the wisdom of preparing world opinion for some of the things we may have to do in case of war." Such attempts might alarm US allies. The president found it "frustrating not to have plans to have nuclear weapons generally accepted."[151] Dulles, nevertheless, continued to believe that "the principal factor restraining local aggression by the Communists was the deterrent nuclear power of the United States." Eisenhower responded that

[T]he theory of retaliation falls down unless we can identify the aggressor. In many cases aggression consists of subversion or civil war in a country rather than overt attack on that country. In such cases it is difficult for us to know whom to retaliate against.[152]

With the Soviet Union acquiring thermonuclear capability in 1954, and with the Soviet nuclear arsenal and delivery capability rapidly increasing, the strategic equation of the postwar years changed profoundly.

adopted on 6

Reflecting this change, NSC 5422/2, ~~dated 7~~ August 1954, explicitly acknowledged the existence of mutual nuclear deterrence. The paper conceded that "the freedom of either side to initiate strategic nuclear bombing against the other" would be curbed by the fear of nuclear retaliation and the prospect that neither side might emerge victorious from an all-out nuclear war. This might create "a condition of mutual deterrence, in which each side would be strongly inhibited from deliberately initiating general war or taking actions which it regarded as materially increasing the risk of general war." In view of this reality, NSC 5422/2, adopted on 6 August 1954, argued:

To permit appropriate flexibility in the capability of deterring or defeating local aggressions, the US should be prepared to defeat such aggressions without necessarily initiating general war. For this purpose the US should be prepared to assist, with US logistical support and if necessary with mobile US forces, indigenous forces supplemented by available support from other nations acting under UN or regional commitments. *However, the US must be determined to take, unilaterally if necessary, whatever additional action its security requires, even to the extent of general war, and the Communists must be convinced of this determination.* (emphasis added)

NSC 5422/2 noted that in order to stop further communist expansion, the United States should adopt "a flexible combination of political, psychological, economic and military actions."[153] Here was "flexible response" (the strategic doctrine that the Kennedy administration adopted) in all but name, less than eight months after the Eisenhower administration enunciated "massive retaliation."

NSC 5422/2 was adopted amidst growing tension in the Taiwan Strait. The first crisis in that theater started in earnest less than a month later. Dismissing the more bellicose recommendations of his military advisers, Eisenhower chose a cautious policy in response to the Chinese shelling of Quemoy. Eisenhower and Dulles hoped that the United Nations would succeed in keeping the situation under control. In the spring of 1955, however, the administration worried that China might launch an invasion of the offshore islands once they had built up their airfields in the coastal area opposite the offshore islands. With a view to preparing domestic and international opinion for possible use of atomic weapons in a likely war with China as well as to deter China, the administration resorted to overt atomic diplomacy.[154]

While reaffirming the possibility of mutual deterrence contained in NSC 5422/2, a November 1954 State Department paper containing "suggestions of the Secretary of State" cautioned against excluding the possibility of inadvertent war. The paper noted that "growing Soviet nuclear power and the devastating nature of total war seemed certain to affect allied and US attitudes toward war and risks of war."[155] While the United States should maintain adequate forces and leave no doubts about its determination to halt communist aggression, the paper recommended, it

should (1) forego actions which would generally be regarded as provocative, and (2) be prepared, if hostilities occur, to meet them, where feasible, in a manner and on a scale which will not inevitably broaden them into total nuclear war. In the conditions facing us, such policies are necessary to assure the support of our allies against aggression and to avoid risks which do not promise commensurate strategic or political gains. *These conclusions have an obvious bearing on basic military strategy and on our policy toward Communist China.*[156] (emphasis added)

Eisenhower's concept of disarmament displayed his understanding of the new reality created by the Soviet nuclear capability. He foresaw no significant military threat to the United States except a nuclear war initiated by the Soviet Union. He was therefore prepared to accept complete nuclear disarmament without simultaneous conventional arms limitations. He believed that "The question of total, as opposed to atomic, disarmament is largely academic." The Soviets would never allow the kind of verification systems required to make either kind of disarmament work. He wanted "all the so-called military experts" to think of what the total elimination of atomic weapons meant for the United States. Atomic weapons favored the side that initiated a surprise attack. "This," asserted the president, "the United States will never do; and let me point out that we never had any of this hysterical fear of *any nation* until atomic weapons appeared upon the scene and we knew that others had solved the secret" (emphasis in original). He said at a meeting of key officials who dealt with disarmament affairs that "if it could be accomplished, he would be willing to cancel out atomic and hydrogen weapons from the armaments of both the US and the USSR." Once the nuclear threat to the country's industrial base was removed, he believed, the United States could take care of any other threat to its security.[157]

Since the New Look made the United States so dependent on nuclear weapons, however, Eisenhower found it impossible to follow his preferred course on disarmament. The administration's disarmament policy became largely one of trying to score propaganda points against the Soviet Union, or crude attempts to freeze US superiority in weapons technology by banning further nuclear tests at a point when the United States was ahead.[158] The JCS opposed even such a course outside of a comprehensive program for the control of *all* armaments. The advantages of a moratorium on testing, they felt, would be transitory. The Soviets could continue scientific research and catch up with the United States. They could neutralize the US advantage by resuming testing based on their research in violation of the agreement. A moratorium on testing would also generate pressures for additional limitations on the military use of atomic energy, without the benefits of a universal, comprehensive system of disarmament.[159] Presidential aide C. D. Jackson concluded that the

[r]eal problem is very deep and goes beyond any disagreement on wording or technical details. [The] real problem is basic philosophy—are we or are we not prepared to embark on a course which may in fact lead to atomic disarmament? Soldier boys and their civilian governesses say no.[160]

The Pentagon feared that talks about disarmament would weaken support for defense spending. Robert Bowie, then director of policy planning at the State Department, later recalled that the military

adopted the somewhat hypocritical position of being in favor of total and complete disarmament as the only way in which to have real peace. But this obviously involved taking the moral high ground, while assuming that there would be no agreements that might jeopardize the U.S. defense program.[161]

In order to give greater momentum to US disarmament efforts, Eisenhower entrusted the job to Harold Stassen, who came in as director for foreign operations. Stassen, however, soon came to the conclusion that "substantial disarmament would not really be in the interest of the United States and that the optimum goal should be to try to stabilize the situation at about the present level."[162] The US delegation to the London meeting of the UN Disarmament Subcommittee made it clear to the Soviets that the United States "would never agree to forego all use of such weapons," although it might agree to limitations such as use only for individual and collective self-defense.[163]

When the Soviets gave up their long-standing proposal to ban *possession* of all nuclear weapons in the spring of 1954 and suggested a simple ban on *use* of such weapons, Washington found itself in an awkward position. If the United States accepted this proposal, a PPS memo cautioned, it would have to forego overt threats to use them. Acceptance of the Soviet proposal would, therefore, be "inconvenient" for the United States. "[I]t might impose a new inhibition on our diplomatic freedom of action, so far as diplomacy consists of making clear, where appropriate for deterrent purposes, what one is prepared to do in case of trouble." The PPS recommended rejecting the Soviet proposal "in calm and reasoned tones," so as to leave the United States a "line of retreat" for the future.[164] Acceptance of this proposal would have ruled out the kind of nuclear diplomacy the administration practiced during the Taiwan Strait crisis only a few months later and again in 1958.

THE ORIGINS OF FLEXIBLE RESPONSE

The failure of disarmament proposals to get off the ground and the depletion of conventional forces under the New Look strengthened the role of atomic weapons in the American force structure. Eisenhower accepted that the superpowers could not fight a serious war without using nuclear weapons. The United States should, therefore, structure its armed forces on the assumption that both sides would use nuclear weapons. He believed that in local wars, "the tactical use of atomic weapons against military targets would be no more likely to trigger off a big war than the use of twenty-ton 'block-busters.' " The United States, he emphasized, would not waste its forces in small peripheral wars. The forces that the United States would deploy to support local forces "would use the most efficient weapons, and over the past several years tactical atomic weapons have come to be practically accepted as integral parts of modern armed forces." He thought that once general war began, movement of large-scale ground forces would be impossible. "If we have been heavily attacked, there would be neither the planes nor the air bases needed" for such movements. Eisenhower "reiterated that planning should go ahead on the basis of the use of tactical atomic weapons against military targets *in any small war* in which the United States might be involved" (emphasis added). He believed that "Massive retaliation . . . is likely to be the key to survival" and he felt "that in the emphasis he has given on the atomic weapons lies the greatest safety and security for our country."[165]

However, as American strategists absorbed the implications of mutual assured destruction, they came to appreciate the need for forces tailored for limited war situations. Prompted by some members of the NSC Planning Board, one of whom referred to the effect upon the Soviet Union and US allies "of our becoming more and more possessors of a vast deterrent power which we may be less and less inclined to use," Eisenhower's special assistant for national security affairs, Robert Cutler, proposed setting up a high-level committee to assess US capabilities to deal with hostilities short of general war.[166] The JCS approved a recommendation by the chief of army staff that a committee of the JCS urgently examine American capabilities to cope with limited war.[167] The Gaither Panel recommended augmentation of US and allied forces for limited military operations and enhancing their mobility, to enable them to deter or promptly suppress small wars. The panel suggested a study, at the national rather than the service level, to develop a doctrine on when and how nuclear weapons could contribute to limited operations.[168] However, a group of State and Defense Department officials, set up following the NSC discussion, came to the rather surprising conclusion that the

United States possessed adequate capability to tackle limited war situations.[169]

In the NSC discussion on the topic, Dulles conceded that in the last five years, "the State Department had sometimes felt a need for the United States to have non-nuclear-equipped forces which could, if necessary, put on a demonstration of US interests in various parts of the world." Eisenhower took the stand that "the important thing was to augment the capabilities of our forces for limited war rather than increasing the size of such forces."[170] Soviet gains in strategic weapons, Dulles admitted, had somewhat neutralized the American nuclear deterrent. This made US allies doubt whether the Americans would in fact use thermonuclear weapons if the United States itself was not attacked. The State Department did not think it could hold the European alliance together for more than a year on the basis of the existing US strategic doctrine. Dulles came to the belated realization that "the decision to 'press the button' for all-out war is an awesome thing, and the possibility that such a decision would not be taken must be recognized." The time had come to ask whether developments in the nuclear field made possible "an area defense based on tactical weapons." Echoing the theme of a recent best-selling book by Henry Kissinger, Dulles saw a need for a doctrine for the use of tactical nuclear weapons.[171]

On 1 April 1958, Dulles raised with Eisenhower the need for a review of the massive retaliation strategy that "too much invoked massive nuclear attack" in response to any conflict with the Soviet Union. He wanted development of "other means short of wholesale obliteration of the Soviet Union." He conceded that the existing policy had led to a "vicious circle," and the creation of a force structure that ruled out any kind of response other than massive retaliation.[172] The administration's latest document of its basic national security policy, NSC 5810/1, reflected the new currents of thought. It proposed that

military planning for US forces to oppose local aggression will be based on the development of a flexible and selective capability, including nuclear capability for use as authorized by the President. When the use of US forces is required to oppose local aggression, force will be applied in a manner and on a scale best calculated to avoid hostilities from broadening into general war.[173]

In the NSC meeting that discussed the new document, Dulles urged the development of small, "clean" tactical nuclear warheads and preparation for small, defensive wars short of the total defeat of the enemy.[174]

American reliance on nuclear weapons, whether tactical or strategic, would continue unabated. This raised the question of public reaction to the use of atomic weapons. Eisenhower felt that "we have moved a long distance since 1953 in reconciling the world to the necessity of using atomic weapons," but he was concerned about "what we would do if some small country called on us for assistance against Communist aggression but did not wish us to use nuclear weapons in providing such assistance."[175] Dulles cautioned that using nuclear weapons anywhere in the Far East would produce "the most serious political repercussions" in countries such as India and Japan. He worried that the United States did not have limited war capability in this area.[176]

The American experience in the Taiwan Straits crisis that started soon after showed that the president was way off the mark, and his secretary of state was only partly right, about the political repercussions of the use of atomic weapons in a limited war situation. The political and diplomatic implications of initiating nuclear war would far outweigh the tactical military advantage that the use of atomic weapons might confer. This crisis also demonstrated how severely the shortage of conventional military assets had affected the American ability to respond to the crisis.[177] Sobered by his latest walk to the nuclear brink, Dulles finally began to wonder "whether we might not be putting too much emphasis on the nuclear deterrent." He also questioned the need to continue the nuclear buildup at the cost of conventional weapons. "Anything beyond the capacity to destroy the enemy," he told the secretary of defense, "would seem excessive and unnecessary." He favored cutting down on nuclear forces and passing on the savings to augment conventional forces.[178]

By the time the Republican Party vacated the White House, American strategic thinking had come full circle. During the Kennedy administration, the line of thinking Dulles had initiated toward the end of his career would gather momentum and endorse the need for a renewed buildup of conventional forces. For the rest of the Cold War, nuclear diplomacy toward non-nuclear states remained in the background.

NOTES

1. *New York Times*, 7 August 1945.

2. McGeorge Bundy, *Danger and Survival: Choices About the Bomb in the First Fifty Years* (New York: Vintage Books, 1988), 3, 58, 132.

3. Martin Sherwin, *A World Destroyed* (New York: Alfred A. Knopf, 1975) Barton Bernstein (ed.), *The Atomic Bomb: The Critical Issues* (Boston: Little, Brown & Co., 1976); Barton Bernstein, "Seizing the Contested Terrain of Early Nuclear History: Stimson, Conant, and Their Allies Explain the Decision to Use the Atomic Bomb," *Diplomatic History* (Winter 1993); Gar Alperowitz, *Atomic Diplomacy* (New York: Simon and Schuster, 1965); Gar Alperowitz and Robert Messer, "Marshall, Truman, and the Decision to Drop the Bomb," *International Security* (Winter 1991/1992), 204–14. For the historiography of this debate, see J. Samuel Walker, "The Decision to Drop the Bomb: A Historiographical Update," *Diplomatic History* (Winter 1990). See also *Nuclear America: A Historical Bibliography* (Santa Barbara, CA: ABC-Clio Information Service, 1984). For recent works co-

inciding with the fiftieth anniversary of Hiroshima, see Martin Sherwin, "The Atomic Bomb and the Origins of the Cold War," in Melvyn Leffler and David Painter (eds.), *Origins of the Cold War: An International History* (New York: Routledge, 1994); Ronald T. Takaki, *Hiroshima: Why America Dropped the Atomic Bomb* (Boston: Little, Brown & Co., 1995); Robert P. Newman, *Truman and the Hiroshima Cult* (East Lansing: Michigan State University Press, 1995); Dennis Wainstock, *The Decision to Drop the Atomic Bomb* (Westport, CT: Praeger, 1996); Gar Alperowitz, *The Decision to Use the Atomic Bomb and the Architecture of an American Myth* (New York: Alfred A. Knopf, 1995). J. Samuel Walker, *Prompt and Utter Destruction: Truman and the Use of Atomic Bombs Against Japan* (Chapel Hill: University of North Carolina Press, 1997), offers a superb bibliographical essay.

4. Sherwin, *A World Destroyed*, 6, 230.

5. Bernstein, "The Atom Bomb and American Foreign Policy: The Route to Hiroshima," in Bernstein (ed.), *The Atomic Bomb*, 96–98.

6. Henry L. Stimson and McGeorge Bundy, *On Active Service in Peace and War* (New York: Harper and Row, 1948), 616.

7. According to historian Herbert Ferrell, contrary to conventional wisdom and Truman's own claim that he did not know about the atomic bomb program before he became president, Roosevelt told his running mate about the bomb on 18 August 1944. See Herbert Ferrell, *Harry S. Truman: A Life* (Columbia: University of Missouri Press, 1994), 172 and 418, note 37.

8. Harry S. Truman, *Memoirs, Vol. 1: Year of Decisions* (Garden City, NY: Doubleday & Co., 1956), 87.

9. Gregg Herken, *The Winning Weapon* (New York: Alfred A. Knopf, 1980), 16.

10. Sherwin, *A World Destroyed*, 193–94.

11. Bernstein, *The Atomic Bomb*, 107.

12. Sherwin, *A World Destroyed*, 190.

13. See Introduction.

14. Sherwin, *A World Destroyed*, 189–90; Bernstein, *The Atomic Bomb*, 106. Oppenheimer's request for a three-day postponement of the test scheduled for 14 July was denied. "The upper crust wants it as soon as possible," General Leslie Groves, the head of the Manhattan Project, informed Oppenheimer. The test could, however, only be done on the 16th. Sherwin, *A World Destroyed*, 222.

15. Ibid., 224; Herken,*The Winning Weapon*, 18.

16. Melvyn Leffler, *A Preponderance of Power* (Stanford, CA: Stanford University Press, 1992), 37.

17. Ibid., 38–39.

18. Bernstein, *The Atomic Bomb*, 110. Byrnes argued that "our possessing and demonstrating the bomb would make Russia more manageable in Europe." Leading atomic scientist Leo Szilard pressed for a delay in dropping the bomb on Japan on the plea that the "interests of peace might best be served and an arms race avoided by not using the bomb against Japan, keeping it secret, and letting the Russians think that our work on it had not succeeded." Byrnes retorted that Congress would insist on seeing the results of the $2 billion spent on the development of the bomb. "How would you get Congress to appropriate money for atomic energy research," he queried, "if you do not show results for the money which has been spent already?" Sherwin, *A World Destroyed*, 202.

19. Robert L. Messer, *The End of an Alliance: James F. Byrnes, Roosevelt, Truman, and the Origins of the Cold War* (Chapel Hill: University of North Carolina Press, 1982), 127–30; Herken, *The Winning Weapon*, 48–49, 56.

20. Bundy, *Danger and Survival*, 137–38.

21. Stimson to Truman, 11 September 1945, and Stimson memo for the president, 11 September 1945, PSF, General File, Box 112, "Atomic Bomb," HSTL.

22. Bundy, *Danger and Survival*, 139–42.

23. JCS Decision on JCS 1471/4, 24 October 1945, CCS 471.6 (8–15–45) Sec. 2, RG 218, NA.

24. Truman, *Year of Decisions*, 527–28; Secretary of Agriculture to Truman, 25 September 1945, PSF, General File, Box 112, "Atomic Bomb," HSTL; Vinson to Truman, 27 September 1945, PSF, Subject File, Box 199, "Atomic Bomb-Cabinet-Fred Vinson," HSTL.

25. Bundy, *Danger and Survival*, 141; Herken, *The Winning Weapon*, 37–38. Groves also advised Truman that the United States and Britain had together cornered the world's known supply of fissionable materials, thus assuring themselves an adequate supply while denying potential competitors access to the vital resource. Ibid., 14.

26. Messer, *The End of an Alliance*, 89.

27. Enclosure to JCS 1477/10, 31 March 1946, CCS 471.6 (8–15–45) Sec. 2, RG 218, NA.

28. The Final Report of the JCS Evaluation Board for Operation Crossroads, 30 June 1947, Student Research File, Box 3, "Decision to Drop Atomic Bomb on Japan, Folder 5," HSTL. Operation Crossroads was a series of atomic bomb tests in the Pacific in which bombs were dropped on the captured Japanese fleet to determine weapons effects.

29. David Alan Rosenberg, "The Origins of Overkill: Nuclear Weapons and American Strategy," in Norman Graebner (ed.), *The National Security: Its Theory and Practice, 1945–1960* (New York: Oxford University Press, 1986), 129.

30. John Lewis Gaddis, *The Long Peace: Enquiries Into the History of the Cold War* (New York: Oxford University Press, 1987), 106.

31. David E. Lilienthal, *The Journals of David E. Lilienthal: The Atomic Energy Years* (New York: Harper and Row, 1964), 391.

32. Ibid., 474.

33. Rosenberg, "The Origins of Overkill," 129–30; Steven Rearden, *History of the Office of the Secretary of Defense* (Washington, DC: Historical Office, Office of the Secretary of Defense, 1984), 434–36. See also Steven Rearden and Samuel R. Williamson Jr., *The Origins of US Nuclear Strategy, 1945–1953* (New York: St. Martin's Press, 1993), 85.

34. NSC 30, 10 September 1948, *FRUS 1948, I*, 624–28; Rearden, *History of the Office of the Secretary of Defense*, 436.

35. Webb memo for the president, 22 July 1948, PSF, Subject File, Box 200, "NSC-Atomic Energy-Budget," HSTL.

36. Walter Millis (ed.), *The Forrestal Diaries* (New York: Viking Press, 1951), 458.

37. Richard Betts, *Nuclear Blackmail and Nuclear Balance* (Washington, DC: The Brookings Institution, 1987), 24–25.

38. Kenneth W. Condit, *The History of the Joint Chiefs of Staff: The Joint Chiefs*

of Staff and National Policy, Vol. II, 1947–1949 (Wilmington, DE: Michael Glazier, 1979), 139.

39. *Newsweek*, 19 July 1948.

40. Memo for president, 16 July 1948, PSF, NSC meetings, Box 220, "NSC Meetings—Memos for the President—Meeting Discussions, 1948," HSTL.

41. Millis, *The Forrestal Diaries*, 457. See also Avi Shlaim, *The United States and the Berlin Blockade, 1948–1949: A Study in Crisis Decision-Making* (Berkeley: University of California Press, 1983), 236–37.

42. Ibid., 237; *Newsweek*, 26 July 1948, 32. For additional documentation on the movement of B-29 bombers to Europe, see Herken, *The Winning Weapon*, 258 60.

43. Quoted in Betts, *Nuclear Blackmail*, 26. Truman admonished those who clamored for the transfer of the custody of the atomic stockpile to the armed forces during the Berlin crisis that "This is no time to be juggling an atom bomb around." Lilienthal, *Journals*, 391.

44. Condit, *The History of the Joint Chiefs of Staff, Vol. II*, 139.

45. David Holloway, *Stalin and the Bomb: The Soviet Union and Atomic Energy, 1939–1956* (New Haven, CT: Yale University Press, 1994), 261.

46. Lilienthal, *Journals*, 215.

47. Memcon 20 November 1948, *FRUS 1948, III*, 281. See also Millis, *The Forrestal Diaries*, 502.

48. The Harmon Committee Report, 11 May 1949, excerpted in Thomas H. Etzold and John L. Gaddis, *Containment: Documents on American Policy and Strategy, 1945–1950* (New York: Columbia University Press, 1978), 361–63. However, this estimate was based on a gross overestimation of Soviet force strength in Europe. See Matthew Evangelista, "Stalin's Postwar Army Reappraised," *International Security* (Winter 1982/1983).

49. Rosenberg, "The Origins of Overkill," 137–38.

50. Leffler, *A Preponderance of Power*, 223.

51. Ibid., 225.

52. NSC 20/4, 23 November 1948, *FRUS 1948, I*, 667.

53. Leffler, *A Preponderance of Power*, 264–65.

54. Ibid., 304.

55. Truman to Souers, 1 July 1949, *FRUS 1949, I*, 350–52.

56. Ernest R. May, *American Cold War Strategy: Interpreting NSC 68* (Boston: Bedford Books, 1993), 3.

57. Pace to Truman, 5 April 1949, PSF, Subject Series, Box 200, "NSC-Atomic Energy-Budget," HSTL.

58. Acheson memo, 20 December 1949, *FRUS 1949, I*, 612.

59. Memcon 3 November 1949, PPS Papers, 1947–1953, Box 50, "Nitze, Paul (Atomic Energy 1948–1950)," RG 59, NA.

60. Draft Kennan memo, 17 February 1950, *FRUS 1950, I*, 164.

61. Ibid., 223.

62. For recent studies of the Soviet nuclear program, see David Holloway, *Stalin and the Bomb* (New Haven, CT: Yale University Press, 1994); Thomas B. Cochran, Robert S. Norris, and Oleg Bukharin, *The Making of the Russian Bomb: From Stalin to Yeltsin* (Boulder, CO: Westview Press, 1995). See also essays and

documents on the Soviet nuclear program in the *Cold War International History Project (CWIHP) Bulletins*, 1991 to 1998.

63. CIA memo for the president, 6 July 1948, NSC Records, Box 1, "NSC-CIA Memoranda—May 31, 1948–August 31, 1950," HSTL.

64. Estimated Allocation of Soviet Atomic Bombs Between War-Making Resources and Retaliatory Force Targets in the United States, PPS Papers, 1947–1953, Box 50, "Nitze, Paul (Atomic Energy 1948–1950)," RG 59, NA.

65. See *FRUS 1950, I*, 126–492; May, *American Cold War Strategy*; Leffler, *A Preponderance of Power*, 355–60.

66. George F. Kennan, *Memoirs: 1925–1950* (Boston: Little, Brown & Co., 1967), 373–75.

67. The "China Lobby" consisted of an assortment of individuals and organizations, largely financed by the Nationalists, that strove to advance the Nationalist cause in the United States. The "China Bloc" refers to the group of US senators and members of the House of Representatives who supported the aims of the China Lobby. See Ross Y. Koen, *The China Lobby in American Politics* (New York: Octagon Books, 1974). A recent study of the China Hands is Paul G. Lauren (ed.), *The China Hands' Legacy: Ethics and Diplomacy* (Boulder, CO: Westview Press, 1987). See also Stanley D. Bachrack, *The Committee of One Million: "China Lobby" Politics, 1953–1971* (New York: Columbia University Press, 1976). For details of the China Bloc's efforts to secure American aid for the Nationalists, see Bradford Westerfield, *Foreign Policy and Party Politics: Pearl Harbor to Korea* (New Haven, CT: Yale University Press, 1955), 346–69; David R. Kepley, *The Collapse of the Middle Way: Senate Republicans and the Bipartisan Foreign Policy, 1948–1952* (Westport, CT: Greenwood Press, 1988). The attack on the administration's China policy was not confined to Republicans alone. Congressman John F. Kennedy charged that "What our young men had saved, our diplomats and President have frittered away." Quoted in Michael Schaller, *The United States and China in the Twentieth Century* (New York: Oxford University Press, 1979), 117. See also Ferrell, *Harry S. Truman*; Robert J. Donovan, *Tumultuous Years: The Presidency of Harry S. Truman, 1949–1953* (New York: W. W. Norton & Co., 1982).

68. Lyman Van Slyke (ed.), *The China White Paper, 1949* (Stanford, CA: Stanford University Press, 1967), 688. The *White Paper* was published by the State Department to explain to the American people what the United States had done to support the Nationalist regime in China and to counter the criticism leveled at it by the Republican right wing. However, by blaming the Nationalists for their failures, the *White Paper* led to continued right-wing criticism of the administration. By explaining in graphic detail how far it had gone to support the Nationalists, it probably aroused the Chinese communists' suspicions of American intentions toward the PRC.

69. Westerfield, *Foreign Policy and Party Politics*, 347.

70. *FRUS 1949 IX*, 263–65, 461–62; Michael Schaller, *The American Occupation of Japan: Origins of the Cold War in Asia* (New York: Oxford University Press, 1985), 174, 208–10.

71. State Department to Taipei, 15 August 1949, *FRUS 1949, IX*, 160–61, 315; note of conversation with Dean Acheson, 15 February 1949, Wellington Koo Papers, Box 130, "Various Interviews, 1949, #39–45," Butler Manuscripts Library, Columbia University.

72. For a view that, by the end of 1949, Acheson had made up his mind against strong opposition from his advisers in the State Department and the Pentagon, to accord diplomatic recognition to the PRC, acquiesce in the communist capture of Formosa, and sever US ties to the Nationalists, see Nancy Bernkoff Tucker, *Patterns in the Dust: Chinese-American Relations and the Recognition Controversy, 1949–1950* (New York: Columbia University Press, 1983); Warren Cohen, "Acheson, His Advisers, and China, 1949–1950," in Dorothy Borg and Waldo Heinrichs (eds.), *Uncertain Years: Chinese-American Relations, 1947–1950* (New York: Columbia University Press, 1980), 13–52. For differing views, see Robert Blum, *Drawing the Line: The Origins of the American Containment Policy in East Asia* (New York: W. W. Norton & Co., 1982) and William Stueck, *The Road to Confrontation: American Policy Toward China and Korea, 1947–1950* (Chapel Hill: University of North Carolina Press, 1987). See also Warren Cohen, "Conversations with Chinese Friends: Zhou Enlai's Associates Reflect on Chinese-American Relations in the Late 1940s and the Korean War," *Diplomatic History* (Summer 1987); and Warren Cohen, *America's Response to China* (New York: Columbia University Press, 1990).

For a view that the administration formulated a "two-China" policy in mid-1949, which it kept secret from the lesser State Department officials, Congress, the American public, and the Nationalists, that Taiwan was never "abandoned," and that the neutralization of the Taiwan Strait after 25 June 1950 was simply an extension of this policy, see June Grasso, *Truman's Two-China Policy, 1948–1950* (Armonk, NY: M. E. Sharpe, 1987). See also Su Ge, *The Horrible Dilemma—the Making of the US-Taiwan Mutual Defense Treaty, 1948–1955* (Ph. D. dissertation, Brigham Young University, 1987).

73. "The evidence of this [US] intention [to recognize the PRC] is as tenuous today as it was then," John Gittings summed up, "but the Chinese were supposed to be capable of seeing it, drawing the right conclusion, and refraining from any measure which might inhibit its eventual fulfillment." John Gittings, *Survey of the Sino-Soviet Dispute* (London: Oxford University Press, 1968), 17.

74. Paradoxically, at the very moment when Acheson seemed to have swung Truman's thinking to his own view, his influence with the president began to decline. Truman's 5 January statement underwent two significant changes from the draft cleared by the State Department. From the sentence "Nor does it have any intention of utilizing its armed forces to interfere in the present situation *or to detach Formosa from China*," Truman deleted the italicized portion. To the sentence "The United States has no desire to obtain special rights or privileges or to establish military bases on Formosa," he added the words "at this time." These changes, made at the insistence of General Omar Bradley, the chairman of the JCS, ran counter to the line Acheson was pursuing so far and foreshadowed the move in the opposite direction that began later in 1950. See Gordon Chang, *Friends and Enemies: The United States, China, and the Soviet Union, 1948–1972* (Stanford, CA: Stanford University Press, 1990), 310–12.

75. Cohen, "Acheson, His Advisers, and China, 1949–1950."

76. Dean Acheson, *Present at the Creation: My Years in the State Department* (New York: W. W. Norton & Co., 1969), 358–60.

77. Alonzo L. Hamby, *Man of the People: A Life of Harry S. Truman* (New York: Oxford University Press, 1995), 521–29.

78. Acheson, *Present at the Creation*, 364. The movement snowballed into what Acheson called the "attack of the primitives." Ibid., Chapter 39.

79. Donovan, *Tumultuous Years*, 165, 170.

80. See Kepley, *The Collapse of the Middle Way*, 75–76; *Time*, 12 June 1950.

81. Robert Divine, *Foreign Policy and US Presidential Elections, 1952–1960* (New York: New Viewpoints, 1974), 170; Thomas J. Christensen, *Useful Adversaries: Grand Strategy, Domestic Mobilization, and Sino-American Conflict, 1947–1958* (Princeton, NJ: Princeton University Press, 1996), 50.

82. *New York Times*, 8 January 1950.

83. See Blum, *Drawing the Line*; Westerfield, *Foreign Policy and Party Politics*.

84. Blum, *Drawing the Line*, 184–87.

85. Schaller, *The American Occupation of Japan*, 253; Chang, *Friends and Enemies*, 71–72.

86. For details of NSC 68, see *FRUS 1950, I.*

87. Dean Rusk, *As I Saw It: As Told to Richard Rusk* (New York: W. W. Norton & Co., 1990), 161; Rosemary Foot, *The Wrong War: American Policy and the Dimensions of the Korean Conflict, 1950–1953* (Ithaca, NY: Cornell University Press, 1985), 43.

88. Chang, *Friends and Enemies*, 70–71.

89. Dulles memo, 18 May 1950, *FRUS 1950, I*, 314–16; Rusk to Acheson, 30 May 1950, *FRUS 1950, VI*, 349–51; Howe to Armstrong, 31 May 1951, ibid., 347. Although no evidence to show that Acheson saw Rusk's memorandum has surfaced yet, Acheson's appointment diary shows that he met Rusk, Nitze, and Dulles on 31 May and 9 June 1950. Bruce Cumings, *The Origins of the Korean War, Vol. 2: The Roaring of the Cataract* (Princeton, NJ: Princeton University Press, 1990), 539.

90. Chang, *Friends and Enemies*, 72, 74.

91. Freeman to Merchant and Rusk, 21 June 1950, 793.52/5–2750, RG 59, NA; Cumings, *Origins of the Korean War, II*, Chapter 16; Chang, *Friends and Enemies*, 72, 74.

92. Notes of conversation with Dulles, 12 June, Koo Papers, Box 180, "Notes of Conversation, 1950," Columbia University Library. Koo, however, worried that the State Department's poor opinion of the Nationalists seemed to have influenced Dulles. Diary entry for 12 June 1950, Koo Papers, Box 217, "Koo Diary, September 9, 1949–June 25, 1950," Columbia University Library.

93. Donovan, *Tumultuous Years*, 194–95; Acheson, *Present at the Creation*, 369.

94. *New York Times*, 13 January 1950. For Acheson's account of the episode, see Acheson, *Present at the Creation*, 355–57.

95. *Time*, 19 June 1950.

96. Donovan, *Tumultuous Years*, 194–95; Acheson, *Present at the Creation*, 407. On the Blair House meeting, see Chapter 3.

97. *New York Times*, 27 June 1950.

98. *New York Times*, 28 June 1950.

99. Acheson, *Present at the Creation*, 364–66.

100. Donovan, *Tumultuous Years*, 182–83.

101. Leffler, *A Preponderance of Power*, 401–3.

102. Ibid., 452–53.

103. For details, see Chapter 3.

104. Savage memo, 12 April 1951, *FRUS 1951, I*, 815, 819.

105. Memo for the president, 25 January 1951, PSF, NSC Meetings, Box 220, "NSC Meetings-Memos for President-Meeting Discussion, 1951," HSTL.

106. Enclosure to NSC 126, 28 February 1952, PSF, Subject, Box 193, "NSC Memo Approvals," HSTL.

107. Chief of Special Projects to the Chairman, AEC, 15 August 1951, PSF, Subject Series, Box 202, "NSC-Atomic Weapons—Atomic Stockpile," HSTL.

108. Summary of discussions of the meeting of the Special Committee of the NSC on Atomic Energy, 16 January 1952, *FRUS 1952–54, II, Part 2*, 854.

109. David Alan Rosenberg, "US Nuclear Stockpile, 1945 to 1950," *The Bulletin of the Atomic Scientists* (May 1982), 26.

110. Ibid., 28.

111. Ibid., 29.

112. Thomas B. Cochran et al., *Nuclear Weapons Databook, Vol. II: US Nuclear Warhead Production* (Cambridge, MA: Ballinger, 1987), 10, 15; Chuck Hansen, *US Nuclear Weapons: The Secret History* (Arlington, TX: Aerofax, 1988), 125–28.

113. Ibid., 131–33.

114. Ibid., 128–31.

115. Ibid., 133–37.

116. Rosenberg, "The Origins of Overkill," 143.

117. Ibid., 138–41.

118. *New York Times*, 1 October 1952; Hansen, *US Nuclear Weapons*, 172–74; John J. Midgley, Jr., *Deadly Illusions: Army Policy for the Nuclear Battlefield* (Boulder, CO: Westview Press, 1986), 22–24; Summary of the Final Report of Project VISTA, 12 February 1952, Psychological Strategy Board Files, Box 30, "Evaluation of Project VISTA, Joint Applications," HSTL.

119. Richard L. Miller, *Under the Cloud: Three Decades of Nuclear Testing* (New York: The Free Press, 1986), 101; Hansen, *US Nuclear Weapons*, 190–91; Kenneth W. Condit, *History of the Joint Chiefs of Staff, Vol. VI: The Joint Chiefs of Staff and National Policy, 1955–1956* (Washington, DC: Historical Office, Joint Staff, 1992), 65. On the early history of US tactical missiles, see Matthew Evangelista, *Innovation and Arms Race: How the United States and the Soviet Union Develop New Military Technologies* (Ithaca, NY: Cornell University Press, 1988), Chapter 4.

120. Summary of the Final Report of Project VISTA, 12 February 1952, Psychological Strategy Board Files, Box 30, "Evaluation of Project VISTA, Joint Applications," HSTL.

121. Marcelle Size Knaack, *Encyclopedia of US Air Force Aircraft and Missile Systems, Vol. I: Post World War II Fighters, 1945–1973* (Washington, DC: Office of Air Force History, 1978), 22, 36–37.

122. Midgley, *Deadly Illusions*, 6–7.

123. James A. Gavin, *War and Peace in the Space Age* (New York: Harper & Brothers, 1958), 112–13.

124. Midgley, *Deadly Illusions*, 8–9.

125. Ibid., 2–4.

126. Ibid., 5. Later, Eisenhower administration spokesmen, led by the president himself, would repeatedly claim that atomic weapons were no different from other weapons. Eisenhower's view on this was perhaps influenced by such briefings while he was chief of army staff.

127. Midgley, *Deadly Illusions*, 5, 15–18.

128. Ibid., 22.

129. Ibid., 24–25.

130. Report of the Oppenheimer panel, *FRUS 1952–54, II*, 1070–72. On Eisenhower's agreement with these conclusions, see Robert Bowie, "Eisenhower, Atomic Weapons, and Atoms for Peace," in Joseph F. Pilat et al. (eds.), *Atoms for Peace: An Analysis After Thirty Years* (Boulder, CO: Westview Press, 1985), 18.

131. For documentation on the Solarium Project, see *FRUS 1952–53, II*, Part 2.

132. For recent studies of New Look, see Saki Dockrill, *Eisenhower's New Look National Security Policy, 1953–61* (London: Macmillan Press, 1996); Robert R. Bowie and Richard H. Immerman, *Waging Peace: How Eisenhower Shaped an Enduring Cold War Strategy* (New York: Oxford University Press, 1998).

133. "Memo of discussion at the 131st meeting of the NSC, 11 February 1953, *FRUS 1952–54, II*, 236. When the three service chiefs predicted grave consequences for American security if the share of their respective services came down, Eisenhower sarcastically suggested a study to determine "whether national bankruptcy or national destruction would get us first." 138th Meeting of NSC, 25 March 1953, ACWF/NSC, Box 4, DEPL.

134. Enclosure to Cutler memo for Hauge, 1 May 1953, WHCF, Confidential File, Subject Series, Box 45, "National Security," DEPL. On 28 September 1950, while he was president of Columbia University, Eisenhower had articulated the concept underpinning his outlook later as president. The Korean War, he had said, was only one episode in a "long deliberate campaign," in waging which the United States "must not go broke." If it did so, "the Russians would have won even a greater victory than anything they could obtain by going to war." Samuel F. Wells, Jr., "The Origins of Massive Retaliation," *Political Science Quarterly* (Spring 1981), 40.

135. Memo of 166th NSC meeting, 13 October 1953, *FRUS 1952–54, II*, 547.

136. Rosenberg, "The Origins of Overkill," 141; "History of the Custody and Deployment of Nuclear Weapons," and "Deployment by Country 1951–1977," NSA website.

137. Ibid., 593. The administration tried out this policy on British and French leaders at the Bermuda summit conference, with not very satisfactory results. Bermuda (dictation 12/6/53)-2," AWF, International, Box 3, "Bermuda—Pres. Notes 12/53 (1)," DEPL.

138. Lay memo, 4 January 1954, OSANSA Files, NSC Series, Subject Subseries, Box 1, "Atomic Weapons, Presidential Approval and Instructions for Use," DEPL.

139. 160th NSC, 27 August 1953, *FRUS 1952–54, II*, 447.

140. Eisenhower memo to Dulles, 8 September 1953, ibid., 461.

141. Memo of discussions in the 165th NSC meeting, 7 October 1953, ibid., 532–33.

142. Thomas B. Cochran et al., *Nuclear Weapons Databook, Vol. I: US Nuclear Forces and Capabilities* (Cambridge, MA: Ballinger Publishing Company, 1984), 15.

143. Robert Bowie, "Commentary," in May, *American Cold War Strategy*, 114.

144. *Public Papers of the Presidents: Dwight D. Eisenhower, 1953–1961* (Washington, DC: 1960–1961), 1954, pp. 6–23.

145. Wells, "The Origins of Massive Retaliation," 33–36.

146. For critical views of the massive retaliation strategy, see William Kaufman, "The Requirements of Deterrence," in Kaufman (ed.), *Military Policy and National Security* (Princeton, NJ: Princeton University Press, 1956); Paul Nitze, "Critique of Dulles's 'Massive Retaliation' Speech," in Steven Rearden and Kenneth W. Thompson (eds.), *Paul H. Nitze on National Security and Arms Control* (Lanham, MD: University Press of America, 1990). See also John Lewis Gaddis, *Strategies of Containment: A Critical Appraisal of Postwar American National Security Policy* (New York: Oxford University Press, 1982).

147. Memo of meeting, 9 May 1954, Dulles Papers, Subject, Box 8, "Indochina May 1953–May 1954 (2)," DEPL; Bundy, *Danger and Survival*, 261–62.

148. McCardle to Dulles, 30 April 1954, Dulles Papers, General Correspondence and Memo Series, Box 2, "Strictly Confidential—C-D (1)," DEPL.

149. Bundy, *Danger and Survival*, 263–65; *FRUS 1952–54, XIII*, 1437.

150. Ibid., 267. See also John Prados, *The Sky Would Fall: Operation Vulture: The US Bombing Mission in Indochina, 1954* (New York: The Dial Press, 1983), 152–56.

151. AWF, NSC, Box 5, "209th Meeting of NSC, 5 August 1954," DEPL; *FRUS 1952–54, II*, 706–7.

152. Ibid., 708.

153. Ibid., 716–19.

154. See Chapter 4.

155. *FRUS 1952–54, II*, 773.

156. Ibid., 774–75.

157. Memo of 166th NSC, 13 October 1953, *FRUS 1952–54, II*, 546; Eisenhower memo to C. D. Jackson, 31 December 1953, ibid., 1322; Summary of Meeting in the White House, 16 January 1954, ibid., 1342–43.

158. See minutes of 195th meeting of the NSC, 6 May 1954, ibid., 1425–28.

159. JCS memo to secretary of defense, 30 April 1954, ibid., 1438–40.

160. Log entry, 27 November 1953, Log 1953 (2), Box 56, C.D. Jackson Papers, "Time-Life-Log-1953 (2)," DEPL.

161. Bowie, "Eisenhower, Atomic Weapons, and Atoms for Peace," 21.

162. Memo of conversation with Stassen, 31 December 1955, Dulles Papers, Subject, Box 4, "Disarmament 1955–56 (2)," DEPL.

163. AWF, NSC, Box 8, "324th meeting of the NSC, 23 May 1957," DEPL.

164. PPS Study, 23 April 1954, *FRUS 1952–54, II*, 1390–92.

165. Goodpaster memcon, 24 May 1956, AWF, DDE Diary, Box 15, "May 1956 Goodpaster," DEPL.

166. Cutler memo for the president, 7 August 1957, AWF, Administration Series, Box 11, "Cutler, General Robert L., 156–57 (1)," DEPL.

167. JCS 1812/82, 23 December 1957, 381 (11–22–57) Sec. 1, RG 218, NA.

168. For the Gaither panel's recommendations on limited war capabilities, see AWF, NSC Series, Box 9, "Discussions at the 352nd meeting of the NSC, 22 January 1958," DEPL.

169. JCS 2285/1, 11 June 1958, 381 (11–22–57), Sec. 2, RG 218, NA. The officials were unduly optimistic. US forces managed to land less than the equivalent of a division of troops in Lebanon just weeks after this study. In historian Ernest May's near contemporary assessment, the operation "fell short of a terrifying display of strength." Ernest R. May, "Eisenhower and After," in May (ed.), *The*

Ultimate Decision: The President as Commander in Chief (New York: George Braziller, 1960), 227–28.

170. AWF, NSC, Box 9, "352nd meeting of the NSC, 22 January 1958," DEPL.

171. Goodpaster memo for the record, 9 April 1958, Staff Secretaries File, Subject Series, Alphabetical Subseries, Box 21, "Nuclear Exchange—September 1957– June 1958 (3)," DEPL; *Henry Kissinger, Nuclear Weapons and Foreign Policy* (New York: Harper & Brothers, 1957). Admiral Arleigh Burke, the Chief of Naval Operations, testified before a Subcommittee of the Senate Committee on Appropriations in June 1958 that "the mutual capability to annihilate each other as we have seen is not a deterrent to Communist aggression by other means. It is in fact likely that the Communists will channel greater effort into the Cold War. . . . Massive destruction will not prevent this type of creeping aggression." Jonathan Howe, *Multicrises: Sea Power and Global Politics in the Missile Age* (Cambridge, MA: MIT Press, 1971), 164.

172. Editorial note, *FRUS 1958–60, III,* 57.

173. NSC 5810/1, 5 May 1958, PPS Files, NND 933301.

174. Memo of 364th NSC meeting, 1 May 1958, *FRUS 1958–60, III,* 85.

175. Memo of 370th meeting of NSC, 26 June 1958, ibid., 121.

176. Ibid., 121–22.

177. For details of this crisis, see Chapter 5.

178. Memo of 8 November 1958, *FRUS 1958–60, III,* 146.

CHAPTER 3

The Limits of Nuclear Coercion: Nuclear Diplomacy in the Korean War

In the 1956 *Life* report, Dulles had claimed that after listening to his presentation on the Korean War aboard the USS *Helena*, President-elect Eisenhower "made his first vital decision" about the war. He "would make every effort to bring an honorable truce" in the negotiations, but if the stalemate continued, "the US would this time fight to win." The report continued, based on information provided by Dulles, that

> in order to save lives in the UN command, Eisenhower decided on the tactical use of atomic arms should hostilities be renewed....
>
> [I]t was urgent to make sure that the Reds would not again act out of miscalculation. Characteristically, Dulles undertook personally to see that this was done....
>
> Dulles told [India's Prime Minister Jawaharlal] Nehru that the US desired to end the fighting in Korea honorably. He also said that if the war continued, the US would lift the self-imposed restrictions on its actions and hold back no effort or weapon to win.
>
> Within two weeks after his trip to New Delhi, Dulles received word from Korea that the Reds appeared to have begun to negotiate seriously.[1]

Stories about the passing of American nuclear threats to China through India had surfaced soon after the signing of the armistice on 27 July 1953. Nehru had, however, denied the rumors.[2] Following the *Life* article, Nehru had instructed the Indian ambassador in Washington to inform the State Department that his record of the meeting with Dulles did not refer to any threat of nuclear attacks and that he had certainly not passed on any such message to China.[3] Nevertheless, the story continued to be widely accepted. It gained further currency after Eisenhower claimed in his memoirs:

The lack of progress in the long-stalemated talks . . . and the nearly stalemated war both demanded, in my opinion, definite measures on our part to put an end to these intolerable conditions. One possibility was to let the Communist authorities understand that, in the absence of satisfactory progress, we intend to move decisively without inhibition in our use of weapons, and would no longer be responsible for confining hostilities to the Korean Peninsula. We would not be limited by any world-wide gentleman's agreement. In India and in the Formosa Straits area, and at the truce negotiations at Panmunjom, we dropped the word, discreetly, of our intention. We felt quite sure it would reach Soviet and Chinese Communist ears.

"Soon," Eisenhower wrote, "the prospects for armistice negotiations seemed to improve."[4] Eisenhower also told Lyndon Johnson on 17 February 1965 that he had sent covert messages to China through the Nationalist government and lower-level officials handling the armistice talks at Panmunjom that "they must agree to an armistice quickly, since he planned to remove the restrictions of area and weapons if the war had to be continued."[5] Prominent members of the Eisenhower administration maintained in later years that Eisenhower's nuclear diplomacy had helped end the Korean War. "The record is clear that the threat to Korea was conveyed," Andrew Goodpaster, Eisenhower's former staff secretary, told author John Newhouse in 1986; "Eisenhower did feel that it helped to end the war."[6]

In contrast to Eisenhower and his former aides, officials who had served under President Truman have been unanimous in keeping under wraps the record of his administration in the field of nuclear diplomacy. Truman himself did not mention any nuclear weapons-related activity of his administration in the Korean War in his memoirs, except for a brief reference to the storm raised by his remarks on 30 November 1950 on the possible use of atomic weapons in the Korean War and the US visit of British Prime Minister Clement Attlee that followed it. Neither did Acheson, although he dealt with the Attlee visit in greater detail in his memoirs. Of the junior-level Truman subordinates involved in policy making during the war, Paul Nitze, then director of policy planning in the State Department, claimed that "No one in the executive branch to my knowledge was pushing for use of nuclear weapons."[7] On the issue of nuclear weapons, Truman's handling of the Korean War seemed to stand in stark contrast to his successor's, prompting historian John L. Gaddis to remark that "one of the most remarkable aspects of the Truman administration's strategy in the Korean conflict is how inconspicuously the atom bomb figured in it." Gaddis found it "curious that the

Truman administration appears never to have considered explicitly threatening the Soviet Union with atomic retaliation as a means of *deterring* its intervention on behalf of the North Koreans and the Chinese" (emphasis in original).[8]

The historiography of the American nuclear diplomacy in the Korean War for long concentrated on whether the Eisenhower administration used nuclear diplomacy to end the war.[9] The debate over the Eisenhower administration's alleged nuclear diplomacy helped obscure the actual circumstances that led to the armistice. The myth of the successful nuclear diplomacy of the Eisenhower–Dulles team also helped obscure the far more extensive and complex nuclear diplomacy undertaken by the Truman administration. The position changed dramatically with Roger Dingman's pioneering study that showed that the Truman administration had indeed practiced nuclear diplomacy during the war and on several occasions had moved nuclear bombers overseas.[10] Dingman argued that Truman employed nuclear diplomacy in order to achieve a variety of diplomatic and domestic political objectives. Evidence that subsequently became available and later studies, in particular Bruce Cumings' account of the origins of the Korean War and Mark Ryan's study of the Chinese side of the nuclear issue in the Korean War, have supplemented Dingman's findings.[11] That the atom bomb did figure prominently in the considerations of the Truman administration during the Korean War is no longer doubted. Nevertheless, the exact nature of this diplomacy and what role it played in the Korean War strategy of the Truman administration have not been fully appreciated.

An analysis of the role of American nuclear diplomacy in the Korean War shows that the confidence in the capability of the American atomic arsenal to deter Soviet entry into the war enabled Truman to make the decision to oppose the communist invasion of South Korea at a juncture when the US conventional forces were inadequate to wage a full-scale war against the communist powers. Truman ordered the overseas movements of atomic bombers in order to deter Soviet intervention in the war and as precautionary steps in case the Soviet Union intervened at critical stages in the war. Senior US officials kept the use of atomic weapons under almost continuous review throughout the war. Some time after China entered the war, the Truman administration approved plans that involved the use of atomic weapons, subject to presidential authorization, in order to extricate US forces from possible disaster. In the first half of 1951 and especially in the fall of 1952, the Truman administration undertook almost exactly the kind of nuclear diplomacy aimed at ending the war that the Eisenhower administration *claimed* it had undertaken. Further, the wide publicity given to American nuclear testing and atomic war preparations throughout the war and the widespread public advocacy of the use of atomic weapons in the war by prominently placed

Americans continuously forced the Chinese and the North Koreans to face the possibility of nuclear strikes against them. The likelihood of American atomic bombing did not deter China from entering the war. Nor did American nuclear diplomacy succeed during the armistice negotiations in securing the concessions that the United States sought. There is no basis for the claim that nuclear diplomacy by the Eisenhower administration ended the war. A change in Soviet policy after the death of Stalin and American moderation, not American nuclear threats, removed the last hurdle in the way of an armistice agreement in the spring of 1953.

DECISION TO INTERVENE

As we have seen in Chapter 2, the domestic political situation in the United States when the war started made it impossible for Truman not to intervene with US forces to stop a communist takeover of the Republic of Korea (ROK).[12] When the war started, the US conventional forces were grossly under strength. The army totaled only 10 divisions. Of these, four divisions, about one-third under strength, were in Japan and one in Germany.[13] On 26 June, Bradley warned that commitments of ground forces to Korea would leave the United States without the manpower required to meet other emergencies without mobilization. The JCS faced the painful choice of "how much risk should be accepted in other parts of the world" in opting to intervene.[14] The war commenced in the middle of a dispute among State Department, Pentagon, and CIA officials on whether the Soviet Union would initiate general war once it had acquired an atomic arsenal. Earlier in the year, the JCS had concluded that Soviet forces could launch a major offensive from "a standing start," so the usual warnings would not be forthcoming.[15] Truman thus faced a situation in which he had to choose American military intervention, but lacked the forces for intervention in case the North Korean invasion of South Korea was part of a wider Soviet offensive.

The use of nuclear weapons figured in the very first meeting at the Blair House on 25 June, called by Truman to discuss the crisis generated by the North Korean attack on the South. Air Force Chief of Staff General Hoyt Vandenberg stated that American air units could destroy North Korean armored forces only if the Soviet Air Force did not intervene. When Truman inquired whether US forces could destroy Soviet air bases in the region, Vandenberg replied that "it could be done if we used A-Bombs." Thereupon, Truman ordered the air force to "prepare plans to wipe out all Soviet air bases in the Far East."[16] Obviously, preventing Soviet intervention in the war was very much in Truman's mind.

In the early days of the war, however, opinion among policy makers did not favor the use of nuclear weapons. CIA Director Admiral Roscoe

Hillenkoetter recommended obtaining UN concurrence before using these weapons. "Mere reference to it [atom bomb] incites more than the discussion of its military potential," he argued. A State Department paper concluded that

[T]he US public would sanction our use of the atomic bomb in Korea if the civilian and military leaders of the country believe this action essential for reestablishing peace and for saving the lives of American boys, and if the atomic bombs were used against military objectives without resultant wholesale destruction of civilians.

However, the paper argued, use of atomic weapons would lead to severe loss of US prestige as long as the Soviet and Chinese role was limited to supply of equipment and advice to North Korea. If the United States used atomic weapons and was still driven out of Korea, it would be disastrous for the United States. UN concurrence in the atomic strikes might strengthen the moral case and serve to deter future aggression by serving as a precedent for the UN authorizing use of atomic weapons against aggression in defiance of world opinion. UN involvement in any decision to use atomic weapons might, however, restrict American freedom of action in future conflicts, and the publicity surrounding a UN debate would help the enemy. General Kenneth Nichols, head of the Armed Forces Special Weapons Project and the leading Pentagon authority on nuclear weapons, concurred with the State Department view. A study by the operations planning division at army headquarters, the G-3, also concluded that the use of atomic bombs in Korea at that stage was "unwarranted from military point of view, and questionable from political and psychological point of view."[17]

NUCLEAR BOMBER MOVEMENTS: PHASE ONE

On 8 July, despite the misgivings within his administration about the use of nuclear weapons, Truman ordered the movement of two medium bomber groups of nuclear-capable B-29 bombers to Britain. A few days later, he authorized these units to carry with them the non-nuclear components of atomic bombs.[18] The British government considered the matter serious enough for a discussion in the Cabinet before approving the stationing of the bombers on British soil. Probably the British government did not want a repetition of the publicity that surrounded the B-29 movement to Britain during the Berlin crisis of 1948. They insisted that the Foreign Office should work out the publicity arrangements with the US Embassy in London. They also insisted that the United States treat this move merely as a normal training rotation. They did not want it linked in any way to the Korean War.[19] At the end of July, 10 nuclear-configured B-29s were moved to Guam. On 13 September, Washington ordered these bombers back home.[20]

As possible motives for these bomber movements, Dingman lists: a desire to impress the British about American resolve; deterring a likely Chinese invasion of Taiwan; and demonstrating toughness in order to blunt Republican criticism. It could also have been a response to the North Korean offensive launched on 30 July.[21] Dingman attributes the restrained reaction by the president's opponents at least in part to knowledge of these bomber movements. While Truman might have hoped for diplomatic and domestic political gains from this move, it is questionable whether these were his primary motives. If the need to deter China had influenced the decision to send the bombers to the Far East, it made no sense to withdraw them while the administration contemplated crossing the 38th parallel in the face of a possible Chinese intervention.[22] Acheson could at best have leaked a decision already taken under military initiative to move the bombers. No evidence has surfaced to indicate that he initiated the idea, that too for purely diplomatic ends. At the most, Acheson sought some diplomatic gain as a bonus out of what had originated as a military move. Truman had already done a great deal to satisfy his right-wing domestic critics by mobilizing the UN to stop the communist invasion of South Korea and ordering the Seventh Fleet to repel a Chinese invasion of Taiwan. The overseas movement of the bombers did not generate any publicity in the media. An action that remained hidden even to scholars for decades could hardly have been calculated to give the president any kind of domestic political advantage.

It is far more likely that Truman approved the movement of the bombers to deter Soviet intervention. After the limited American ground forces committed in Korea failed to stop the North Korean advance, MacArthur "jolted" the JCS on 9 July with the news that the battlefield situation was "critical." He went on to add that

This [North Korean] force more and more assumes the aspect of a combination of Soviet leadership and technical guidance with Chinese Communist ground elements. While it serves under the flag of North Korea, it can no longer be considered as an indigenous North Korean military effort.

He ended by asking for at least four full divisions to reinforce the force at his command.[23]

Truman formally approved the decision to send the B-29s to Europe after MacArthur's message reached Washington. In fact, one B-29 squadron sent to the Far East had an assigned role in the US global war plan.[24] Soviet intervention at this stage would have easily driven the US forces off the Korean peninsula altogether. The JCS held the view that if the Soviet Union intervened, or appeared to intervene, the United States should curtail its role in Korea and go ahead with its plans for global war. They did not want US forces to be bogged down in a theater, operations in which would not decisively affect the outcome of a global war. If sizable American forces got pinned down in Korea, they worried, it would actually further Soviet interests.[25] Truman himself feared that "if we just stand by, they'll move into Iran and they'll take over the whole Middle East." To his aide George Elsey, Truman "appeared sincerely determined to go very much further than the order that he had approved for General MacArthur" initially.[26] However, even while authorizing American military intervention in the war, Truman "wanted to be sure that we were not so deeply committed in Korea that we could not take care of other situations which might develop."[27] Since the United States lacked the conventional forces required to stop a North Korean invasion of South Korea with direct Soviet participation, the only way Truman could deter Soviet intervention in Korea or prevent "other situations" from developing was to rely on the US nuclear forces.[28] Without the backing of his nuclear arsenal, it is highly unlikely that Truman would have risked American forces for the defense of South Korea. Given that a serious war was going on in which the United States rarely had an inkling of what the Soviet Union was up to, and the fact that Soviet entry would have triggered American global war plans in which the atomic bombers ordered abroad would have participated anyway, the movement of these bombers closer to their targets should be considered military steps either to deter hostile Soviet moves or, if deterrence failed, as preparation for their actual employment in the war.

BATTLEFIELD USE OF NUCLEAR WEAPONS

With the movement of nuclear-capable forces overseas, the Pentagon simultaneously began to examine the feasibility of using atomic weapons in Korea. Early in July, Bradley proposed providing MacArthur with nuclear weapons. The JCS, however, did not proceed with the idea.[29] When Chief of Army Staff General Lawton Collins visited Korea in mid-July along with Vandenberg, army headquarters sent him a message asking him to ascertain MacArthur's opinion on the military effectiveness of using atomic bombs in a ground support role in Korea. Army headquarters also sought information such as types of targets for atomic strikes, and the political and psychological implications of atomic strikes. The army's G-3 did not get any feedback on this, except for a memorandum of a conversation between MacArthur and Collins in which MacArthur talked about using atomic bombs to destroy the bridges and tunnels connecting the Korean peninsula with Manchuria and Vladivostock. MacArthur saw "a unique use for the atomic bomb—to strike a blocking blow—which would require a six months' repair job." Curiously, Collins denied having had any such conversation with MacArthur and directed that the records should be amended to delete any reference to the quote in question. He saw no need for an immediate decision on the use of atomic weapons or to secure presidential approval of their use.[30]

Collins' strong reservations about the use of atomic weapons in Korea possibly reflected disagreement among planners on whether the US atomic stockpile was adequate for use in the Korean War. The latest Pentagon plan for global war, OFFTACKLE, called for an atomic strike at Soviet targets using 292 bombs. The stockpile in July 1950 contained barely this number of bombs.[31] G-3 did not consider that the use of 10 to 20 bombs in Korea would "unduly jeopardize" American global war plans. Nitze and Brigadier General Herbert B. Loper, assistant for atomic energy at army headquarters, however, thought that "the stockpile was not large enough to mount an effective attack against China and still have sufficient weapons to deal with the Soviets if they too decided to intervene."[32] In any case, G-3 did not consider MacArthur's idea of atomic bombing to destroy bridges and tunnels feasible. The airburst-type bombs then available were not suitable for destroying such targets. Sound military reasons thus ruled out the use of atomic bombs in the early days of the war.

CHINESE DECISION TO INTERVENE

The withdrawal of the North Korean forces north of the 38th Parallel began the second phase of the Korean War, which was dominated by China's entry in the war. American field intelligence indicated that the Chinese leadership was "absolutely confident" that the United States would not use atomic weapons against China and "when pushed back to 38th Parallel will either withdraw from Korea entirely or reach agreement with Chinese." A Chinese Democratic League leader, who defected to Hong Kong, recalled that while the Chinese communist leader Mao Zedong "hoped for a good outcome, he prepared for a bad outcome, even to the extent of reckoning that the US might use the atomic bomb against China." Mao had reportedly paced up and down in his room for three days and nights before finally making the decision to intervene.[33] MacArthur alleged that China received information about American unwillingness to use atomic weapons in the Korean War through communist spies in British service.[34] Kim Philby, Guy Burgess, or Donald Maclean, all of whom occupied pivotal positions in the British diplomatic service and might well have come into possession of confidential information relating to top-level policy discussions on the war, later turned out to have been Soviet spies. However, no evidence to substantiate MacArthur's charge has surfaced yet.[35]

For long, Allen Whiting's 1960 study of China's decision to intervene in the war dominated the historiography of this topic.[36] Whiting discounts the possibility that "Beijing would have taken so serious a step as entry into the Korean War on the basis of a foreign agent's report about American intentions, particularly in view of past reversals of US policy both on Taiwan and Korea." He argues that "intervention was decided upon with at least some realization that it might trigger US retaliation through nuclear as well as non-nuclear air attack." In his view, "the Chinese accepted a calculated risk, which they felt to be justified by the overriding considerations favoring intervention." Intercepted Chinese radio broadcasts indicated that Chinese leaders expected atomic bombing of their cities and industries. Old China hand John P. Davies of the PPS speculated that the Chinese leadership took into account possible American military reprisals, including bombing of targets in China, before they decided to intervene.[37]

Our understanding of the Chinese and Russian role in the Korean War is undergoing rapid changes as more and more documents are made available in Beijing and Moscow. Although much has been learned, there still is a great deal more to be learned about the decision making in Moscow, Beijing, and Pyongyang before one can come to definitive conclusions. One critical question is whether China had advance knowledge of North Korean leader Kim Il Sung's plans to attack the South. Based on sources initially released, scholars had concluded that Mao had some knowledge of Kim's military plans for unifying Korea, and that Mao had discussions with Stalin and Kim on these plans during his Moscow visit in January 1950.[38] Questions have since been raised about whether Stalin informed Mao that he had already approved Kim's plan for invading South Korea.[39]

In any case, currently available evidence shows that the Chinese had no knowledge of the actual timetable for Kim's invasion plans. Kim did not formally inform China of the invasion until after his forces occupied Seoul on 27 June. Not only did China lack accurate information during the first two weeks of the war, in the less-than-friendly state of China's relationship with the Kim regime, Chinese Prime Minister Zhou Enlai had to send military officers to Korea to report on the war in the role of embassy staff rather than as military observers.[40] The American decision to intervene and the dispatch of the Seventh Fleet to the Taiwan Strait seemed to Chinese leaders to pose a threat to their northeast frontier. The Chinese Communist Party (CCP) leadership believed that the US actions were part of an elaborate American plan for aggression against China. According to Chai Chengwen, newly appointed political counselor in the Chinese Embassy in Pyongyang, Chinese leaders feared American encirclement of China. MacArthur had commented, during his Taiwan visit toward the end of July, that "arrangements have been completed for effective coordination between American forces under my command and those of the Chinese government." Chinese leaders viewed this as evidence of an American plan to encircle communist China. Mao and other CCP leaders felt that they had to be prepared for the worst outcome: American success in Korea followed by an advance to the Yalu, which would give a fillip to reactionary forces in mainland China and Taiwan.[41]

Early in July, China decided to create the Northeast Border Defense Army (NEBDA), with orders "to defend the borders of the Northeast, and to prepare to support the war operations of the Korean people's army if necessary." By the end of July, the PLA had concentrated more than a quarter of a million troops along the Yalu.[42] At a meeting of the Politburo on 4 August, Mao raised the need to intervene in the war. An American victory, he argued, would threaten China. "We must lend them [the North Koreans] our hands in the form of sending our military volunteers there. The timing could be further decided, but we have to prepare for this." Zhou supported Mao's arguments. The Politburo concluded that China had to be prepared for a long and expanded war, in which the United States might use atomic bombs. Mao ordered the NEBDA to be ready to carry out operations by the end of August. In view of the difficult task involved, he later postponed the deadline by a month.[43]

When MacArthur began to concentrate ground and naval forces in Japan, the Chinese concluded that an American landing behind the North Korean lines appeared imminent, with Inchon the most likely landing site. A successful American landing, they feared, could reverse the current battlefield situation. US Ambassador Warren Austin's statement in the UN suggesting that the UN forces would aim for the unification of Korea heightened Chinese suspicions. China warned North Korea of a possible American landing in Inchon. Kim, however, ignored the Chinese warning.[44]

Several senior Chinese leaders had serious reservations about intervening in the war. But Mao argued in favor of intervention in his address to the Ninth Session of the Central People's Government Council in early September.[45] On 15 September, MacArthur's forces landed at Inchon. The threat to China's industrial heartland now appeared more imminent. By the end of September, Stalin agreed to give China arms and Soviet air cover for Chinese forces if the PLA entered the war.[46]

When it appeared that UN forces would cross the 38th Parallel and invade North Korea, China began to signal that it would consider such a move a threat to its security and would intervene in the war. As the Indian ambassador to China, KM Panikkar, later recalled, the People's Liberation Army's Acting Chief of Staff General Nie Rongzhen told him on 25 September that "the Chinese did not intend to sit back with folded hands and let the Americans come up to their border." Asked by Panikkar "whether he realized the full implication of such an action," Nie said, "We know what we are in for, but at all costs American aggression has to be stopped. The Americans can bomb us, they can destroy our industries, but they cannot defeat us on land." Dismissing Panikkar's warning that American bombing could "put China back by half a century," Nie confidently replied,

We have calculated all that. They may even drop atom bombs on us. What then? They may kill a few million people. Without sacrifice, a nation's independence cannot be upheld. . . . After all, China lives on the farms. What can atom bombs do there? Our economic development will be put back. We may have to wait for it.[47]

On 30 September, South Korean forces crossed the 38th Parallel. On 1 October, Kim finally requested Chinese assistance. Opposed by dissenters within the CCP, Mao argued that China must intervene.[48] The same day, Stalin sent the Chinese leaders a telegram requesting China to send at least five or six divisions designated as volunteers to defend North Korea.[49] That day, Zhou declared in a speech to the Chinese People's Political Conference that "the Chinese people absolutely cannot tolerate foreign aggression, nor can they stand idly aside while their neighbors are outrageously invaded by imperialists." The *Renmin Ribao* carried the text of the speech on 1 October.[50] On 2 October, the CCP Politburo's Standing Committee discussed the situation. Apparently Mao encountered strong opposition to Chinese intervention from senior CCP leaders, including Zhou and Lin Biao.

The publication by China in 1992 of what was claimed to be the text of a telegram Mao sent Stalin on 2 October had led scholars to believe that Mao had communicated to Stalin China's decision to intervene on 2 October, after which Stalin backed out of his commitment to give China air cover by the Soviet Air Force. The telegram Mao purportedly sent, it now turns out, might at best have been the draft of what Mao had intended to send, but in fact never sent.[51] Mao's actual message to Stalin was conveyed the next day by the Soviet ambassador in Beijing, N. V. Roschin. In this message, Mao conveyed China's inability to accede to Stalin's request for Chinese intervention on the plea that a small number of poorly equipped Chinese divisions would collapse before the US forces. This would drag the Soviet Union into the war and derail China's own domestic goals. A visit to the Soviet Union by Zhou and Lin and two days of discussions with Stalin failed to solve Sino-Soviet differences.[52]

After the Politburo meeting, Zhou informed Panikkar on the night of 2 October, in carefully chosen words, that "The American forces are trying to cross the 38th Parallel and to expand the war. If they really want to do this, we will not sit still without doing anything. We will be forced to intervene."[53] On 4 and 5 October, the Politburo discussed the decision to enter the war. Mao was probably the only one who steadfastly favored intervention. Even Zhou expressed reservations, and others like Lin Biao and Gao Gang strongly opposed intervention.[54] On 7 October, US forces crossed the 38th Parallel. On 13 October, the Politburo finally decided to intervene so as not to allow the enemy to advance to the Yalu "and (allowing) the arrogance of reactionaries at home and abroad to grow." Mao reiterated that "we should enter the war; we must enter the war; entering the war will have great benefits; the harm inflicted by not entering the war would be great."[55] When the UN forces advanced rapidly northward, on 18 October, Mao ordered the People's Volunteers (CPV) to cross the Yalu. The Chinese forces crossed the river on 19 October.[56]

Historian Chen Jian argues that while the UN decision to cross the 38th Parallel offered China a "justification" to intervene, China's decision was influenced more by its domestic and revolutionary needs. In a recent study based on newly available Soviet documents, Vladislav Zubock and Constantin Pleshkov argue that Mao "crumbled" under Stalin's pressure.[57] This study considers neither argument convincing. Even if China had wanted to intervene, and granted, Chinese preparations for intervention had begun as soon as the war started, China could not have intervened without North Korean concurrence and Soviet support, neither of which was certain until after Inchon. Whatever China's domestic imperatives were, they were not pressing enough to risk war with the United States. Pressure from Stalin was also not necessary. Mao very much favored intervention. His problem was opposition within his own ranks.

Whatever the motives behind China's decision to enter the war were, American nuclear capability did not deter China from deciding to intervene. Mao and the CCP had lived in the shadow of a perceived American atomic threat right from the dawn of the nuclear age. Mao's skeptical view of the power of the atom bomb had begun to form within days of the dropping of the bomb on Hiroshima. He formulated his "paper tiger" thesis in 1946 partly with the aim of countering the fear in the PLA ranks about confronting the Nationalists backed by a nuclear-armed United States.[58] Published information on the effects of atomic bombs did not present an image of these weapons sufficient to scare the Chinese leadership.[59] Before the Korean War began, China had actively participated in the worldwide signature campaign against nuclear weapons, known as the Stockholm Peace Appeal. Once the war began, this Chinese campaign merged with the campaign against the American role in the war. The Chinese hoped the signature campaign would inhibit American use of nuclear weapons in Korea.[60] Nie Rongzhen told a conference of the Central Military Commission of the CCP that since the Americans had lost their atomic monopoly, "they may be less eager to use it [atomic bomb] nowadays." However, Nie did not altogether rule out the possibility of American nuclear attacks.[61]

Before China's decision to intervene, senior PLA officers examined the question of possible American use of atomic weapons. Echoing the party line on atomic weapons, they concluded that human forces would ultimately prevail over atomic weapons. Tactically, they believed, use of atomic weapons would harm American forces too; strategically, the impact on world opinion would be critical.[62] Mao proclaimed at the ninth meeting of the Council of the Central People's Government on 5 September: "You [the United States] can use the atomic bomb. I will respond with my hand grenade. I will catch the weak point on your part, hold you, and finally defeat you."[63] Peng Dehui told the Central Committee that "If China is devastated in war, it only means that the Liberation War will last a few years longer. The US will find a pretext at any time to invade China if its troops are poised on the bank of the Yalu River and in Taiwan."[64] Just before launching its offensive against MacArthur's forces, the PLA strengthened air defense in the eastern and southern areas.[65]

Mao's 2 October draft telegram to Stalin, despite its questionable authenticity, offers crucial evidence that Mao had in fact thought through the consequences of Chinese intervention. In the draft telegram, Mao stated that China

must be prepared for the United States to declare and enter a state of war with China; we must be prepared [for the fact that] the United States may, at a minimum, use its air force to bomb many major cities and industrial centers in China, and use its navy to assault the coastal region.

While he was optimistic that the war would not last long and would end with the Chinese forces destroying the American army, Mao did acknowledge the possibility that in the worst case the war might become a stalemate, with the United States in a state of open war with China. This could seriously hurt China's economic development plans and encourage malcontents.[66] Clearly, China considered the threat to its security posed by the rapid American advance toward its own borders serious enough to risk military intervention, even in the face of possible American atomic attacks. That Mao did not take the plunge lightly in a fit of "revolutionary romanticism" is borne out by the report that he pondered over the problem for 60 sleepless hours.[67]

Once reports reached Washington of Chinese threats to intervene in case UN forces crossed the 38th Parallel, Truman modified MacArthur's orders to take into account the possibility of Chinese intervention.[68] Nevertheless, Truman made no overt or covert nuclear threats to deter a Chinese intervention.[69] In the context of nuclear diplomacy, what the Truman administration *did not do* on this occasion is as significant as what it, and its successor, did do in the rest of the war. Truman's refusal to contemplate nuclear diplomacy to deter Chinese entry into the war at this juncture is possibly the best argument against the claim that he moved B-29s to the Far East toward the end of July to deter a Chinese invasion of Taiwan. It is difficult to imagine Truman dispatching nuclear bombers to save the Nationalists in Taiwan, whom he despised, but not the US forces in Korea.

THE US RESPONSE TO CHINESE INTERVENTION

The catastrophe brought about by the Chinese intervention confronted the Truman administration for the second time with a situation it was ill prepared to deal with in the absence of atomic weapons. Bradley reported that within 48 to 72 hours, the battlefield situation might reach "a crash state."[70] The *New York Times* observed that "Not even on the fateful night twenty-three weeks ago when the Korean War started was the atmosphere more grim."[71] The Eighth Army suffered casualties in excess of 11,000 men on 30 November and 1 December, with the 2nd Infantry Division alone losing 6,380 men. About 110,000 UN troops faced an enemy force of 266,000, the vast majority of them Chinese.[72] There was only one army division left in the United States. Another division being formed would not have been ready for operation until the spring.[73]

If the situation was so grim, why did Truman not decide to pull the US forces out of Korea? The president turned to what by now had become a tried and trusted asset: atomic weapons. On 30 November, he said at a news conference that the United States would "take all necessary steps to meet the military situation." Asked whether that included the atom bomb, the president replied, "That would include every weapon that we have." Truman went on to say that "Always there had been active consideration" of use of atom bombs and that the theater commander would be in charge of their use.[74]

Truman's remark might not have been entirely off-the-cuff. Rattling the atom bomb was his best option under the circumstances. A withdrawal from Korea forced by the Chinese would have been politically calamitous. If the Chinese forced the remnants of a defeated Eighth Army to surrender, it would have been even worse. The Chinese intervention in force was a major escalation by the communists. No American president in 1950 could have withdrawn from Korea in the face of a communist advance without using the atom bomb—either militarily or diplomatically. Although the US forces stopped the Chinese advance and stabilized the front using only conventional forces, there was no certainty that the communists would not escalate in some other way. If the Soviet Air Force entered the war, it is unlikely that conventional means would have sufficed, as Vandenberg had foreseen. Truman had already ordered the US Air Force to plan for neutralizing the Soviet Far East Air Force using atomic weapons. When Truman said that he would take "all necessary steps to meet the military situation," he said enough to ensure that US forces could remain in Korea without fear of a forced evacuation.

The United States went a great deal beyond merely verbal nuclear threats. Army G-3 concluded, after the CPV first appeared on the battlefield, that "from the military point of view, the situation is more favorable for employment of atomic weapons than it was in July." Accordingly, they recommended commencement of preparations to provide MacArthur with the capability to use these weapons.[75] G-3 did not contemplate a "tactical necessity" for use of the bomb in Manchuria in the aftermath of the rout of MacArthur's forces. However, G-3 suggested on 1 December that if the UN forces in Korea faced disaster, the JCS should recommend to the president the use of atomic bombs. They wanted that completion of arrangements for the prompt use of atomic weapons, if required, should proceed on an urgent basis.[76] Collins felt that

[I]n the event of an all-out effort by the Chinese Communists, the use of atomic bombs against troops and material concentrations might be the decisive factor in enabling the UN forces to hold a defensive position or to effect the early drive to the Manchurian border.

He wanted the JSSC to study conditions under which atomic weapons could be used in Korea.[77] On 29 November, the JSSC recommended not using of nuclear weapons, except "under the most compelling military circumstances" such as the need to prevent UN forces in Korea from being routed by the communist forces. On 3 December, the JSPC recommended the use of atomic weapons to cover an American evacuation following direct Soviet participation in the war. The committee also wanted immediate preparation to begin for the employment of atomic bombs in such a contingency. The JCS did not act on these reports and withdrew them from circulation.[78] Karl Bendetsen, then deputy secretary of the army, later recalled that

I did make specific and affirmative detailed recommendations urgently for employment of a precise number of atomic weapons in carefully delineated areas, the use of which would remain valid during a specified and limited time zone. These recommendations were not carried into execution although preliminary steps were taken.[79]

An NSC document prepared by the Eisenhower administration early in April 1953 contains an intriguing statement that according to restrictions then in force in the Korean War, "Employment of atomic weapons is *authorized* only in the event our forces in that area would otherwise be faced with a military disaster, and upon approval of the President" (emphasis added).[80] The document does not specify when, and under what circumstances, this was "authorized." The period following the Chinese intervention would have been the most logical occasion for such a decision. The withdrawal of the JSSC and the JSPC recommendations from circulation might well have been related to the need to keep such a decision under wraps for obvious reasons. The use of atomic weapons in the war continued to attract JSSC interest in subsequent months, but this could well have been because approval of the plans involving use of nuclear weapons were not passed down to the lower levels. Based on currently available evidence, this decision is the closest to a decision to use atomic weapons ever taken during the Korean War. This authorization did not amount to a decision *to* use atomic weapons, but it seems to have been somewhat more than mere contingency planning of the kind the JCS undertook throughout the war.

On an inspection trip to the Far East a few days after the Chinese intervention began, Collins found that while the situation "remained serious, it was no longer critical."[81] Atomic weapons, however, figured in his final conference with MacArthur and his senior officers. MacArthur stated that holding out against an all-out Chinese offensive would involve the "possible use of atomic weapons" (along with a naval blockade of China, air attacks on the mainland, and use of Nationalist troops). General George Stratemeyer, commander of the Far East Air Force, asked for more planes, including two medium bomber groups with atomic capability, to be positioned at Guam or Okinawa if operations were to continue in Korea.[82] On 9 December, MacArthur sought "commander's discretion to use atomic weapons." He also sent a list of "retardation targets" and requested Washington to provide him with a total of 34 atom bombs to drop on these targets as well as on enemy invasion forces and air force concentrations.[83] Collins, however, saw nothing during his Korea trip that seemed to necessitate the use of atomic weapons.[84] Nationalist Chinese leader Chiang Kai-shek in Taiwan also expressed doubts about the military effectiveness of nuclear bombing, although he refused to "speculate" about the effect of atomic bombing on the Chinese people.[85]

In the meantime, Truman's 30 November statement provoked a widespread outcry abroad. A quick White House clarification, that any use of atomic weapons would require presidential authorization, did little to calm down the diplomatic storm. Most delegates to the UN, with the exception of the Latin Americans, reacted adversely. A reporter characterized the European reaction as "one of the most amazing political upheavals in Europe since the war."[86] In Britain, the *New York Times* reported "an increasing demand that Britain, now in the process of economic recovery, should assert her independence of United States leadership lest her voice in the councils of nations be mistaken for that of a ventriloquist's dummy."[87] The British press took the view that the United States could not unilaterally decide to use atomic bombs in the war.[88] Prime Minister Attlee considered the furor serious enough to announce his intention to visit Washington with the aim of restraining the United States. Before crossing the Atlantic, Attlee met visiting French Prime Minister Rene Pleven on 2 December. The two leaders established a "general identity of views."[89]

The State Department's position paper for the meeting with Attlee had recommended that "no *commitment* be made restricting the action of the US" and to stress "our *desire*" not to use the bomb (emphasis in original).[90] The JCS suggested informing Attlee that the United States had "no intention" of resorting to atomic weapons in Korea, except in a purely defensive role for the protection of the evacuating UN forces or for preventing "a major military disaster."[91] In his private meeting with Attlee, however, Truman went on to say that "the Governments of the United Kingdom and the United States had always been partners in this matter [the atom bomb] and that he would not consider the use of the bomb without consulting with the United Kingdom."[92] Acheson, however, intervened, and he persuaded Truman to retract his promise to Attlee and merely undertake to keep in close touch with the prime minister in threatening situations.[93]

Within the United States, use of nuclear weapons enjoyed substantial popular support. While some opposed the bomb on moral grounds or out of fear of retaliation or the outbreak of general war, many argued that since the United States had spent so much money developing the bomb, it should use it. Some felt that "God gave us the bomb and therefore its use was justified." A *Washington Post* editorial cautioned that the president "was well advised to emphasize that it is a usable weapon, not a museum piece."[94]

China's entry into the war, however, made the State Department even more hesitant than earlier about playing the nuclear card. John Emmerson of the Bureau of Far Eastern Affairs pointed out that

regardless of the fact that military results achieved by atomic bombardment may be identical to those attained by conventional weapons, the effect on world opinion would be vastly different. The A-bomb has the status of a peculiar monster conceived by American cunning and its use by us, in whatever situation, would be exploited to our serious detriment.

Emmerson argued that if the United States used atomic bombs, American efforts to win over Asians would fail and American influence among the non-communist nations of Asia would disappear.[95] O. Edmund Clubb, director of the Office of Chinese Affairs, acknowledged that strategic bombing of Manchuria, including atomic bombing, would "shake the Chinese aggressor," especially if the United States declared in advance that it would target major cities in Manchuria. Atomic bombing, however, needed the concurrence of the allies, which would be "practically impossible to get."[96]

After consulting with Loper, Nitze informed Acheson that atomic bombs would be effective against troop and artillery concentrations and would not inflict large civilian casualties. Use of the bomb might also deter further Chinese participation. However, targets appropriate for atomic strikes would not appear in the normal course. UN forces would have to draw out sizable concentrations of enemy forces through tactical maneuvers. Few such targets could be created this way; using a small number of atomic bombs would not produce decisive results. The use of atomic bombs might provoke Soviet intervention and antagonize other Asians. Strategic use of the bomb against Manchurian cities might cause massive civilian casualties and invite Soviet intervention.[97] Therefore, use of atomic weapons in the war simply did not make tactical or strategic sense.

NUCLEAR BOMBER MOVEMENTS: PHASE TWO

Soon after the UN Command recovered from the reverses inflicted by the Chinese and stabilized the front, a new crisis occurred. On 10 March 1951, MacArthur, citing evidence of a Chinese and Soviet buildup that pointed to a possible invasion of Japan, asked the JCS to provide him with atomic weapons he could use on "D Day."[98] Gordon Dean, chairman of the AEC, learned from Robert LeBaron, chairman of the AEC's Military Liaison Committee, on 26 March that the situation in Korea had worsened. The Chinese seemed to be concentrating their forces for an offensive. It appeared that with Soviet support, China might use its air force for the first time. US intelligence reported that the Soviet Union had moved three divisions into Manchuria and was readying other forces for a possible attack on Japan. Fearing a Russian and Chinese decision to invade Japan, the JCS sought presidential authorization for the transfer of nuclear bomb cores to the military.[99] On 4 April, Dean came to know that the JCS might make an immediate request for the transfer. Two days later, Truman informed Dean that he had decided to approve the transfer of nine nuclear bomb cores to the air force. He had not made a decision to use them, however, and promised that "in no event would the bomb be used in Northern Korea where . . . they would be completely ineffective and psychological 'duds.' "[100] Before relieving MacArthur from his command, Truman decided to send to Okinawa B-

29s carrying complete nuclear bombs.[101] The Far East Air Force had already readied loading pits for atomic bombs in Okinawa.[102] The bombers were, however, stopped at Guam and the unit's commander was ordered to remain at the SAC headquarters. The nuclear weapons were prepositioned in Okinawa. Toward the end of April, following a renewed communist offensive, Truman ordered more atomic bombers to the Far East.[103]

Dingman has argued that Truman ordered the dispatch of the atomic bombers in order to improve his domestic standing. He has cited in support of this conclusion Truman's waning popularity and the fact that the decision to transfer the bombers was known to 18 legislators, including the president's critics. Truman, according to Dingman, exaggerated the extent of the communist threat. It appeared that MacArthur's headquarters did not consider the situation all that serious after all.[104]

Here again, the initiative for the movement had come from the military. Similar movements of nuclear bombers in July 1950 had done nothing to improve Truman's popularity. Moreover, the possibility of Soviet air action continued to worry the JCS well into April. On 27 April, General Matthew Ridgway, MacArthur's replacement as CINFE, requested authority to strike air bases in Manchuria and the Shantung Peninsula in the event of an air attack on his forces from those regions. He cited "increasing scope and rate of buildup of enemy capabilities of an air attack" and "the increasing probability of such an attack in support of his present major ground offensive." In response, the JCS passed on to him presidential authorization to hit air bases in Manchuria and nearby China in the event of a major attack.[105]

In this context, one should remember that it was the Far East Command (FECOM) that had first raised the alarm about a possible invasion of Japan. It is questionable whether Truman would have put much faith in the judgment of FECOM on such a critical matter, considering FECOM's monumental failure in assessing Chinese intentions only a few months earlier.[106] As Bradley told Lord Tedder, head of the British Joint Services Mission in Washington, he himself doubted that a new communist offensive could take place before June, but "one could never be sure." An intelligence report he had received, Bradley told Tedder, specifically mentioned 16 April as the date the communist campaign would begin. The Chinese offensive at the end of April was strong enough to force the Eighth Army to retreat as much as 35 miles in one sector, bringing the frontline as close as five miles to Seoul. Another massive Chinese offensive followed on 16 May.[107] Unlike the earlier B-29 movements in the war, the latest movements were not reported in the press. The Chinese probably never learned of the bomber movement. One possible explanation for the secrecy is that while the bombers sent in 1950 carried only the non-nuclear components of the bombs, the bombers this time carried complete nuclear bombs. If the Soviet Union had entered the war and the communists had learned the whereabouts of these bombers, they would surely have been the first targets for the Soviet Air Force in the Far East. One doubts that Truman would have exposed these bombers and the fully assembled atomic bombs to such a risk for purely political gains.

RENEWED CONSIDERATION OF BATTLEFIELD USE OF NUCLEAR WEAPONS

Meanwhile, experts continued to study and debate the use of nuclear weapons in the war. A team from Johns Hopkins University, working with FECOM's Operations Research Office, examined the feasibility of atomic strikes in support of ground operations in Korea. The study estimated that, on average, an airburst of a 40-kiloton atomic bomb would kill at least 600 enemy troops and seriously injure 400 more. Three such bombs would destroy 30 percent of an enemy division. FECOM's intelligence branch reported at least two target concentrations of 2,000 or more enemy troops daily. One sortie of atomic bombing would do as much damage to the enemy as 300 sorties of carpet bombing by B-29s or 5,900 sorties by tactical aircraft. "Only the atomic bomb," the report argued, "can deliver the attack on large area targets in a short enough time actually to achieve appreciable enemy casualties before the enemy disperses. The bomb is therefore a new, exceedingly powerful, and unique type of tactical weapon."

The study concluded that "If used in sufficient quantity, atomic weapons can be delivered effectively against Chinese Communist forces in Korea and could be decisive in offense, defense, or disengagement." For a "decisive effect" against 120 enemy divisions, the study recommended the use of 360 bombs; for holding a defensive line of 50 miles, 120 bombs; and for aiding a withdrawal from a perimeter defense such as the Pusan line, 25 bombs. The study recommended that for tactical use in Korea, enemy personnel would be the ideal targets. The average cost of killing enemy troops was approximately $100,000 per enemy killed in World War II. In Korea, it was estimated at $150,000. Killing 600 enemy soldiers in Korea would thus cost $90 million using conventional means. An atomic bomb would achieve the same result at a cost of only $2.5 million, provided the bomb was used against a large enough troop concentration.

Battlefield use of atomic weapons in Korea, however, did have its drawbacks, the experts conceded. Enemy forces were rarely deployed in depth, and American tactical air power forced the enemy to fight in close contact with US forces. To use the bomb, it would be necessary to induce enemy troops to dispose themselves so as to present a "remunerative" target. This could only be done in exceptional circumstances. To facilitate an atomic attack, combat intelligence must identify and locate with great precision suitable targets occurring simultaneously, and estimate the time during which the target would persist. In response to an atomic attack, the enemy might alter ground tactics and use more air power, making future targets increasingly difficult to find. Dispersal of enemy forces would, however, be useful, as it would prevent the mounting of concentrated attacks. UN forces would rarely find or contrive a sizable concentration of enemy forces, except when they themselves were exposed to similar attacks. Thus, in situations that favored atomic attacks against the enemy, UN forces themselves would be vulnerable.[108]

What impact this report produced is not clear. AEC and army officials, however, initiated action on some of the issues raised in the report a few months later. In July 1951, Frank Pace, secretary of the army, and his deputy, Karl Bendetsen, discussed with Secretary of Defense Marshall and his deputy, Robert Lovett, the question of transferring to the armed forces nuclear and non-nuclear components of some bombs for use by the field commander when field intelligence detected suitable targets. On such occasions, there would not be time to seek presidential authorization for atomic strikes before the targets disappeared. At a meeting on 12 July, Dean, Bendetsen, Frank Nash of the Department of Defense, and Brigadier General James McCormack, director of the AEC's division of military applications, decided that McCormack and Nash should prepare a memorandum for Truman and Marshall recommending that the president refer this matter to the Special NSC Subcommittee on Atomic Weapons. Dean felt that tactical use of atomic weapons in Korea would not provoke the Soviets into making a major move in Europe. It might even prevent such a step by making them fear that the United States might use atomic weapons against them. The American people, he believed, would approve such an action. Frustrated by the stalemate in Korea, Americans would applaud the use of nuclear weapons in the war if it led to the withdrawal of Chinese forces from Korea. One of the "real hurdles" was that some people, including Truman, associated atomic weapons with strategic bombing that would kill civilians rather than troops. Therefore, the memo should use appropriate terminology to make the distinction clear. The officials discussed several alternatives such as "small bang weapons" and "Nevada bombs." None, however, sounded suitable. It is not certain whether the officials ever wrote the memo or discussed the matter with the president.[109]

The JCS began to look seriously at the use of atomic weapons in Korea in the summer of 1951. In June, Collins endorsed an army study that recommended creation of capabilities and training for US forces for using atomic weapons in the war. A JSPC study completed on 11 August recommended that "under current conditions atomic weapons should be employed in the Far East *only* in the event our forces in that area would otherwise be faced with military disaster." The study opposed taking any premature decision, "thus giving present and potential enemies opportunity to develop defenses against what would be a new employment of an existing weapon." As US forces had no experience in providing battlefield atomic support, the study recommended staging "simulated" tactical atomic strikes in Korea using atomic bombs minus their nuclear components, except "actual flights over enemy territory." US forces practiced such simulated strikes in the "Hudson Harbor" exercise that took place in September and October 1951 in Korea, with presidential approval.[110] This exercise must rank as the strongest nuclear signal communicated throughout the Korean War, or for that matter, in any other case of nuclear diplomacy.

The G-3 team that evaluated Operation Hudson Harbor reported that "the policies, procedures, and the means available for Operation 'Hudson Harbor' were inadequate for successful tactical employment of atomic weapons." Ground intelligence could seldom detect large masses of enemy troops. Enemy forces in the frontlines were too well dug in to be affected by airburst atomic bombs. CINFE needed to develop more effective methods for acquiring combat intelligence for atomic strikes. The team recommended that, as a matter of policy, the army use atomic weapons (1) if necessary to save the Eighth Army from disaster or to cover its evacuation, (2) to destroy all communist forces in the Far East in the event of a general war, or (3) in the event that political or military developments forced its use. In the meantime, G-3 recommended, CINFE should prepare plans for atomic strikes and be ready to implement the plans when authorized.[111]

In July 1952, Collins publicly came out against the use of atomic weapons in Korea. He claimed that although US forces in Korea had the "capability" to use tactical nuclear weapons, he considered their use in Korea "impractical."[112] The state of the US nuclear arsenal perhaps was responsible for Collins' skepticism. American forces acquired the capability to use atomic weapons in tactical roles only after the Truman administration left office.[113]

DOMESTIC CALLS FOR USE OF NUCLEAR WEAPONS

Throughout the war, influential Americans kept up a continuous barrage of calls for using atomic weapons in the war. As early as 27 June 1950, Representative L. Mendel Rivers of the House Armed Services Committee proposed dropping an atomic bomb on Pyongyang.[114] Rep. Lloyd Bentsen called on Truman to give the communists a week's time to withdraw or face atomic attacks on their cities. Republican Senator Owen Brewster wanted MacArthur to be given the authority to use nuclear weapons at his discretion. Eisenhower also spoke in favor of using atomic weapons against military targets. Truman, however, refused to accept such advice.[115]

After the war degenerated into a stalemate, call for the use of atomic weapons and publicity for advances in American atomic weapons programs increased. Secretary of the Army Frank Pace told reporters that the army would be equipped with tactical atomic weapons. The AEC's semi-annual report to Congress referred to the progress in the development of "smaller weapons."[116] The next month, Admiral Lynde McCormick, commander of the US Atlantic Fleet, disclosed that his fleet would practice simulated tactical use of atomic bombs that carrier-borne aircraft would soon be able to deliver. Truman himself publicly spoke of "fantastic new weapons," including new atomic weapons under development.[117] On 5 October 1951, AEC Chairman Dean announced, in a speech that the Voice of America broadcast worldwide, that tactical nuclear weapons were "already here." He said that the United States possessed atomic weapons that would neutralize any enemy's manpower superiority. The number and variety of nuclear weapons available to the United States, he claimed, enabled their use "in different ways heretofore not possible."[118] Much of this activity was independent of the Korean War and was the result of programs initiated before the war began. The publicity, however, helped keep the American nuclear sword dangling before the Chinese.

On 11 October, Senator Henry Cabot Lodge called for the immediate use of atomic artillery or other tactical nuclear weapons.[119] When the AEC members met Lovett, the press speculated that the administration was actively considering using nuclear weapons in the war. Bradley had, reports claimed, "studied" the battlefield use of atomic weapons during his Far East trip.[120] The press also carried reports of JCS consideration of use of nuclear weapons.[121]

In late 1951 and the early months of 1952, amidst considerable publicity, army exercises held in the United States simulated offensive use of tactical nuclear weapons. On 1 November 1951, 800–900 troops were placed in foxholes and bunkers 6.8 miles from ground zero of a 21-kiloton test. After the detonation, the troops attacked an objective 500 feet from ground zero. Scientists studied the effects of exposure to the explosion on animals and equipment. Army analysis of the tests concluded that "combat troops can safely cross the area of a nuclear explosion within minutes." The army commander of the exercise told the press that "Through this operation an appreciable forward step has been taken toward relative military tactics to the employment of atomic weapons [sic]."[122] General Mark Clark, chief of Army Field Forces, announced that the army was being trained in the battlefield use of atomic weapons. In one 17-day exercise (the largest since World War II) that simulated tactical atomic strikes, 115,00 men and 750 aircraft participated.[123] As part of an atomic test in April 1952, troops were stationed close to ground zero. The *New York Times*'s Hanson Baldwin wrote that this indicated that US forces now had nuclear weapons for use against troop concentrations. Baldwin added that atomic weapons small enough to be carried by fighter-bombers were reportedly available.[124] In Operation Mushroom, conducted in Korea itself with a great deal of publicity in May 1952, 10,000 troops participated. According to press releases, the exercise, in which troops burrowed underground, involved testing defense against atomic weapons.[125] In tests in 1953, the army placed troops in trenches as close as two miles from ground zero. For the test of a 16-kiloton warhead on 17 March, troops and a group of reporters, dubbed "men of extinction," were stationed two miles from ground zero and, after the detonation, moved to within 700 yards of ground zero.[126] In later tests of the series, volunteer soldiers were positioned just over a mile from ground zero, and in one case, as close as half a mile.[127]

CHINESE RESPONSE TO AMERICAN NUCLEAR DIPLOMACY

To deal with the threat of nuclear war directed at them from such a variety of sources, the Chinese adopted a wide range of countermeasures.[128] They had to take action on two fronts—psychological and physical. At the psychological level, the CCP adopted what Mark Ryan calls "a systematic, integrated party line dealing with nuclear weapons" and gave it wide domestic and international publicity. This line provided guidelines to the party propaganda machine and served as a framework for interpreting American press reports on nuclear weapons. The party line maintained that nuclear weapons would not compensate for US conventional weakness in Korea in areas such as manpower, motivation and training, and logistics; nuclear bombing could not be decisive militarily despite its destructiveness; the United States itself was vulnerable, perhaps more vulnerable, to nuclear weapons; and the nation that first used these weapons should be punished for war crimes. The purpose of this propaganda line was to transform the fear of the Chinese people about atom bombs into confidence and to demonstrate China's invulnerability to atomic blackmail.[129] The Chinese based their counterstrategy mainly on the technical data on nuclear weapons released in the West and Western analysis of the effects of atomic weapons.[130] The Chinese also had access to published American studies of the effects of the atomic bombs dropped on Japan. In addition, the PLA began training and indoctrinating its troops to face nuclear warfare.[131] The indoctrination of the troops emphasized the military insignificance of nuclear weapons and the deterrent capability of Soviet nuclear weapons. This program apparently was not a resounding success. A Rand Corporation study, based on the interrogation of Chinese POWs, showed that the Chinese troops still retained exaggerated ideas of the power and range of atom bombs.[132]

At the physical level, the Chinese reportedly began construction of air-raid shelters in the Mukden area as early as October 1950 and by November began building such shelters and conducting air-raid drills in major cities in northeast China. They adopted other tactics such as breaking up formations into smaller units and stockpiling supplies in scattered hidden storage sites. In late October, they deployed MiG fighters along the Yalu. Reports also surfaced, many of them confirmed by US intelligence, of movement of population and industrial machinery from coastal cities to the interior. Once the battlefield situation stabilized, such reports tapered off.[133]

The principal Chinese countermeasure against atomic weapons was, however, tunnelling. The PLA began erecting fortifications near the 38th Parallel in January 1951 to defend against possible UN counterattacks. In the next few months, they replaced or supplemented these surface installations with underground fortifications. After the armistice talks began in July 1951, they extended and consolidated these into a network from which they could conduct offensive as well as defensive warfare. This network comprised a total of 1,250 kilometers of tunnels stretching from coast to coast and over 6,000 kilometers of trenches. The tunnels were reportedly elaborate affairs with massive storage, cooking, and heating facilities. By mid-1952, the Chinese press began to describe the tunnels as impervious to American attacks. The information the Chinese received through the widespread reporting of American atomic testing and exercises involving atomic weapons helped confirm the adequacy of these tunnels. Civil defense booklets published in China specifically referred to the ability of tunnels and concrete bunkers to withstand nuclear explosions and shield the troops within from heat, blast, and radiation. A Chinese press dispatch, published to coincide with the inauguration of President Eisenhower, described the tunnels as "an impregnable line never before seen in the history of war."[134] The "underground Great Wall" largely neutralized the UN's conventional firepower, thus facilitating the battlefield stalemate. The tunnels also made the battlefield use of atomic weapons by US forces unfeasible.[135]

THE FAILURE OF NUCLEAR COERCION

Once the threat of a forced withdrawal from Korea ended, the Truman administration turned its attention to finding ways of securing an honorable way to get out of the war. One of the tactics it tried was nuclear diplomacy. With Acheson's knowledge, Charles Burton Marshall of the PPS carried on a series of exchanges with a former Chinese soldier who claimed to be associated with non-communist elements in China. Pro-

fessor George Taylor of the University of Washington acted as the intermediary in these secret dealings. In these contacts, spread over several
months in the first part of 1951, Marshall passed on the warning that the
United States had the ability to "lay waste their [Chinese] cities and
destroy their industries." Marshall added that "If war comes, and China
is still acting in Moscow's interest, China could certainly count on no
immunity from our wrath. . . . The consequences for China would be terrible."[136]

After this contact proved fruitless, Marshall went to Hong Kong with
the aim of establishing contacts with Chinese agents. When a Chinese
representative finally contacted him, Marshall warned him that if a
world war started with China in the enemy camp, it "would have to
suffer the consequences to the bitter end. We could not afford to show
it mercy or consideration. It would probably mean that the Chinese
would be set back a century or more in their progress." The best way
for China to avoid this fate was to act independently of Moscow. Marshall repeated his old argument about the United States restraining itself
so far from acting on its emotions, despite calls to "Let's give the Chinese
what they are asking for."[137]

After the failure of the fifth Chinese offensive in late March, Mao realized the futility of striving for a military victory. On 3 June, Kim held
discussions with Mao and Zhou. High-level discussions within the CCP
followed, leading to a consensus to start negotiating. On 23 June, the
Soviet ambassador to the UN publicly suggested negotiations, a suggestion the Chinese press quickly endorsed. Armistice negotiations started
on 10 July 1951.[138] Fairly soon, the two sides reached agreement on the
ceasefire line and on all other related issues, except the repatriation of
the prisoners of war. The unwillingness of large numbers of Chinese and
North Korean POWs to go back to their own countries complicated the
problem.[139] Departing from the all-for-all exchange of prisoners dictated
by the Geneva Convention, the United States proposed a voluntary or
non-forcible repatriation of the prisoners. The communist side rejected
this approach.[140]

With the negotiations stalled, the United States increased military pressure, on the reasoning that "the best chance of breaking the deadlock at
Panmunjom is to hit the enemy with the forces at our command." On 8
May, US bombing destroyed the supply depot at Suan in the "biggest
single attack since the beginning of the Korean conflict." In the last week
of June, US air attacks destroyed 90 percent of North Korea's power
supply.[141]

The US bombing killed a promising opening in the negotiations. In
June 1952, Constantin Zichenko, a Soviet official working in the UN, had
proposed to Ernest Gross of the US delegation agreement on the basis
of the Geneva Convention. If some prisoners refused repatriation after

that, Zichenko suggested, "this could be taken into account." Meanwhile, Zhou made a similar proposal to Panikkar in Beijing. Zhou proposed agreement on the basis of the Geneva Convention, with the understanding that those prisoners who did not wish to be repatriated should be brought to Panmunjom and interrogated by representatives from the four neutral nations identified to supervise the armistice and Red Cross personnel from both sides.[142] After the United States escalated bombing of North Korea, the Chinese withdrew their offer and reverted to their demand for the repatriation of all Chinese prisoners of war. Zichenko also broke off contacts with Gross.[143]

In July, the UN Command increased bombings again. On 11 July, US planes bombed Pyongyang with napalm, causing 7,000 casualties. The UN command issued warnings of similar raids in 78 localities to "increase the pressure on the Communist negotiators at Panmunjom." The communists replied that indiscriminate UN bombing would only make them fight harder.[144] General Mark Clark, commanding the UN forces, blamed the stalemate on the US failure to increase military pressure on the enemy. He called for an extension of the bombing into Manchuria and if that did not succeed, ground operations designed to reach the Yalu.[145] Clark also asked for removal of restrictions on military actions and authorization to use tactical nuclear weapons. The JCS, however, decided to wait until the new administration took over after the elections before acting on Clark's demands. Pace warned that "any course of action involving the extensive use of UN ground troops for forcing a decision in Korea prior to 1954 is simply out of the question because of manpower and budgetary considerations."[146]

Expansion of the war with the presidential election just around the corner was not an attractive option for Truman. Instead, the administration once again resorted to nuclear diplomacy to break the deadlock. When a Chinese delegation led by Zhou Enlai arrived in Moscow in mid-August, George Kennan, US ambassador in Moscow, suggested that this offered a "unique opportunity" to frighten the Chinese and to increase Chinese demands on the Soviet Union for assistance. He recommended "something in the nature of increased military threat or feint," balanced by "some sort of conciliatory gesture" to the Soviets.[147] The State Department, however, heard from FECOM that "everything possible already is being done to induce the Chinese to make panicky demands on the Russians." On 3 September, the State Department approved a suggestion for a covert operation to spread rumors in Korea, Japan, and China that an amphibious operation was being planned. The department also recommended a similar operation to circulate the following rumor:

The US has consistently refused to accept prohibitions on the atomic weapons. The reason for this is that the atomic bomb is our real ace in the hole in Korea, but the US Government has been against their use. But pressure from some elements in the US is intense to use them. The present saturation bombings in Korea have been launched in an effort to restrain these elements by satisfying them that we are taking vigorous action. But the saturation bombing is obviously not going to be decisive. A presidential campaign is on and already one party is demanding more decisive action. As the presidential campaign grows, this pressure will get much greater. The government probably will not be able to resist it. There is one way to prevent the use of atomic weapons in Korea. This is to get an armistice without delay. If that is not done and atomic weapons are used, they may not prove decisive since they have never been tried on troops in the field. If that happens, then the same pressure undoubtedly will be exerted to extend the bombings to China, using atomic weapons.

This memo went to the CIA with a request to implement the suggestions "on an urgent basis."[148]

On 28 September, General William K. Harrison, the UN chief negotiator, presented three alternative plans to the communist negotiators, all of which called for voluntary repatriation. When the communist side rejected these, Harrison, under instructions from Washington, recessed the talks.[149] Soon after, Chester Bowles, the US ambassador in India, warned the Indian government that "we would continue to expand the war in Korea until we had won it," unless a "satisfactory settlement" was reached.[150] In November, Lovett told British and Canadian foreign ministers that in the absence of an acceptable settlement, "the US would seek a military conclusion." He hinted that "alternatives, although disagreeable, were under consideration."[151] Taken together, these American signals look remarkably like the signals the Eisenhower administration claimed it had sent in the spring of 1953. Equally significant, the outcome was negative. Instead of compromising, the communists stepped up their operations in October.[152]

In opting for a strategy of compelling China to capitulate in the negotiations, the Truman administration completely misjudged the position of the adversary. New evidence now available suggests that China was looking for a face-saving formula to compromise. In his talks with Stalin in Moscow in the fall of 1952, Zhou proposed that the communist side should accept if the Americans made "some sort of compromise, even if they were small." Even if all POWs were not returned, they could accept, provided a face-saving method was devised to decide the fate of the remaining POWs, such as mediation by a neutral country or transferring the POWs to the neutral state as an interim measure. The documents make it clear that Stalin had the decisive say, and he did not clearly reveal his hand. The Chinese were in no position to take a line independent of the Soviet supremo, given their complete dependence on Soviet equipment supplies. Stalin did concede that "if the Americans back down a little, then you can accept." By the time Zhou met him a month later, however, Stalin had changed his mind. He insisted on the return of all POWs.[153]

In November, after the presidential elections in the United States, India introduced a resolution in the UN General Assembly for settling the POW issue. India had initiated the move after consulting the Chinese, and elements of the Indian plan were similar to the views that Zhou had expressed to Stalin. Under strong American pressure, this resolution in its final form moved far too close to the American position from the communist point of view. The Soviet Union rejected it outright.[154] The Truman administration bowed out of office soon after, with the armistice no nearer than a year earlier.

DOING SOMETHING OR OTHER

Eisenhower assumed the US presidency uniquely qualified to tackle the problem posed by the Korean War. He commanded enormous prestige worldwide, stemming from his command of the allied forces against Nazi Germany. As chief of army staff, the first chairman of the JCS, and supreme commander of the NATO forces, he had actively participated in the debates and the planning on the use of atomic weapons. His knowledge of national security issues was unrivalled. After two and a half years of fighting that in no way changed the status quo in the Korean peninsula, the nation longed for peace.[155] If Eisenhower could not win national support for a peace initiative, no one else could have.

The international situation favored the new president. The papers on Christmas morning headlined Stalin's willingness to cooperate with the incoming Eisenhower administration on a new diplomatic approach to end the Korean War, expressed in his replies to columnist James Reston's questions. The Soviet supremo declared that war between the United States and the Soviet Union "cannot be considered inevitable," and he expressed his interest in a meeting with Eisenhower.[156]

The extensive international experience of Dulles, the new secretary of state, should have been a great asset for the new president. Dulles, however, came with ideas of his own that hardly helped advance the prospect of a peace settlement. He had believed for some time that the US objective should be to extend the boundaries of the Republic of Korea to the so-called "waistline" of Korea. Since the communists would not quietly pull back their forces north of this line, this meant a massive new offensive. Dulles also considered non-forcible repatriation of the POWs important for the purpose of encouraging defections in other communist countries.[157]

When Eisenhower went to Korea in early December in fulfillment of his campaign pledge, Clark was ready with Oplan 8–52. Under this plan, the Eighth Army in Korea would advance to the waist of Korea, and US forces would launch air and sea attacks on China in order to force China to end the war on American terms. The attacks would include the use of nuclear bombs. The plan included an amphibious landing and a naval blockade of China.[158] The "most significant thing about the visit of the President elect" to Clark was that he got no opportunity to present his plan for victory to Eisenhower. As he recalled, "It soon became apparent, in our many conversations, that he would seek an honorable truce." Bradley, who had accompanied Eisenhower on this trip, got the impression that Eisenhower deliberately denied Clark the opportunity to present the "MacArthuresque" plan. FECOM officers "were quite naturally miffed."[159]

Upon his return home, Eisenhower announced that he believed he could end the war by initiating actions that would "induce" the communists to make peace. In a prepared speech delivered at La Guardia Airport, he declared that "we face an enemy whom we cannot hope to impress by words, however eloquent, but only by deeds—executed under circumstances of our own choosing."[160] This speech has now become part of the Eisenhower lore, but there is, as yet, no evidence that it had any impact on the armistice settlement.

As Eisenhower later explained, breaking through the communist lines would have presented great tactical difficulties. "Moreover, if the purpose were to occupy the major part of the peninsula of Korea, success would put us in an extremely awkward position, with a substantial occupation of territory but no ability to use our weapons to complete victory," unless the war was carried into Manchuria. This, however, posed the risk of expanding the war. "An attack launched merely to move the line of contact to the narrow waist of the peninsula between Sinanju and Hungnam would not in itself prove decisive and would never merit the cost in lives." Eisenhower concluded that "Clearly, then, a course of action other than a conventional ground attack in Korea was necessary." Further, a conventional attack was "the least attractive of all plans."[161]

Although Eisenhower failed to acknowledge it, this was more or less the reasoning that had prompted the Truman administration to accept the futility of striving for a military victory. From the available documentary evidence, it is hard to make the case that Eisenhower started out with the assumption that a drive to the waist was not worth the cost. The corollary to such an assumption would have been an initiative to break the logjam in the talks, or hunkering down for an indefinite stalemate. Eisenhower had already rejected acceptance of the stalemate. He took absolutely no initiative to start the talks that the UN delegation had broken off in the fall of 1952. Instead, he ordered planning for a renewed offensive that might involve the use of nuclear weapons. As a result, talk of nuclear weapons dominated internal administration discussions in the early months of 1953, while the peace process, which resumed in the spring on a communist initiative, moved on parallel tracks.

If Eisenhower had indeed found the drive to the waist not worthwhile and had made up his mind to pursue a peaceful solution, an episode narrated by presidential aide Emmet Hughes demonstrated that he had neglected to take his secretary of state into his confidence. Hughes had asked Dulles what the administration's reaction would be if the communists accepted a compromise settlement. Dulles had replied: "We'd be sorry. *I don't think we can get much out of a Korean settlement until we have shown—before all Asia—our clear superiority by giving the Chinese one hell of a licking.*" When Eisenhower heard about it, he "snapped out" that

If Mr. Dulles and his sophisticated advisers really mean that they can *not* talk peace seriously, then I am in the wrong pew. For if it's *war* we should be talking about, I *know* the people to give me advice on that—and they're not in the State Department. Now either we cut out all this fooling around and make a serious bid for peace—or we forget the whole thing.[162]

The divergence in thinking between Eisenhower and Dulles was all the more surprising, as Dulles had accompanied Eisenhower on his Korean trip and should have been aware of Eisenhower cold-shouldering the Clark plan for a renewed offensive. Either the communication gap between the president-elect and his secretary of state–designate was alarmingly wide, or Dulles had confidently expected to bring the president around to his own line of thinking.

If one wanted evidence to corroborate Hughes' account, Dulles's first meeting with British Foreign Secretary Anthony Eden on 5 March provided it. Dulles raised the "necessity of creating a threat of pressures" against mainland China to reduce the possibility of China sending its forces to help the communists in Indochina or increasing their forces in Korea. He argued that the South Koreans could not bear further sacrifices if they had no hope of creating a viable country. Moving the boundary up to the waist would bring 85 percent of the population of Korea and the industrial complex north of the 38th Parallel within the Republic of Korea. Dulles emphasized that for such an operation, he did not rule out bombing targets in Manchuria.[163]

Eisenhower's campaign promises and trip to Korea had helped raise public expectations from his presidency. Unaware of the president's thinking, the public continued to expect that the new president would soon take new initiatives to end the war. Weeks passed, however, with nothing happening. U. Alexis Johnson, deputy assistant secretary of state for Northeast Asian affairs, later recalled that Eisenhower and his team "were clearly groping their way" and did not have "the finely crafted plan for ending the war the Republicans had intimated they possessed."[164] On a visit to the United States in January 1953, Churchill gained the impression that the Eisenhower administration had no plan to end the war, "apart from doing something or other."[165]

Eisenhower brought up the use of nuclear weapons in his very first National Security Council meeting on 11 February. When Bradley raised the problem of Chinese infiltration of the Kaesong "sanctuary," Eisenhower suggested that the Kaesong area offered a good target for the use of tactical atomic weapons. He added that "we could not go on the way we were indefinitely." Dulles raised "the Soviet success to date in setting atomic weapons apart from all other weapons as being in a special category" and the "inhibitions" this placed on the use of the bomb. He wanted to "break down this false distinction." Bradley thought it premature to talk to the allies about use of atomic weapons. Eisenhower retorted that "if they [the allies] objected to the use of atomic weapons we might well ask them to supply three or more divisions needed to drive the communists back, in lieu of use of atomic weapons." However, in the end, he decided against raising the issue with the allies.[166]

On 21 March, Eisenhower ordered the Pentagon to study "what it would cost" to launch a new offensive in Korea with the objective of securing a line at the waistline of Korea. If the plan required atomic strikes against military targets, he had no objections.[167] Ten days later, he admitted in the NSC that if the United States increased its forces to the level required to achieve a tactical goal such as reaching the waist of Korea, Russia might retaliate by strengthening the communist forces in Korea. If the United States still wanted to proceed with a conventional offensive, it would push the country very close to general mobilization. Bradley agreed with this assessment.[168]

In an NSC meeting, Eisenhower argued that although there were not many suitable targets in Korea, "it would be worth the cost if, through use of atomic weapons," the United States could defeat the communist forces and go up to the waist of Korea. Deane Mallot, one of the NSC consultants,[169] recommended the use of a couple of atomic weapons in Korea. Contradicting his statement earlier in the meeting, Eisenhower replied that the impact of such a decision on US allies ruled it out. The president and Dulles, however, agreed that "somehow or other the tabu [sic] which surrounds the use of atomic weapons would have to be destroyed." Dulles "admitted that in the present state of world opinion we could not use an A-bomb," but he felt that "we should make every effort now to dissipate this feeling."[170] Eisenhower inquired whether the airfields in North Korea were not good targets for atomic bombs. He wished "to consider the atomic bomb as simply another weapon in our arsenal." Bradley, however, did not consider the airfields suitable as targets for atomic bombs.[171] In a meeting of State Department officials and the JCS on 27 March, Collins reiterated his known skepticism about the tactical use of atomic weapons in Korea. The communist forces, he pointed out, were dug in in depth over a long front. Recent tests had shown that men well dug in very close to atomic explosions could survive. Vandenberg argued that atomic weapons would be effective against air bases in Manchuria. Collins retorted that Pusan and Inchon presented better targets for enemy atomic weapons. A US amphibious operation would offer a perfect target for an atomic bomb.[172]

NSC 147, dated 2 April, examined six alternative courses of action to be pursued in Korea, five of which permitted, but did not require, the use of atomic weapons.[173] On 6 April, Johnson recommended to Dulles adoption of the option that called for aggressive air and naval activity and coordinated ground operations, followed by a drive to the waist.[174] Ironically, this alternative was on the broad lines of the Clark plan that Eisenhower had disdained to even look at only months earlier. The NSC meeting on 8 April did not examine the alternatives in view of a new turn of events in the negotiations.[175]

On 13 May, JCS representatives told the NSC that atomic weapons would have to be used if the administration chose options that involved operations outside Korea. If atomic weapons were used, "they must be used in considerable numbers in order to be truly effective." Korea itself, in their view, offered no good targets for atomic weapons. The view that atomic weapons would not dislodge the Chinese from their tunnels did not satisfy Eisenhower. General John E. Hull, representing the chairman of the JCS in the NSC meeting, revealed that the test of a ground-penetrating atomic bomb had produced an effect similar to an earthquake. It was, however, doubtful whether the use of such warheads would result in significant destruction of enemy forces. Eisenhower thought that "it might be cheaper, dollar-wise, to use atomic weapons in Korea than to continue to use conventional weapons" against the entrenched communist positions, especially in view of the cost of transporting conventional munitions across the Pacific. Asked by Eisenhower what effect a broadening of the war would have on NATO, Under Secretary of State Walter Bedell Smith replied that "in all probability NATO and our European system of alliances would all fall to pieces temporarily." However, if the United States succeeded in its bold line of action, and did so while avoiding global war, it could rebuild the alliance. Smith raised the possibility that soon after an armistice, the American public and Congress might add up the results of two years of fighting and bitterly criticize the meager result of the costly effort. The prospect of such criticism irritated Eisenhower, prompting him to retort that "If people raised hell when they contemplated the results, the thing to do would be to ask them to volunteer for frontline action in a continued Korean War."[176]

Bradley briefed the NSC on 20 May on the JCS plan for an expanded war. The plan involved enhanced military operations, including air and naval attacks directly against China, an offensive to establish a line at the waist of Korea, and "extensive tactical and strategic use of atomic bombs." Eisenhower expressed his worry about the danger of Soviet air attacks "on the almost defenseless population centers of Japan." This, he said, "was always in the back of his mind." Collins replied unhelpfully that "there was no clear answer to the President's anxiety." The president concluded the discussion stating that if the United States was forced to expand the war in Korea, "the plan selected by the Joint Chiefs of Staff was most likely to achieve the objective we sought."[177]

Eisenhower's apparent endorsement of the JCS plan for expanded war glossed over the practical difficulties involved. An analysis in *Life* before Eisenhower took over estimated that breaching the Chinese defenses for a drive to the waist would cost the Eighth Army 25,000 to 40,000 casualties. Success in this operation, in any case, would not end the war, as the Chinese would continue fighting. A push to the Yalu would lengthen the UN lines of supply (while shortening the Chinese lines) and extend the front from 145 miles to 450 miles. The invasion and occupation of China was "wholly beyond possibility." Blockade of the sea lanes would not help, as China could continue to get supplies from the Soviet Union overland. It would require internal bombing of China to achieve the objectives of a blockade. The Chinese appeared to have prepared for this by widely dispersing their MiG fighters. With over 2,500 planes, the Chinese Air Force had become the fourth largest in the world.[178] An air campaign in China would lead to severe attrition of US aircraft. Vandenberg had testified before Congress that the US Air Force could not take on both China and the Soviet Union at the same time. Intensive bombing in Korea had not succeeded in curtailing supplies to the communist forces. As for the use of nuclear weapons, in addition to alienating world opinion, it would require a considerable increase in air power in the theater, which would unbalance US forces in Europe.[179] While the use of tactical nuclear weapons would not guarantee a breakthrough against the Chinese frontlines, the success of a strategic nuclear offensive against China was equally doubtful. Such an offensive would encounter strong Chinese air defenses. The communist MiG 15s might have been inferior to the US F-86 fighters, but they had proved quite effective against the US strategic bombers. After they shot down three B-29s and damaged five others in one raid, FECOM decided to use the bombers only in night raids, which were not as effective as day operations.[180]

THE BREAKTHROUGH

In any event, a breakthrough in the negotiations made the talk of a new offensive pointless. On 22 February, Clark wrote to Nam Il, leader of the communist delegation at the talks, proposing a mutual exchange of sick and wounded POWs. Stalin died on 5 March. The new leadership in Moscow quickly signalled its desire to bring the war to an end. The Soviet Council of Ministers resolved within days of Stalin's death that a change in the communist stand in the negotiations would best serve the interests of the Soviet Union, China, and North Korea. The council suggested an immediate favorable response to Clark's letter, a statement by Zhou calling for the resumption of negotiations, statements in Moscow and Pyongyang in support of such a statement by Zhou, and action by the Soviet UN delegation to advance the new line. The Council of Ministers resolution practically dictated what Zhou and Kim should say, showing how decisive Moscow's say was in communist decision making.[181]

This development started the process that finally led to the conclusion of the armistice. Although Mao seems to have interpreted the Clark letter as the beginning of a new American policy, Clark did not send the letter as part of a premeditated plan. According to Eisenhower, the letter was a "routine" one and the "sending of this kind of letter was almost a common practice."[182] Even if the Chinese had simply accepted the proposal, there would still have been no breakthrough. The key event was the Chinese initiative to resume the talks, taken under Soviet instructions.

Events now began to move quickly. On 28 March, Nam Il accepted Clark's proposal.[183] On 30 March, Zhou publicly proposed resumption of the talks. Zhou's suggestion that those POWs who wished repatriation should be repatriated and others should be handed over to a neutral nation signalled virtual public acceptance of the principle of voluntary repatriation.[184] Now only procedural details remained.

Far from grasping this opportunity to move toward an armistice, Washington's initial response was to harden its own stand. Taking a very dim view of the latest development in the negotiations, Dulles told National Security Adviser Robert Cutler on 7 April that "someone should speak at [the] NSC tomorrow *on the armistice agreement that we are being sucked into in Korea*" (emphasis added). He "does not believe that the President knows what it is all about and feels that they are liable to criticism if they do not warn him now."[185] Sure enough, Dulles pointed out in the NSC on 8 April that in view of the "changed situation" and the "possible desire of the Communists for an armistice," the new administration could secure "a much more satisfactory settlement in Korea" than what it had inherited. He questioned whether the administration should feel bound by the provisions in the armistice that its predecessor had accepted. An armistice at the 38th Parallel "would leave a divided Korea not economically viable nor politically acceptable to the South Koreans." US allies were "desperately anxious to see the fighting stopped." However, he insisted, "we should certainly be able to secure a better armistice in view of our much greater power and the Soviet Union's much greater weakness currently."[186]

Eisenhower opposed voiding the agreements already arrived at and a resumption of full-scale war. "The American people," he pointed out, "would never stand for such a move." Still, Dulles persisted, "our current trading position is a great deal better." He wanted to tell the communists that unless they agreed to divide Korea at the waist instead of at the 38th Parallel, Washington "would call off the armistice." What the United States really wanted, he argued, was "a satisfactory settlement of the Korean problem," and it should not accept any armistice that promised less. Eisenhower finally conceded that the American negotiators should state that "in certain circumstances and on due notice, the armistice could be ended." The NSC decided that the administration should make it clear that, "without revising provisions already agreed upon, the United States interprets the purpose of the armistice to be the achievement of a political settlement in Korea," and that, if this was not reached "within a reasonable time," it might void the armistice.[187]

Early in April, Dulles gave a background briefing to the press. Misinterpreting Dulles's "loud thinking" as the administration's views on a possible settlement of the Far East issues and explicitly identifying Dulles as the source, the *New York Times*, on 9 April, reported that the United States was "willing to accept a settlement in Korea based on a boundary at the narrow waist of the peninsula," about 90 miles north of the 38th Parallel. The report claimed that the administration was considering putting Taiwan under a UN trusteeship as part of an overall settlement in East Asia. The press abroad interpreted this as signaling a sharp, dramatic reversal of the US Far East policy. Foreign diplomats in Washington expressed the fear that an American demand for a boundary at the waist of Korea would make a settlement impossible.[188] Within the United States, the reaction was equally vehement, but in the opposite direction. Senator William Knowland, Senate Republican leader and a leading light of the China Bloc, expressed his alarm and charged the administration with planning "a Far East Munich." He threatened to call a conference of Republican senators if the administration did not disavow the story. Dulles told presidential spokesman James Hagerty to issue a statement that the United States still sought a united Korea.[189] The story, however, did not die off before speculation surfaced about Dulles's future in the cabinet. This episode probably made Dulles even more disinclined to consider concessions in the negotiations.[190]

The communists' formal proposal at Panmunjom gave a further push to the peace process. On 7 May, Nam Il presented an eight-point plan that closely resembled the Indian-sponsored UN resolution that the communists had rejected in December, with the additional provision that India should be the chairman of the Neutral Nations Repatriation Commission (NNRC).[191] The president, secretary of defense, acting secretary of state, and General Hull discussed the new communist proposal the same day. They concluded that it represented "a significant shift" in the communist position and might break the deadlock.[192] The United States, however, had to take into account the South Korean leader Syngman Rhee and Republican congressional opinion, both highly suspicious of India. The United States proposed that the NNRC should take substantive decisions on the basis of unanimous voting, and that Korean POWs would not be handed over to the NNRC but released as soon as the armistice was signed.[193] The proposed release of the North Korean POWs constituted a significant departure from the UN resolution. The administration decided to insist on unanimity of voting after Dulles consulted with congressional leaders.[194]

The US proposal provoked sharp reactions from the Chinese, neutral nations, and even American allies. Lester Pearson of Canada was restrained from "making a public denunciation of the UNC [UN Command] stand" only with "great difficulty." Churchill criticized the American stand in the House of Commons. Attlee commented caustically on Senator McCarthy's influence on the new administration's policy. The Psychological Strategy Board reported a "disappointing deterioration" in public support for the US position among European allies, who deplored the "anti-Communist 'hysteria' " that seemed to dominate American policy.[195] Robert Murphy, the political adviser to Clark, cabled the State Department that the "UN technically does not have a foot of ground to stand on" on the question of releasing the Korean POWs. He doubted that there would be peace if the United States insisted on releasing the North Korean POWs. He bluntly informed the State Department that "personally I find it incomprehensible that we put up a twelfth hour stand for the outright release of North Koreans merely because of apprehension over violent ROK [Republic of Korea] reaction which at best is speculative." He advised Clark that if the United States had to choose between an armistice and a dissatisfied Rhee, "we must face the latter philosophically as the lesser of the two evils."[196]

Zhou Enlai informed Nehru that the new American proposals were "utterly unacceptable" and that the Chinese planned to withdraw their recent concessions. Nehru expressed his unhappiness at the turn the negotiations had taken. The British transmitted Nehru's message to Washington, with a message from Churchill that he "felt it important" to give Nehru some "assurance."[197]

Dulles left on an Asian tour in mid-May. The international reaction to the US proposal in the negotiations had a sobering effect on everyone left in Washington. In a State-JCS meeting on 18 May, U. Alexis Johnson argued that the United States could not sustain its stand that the Korean prisoners should be released to civilian status once the armistice was signed. This demand, he asserted, was "really so illogical that it tends to weaken our whole position." Echoing the communist criticism, Collins wondered how the NNRC could function if it operated under the unanimity principle. The new assistant secretary of state for Far Eastern Affairs, Walter Robertson, conceded that obtaining clear terms of reference for the NNRC, not the unanimity clause, was the important factor. In Johnson's opinion, the US position would not look good if Washington continued what the allies called "haggling over details" after the communists had accepted the main points for a settlement. Bradley added that already the American press "was blaming the JCS for blocking an armistice by haggling over details." The United States had to change its stand on the Korean POWs if it wanted an armistice. Johnson pointed out that Eisenhower had publicly accepted the UN resolution. Henry Cabot Lodge, the US ambassador to the UN, had called it "a standard to which all honest men could repair." The United States could now hardly object if the communists proposed similar terms.[198]

In a memorandum to the president on 18 May, Bedell Smith, acting as secretary of state while Dulles was on an Asian tour, put the position bluntly: "The Korean negotiations are at a crisis. Our position vis-à-vis our allies is deteriorating daily." He recommended agreeing to hand over the Korean POWs to the NNRC along with the Chinese POWs and giving up the American insistence on unanimous voting by the Commission. The United States should present this as its final offer, and if the communists did not accept it within one week, Washington would terminate, not simply recess, the negotiations, withdraw from all previous agreements, and promptly release all Korean and Chinese POWS opposed to repatriation. Simultaneous with this offer, Ambassador Charles Bohlen in Moscow would make a confidential approach to Molotov.[199]

Smith cabled Dulles, who was in Saudi Arabia, on the lines of his memo to the president and added that the final decision would be taken after consultation with allies and congressional leaders. Smith did not solicit Dulles's opinion. Nevertheless, on receipt of Smith's cable, Dulles tersely cabled back "approved."[200] After Johnson and Robertson talked to the congressional leaders, Smith cabled Dulles on 22 May that these leaders, including Knowland and Walter Judd, another prominent Asia firster, agreed with the new US position.[201]

The next event was the celebrated Dulles–Nehru meeting in New Delhi. According to Dulles's memo of his conversation with Nehru on 21 May,

Mr. Nehru urged the importance of concluding an armistice, stating that he feared otherwise the fighting would extend. I agreed with his estimate, stating that if the armistice negotiations collapsed, the United States would probably make a stronger rather than a lesser military exertion, and that this might well extend the area of conflict. (*Note*: I assumed this would be relayed.) I said that we were, however, sincerely trying to get an armistice and that only crazy people could think that the United States wanted to prolong the struggle, which had already cost us about 15,000 casualties and 10 to 15 billion dollars of expenditure.[202]

In their meeting the next day, according to Dulles,

Mr. Nehru brought up the subject of the Korean armistice, referring particularly to my statement of the preceding day, that if there was no armistice hostilities might become more intense. He said that if this happened it would be difficult to know what the end might be. He urged withdrawal of our armistice proposals inconsistent with the Indian resolution, notably the provision regarding the Korean POWS and unanimity. . . . He brought up again my reference to intensified operations, but I made no comment and allowed the topic to drop.[203]

When Dulles reported to the NSC on his return from his tour, he did not in the least mention that he had attempted to pass on nuclear threats to China through Nehru. Instead, he stressed that the talks with Nehru "had been valuable in clearing away misapprehensions" in Nehru's mind. He "had done his best to indicate that the United States really desired an armistice and was not resorting to technicalities to avoid one."[204] A few days later, Dulles told Senator Walter George that his conversations with Nehru "had a great deal of weight in getting the armistice."[205] Whether Dulles meant that his threats to expand the war, or his attempts to reassure Nehru that the United States genuinely sought peace, was decisive, is not clear.[206]

In any case, conveying nuclear threats to China with the intention of ending the war simply did not fit in with the logic of Dulles's own interpretation of the inner workings of the communist side. As he suggested to President-elect Eisenhower in November 1952,

It is probable that the dominant will with which we have to deal is that of the Soviet Union. . . . If this conclusion is sound, the considerations which determine whether or not the Communists will continue the war are global considerations and not considerations limited merely to the battle line in Korea or the desires of the North Koreans or Chinese Communists.[207]

The United States formally presented its revised proposal on the lines approved by Eisenhower on 25 May in executive session at Panmunjon. It proposed that 120 days after the POWs were handed over to the commission, any prisoner remaining would be handed over to the UN General Assembly for final disposal.

Under instructions from the State Department, Ambassador Bohlen met Molotov on 27 May. Bohlen emphasized that the latest US proposals were "the extreme limit of possible concessions" and explained how far the United States had accommodated the communist demands. He told Molotov that rejection of the new American proposals would "lead to the creation of a situation which the United States government was most sincerely and earnestly attempting to avoid." While presenting his credentials to Soviet President Voroshilov, Bohlen remarked that the "success or failure of the truce talks at Panmunjon would be the real test of whether . . . relations between the United States and the Soviet Union could improve." On 3 June, Molotov told Bohlen that "as you know, the outcome of these talks does not depend on us but it has been noted with satisfaction that the path to the successful conclusion of these armistice talks has been mapped out."[208] The communist reply on 4 June proposed that after 120 days the prisoners would be released to civilian status. Murphy described this as exceeding "our most optimistic expectations." After more haggling over minor details, the two sides finalized the armistice agreement on 8 June. The POW issue was at last solved. Rhee, however, tried to sabotage the conclusion of peace by releasing over 25,000 North Korean POWs on 17 June. He released more North Korean POWs in the next few days. By a mixture of carrots and sticks, the United States finally persuaded Rhee to refrain from further efforts to destroy the peace.[209]

CHINESE PREPARATION TO FACE EISENHOWER

Newly available Chinese sources show no evidence that American nuclear threats had compelled the Chinese leadership to make peace. Mao calculated that the military situation in Korea was not serious enough to force the United States to end the war. The incoming administration might, therefore, launch a new offensive in the spring. Based on Eisenhower's public pronouncements, Chinese leaders assumed that he would "intensify" fighting. From their analysis of available information, the PLA General Staff concluded that the UN forces might attempt a landing in the spring behind the communist lines. They estimated that the United States had four options: a massive frontal assault, strategic bombing of North Korea and northern China along with a naval blockade of the Chinese coastline, atomic bombing, and an amphibious landing behind the Chinese lines. They dismissed the likelihood of ground attacks and strategic bombings, as both had been tried in the past. They considered the use of atomic weapons unlikely because of adverse world opinion and possible Soviet retaliation. The Chinese leadership apparently perceived no clear signals that the United States might use atomic weapons.[210] The CPV officers studied Eisenhower's background, including the Normandy landings under his command. They also noted Mark Clark's and Van Fleet's interest in amphibious operations and the UN forces' capabilities for such missions.[211] From all of these, Mao anticipated that Eisenhower would resort to amphibious operations behind Chinese lines rather than a frontal attack. It is quite likely that the campaign of rumors that the Truman administration probably planted in the fall of 1952 had contributed to this conclusion by the Chinese.[212]

To deal with possible US military moves, the Chinese took several countermeasures. Mao judged that if the CPV could beat off the anticipated American landings and "take tactical offensives in the frontline to decimate more enemy troops," the tide of war would turn in China's favor. He wanted the assumption that "the enemy will land at our rear, at the western coast, and in the area between the Chongchon and the Han rivers" to guide the CPV's planning. On 20 December, the CCP Central Committee issued the "Instructions on Preparing All Possible Conditions to Smash the Enemy's Amphibious Operations and Increase the Magnitude of Victory in Korea." This order, drafted by Mao himself, anticipated UN landings "along the western coast between the Han and Yalu rivers" and ordered completion of all defensive arrangements by April 1953. Mao expected the UN amphibious operation to be the last American operation in the war. He hoped that if the PLA could repel it, "the enemy's final defeat will be assured."[213]

A four-day conference of the CPV leaders from 17 to 21 December 1952 drew up the "Military Plan for Smashing the Enemy's Amphibious Offensive." The CPV Command completed preparations by the end of April. When the anticipated American landings did not come, Chinese analysts attributed it to three possible reasons: the United States could not muster sufficient domestic and allied support for the operation; the administration needed more time to prepare an offensive (so the resumption of talks was a cover to buy more time); and the United States might still seek a militarily advantageous situation in order to obtain more favorable terms in the negotiations. The Chinese leaders concluded that the United States had to be forced militarily to negotiate. So they proposed tactical offensives along the front. The Central Military Commission (CMC), headed by Peng Dehui, approved this idea and suggested that the offensives start in mid-May after full preparation. Mao agreed, with the caveat that if the talks made progress, the decision could be modified. The CPV headquarters ordered preparations to be completed by the end of May so that operations could start early in June. A senior CPV general later recalled that "[we] just wanted to impress the enemy with the 'iron' facts that we were capable and not afraid of fighting the war."[214]

The uncompromising American stand at Panmunjom on 13 May apparently prompted the CPV headquarters to start the tactical offensives straight away. Without obtaining Beijing's approval, some local commanders started operations on 13 May itself. On 16 May, the CMC ordered that the operations already started should be limited in scope, so as not to attract an unfavorable international reaction. The CMC also insisted on adherence to the original schedule for the offensive. Historian Shu Guang Zhang argues that the CPV tactical offensive "had a big impact on the truce talks."[215] American documents, however, reveal no such effect. The decisive factor in modifying the American stand was the conviction by State Department officials and the JCS that the American position contained in its 13 May proposal was untenable.

NUCLEAR DIPLOMACY IN THE KOREAN WAR

Amidst the debates generated by the claims of Dulles and other Eisenhower administration officials, and Dingman's findings on the nuclear diplomacy of the Truman administration, historians have lost sight of the most important role that atomic weapons played in the Korean War. This war broke out at a critical time from the perspective of policy makers in Washington. They feared that once the Soviet atomic arsenal reached the level at which it could inflict substantial damage on the United States, the Soviet Union might be tempted to give free rein to its expansionist tendencies. The Korean War seemed to many in Washington to be the first shot in a new drive by international communism for territorial gains. The United States did not have the conventional forces required to counter this. Truman had not yet approved the massive rearmament program that NSC 68 called for. He took the decision to intervene to defend South Korea with the full knowledge that if the Soviet Union entered the war, the US forces would be easily driven off the peninsula. Truman's order to the air force to plan for neutralizing the Soviet Far East Air Force shows his consciousness of this possibility as well as the strategic importance of atomic weapons. The only force that could deter the Soviets from intervening was the American atomic arsenal. The American atomic capability facilitated the US decision to oppose the North Korean invasion. This does not mean that Truman would not have decided to intervene in the absence of atomic weapons, just that atomic weapons made it easy for Truman to decide on intervention and to win public and congressional support. After the Chinese intervention, atomic weapons gave US leaders the confidence that these weapons could be used to prevent US forces from being driven off the peninsula, and so allowed the United States to continue fighting in Korea. Truman did not "explicitly" threaten the Soviets with atomic weapons in order to deter them from intervening in the war. Until one has access to the relevant Soviet documents, it is impossible to pass a definitive judgment on what lessons Soviet leaders drew from Truman's overseas movements of atomic bombers. One might, however, hazard a guess that Stalin did not consider the absence of an "explicit" atomic threat particularly reassuring.

The state of nuclear weaponry ensured that use of tactical nuclear weapons on a scale needed to overcome the communist defenses in the war was never a serious option for the Truman administration. Truman was also noticeably slow to resort to nuclear diplomacy against China during the war. Even when the administration attempted nuclear diplomacy, its nuclear threats had no effect on Chinese decision making. Except for cursory references to atomic weapons in the Chinese debates on intervening in the war in the fall of 1950, no documentary evidence on what Chinese leaders thought about specific acts of American nuclear diplomacy has surfaced. It is, however, clear that in the fall of 1950, atomic weapons did not represent a threat strong enough to deter China from intervening in the Korean War. Chinese leaders considered the threat to China's security so critical that they were prepared to risk atomic bombing rather than stand by and see American forces approach their borders. What the Chinese leaders knew of the destructive power of the early generation US atomic weapons, and their conviction that their country, ravaged by decades of war and civil strife, did not offer targets for atomic bombing, was probably sufficient to enable them to defy the atomic bomb. Later, the Chinese countermeasures that significantly neutralized the American nuclear advantage enabled them to stand firm in the face of what would otherwise have been overwhelming pressure. American nuclear diplomacy failed, when faced with an enemy who was prepared to risk American atomic bombing and did what it could to mitigate the consequences of such bombing.

If the communist initiative to offer to reopen the talks set in motion the train of events that led to the armistice, the US decision taken in late May to drop its insistence on unanimity of voting in the NNRC and hand over the Korean POWs also to the commission was the critical event in clinching the agreement. This decision went against Dulles's well-known views about not offering the communists any further concessions. Further, this decision was taken in the absence of Dulles. Far from having masterminded the armistice settlement, Dulles had no role in the events leading up to the final settlement. When the Eisenhower administration took its most significant decision about the war, Dulles was on exactly the other side of the globe.[216]

Eisenhower himself had made no plan to end the war before his inauguration. After he assumed office, he made no plan either. The extended discussions in the NSC have the appearance of a charade played out in slow motion. These deliberations did not disclose anything that a few hours of discussions with Bradley, Vandenberg, and Collins during the transition would not have disclosed. With his military background, Eisenhower did not need to ask these questions anyway. The discussions did, however, serve to confuse the record so thoroughly as to make it all but impossible to pin Eisenhower down. With no apparent order, he sounded tough, as well as moderate. He spoke in favor of using nuclear weapons, as well as against using them. If a latter-day McCarthy wanted to charge Eisenhower with the loss of Korea, he would have had a hard time making out a coherent case. Eisenhower revisionists have claimed that the newly elected president's thinly veiled pre-inauguration threats to expand the war forced the communists to moderate their stand. It appears that the Chinese leadership took these threats quite seriously. However, the Chinese response was to hunker down for another round of fighting, not to succumb to military pressure. All that can be said about Eisenhower's contribution to ending the Korean War is that he did not show much enthusiasm for an expanded war. When a sensible plan for peace was presented to him, and Dulles was conveniently absent, he quickly approved it. On his own, he took no initiative to end the war.

Why did the Eisenhower administration indulge in loud talks of having used nuclear diplomacy to end the war, when the record shows that it did not undertake any such diplomacy in the spring of 1953? Just when Dulles claimed he was passing on nuclear threats to China through Nehru, officials in Washington, with the president's approval, were, in fact, putting the final touches on the American concessions that finally ended the war. Dulles had good reasons to fear a political backlash for these concessions. The claims of masterful nuclear diplomacy might well have been advanced as a smokescreen to cover these concessions.

What is most remarkable about the historiography of the American nuclear diplomacy in the Korean War is the striking similarity between what the Eisenhower administration claimed it had attempted and what the Truman administration actually did. Documentation on the nuclear diplomacy of the Truman administration has long been available. This makes the prolonged life of the myth of the Eisenhower administration's ending of the Korean War through nuclear diplomacy,[217] while the history of the actual nuclear diplomacy practiced by the Truman administration languished in obscurity, all the more surprising.

NOTES

1. *Life* (16 January 1956). See also Chapter 1. The *Helena* meeting took place at the end of Eisenhower's visit to Korea in fulfillment of his campaign pledge.

2. Sarvepalli Gopal, *Jawaharlal Nehru: A Biography, Vol. II, 1947–1956* (Cambridge, MA: Harvard University Press, 1979), 148.

3. Escott Reid, *Envoy to Nehru* (New Delhi: Oxford University Press, 1981), 45.

4. Dwight D. Eisenhower, *The White House Years: Vol. I: Mandate for Change, 1953–1956* (Garden City, NY: Doubleday & Co., 1963), 181.

5. Edward C. Keefer, "President Eisenhower and the End of the Korean War," *Diplomatic History* (Summer 1986), 280.

6. John Newhouse, *War and Peace in the Nuclear Age* (New York: Alfred A. Knopf, 1989), 98. Dean Rusk, however, told Newhouse that "What was actually said to China was very vague and ambiguous." He had looked at the files after he became secretary of state in 1961. "What has been claimed for that episode," he thought, "is quite an exaggeration." Ibid., 98–99. See also Dean Rusk, *As I Saw It: As Told to Richard Rusk* (New York: W. W. Norton & Co., 1990), 170. U. Alexis Johnson, who had handled Korean War affairs in the Truman administration and continued to do so until the summer of 1953 as deputy assistant secretary of state for Far Eastern Affairs, also did not think that Dulles's meeting with Nehru played a decisive role. "Dulles never mentioned this [the alleged message through Nehru] to me or anyone else at the time," Johnson recalled in his memoirs. See U. Alexis Johnson, *The Right Hand of Power* (Englewood Cliffs, NJ: Prentice-Hall, 1984), 165.

7. Harry S. Truman, *Memoirs, Vol. 2: Years of Trial and Hope* (New York: Doubleday & Co., 1956), 410–13; Dean Acheson, *Present at the Creation: My Years in the State Department* (New York: W. W. Norton & Co., 1969); Newhouse, *War and Peace*, 83.

8. John Lewis Gaddis, *The Long Peace* (New York: Oxford University Press, 1987), 115, 117.

9. For a summary of this debate, see Rosemary Foot, "Making Known the Unknown War: Policy Analysis of the Korean Conflict in the Last Decade," *Diplomatic History* (Summer 1991).

10. Roger Dingman, "Atomic Diplomacy During the Korean War," *International Security* (Winter 1988/1989).

11. Bruce Cumings, Origins of the Korean War, Vol. II (Princeton, NJ: Princeton University Press, 1990); Mark Ryan, *Chinese Attitudes Toward Nuclear Weapons: China and the United States During the Korean War* (Armonk, NY: M. E. Sharpe, 1989).

12. See also D. Clayton James (with Anne Sharp Wells), *Refighting the Last War: Command and Crisis in Korea, 1950–1953* (New York: The Free Press, 1993), 139–40.

13. James F. Schnabel and Robert J. Watson, *The History of the Joint Chiefs of Staff: The Joint Chiefs of Staff and National Policy, Vol. 3: The Korean War, Part 1* (Wilmington, DE: Michael Glazier, 1979), 44–46, 180.

14. Ibid., 91.

15. Harvey to Armstrong, 23 June 1950, PPS papers, 1947–1953, Box 7, "Atomic Energy—Armaments, 1950," RG 59, NA; Record of Eighth Meeting (1950) of the PPS, 2 February 1950, *FRUS, 1950, I*, 143.

16. *FRUS 1950, VII*, 159–60.

17. Hillenkoetter memo to Truman, 6 July 1950, PSF, Intelligence, Box 250, "CIA Memo 1950–1952," HSTL; memo by Carlton Savage, "The Question of US Use of Atomic Bombs in Korea," 15 July 1950, PPS papers, 1947–1953, Box 20, "Korea 1947–50," RG 59 (National Archives), NA; Nitze to Acheson, 17 July 1950, ibid; Report by an Ad Hoc Committee, G-3/Plans Div./73772, Army—Operations General Decimal File, 091. Korea, Box 34-A, "OPS 091. Korea TS (Sect. III-A) Case 42, Book II," RG 319, NA.

18. LeMay diary entry for 8 and 10 July, LeMay Papers, Box 103, "LeMay Diary #2–1 July to 31 December 1950," Library of Congress (LC); Dingman, "Atomic Diplomacy," 57.

19. Redline from Norstad to Johnson, 9 July 1950, Johnson to Washington, Norstad to LeMay, Johnson to Norstad, 10 July, in Vandenberg Diary, Box 86, "July 1950," LC.
On the night of 23–24 July, British troops guarding the B-29s sabotaged four of the aircraft at Lakenheath air base in Britain. The damage was minor, such as the puncturing of tires by bayonets. The reported reason was dissatisfaction of the draftees with being ordered overseas. The soldiers were also reportedly "teed off" at their sergeant for posting them to the duty and were drunk. COMGEN-SAC to CS USAF, 26 July 1950, Redline Johnson to Norstad, 27 July, Vandenberg Diary, Box 86, "July 1950," LC. If this was indeed a coincidence, it was too close for comfort.

20. LeMay diary entry, 29 July 1950, 13 September 1959, LeMay Papers, Box 103, "LeMay Diary #2–1 July to 31 December 1950," LC; Dingman, "Atomic Diplomacy," 61–64.

21. Dingman, "Atomic Diplomacy," 58–65. Dingman laid particular stress on Acheson's leaking of the second movement of the bombers to the press.

22. On the possibility of Chinese intervention, see NSC 81-1, 9 September 1950, *FRUS 1950, VII*, 714.

23. Schnabel and Watson, *The History of the Joint Chiefs of Staff*, 183–84.

24. Comments on the initial atomic strike capabilities of SAC, 11 September 1950, LeMay Papers, Box 197, "B-7081," LC.

25. JCS memo for secretary of defense, 10 July 1950, *FRUS 1950, VII*, 346.

26. Elsey Notes, 26 June 1950, George M. Elsey Papers, Subject Series, Box 71, "Korea—June 26, 1950," HSTL.

27. Summary of discussions at the 59th NSC meeting, 30 June 1950, PSF, NSC Meetings Series, Box 220, "NSC Meetings—Memos for President, Meeting Discussion, 1950," HSTL.

28. See Savage memo, "Use of Atomic Weapons," 28 February 1950, PPS Files, 1947–1953, Box 6, "Atomic Energy—Armaments, 1950," RG 59, NA.

29. Dingman, "Atomic Diplomacy," 57.

30. Bolte to Collins, 13 July 1950, Bolte to Gruenther, 25 July, More to Bolte, 21 August 1950, all in Army—Operations General Decimal File, Box 34-A, "Ops 091. Korea TS (Sec. III-A) Case 42, Book II," RG 319, NA. According to Dingman, Collins did not raise the issue with MacArthur. MacArthur, however, brought up the question of atomic bombing in reply to a query by Vandenberg and wanted Vandenberg to "sweeten up" his B-29 force for this task. Vandenberg reportedly agreed. Dingman, "Atomic Diplomacy," 62.

31. Walter S. Poole, *The History of the Joint Chiefs of Staff: The Joint Chiefs of Staff and National Policy, 1950–1952, Vol. IV* (Wilmington, DE: Michael Glazier, 1980), 163–65; Rosenberg, "US Nuclear Stockpile," 26.

32. Paul H. Nitze, *From Hiroshima to Glasnost: At the Center of Decision: A Memoir* (New York: Weidenfeld & Nicholson, 1989), 110; Newhouse, *War and Peace*, 83.

33. Korean War Command G-2 Daily Intelligence Summaries, quoted in Ryan, *Chinese Attitudes*, 30. See also Betts, *Nuclear Blackmail*, 35–36.

34. Douglas MacArthur, *Reminiscences* (New York: McGraw-Hill, 1964), 374–75; Joseph Goulden, *Korea: The Untold Story of the War* (New York: Time Books, 1982), 247.

35. Philby was first secretary in the British Embassy in Washington; Burgess was second secretary and later head of the China desk in the Foreign Office in London; Maclean was head of the US desk in the Foreign Office. They all later defected to the Soviet Union.

36. Allen Whiting, *China Crosses the Yalu: The Decision to Enter the Korean War* (New York: The Macmillan Co., 1960). For a comprehensive listing of other works on this topic, see the footnotes to "Introduction" in Chen Jian, *China's Road to the Korean War: The Making of the Sino-American Confrontation* (New York: Columbia University Press, paperback edition, 1994).

37. Whiting, *China Crosses the Yalu*, 122, 134–36, 142–43; Ryan, *Chinese Attitudes*, 30, 31; Draft Davis memo, 7 November 1950, *FRUS 1950, VII*, 1,079. For a view similar to Whiting's, documentation on contemporary Chinese debates that surfaced, and Chinese countermeasures to cope with possible American retaliation, see Tang Tsou, *America's Failure in China* (Chicago: University of Chicago Press, 1963), 575–80.

38. Michael Hunt, "Beijing and the Korean Crisis, June 1950–June 1951," *Political Science Quarterly* (Fall 1992); Sergei N. Goncharov et al., *Uncertain Partners: Stalin, Mao, and the Korean War* (Stanford, CA: Stanford University Press, 1993), 153, 159; Chen Jian, *China's Road*, 85–90.

39. See Dieter Heinzig, "Stalin, Mao, Kim and Korean War Origins, 1950: A Russian Documentary Discrepancy," *CWIHP Bulletin* (Winter 1996/1997), 240.

40. Chen Jian, *China's Road*, 134–35.

41. Ibid., 127–34, 142.

42. Ibid., 136–37.

43. Ibid., 142–45.

44. Ibid., 147–49. After the Inchon landing, Kim also ignored Stalin's warnings about the strategic significance of the American operations and Soviet advice on how best to deal with it. See Alexandre Y. Mansourov, "Stalin, Mao, Kim, and China's Decision to Enter the Korean War, September 16–October 15, 1950: New Evidence From the Russian Archives," *CWIHP Bulletin* (Winter 1995/1996), 95–97.

45. Chen Jian, *China's Road*, 153–54.

46. Ibid., 161. On possible dissensions within the North Korean camp and the possibility that a faction opposed to Kim might have sought Chinese assistance to get rid of Kim and to defend North Korea, see ibid., 162–63.

47. K. M. Panikkar, *In Two Chinas: Memoirs of a Diplomat* (London: Allen and Unwin, 1955), 108.

48. Chen Jian, *China's Road*, 171–73.

49. Mansourov, "Stalin, Mao, and Kim," 114.

50. Excerpts in Michael H. Hunt, *Crises in US Foreign Policy* (New Haven, CT: Yale University Press, 1996), 206–7.

51. See Shen Zhihua, "The Discrepancy Between the Russian and Chinese Versions of Mao's 2 October 1950 Message to Stalin on Chinese Entry into the Korean War: A Chinese Scholar's Reply," *CWIHP Bulletin* (Winter 1996/1997), 237–42. Even before the publication of the purported Mao telegram to Stalin,

Chinese scholars had claimed, on the basis of interviews with former officials, that Stalin had delayed his offer of air cover to the PLA until after the CMC issued the order to send the Chinese volunteers to Korea. See Hao Yufan and Zhai Zhihai, "China's Decision to Enter the Korean War: History Revisited," *China Quarterly* (March 1990), 110.

52. Mansourov, "Stalin, Mao, and Kim," 102–3, 114–15.

53. Chen Jian, *China's Road*, 180. See also Panikkar, *In Two Chinas*, 110.

54. Chen Jian, *China's Road*, 181–84, 281 note 78.

55. Mao's telegram to Zhou in Appendix to Thomas J. Christensen, "Threats, Assurances, and the Last Chance for Peace: The Lessons of Mao's Korean War Telegrams," *International Security* (Summer 1992), 151–53. See also Chen Jian, *China's Road*, 202.

56. Hunt, "Beijing and the Korean Crisis," 459–63; Mao's telegram to Zhou, 14 October 1950, Appendix, Christensen, "Threats, Assurance, and the Last Chance for Peace," 152–53; Chen Jian, *China's Road*, 208.

57. Ibid., 213ff; Vladislav Zubock and Constantine Pleshakov, *Inside the Kremlin's Cold War: From Stalin to Khrushchev* (Cambridge, MA: Harvard University Press, 1996), 69.

58. On the evolution of Mao's opinion of the atom bomb, see Ryan, *Chinese Attitudes*, Chapter 1.

59. In a British House of Commons debate in 1948, it was stated that very little was needed by way of protection against the effects of atomic weapons. Even a sheet of brown paper would protect against the flash of the explosion; sandbags offered adequate protection against radiation; radioactivity would dissipate in a matter of hours; shelters not much thicker than conventional bomb shelters would suffice. Reports also suggested that the Eniwetok tests showed that radiation effects were less than was previously assumed. *Newsweek*, 5 April and 19 July 1948.

Ansley J. Coale wrote in 1947 that proper disposition of troops and trenches and similar shelters might mitigate the "spectacular anti-personnel properties" of atomic weapons. See Ansley J. Coale, *The Problem of Reducing Vulnerability to Atomic Bombs* (Princeton, NJ: Princeton University Press, 1947), 14. P.M.S. Blackett, the British physicist-turned peace activist, wrote along similar lines. In his view, the Chinese "are not deterred by America's stockpile of bombs because they know that even if they were used against them, they would not be effective." P.M.S. Blackett, *Fear, War, and the Bomb: Military and Political Consequences of Atomic Energy* (New York: Whittlesey House, 1948), 203.

60. Ryan, *Chinese Attitudes*, 27.

61. Russell Spurr, *Enter the Dragon: China's Undeclared War Against the United States in Korea, 1950–51* (New York: New Market Press, 1988), 62.

62. Chen Jian, *China's Road*, 144.

63. Ibid., 153–54.

64. Peng Dehui, *Memoirs of a Chinese Marshall: The Autobiographical Notes of Peng Dehui (1898–1974)*, translated by Zhang Long (Beijing: Foreign Language Press, 1984), 474.

65. Thomas J. Christensen, "A 'Last Chance' for What? Rethinking the Origins of US-PRC Confrontation," *Journal of American–East Asian Relations* (Fall 1995), 260.

66. Chen Jian, *China's Road*, 175–77; Mao's Telegram to Stalin, 2 October 1950, in Appendix to Christensen, "Threats, Assurances, and the Last Chance for Peace," 151–52. Christensen argues that the possibility of American air attacks on China while Chinese forces were bogged down in Korea might have prompted Mao to seek a quick, total victory in Korea. Ibid., 137.

67. Hao Yufan and Zhai Zhihai, "China's Decision to Enter the Korean War," 111.

68. *FRUS 1950, VII*, 911, 915.

69. Some officials in the State Department's Policy Planning Section considered a plan for Ambassador Loy Henderson in New Delhi to drop the word to Indian diplomats that if China intervened, the United States would retaliate with air and naval action against targets in China. Davies memo, "Calculated Indiscretion to be Committed by Ambassador Henderson" and Feis' notes on this memo, both dated 12 July 1950, PPS Files, 1947–1953, China II, RG 59, NA. There is some evidence that China received this message. See Christensen, "A 'Last Chance' for What," 267.

70. Jessup memo, 3 December 1950, *FRUS 1950, VII*, 1,312.

71. *New York Times*, 4 December 1950.

72. Schnabel and Watson, *The History of the Joint Chiefs of Staff*, 356.

73. Minutes of the president's meeting with congressional leaders, 13 December 1950, PSF, B File, Box 42A, "The Korean War: The United States' Response to Communist China's Intervention (1 of 1)," HSTL.

74. *New York Times*, 1 December 1950.

75. Memo for Chief of Staff, US Army, 16 November 1950, Army-Operations Decimal File, 091. Korea, Box 34-A, "OPS091. Korea TS (Section III-A Case 42) Book II, RG 319, NA.

76. G-3 Recommendations With Respect to Military Course of Action, 1 December 1950, RG 319, 1950–51, 091. Korea, Box 34, "G-3–091. Korea TS (Sec. 1B) Case 14," NA.

77. JCS 2173, 21 November 1950, enclosing Collins memo dated 20 November 1950, UPA, RJCS 1946–1953, Reel 9.

78. JCS 2173/1, dated 29 November 1950, and JCS 2173/2, dated 3 December 1950, quoted in Ryan, *Chinese Attitudes*, 35; Schnabel and Watson, *The History of the Joint Chiefs of Staff*, 372–73.

79. Karl Bendetsen Oral History, HSTL, 261. Bendetsen also stated that "very detailed and penetrating studies of high resolution photography were carefully considered." He added pointedly that "If I were to respond more fully, I have a great deal to say of hitherto unrevealed substance."

80. "Analysis of Possible Courses of Action in Korea—General Considerations," Enclosure to NSC 147, *FRUS 1952–54, XV*, 844.

81. Omar Bradley and Clay Blair, *A General's Life: An Autobiography* (New York: Simon and Schuster, 1983), 606; Schnabel and Watson, *The History of the Joint Chiefs of Staff*, 351.

82. Collins memo for the JCS, 8 December 1950, University Publications of America, *Records of the Joint Chiefs of Staff*, Reel 9. See also Acheson, *Present at the Creation*, 477.

83. Foot, *The Wrong War*, 114–15.

84. Schnabel and Watson, *The History of the Joint Chiefs of Staff*, 366–68; Bradley and Blair, *A General's Life*, 606; Ryan, *Chinese Attitudes*, 38.

85. *US News and World Report*, 15 December 1950, 17.

86. Burton I. Kaufman, *The Korean War: Challenges in Crisis, Credibility, and Command* (Philadelphia: Temple University Press, 1986), p. 111; Austin to Secretary of State, 1 December 1950, *FRUS 1950, VII*, 1,300. A columnist reported that "secret high-level discussions held in Washington in the past 48 hours" indicated that the administration contemplated the use of the atom bomb and the introduction of Nationalist troops into the war. Constantine Brown report, *Washington Star*, 2 December 1950.

87. *New York Times*, 2 December 1950.

88. Press summary in London to Department of State (DOS) #3208, 1 December 1950, Selected Korean War Records, Box 8, "Reactions to President's Statement Re Possible Use of Atom Bomb," HSTL.

89. Schnabel and Watson, *The History of the Joint Chiefs of Staff*, 373.

90. Position Paper Prepared for the Truman–Attlee Talks, *FRUS 1950, VII*, 1465.

91. JCS 2173/3, RJCS, UPA, Reel 9.

92. Jessup memo for the record, 7 December 1950, *FRUS 1950, VII*, 1462. Attlee asked "whether this agreement should be put in writing." Truman replied negatively, adding "that if a man's word wasn't any good it wasn't made any better by writing it down." Ibid.

During the Attlee visit, US early warning radar picked up a formation of unidentified objects on a flight path that would have brought them over Washington in a matter of hours. US air defense forces went on alert, and Acheson informed British Ambassador Oliver Franks, to give him "fair warning and the opportunity for prayer." The objects probably were geese. Acheson, *Present at the Creation*, 479–80.

93. Acheson, *Present at the Creation*, 484; *FRUS 1950, VII*, 1,464.

94. Analysis of public comment contained in communications to the president, received 4 to 8 December, 1950, 12 December 1950, Elsey Papers, Subject, Box 73, "Korea—National Emergency Proclamation, December 15, 1950 (folder 1)," HSTL; *Washington Post*, 1 December 1950. A Gallup Poll in November 1951 showed that 41 percent approved of the use of nuclear weapons in Korea, 10 percent gave qualified approval, and 37 percent opposed, while 12 percent had no opinion. George H. Gallup (ed.), *The Gallup Poll: Public Opinion, 1935–1971*, *Vol. II* (New York: Random House, 1972), 1,027.

95. *FRUS 1950, VII*, 1098–1100.

96. Clubb to Rusk, 7 November 1950, Ibid., 1,090.

97. Nitze memo, 4 November 1950, *FRUS 1950, VII*, 1041–42.

98. Michael Schaller, *Douglas MacArthur: The Far Eastern General* (New York: Oxford University Press, 1989), 231.

99. Roger M. Anders (ed.), *Forging the Atomic Shield: Excerpts from the Office Diary of Gordon E. Dean* (Chapel Hill: University of North Carolina Press, 1987), 127; Dingman, "Atomic Diplomacy," 69.

100. Anders, *Forging the Atomic Shield*, 134, 137.

101. Dingman, "Atomic Diplomacy," 72–73.

102. Cumings, *Origins of the Korean War*, 751.

103. Dingman, "Atomic Diplomacy," 75.

104. Ibid., 70–75. See also *New York Times*, 5 April 1951, for reports about lack of concern in MacArthur's headquarters and in the United Kingdom over a looming communist offensive. In contrast, Senator Sam Rayburn came out of a White House meeting muttering about an impending World War III. Ibid.

105. Ridgway to JCS, 27 April 1951, and JCS to Ridgway, 28 April 1951, *FRUS 1951, VII*, 385–86. The JCS had secured this presidential authority weeks earlier, but kept it secret from MacArthur, fearing that he might "make a premature decision in carrying it out." Bradley, quoted in Schnabel and Watson, *The History of the Joint Chiefs of Staff*, 535; *FRUS 1951, VII*, 309 note 6.

106. FECOM was not the only source of information on a possible Soviet intervention. The FBI received a letter from an anonymous source claiming to be in contact with a communist bloc diplomat at the UN stating that the Soviet Union intended to make a full-scale entry into the war in April. Edgar Hoover memos to Lay, 1 March and 9 April 1951, PSF, Subject File-NSC, Box 194, "Miscellaneous Data," HSTL.

107. Nitze memcon, 12 April 1951, *FRUS 1951, VII*, 339; Bradley and Blair, *A General's Life*, 629–30, 641.

108. "Tactical Employment of the Atomic Bomb in Korea," 22 December 1950, enclosed to memo from Acting Chief of Staff, FECOM, to the C-in-C, FECOM, 23 January 1951, NA.

109. Anders, *Forging the Atomic Shield*, 157–61. The Special NSC Subcommittee on Atomic Weapons consisted of the secretary of state, the secretary of defense, and the chairman of the Atomic Energy Commission.

110. Bradley and Blair, *A General's Life*, 649–50; Schnabel and Watson, *The History of the Joint Chiefs of Staff*, 613–14.

111. Report on the G-3 team's Far East visit, quoted in Ryan, *Chinese Attitudes*, 52–53. Probably acting on this, the army arranged for more photo interpreters. Ibid., 53.

112. *New York Times*, 9 July 1952.

113. On the atomic war capabilities of American forces during this period, see Chapter 2.

114. Ryan, *Chinese Attitudes*, 26.

115. *New York Times*, 13, 21, 28 July 1950.

116. *New York Times*, 1 August 1951; Anders, *Forging the Atomic Shield*, 151.

117. Ibid., 174; *New York Times*, 11 September 1951.

118. *New York Times*, 6 October 1951. Taking a contrary stand, Rep. James E. Van Zandt, member of the Congressional Atomic Energy Committee, declared that "Dean is kidding the American people that they [tactical nuclear weapons] are available immediately. He knows that those weapons are a long way off." The same day the paper carried calls by three senators for use of atomic weapons in the war. One of them queried, "if we have them [tactical atomic weapons] what are we waiting for?" As if in response, Stalin announced that the Soviet Union was developing atomic weapons of "various calibers." Ibid.

119. *New York Times*, 12 October 1951. Rep. Overton Brooks, Acting Chairman, House Armed Services Committee, demanded that the United States should use atomic weapons in the war. He claimed that the administration was indeed "se-

riously thinking" of resorting to nuclear weapons if the armistice talks failed. *New York Times*, 14 October 1951.

120. *New York Times*, 11 and 12 October 1951.

121. Ryan, *Chinese Attitudes*, 134.

122. *New York Times*, 2 November 1952.

123. *New York Times*, 4, 6 January; 16, 17 February; 26, 27 March; 12 April 1952.

124. *New York Times*, 22 April 1952.

125. *New York Times*, 18 May 1952.

126. Hanson Baldwin's front page report, *New York Times*, 18 March 1953.

127. Miller, *Under a Cloud*, 163, 167, 169.

128. This part of the study closely follows the analysis by Ryan, *Chinese Attitudes*.

129. Ibid., 39–40.

130. Ibid., 73.

131. Ibid., 133–35.

132. H. Goldhamer, *Communist Reaction in Korea to American Possession of the A-Bomb and Its Significance for US Political and Psychological Warfare*—Rand Research Memorandum #RM-903 (Santa Monica, CA: The Rand Corporation, 1 August 1952), 6–9, 37–38.

133. Ryan, *Chinese Attitudes*, 107–9.

134. Ibid., 129–31.

135. See Collins's remarks in State-JCS meeting, *FRUS 1952–54, XV*, 817–18; Ryan, *Chinese Attitudes*, 132.

136. Marshall memcon of meetings on 6, 7, 12, and 13 January 1951, *FRUS 1951, VII*, 1,480; Charles Burton Marshall Oral History, HSTL; Dingman, "Atomic Diplomacy," 76–77; Nitze, *From Hiroshima to Glasnost*, 112. Marshall and the Chinese contact also discussed dropping propaganda leaflets over China, which some US officials considered a good idea. One official suggested starting the leaflets with the statement, "It might have been a bomb." Others, however, disapproved of such bluntness. Marshall memcon, 30 January 1951, *FRUS 1951, VII*, 1535.

137. *FRUS 1951, VII*, 1,658–62; Marshall Oral History. The Chinese contact stated that when US forces crossed the 38th Parallel, the Chinese were certain that other US forces would land in Shanghai and were prepared to face it.

138. Hunt, "Beijing and the Korean Crisis," 468.

139. The "persuasive ability" of their captors played no small part in this "unwillingness."

140. For details of these negotiations, see Rosemary Foot, *A Substitute for Victory: The Politics of Peacemaking at the Korean Armistice Talks* (Ithaca, NY: Cornell University Press, 1990).

141. Ibid., 136–37; *Time*, 30 June 1952.

142. Gross to State Department, 30 June 1952, *FRUS 1952–54, XV*, 365–67; McClurkin memcon, 18 June 1952, ibid., 340–41; Hickerson memcon, 19 June 1952, ibid., 344–46.

143. Foot, *A Substitute for Victory*, 137.

144. Ibid., 137–38.

145. Ibid., 151–52.

146. Schnabel and Watson, *The History of the Joint Chiefs of Staff*, pt. 2, 932–34.

147. Moscow cable, 19 August 1952, *FRUS 1952–54, XV,* 484 note 2.

148. Phillips to MacKnight, 3 September 1952, ibid., 484. The planting of the rumor of an amphibious invasion might well have been behind the conclusion the Chinese reached that the incoming Eisenhower administration might launch a sea-borne invasion of communist-held areas. See Shu Guang Zhang, *Deterrence and Strategic Culture: Chinese-American Confrontations, 1949–1958* (Ithaca, NY: Cornell University Press, 1992), 131–33.

149. *FRUS 1952–54,* 545–48, 554–57.

150. Chester Bowles, *Ambassador's Report* (New York: Harper & Brothers, 1954), 242.

151. Draft memcon, 16 November 1952, *FRUS 1952–54, XV,* 644.

152. Clay Blair, *The Forgotten War: America in Korea, 1950–1953* (New York: Time Books, 1987), 970.

153. Record of Stalin–Zhou conversation, 20 August 1952, *CWIHP Bulletin* (Winter 1995/1996), 12–14; Record of Stalin–Zhou conversation, 19 September 1952, ibid., 17–18.

The North Koreans saw no advantage in prolonging the war, as they were suffering greater casualties than the number of POWs whose return they were negotiating. North Korea, Zhou told Stalin, was "wavering somewhat.... Among certain elements of the Korean leadership one can detect a state of panic, even." Ibid., 14.

154. On the Indian resolution, see William Stueck, *Korean War: An International History* (Princeton, NJ: Princeton University Press, 1995), 298–305.

155. As Alexis Johnson recalled, "When the armistice negotiations bogged down over esoteric issues like the neutrality of the conference site, rehabilitation of airfields, voluntary repatriation and riots in the POW camps, we could sense the national eye beginning to glaze." Johnson, *The Right Hand of Power,* 150.

156. *New York Times,* 25 December 1952; *Time,* 5 January 1953.

157. Dulles to Eisenhower, 26 November 1952, Dulles Papers, Subject Series, Box 8, "Korea," DEPL. The "waistline" referred to the line from Sinanju to Hungnan, where the front was one-third shorter than the agreed armistice line. There is no indication, however, that Dulles understood the full implications of a renewed offensive to secure this line.

158. Schnabel and Watson, *The History of the Joint Chiefs of Staff,* pt. 2, 932.

159. Mark W. Clark, *From the Danube to the Yalu* (New York: Harper & Brothers, 1954), 233; Bradley and Blair, *A General's Life,* 658.

160. *New York Times,* 15 December 1952.

161. Eisenhower, *The White House Years. Vol. 1: Mandate for Change,* 179.

162. Emmet Hughes, *The Ordeal of Power: A Political Memoir of the Eisenhower Years* (New York: Atheneum, 1963), 104–5. Emphasis in original.

163. Dulles memo to Eisenhower, 6 March 1953, *FRUS 1952–54, XV,* 805–6. According to Dulles's account of the meting, Eden merely commented that "he hoped that before any major action was taken his government would be consulted. He said he did not necessarily want to impose a veto on any action but merely wanted to insure that Britain not be taken by surprise." Dulles, however, left with the impression that Eden agreed with the general line taken by him. Ibid.

Not much remained of the industrial complex north of the 38th Parallel by now. The Far East Air Force had already run out of "worthwhile targets" in Korea to bomb. Blair, *The Forgotten War*, 973.

164. Johnson, *The Right Hand of Power*, 162.

165. Churchill to Eden, 6 January 1953, FO 371/105478/10345/1G, PRO. Churchill's criticism was somewhat unfair, considering that he had urged Eisenhower that "on this and indeed on other matters it would be wise to take a few months and let us pool our brains meanwhile." Churchill had left with the feeling that Eisenhower "liked the idea." Ibid.

166. Memo of 131st NSC meeting, *FRUS 1952–54, XV*, 769–70. The Kaesong sanctuary consisted of about 28 square miles around the conference site where, by mutual agreement, hostile actions were prohibited. Clark had asked for authority to attack it as soon as a communist attack from that spot appeared imminent.

167. Cutler memo for Wilson, 21 March 1953, ibid., 815.

168. Memo of the special NSC meeting, 31 March 1953, ibid., 826. In the NSC meeting on 28 April, Eisenhower said that the United States might "at least appear to be increasing our build-up in Korea even though we sent out only skeletonized units or headquarters units in place of the real thing," and publicize this buildup. Allen Dulles, director of the CIA, agreed that it might be possible "to initiate some kind of deception tactics" to implement the president's suggestion. In the NSC on 6 May, Bradley said that the JCS were convinced that "a fake buildup" would not fool the communists. Ibid., 946, 976. Bradley also warned that sending reinforcements to Korea would "seriously affect any commitments in other vital areas and would require more funds and higher force levels." Ibid., 976.

169. An ad hoc committee of civilian consultants was established on 25 February 1953 to study and advise the NSC on basic national security policies and programs in relation to their costs.

170. Minutes of special NSC, 31 March 1953, *FRUS 1952–54, XV*, 826–27.

171. 143rd meeting of the NSC, 6 May 1953, ibid., 977.

172. Memo of State-JCS meeting, *FRUS 1952–54, XV*, 817–18.

173. Ibid., 839–45.

174. Johnson memo, 6 April, ibid., 880–82, 839–40.

175. Memo of NSC, 8 April 1953, ibid., 893.

176. Memo of 144th NSC, ibid., 1014–17.

177. Memo of 145th NSC, ibid., 1065–67. See also ibid., 1062.

178. The Chinese took some pains to impress the United States with their new air power. On 22 April, UN reconnaissance observed 800 to 1,000 planes, mostly MiG-15s, concentrated in Chinese airbases near Antung (on the Chinese side of the Yalu). This was double the number reported earlier in these fields. The US Far East Air Force concluded that the communists were putting their fighter strength on display. Aerial photography also disclosed what looked like a V-1 rocket launcher. The British speculated that the Chinese wanted the rocket launcher to be discovered, too, and that it might even have been a dummy. British Embassy, Washington, to FO, 30 April 1953, FO 371/105547/K1095/23, PRO; British Military Attache, Korea, to Director, Military Intelligence, 22 May 1953, FO 371/105547/1095/27, PRO.

179. Charles JV Murphy, "What Ike Faces in Korea," *Life* (1 December 1953), 51–64.

180. Philip S. Meilinger, *Hoyt S. Vandenberg: The Life of a General* (Bloomington: Indiana University Press, 1989), 185. On the development of the PLA Air Force, see Kenneth W. Allen et al., *China's Air Force Enters the 21st Century* (Santa Monica, CA: The Rand Corporation, 1995), 40–54.

181. Resolution of the USSR Council of Ministers, 19 March 1953, *CWIHP Bulletin* (Winter 1995/1996), 80.

182. Zhai Qiang, *The Dragon, the Lion, and the Eagle: Chinese-British-American Relations, 1949–1958* (Kent, OH: Kent State University Press, 1994), 129; Eisenhower, *The White House Years. Vol. 1: Mandate for Change*, 181.

183. Clark to JCS, *FRUS 1952–54, XV*, 818–19. An NSC study late in March had considered it unlikely that the communists would take the initiative to reach an agreement in the negotiations. Their "most probable course" appeared to be to hold their positions and drag along the negotiations. US military action against China proper, the study anticipated, would increase the risk of "general war." The Chinese might react to a naval blockade by attacking the blockading forces and launching "new acts of aggression." In case a blockade or bombing threatened the survival of the PRC, the Soviets might intervene. US atomic superiority would neutralize the communists' conventional superiority. However, use of atomic weapons in Korea posed serious disadvantages. "Future Courses of Action in Connection with the Situation in Korea," 28 March 1953, OSANSA, Policy Papers, Box 2, "NSC 118/2-Korea," DEPL.

184. Editorial note, *FRUS 1952–54, XV*, 824.

185. Memo of telephone conversation with Cutler, 7 April 1953, Dulles Papers, Telephone Calls Series, Box 1, "Telephone Memoranda (except to or from White House) 1953–April (1)," DEPL.

186. Memo of 139th NSC, 8 April, *FRUS 1952–54, XV*, 893–95.

187. Ibid., 893–95. A special intelligence estimate that day stated that if the United States employed atomic weapons, the communists would recognize it "as indicative of Western determination to carry the Korean War to a successful conclusion." The analysts were unable to estimate whether this recognition might make the communists offer the concessions necessary to conclude an armistice. Special Estimate SE-41, 8 April 1953, ibid., 892.

188. *New York Times*, 9, 10 April 1953.

189. Telephone Conversation Re: *New York Times* story, 9 April, Dulles Papers, Telephone Calls Series, Box 1, "Telephone Memoranda (except to or from White House) 1953–April (1)," DEPL.

190. *Newsweek*, 20 April 1953, 27.

191. Clark to JCS, 7 May 1953, *FRUS 1952–54, XV*, 980–81.

192. Collins to Clark, 7 May 1953, ibid., 982.

193. *State Department Bulletin*, 25 May 1953, 755–57.

194. Memcon of State-JCS meeting, 18 May 1953, *FRUS 1952–54, XV*, 1038.

195. Foot, *Substitute for Victory*, 171–72.

196. Murphy to DOS, 19 May 1953, *FRUS 1952–54, XV*, 1057.

197. Johnson Memcon, 695.0029/5-1653, RG 59, NA. It appeared to Johnson that Zhou was attempting "a little psychological warfare against Nehru." The Dutch Foreign Office felt that as long as the principle of non-forcible repatriation

was upheld, the procedural aspects were secondary; world opinion would not understand why the negotiations broke down on secondary issues. When Johnson argued that the communists might offer better terms if they got the impression that the UN was not "overanxious" for an armistice, Dutch officials countered that the communists might conclude that the UN did not in fact want an armistice and give up their efforts for a settlement. They had perceived a feeling among the Russians that the United States did not want a settlement in Korea. The Dutch Foreign Office had heard that Ambassador Murphy in Tokyo had left the impression that Washington would make one final effort to obtain an armistice, after which military operations would resume in full swing. Memcon of meeting with Dutch embassy officials, 6 May 1953, 695.0029/5–653, RG 59, NA.

198. Memcon 18 May 1953, *FRUS 1952–54, XV*, 1038–46.

199. Ibid., 1046–48. The threats would appear to have been superfluous. The American concessions more or less met the latest Chinese demands.

200. Smith to Dulles (in Riyadh), 18 May 1953, *FRUS 1952–54, XV*, 1050–52; Baghdad to DOS, 795.00/5–1853, RG 59, NA.

201. Memo of State-JCS meeting, 22 May 1953, *FRUS 1952–54, XV*, 1075–76; Smith to Dulles, 22 May 1953, ibid., 1079–80.

202. Ibid., 1068–69.

203. Ibid., 1071.

204. AWF, NSC, Box 4, 147th meeting of the NSC, 1 June 1953, DEPL. *Time* reported that Dulles was "startled to find that India's Prime Minister Jawaharlal Nehru was convinced that the US really did not want a truce." *Time*, 15 June 1953, 19.

205. Memo of telephone conversation, 4 June 1953, Dulles Papers, Telephone Calls Series, "Telephone Memoranda (except to or from White House) May–June 1953 (2)," DEPL.

206. James Reston claims in his memoirs that "Dulles allowed me to know not only that they were considering the use of atomic weapons in an expanded war, but also that specific actions had been taken to move nuclear weapons and the appropriate bombers to bases close to China's mainland." James Reston, *Deadline: A Memoir* (New York: Random House, 1991), 231.

207. Dulles to Eisenhower, 26 November 1952, Dulles Papers, Subject Series, Box 8, "Korea," DEPL.

208. Charles E. Bohlen, *Witness to History, 1929–1969* (New York: W. W. Norton & Co., 1973), 349–51. See also DOS to Moscow, 26 May, *FRUS 1952–54, XV*, 1103–4; Moscow to DOS, 28 May, ibid., 1109–11; Moscow to DOS, 3 June, ibid., 1133–34. The Indian ambassador in Moscow told Bohlen that Molotov had inquired whether India was willing to serve on the NNRC. Molotov had mentioned that the Soviet government attached great importance to India's membership of the commission. See Moscow to DOS, #1606, 795.00/5–1953, RG 59, NA.

209. Editorial note, *FRUS 1952–54, XV*, 1196–97. For documentation on US efforts to restrain Rhee, see ibid., 1199ff.

210. Zhang, *Mao's Military Romanticism*, 232–35; Zhang, *Deterrence and Strategic Culture*, 131–33. A former CPV intelligence official told Zhang in an interview in 1988 that the Chinese did not expect the Eisenhower administration to resort to atomic strikes in Korea or Manchuria. The CPV headquarters did not receive any

intelligence or warnings about the presence of such weapons in the Far East, or that they would be used. Ibid., 133 note 59. See also Xiao Jingguang, "Chinese Generals Recall the Korean War," *Chinese Historians* (Spring and Fall 1994).

211. Zhang, *Mao's Military Romanticism*, 234.

212. The 15 December 1952 issue of *Life* carried a report about a new American amphibious landing vehicle. The report described the ability of this vehicle to quickly disperse inshore with loads as heavy as 100 tons and called the vehicle a partial answer to the threat of atom bombs against landing beaches full of supplies and grounded craft.

213. Zhang, *Deterrence and Strategic Culture*, 134; Zhang, *Mao's Military Romanticism*, 235–36.

214. Ibid.

215. Ibid., 138–39.

216. A few days before Eisenhower's inauguration, a State Department official told Judd that some officials in the department who did not like the election result thought that they could continue as before by giving Dulles the "Jimmy Byrnes treatment." This involved sending Dulles abroad and confronting him with *fait accompli* when he returned. Judd claimed that he advised Dulles not to go abroad until he had set his house in order. What happened to Dulles in this case had all the hallmarks of the "Jimmy Byrnes treatment," although it is not clear who had initiated the overseas trip of Dulles at such a convenient time. Walter Judd Oral History, Part 4, 110–11. It is likely that Judd mentioned this to Eisenhower also. Judd's scrapbook notes of his meetings with Eisenhower contain the words "Byrnes treatment." Judd Papers, Box 79, "Notes—Eisenhower, Dwight D., 1952–1955," Hoover Institution on War and Peace, Stanford.

217. The myth seems to have survived the considerable scholarly work in recent years based on archival evidence. See James, *Refighting the Last War*, 206, 237.

CHAPTER 4

A "Rash and Quixotic Policy":
The Taiwan Strait Crisis of
1954–1955

On 3 September 1954, China launched an artillery attack on Quemoy, the largest of the offshore islands held by the ROC. The Chinese firing set off the first Taiwan Strait crisis. In his memoirs, Eisenhower described this Chinese action as

the commencement of a sequence of events which was to extend through nine months, threaten a split between the United States and nearly all its allies, and seemingly carry the country to the edge of war, thus constituting one of the most serious problems of the first eighteen months of my administration.[1]

and others in US admin

Dulles foresaw "at least an even chance" of war breaking out between the United States and China before the crisis ended.[2] He could not help thinking "how fortunate it would be if these islands sank to the bottom of the sea."[3] The Eisenhower administration felt that defense of the off-shore islands involved issues critical for American national security. The rest of the world, however, looked upon these islands, in the words of Robert Bowie, the State Department's director of policy planning, as "a futile hostage to fortune and the symbol of a rash and quixotic policy."[4]

Twice during this crisis, the more hawkish among his advisers pressed Eisenhower to use nuclear weapons to defend Quemoy and Matsu against an anticipated Chinese invasion. In September 1954, Eisenhower overruled them and decided to take the dispute to the United Nations. Six months later, as tensions again rose, he decided that if the United States had no choice but to intervene in the crisis, it would initially rely on conventional weapons and use nuclear weapons only as a last resort. American leaders, however, held out overt threats of nuclear strikes against China. Eisenhower claimed that his administration resorted to this tactic in order to deter China from launching an invasion during a 10-day period in the middle of March, when the offshore islands appeared most vulnerable.[5] This study, however, concludes that the goal of the American nuclear diplomacy in the spring of 1955 was to set the stage for employing nuclear weapons against China in a war over the offshore islands that Dulles anticipated might occur later that year. If the Chinese did not start a war, Dulles contemplated "egging them on" to start one.

The crisis that began in the fall of 1954 was an extension of the Chinese civil war. With the Nationalist forces driven out of mainland China in 1949, the PRC planned to occupy the offshore islands before Chiang Kai-shek could consolidate his hold on the islands with American support. The total defeat of an ill-prepared Chinese attack on Quemoy island on 24 October 1949 upset Mao's plans. Not wanting another fiasco, he ordered the postponement of the attack on Hainan. The attack finally took place on 16 April 1950 and by 1 May, the communists took control of the island.[6] In February 1950, Mao ordered certain PLA units, including paratroops, to train for an invasion of Taiwan.[7] On 10 May, the Nationalists evacuated the Chusan islands in the face of a threatened communist attack.

Preparations for the invasion of Taiwan did not proceed as fast as the Chinese desired.[8] China's CMC, therefore, postponed the operation by a year. Some preparations for the invasion, however, went ahead. The beginning of the Korean War on 25 June 1950 further upset the Chinese timetable. The CMC later decided to postpone the operations against the offshore islands also. On 11 August, the Chinese leadership finally postponed the invasion of Taiwan until 1952. After September, the CCP did not consider a definite plan for this campaign.[9]

The Korean War led to a fundamental change in the American policy toward Taiwan. The JCS, who wanted to use Taiwan as a base in case of a full-scale war with China, successfully opposed Acheson's plan to take the issue of Taiwan's future to the UN.[10] On the ground that the loss of Taiwan to the Chinese would be "seriously detrimental" to American security, they urged American military assistance to the Nationalists. Acheson and Truman agreed to provide $14 million in military aid to the ROC but refused to allow deeper American involvement in the defense of Taiwan.

With the war in Korea bogged down in a stalemate, the State Department came around by the spring of 1951 to the view that the United States "should attempt to develop Formosa as an instrument for accomplishing our objective of breaking China's alignment with the Soviet Union." The ROC could be developed as a competitor for power in the mainland. The State Department favored strengthening the forces on Formosa so that they would have the military capability of attacking the mainland with good prospects for establishing and holding a beachhead. . . .

[W]hen the necessary political and military capabilities have been developed and if circumstances are such that an offensive against the mainland would be in our interest, then the restrictions which have been imposed on such actions shall be removed.[11]

NSC 48/5, dated 17 May 1951, concluded that "The interests of the United States would be served by the emergence of a non-communist government controlling both China and Formosa." It recommended American military and economic aid to strengthen the Nationalist forces for defending Taiwan as well as for operations elsewhere.[12] Reflecting the new thinking in Washington, American aid for Taiwan increased substantially. In fiscal year 1952, it amounted to as much as $300 million, the largest American aid program until then on a per capita basis.[13]

In March 1952, the JCS recommended that the United States should take steps, including use of the Seventh Fleet, "to deny Formosa to any Chinese regime aligned with or dominated by the USSR" and "to insure the continued availability of Formosa as a base for possible United States operations." They insisted that these military views "should be overriding and should govern United States policy" in the future, including in the Korean War negotiations. They also proposed continued assistance to the Nationalists to defend Taiwan and to create Nationalist units capable of operations outside the island.[14] Small-scale Nationalist raids on the mainland, stopped by Truman in June 1950, soon resumed, with Washington's tacit approval.[15]

UNLEASHING CHIANG

Within days of his inauguration, Eisenhower declared in his state of the union address that the Seventh Fleet "would no longer be employed to shield Communist China."[16] This "unleashing of Chiang" provoked a Chinese outburst as well as apprehension among US allies. It also raised Nationalist expectations. Wellington Koo, the ROC ambassador in Washington, made it clear in a discussion with Assistant Secretary of State for Far Eastern Affairs John Allison that the Nationalists would increase their raids on China. Koo inquired whether the Seventh Fleet would, under its new directive, take action against Chinese operations in retaliation for Nationalist raids. Allison's "offhand" judgment was that the Seventh Fleet would, under such circumstances, intervene.[17] Koo argued that it was a "natural corollary" of the presidential order that US forces would shield the Nationalists from Chinese counterattacks. Allison "emphasized" that the purpose of the President's order was to release the [Nationalist] Chinese Government forces for any action which they might wish to take against the Communist mainland, while the Seventh Fleet would continue to help ensure the security of Formosa and the Pescadores against any attack by the Communists.[18]

Following Eisenhower's announcement, General William Chase, the chief of the Military Assistance and Advisory Group (MAAG) in Formosa, advised the Nationalists to plan "to increase the frequency of raids not only from the 'off-shore' islands, but also from Formosa and the Pescadores and that both little raids and big ones be planned and executed on a wide front in order to obtain prisoners and worry and confuse the Communist coastal defenses." Chase suggested immediate planning for a blockade of the mainland coast from Swatow to Dachen, and promised American assistance "to the maximum degree." His only condition was that the ROC forces not launch major raids on Chinese territory without consulting him in advance.[19]

The Nationalists could hardly be blamed if they interpreted Chase's letter as American encouragement for increased raids on the mainland. Whether Dulles himself appreciated the implications of this is not clear. At a State-Defense meeting to discuss new directives to Admiral Arthur Radford, Commander-in-Chief, Pacific (CINPAC), for the defense of Taiwan, General Hoyt Vandenberg, Chief of the Air Force Staff, warned that if the Nationalists attacked the mainland and the Chinese retaliated with attacks on Taiwan, it might draw the United States and the Soviet Union into the war. He cautioned that "we should fully understand the kind of flypaper that we are stuck on."[20] Following this, the JCS issued supplementary orders to CINPAC, instructing him to secure a commitment that Nationalist forces would not engage in offensive operations that were not in the United States's interest. Radford was to make it clear that the United States undertook no commitment to intervene in case the Chinese retaliated against Nationalist operations undertaken without American approval.[21]

Unlike Taiwan, which was part of the Japanese empire from 1895 to 1945, the offshore islands had always been under the sovereignty of mainland China. After the Nationalists fled the mainland in 1949, they managed to retain their hold on many of these islands. Control of the offshore islands chain, stretching from the Miao Island group near the Shantung Peninsula to Hainan in the south, enabled the Nationalists to blockade the ports of Canton, Swatow, and Shanghai through air and naval action. These raids convinced the Chinese of the necessity of capturing some of these islands. In the spring of 1950, they seized the major islands of Miap Tao, the Che Shan, the Saddle, and the Lima groups, and Hainan. By 1950, these Chinese successes, achieved despite massive losses, reduced the Nationalist holdings to the area from the Dachens in the north to the Lamock islands in the south. Because of their commitments in the Korean War and elsewhere, the Chinese did not undertake any major campaign against the offshore islands after 1950 and limited themselves to small raids on some islands. The fear of communist attacks, however, made the Nationalists abandon several islands, including Tung T'ou Shan, Nan-juih Tao, and the Chih-chu Tao and Lamock groups. This left only the Quemoy, Matsu, and Dachen groups under Nationalist control. China had seriously considered taking the offshore islands in 1952 but refrained from doing so when the Korean War drew to a close. If the Nationalists did not get outside assistance, China had the capability to take all of these islands, but at a very high cost.[22]

While neutralizing the Taiwan Strait in 1950, Truman did not make an American commitment to the defense of the offshore islands.[23] As the Korean War dragged on, the US policy perceptibly shifted. On 9 May 1952, the State Department advised the embassy in Taipei that, although the United States would intervene to defend only Taiwan and the Pescadores, it hoped that the ROC would defend the offshore islands. While avoiding commitments to the Nationalists beyond those covered by the presidential directive to the Seventh Fleet neutralizing the Taiwan Strait, the State Department advised US military officials in Taiwan to give the Nationalists "whatever encouragement and advice they can" for the defense of Quemoy, Matsu, and Dachen islands, and to allow the Nationalists limited use of American supplies for this task.[24]

The Eisenhower administration began with no clear policy with respect to the offshore islands. It faced no demand to extend the "unleashing" of Chiang to include a US commitment to the defense of the offshore islands.[25] Allison confirmed to a British diplomat in Washington that neither the original Truman order to the Seventh Fleet nor the revised order issued by Eisenhower covered the offshore islands.[26] "[F]rom a strictly military standpoint," the JCS, led by Bradley, did not consider the islands "particularly important for the defense of Formosa." [27]

NSC 146/2, dated 6 November 1953, proposed preventing hostile forces from gaining control of Formosa and the Pescadores, "even at the grave risk of general war." A revised policy approved by the NSC on 18 August 1954 recommended "measures designed to reduce the power of Communist China in Asia, even at the risk of, but without deliberately provoking, war." The policy envisaged reacting "with immediate, positive, armed force *against any belligerent move by Communist China*" (emphasis added).[28] On the offshore islands, however, the provision in NSC 146/2 only stated:

Without committing US forces, unless Formosa or the Pescadores are attacked, encourage and assist the Chinese national Government to defend the Nationalist-held off-shore islands against Communist attack and to raid Chinese Communist territory and commerce.[29]

The offshore islands under Nationalist control in 1954 consisted of the Quemoy, Matsu, and Dachen groups. While Taiwan is situated about 90 miles from mainland China, Quemoy is only two miles away from the China coast and blocks the entrance to the port of Amoy. The Matsus are 10 miles away from the mainland and cover the entrance to the port of Foochow. All of these islands are within artillery range from mainland China. The Dachens are about 200 miles to the north of Formosa. The offshore islands were important to the Nationalists as sources of intelligence, centers for supplying and maintaining contact with Nationalist guerrillas on the mainland, and bases for interdicting communist coastal shipping through the ports of Amoy, Foochow, and Hangchow. If the communists gained control of all of the offshore islands, their merchant and fishing fleets would have gained freedom of movement in the coastal areas.

When the crisis began, the Nationalists had around 42,000 regular troops and 6,000 guerrillas in the Quemoy islands. They had a total of 9,000 regulars and guerrillas in the Matsus. The Chinese had several armies totalling 160,000 to 200,000 men within 150 miles of Quemoy and enough troops for an invasion of Matsu in its vicinity. This Chinese buildup in the coastal region could well have been, at least in part, in response to the "unleashing" of Chiang. Chinese jet aircraft, however, were deployed too far away to provide effective air cover for operations over Quemoy or Matsu. Only light piston-engined aircraft were based in Chinese airfields close to these islands. Chinese naval strength in the area consisted of only six minor patrol boats and 15 to 20 motorized junks. In addition, the Chinese had 400 or 500 civilian junks normally used for fishing and coastal transport. Other than the junks, the Chinese did not have the means for reinforcing their invasion forces or for re-supplying an operation against these islands. An invasion of Quemoy would require the assembly and movement of 150,000 men and would entail heavy losses. Fortifications, the small size of the beaches, wide dispersal of the Chinese air force, and unfavorable weather conditions from October to March further complicated the problems an invading force would have faced.[30]

In the Dachens, the Nationalists had 15,000 troops, including one of their best divisions. China had at least three armies within striking distance of the Dachens, any one of which could take these islands. This included a Chinese division that had moved into a port directly opposite the Dachens. The Chinese had a large number of aircraft in the Shanghai area that could attack these islands. They had the capability to reinforce an operation in this area and provide air cover for it.[31] Situated over 200 miles from Formosa and only 60 miles from mainland China, these islands were beyond effective Nationalist air cover. Clearly, the Dachens were the most vulnerable of the offshore islands.

PRELUDE TO THE CRISIS

Nationalist raids and flights over the mainland for dropping supplies to guerrillas began soon after the unleashing of Chiang.[32] The British consulate in Taiwan speculated that the United States hoped for "some diversionary effects" from increased Nationalist raids against China and might even assist in the planning of some such operations. As the Nationalists lacked the means to implement their threats to invade the PRC, British officials foresaw "nothing spectacular" to come out of Eisenhower's "unleashing" of Chiang. They did, however, expect some intensification of Nationalist raids against the PRC.[33] Ambassador Karl L. Rankin in Taipei expressed misgivings over the guerrilla activity supported by MAAG:

It was one thing to carry out diversionary raids while fighting was in progress in Korea; it is something else to do so today when the Korean shooting has stopped and the Fujian-Zhejiang coast is much more strongly held. . . . [T]he activities now envisaged under MAAG auspices seem to me somewhat like Uncle Sam tickling the Communist tiger with a feather duster.[34]

The Chinese reacted to the Nationalist raids by capturing some of the smaller offshore islands. Eisenhower suggested giving the ROC some light US naval vessels for intercepting the small crafts and motorized junks that the Chinese used for their attacks. CIA chief Allen Dulles pointed out that the offshore islands still under Nationalist control were "doomed unless they could be defended by air and sea."[35] On 11 July, American MAAG officials advised Chiang to use his air force and one of his better infantry divisions for the defense of the Dachen islands. Chiang questioned the wisdom of trying to defend the islands and hesitated to deploy such a division there.[36]

Chiang had never abandoned his hope of returning to the mainland. In his New Year's message for 1954, he promised his people an early attack on the mainland. Chiang followed it up by calling for a "holy war" against communism in his Easter message. Soon after, South Korean President Syngman Rhee, in his address to the US Congress, called for US support for an attack on China by South Korea and the ROC.[37] In May, Chiang declared in the presence of US Defense Secretary Charles E. Wilson that with "a reasonable amount of moral and material support from the free world," the Nationalist forces could recover the mainland.[38]

Anti-Chinese speeches by US leaders and officials and the string of military alliances that Washington fashioned around China worried Chinese analysts. They saw the US Taiwan policy as a long-term plan to encircle China and subject it to continuous military pressure. Zhou Enlai told the First National People's Congress of the CCP on 23 September 1954 that the United States aimed to "ensure that Asians would fight Asians." Zhou charged that the United States planned to intervene in revolutionary movements in Southeast Asia, grab strategic markets, and "legalize" its military action under the guise of "defending" these areas.[39]

In early 1954, the Chinese government approved the plan of the East China Military Command to take the Dachens. In July, the CCP Politburo resolved that China must immediately proclaim its intention to liberate Taiwan in order to forestall a US-ROC alliance from taking concrete shape. When Zhou was on his way back from the Geneva Conference in July 1954, Mao informed him that China could not further delay its plan to liberate Taiwan. The Chinese propaganda campaign began with an editorial in the Chinese paper *Renmin Ribao* on 23 July, titled, "We must liberate Taiwan." Mao, following the ancient Chinese strategist Sun Tze, decided that "the best strategy of war is to destroy the adversary's strategy before it is put into effect." The PLA decided to take Yijiangshan island first in order to get within artillery range of Dachen and to undermine the morale of the Nationalists. Chinese leaders adopted the plan "from small to large, one island at a time, from north to south, and from weak to strong." The plan was to attack only the Dachens. No evidence of any Chinese plan for an attack on Quemoy or Matsu has yet surfaced.[40]

From 10 May 1954, US intelligence observed the Chinese massing air and naval forces, including landing crafts, along the Zhejiang coast opposite the Dachens. This rendered them capable of amphibious attacks with air support on the Dachens. On the night of 15 May, the Chinese occupied four small islands near the Dachens and fired on a few others.[41] US officials estimated that if the Chinese mounted an invasion of the Dachens with 25,000 troops, the Nationalists would not be able to hold them without US air support.[42] Allen Dulles saw a threat of the major offshore islands falling to China. By the end of May 1954, the CIA concluded that the Chinese were preparing for an attack on the Dachens.[43]

The threat to the Dachens appeared serious enough to merit consideration by a high-level meeting at the White House. Admiral Radford, who had taken over from Bradley as chairman of the JCS, and Dulles agreed that it would seriously damage American standing in Asia if the United States failed to stop the Chinese from capturing the offshore islands. Dulles, however, did not favor publicly committing American prestige to holding the islands, as many of them could not withstand a sustained Chinese attack. Eisenhower also agreed that an American involvement in the defense of the Dachens carried "too big a commitment of US prestige and forces." To deter China from aggravating the situation, he ordered the Seventh Fleet to go on reconnaissance trips to the Dachens and to make a show of force.[44] Following the shooting down by the Chinese of a British-owned Cathay-Pacific airliner, the United States ordered two aircraft carriers to the area. Eisenhower did not at first favor hot pursuit of Chinese aircraft by US Navy planes. He did not want "our planes flying into Chinese Communist air in order to seek a fight." After some persuasion by Dulles, however, he authorized hot pursuit.[45] Considerable publicity accompanied American naval maneuvers. A report in *Newsweek* described the new policy as one of "instant retaliation" for any Chinese provocation. US air and naval forces were shifted from the North Pacific to the South China Sea. In an encounter with the Chinese air force, US planes shot down two Chinese fighters. Admiral Stump, Radford's successor as CINPAC, explained that the new policy meant that "if the Chinese shot down one of our planes, we should be ready to shoot down one of theirs at the first convenient opportunity." Stump insisted that "they [US pilots] should be quick on the trigger."[46] The US naval presence convinced Mao to order Chinese forces to exercise caution and avoid clashes with US forces.[47]

Heightened tension in the region in August once again called for the attention of American policy makers. Fearing that the Chinese might assemble forces for an invasion of the offshore islands, the Nationalists began air and naval attacks against mainland targets in order to disrupt Chinese plans.[48] Eisenhower commented in an NSC meeting that "if the Chinese tried an invasion of Formosa by a fleet of junks, this might make a good target for an atomic bomb.[49] Questioned at a press conference on 17 August, he declared that "any invasion of Formosa would have to run over the Seventh Fleet." This was not an empty threat. US aircraft carriers had moved close to the Chinese coast on 1 July while the Chinese attacked one of the smaller Dachen islands. Four American destroyers sailed within sight of the mainland late in August. Stump landed in the Dachens and stayed there for one day.[50] In the NSC meeting on 18 August, Radford called for American intervention to defend all of the offshore islands. The United States, he argued, could not tolerate further communist territorial gains in the region. Moreover, the offshore islands contained radar installations that aided the Seventh Fleet's mission of defending Taiwan. Eisenhower favored the United States going as far as "world opinion" permitted it to defend the offshore islands. Dulles did not consider the offshore islands as critical to US security as Taiwan. However, he thought that the United States could ill afford the loss of prestige that might result from failure to oppose Chinese territorial gains in the area. Therefore, he supported a firm policy, including military action, without committing the United States in the long term to the defense of the offshore islands.[51]

THE CRISIS BEGINS

In late August 1954, the Chinese leadership ordered the local commander to bombard Quemoy. The Chinese apparently had no plan to invade Quemoy or Matsu. Chinese forces began the artillery bombardment of Quemoy on 3 September 1954. According to Ye Fei, then commander of the Fujian Military Command (FMC), his forces had only two artillery regiments when he began the shelling. The PLA Air Force had no air base in the vicinity and no naval forces to support the army. Ye later claimed in his memoirs that the choice of the date to start the shelling was his own decision; he chose 3 September, as he expected supply ships to reach Quemoy that day.[52] The Chinese poured in 6,000 rounds during a five-hour barrage. The casualties included two American servicemen belonging to MAAG, Formosa.[53] An American intelligence report indicated that the Chinese would invade Quemoy the next morning. The Pentagon alerted CINPAC and ordered him to position aircraft carriers in case the United States decided to intervene.[54] By the morning of 5 September, the United States assembled three carriers, one cruiser, and three destroyer divisions near Quemoy.[55] Washington also permitted Nationalist air and naval attacks on Chinese mainland installations.

Dulles cabled from Manila, where he was attending the inaugural meeting of the South East Asia Treaty Organization, that the fall of Quemoy would jeopardize the entire US position in the Far East. He thought that a successful defense of Quemoy would cancel out the loss of prestige from the French defeat at Dien Bien Phu. He was prepared to accept the risk that commitment of US forces and prestige might lead eventually to American military operations against the mainland. However, he did not "want to duplicate the French mistake of making a symbol of what cannot be held in the face of Communist willingness to accept immense casualties to gain political objectives." The key question for him was whether the island was defensible.[56] Eisenhower doubted whether Quemoy could be held in view of its proximity to the mainland. He considered it "a great mistake" to undertake to defend it.[57]

In Washington, the Intelligence Advisory Committee did not reach a clear conclusion about whether China planned to push ahead with a full-scale invasion. So far, the Chinese had restrained themselves. They had avoided clashes with US forces and did not appear to be preparing their forces for an invasion of Quemoy. Nationalist raids against the mainland caused a loss of face for China and appeared to the CIA to increase the chances of Chinese retaliatory action against the offshore islands.[58] On 10 September, a Special National Intelligence Estimate concluded that the Chinese "objective is to take over" the offshore islands "at some time." China had the capability to overcome the Nationalist forces but was deterred by the risk of war with the United States. Although "the Chinese desire to avoid a war with the US," they might attempt to probe American intentions.[59]

The JCS was split on the question of defending the offshore islands. The majority felt that these islands, although not essential to the defense of Taiwan, *were* important. Further loss of territory to China, in their view, would have adverse psychological consequences for the United States. They recommended US action to defend the islands, including strikes against the Chinese air bases and artillery installations opposite Quemoy; they opposed any restrictions on military operations and on allowing sanctuaries for Chinese forces as had happened in Korea; they wanted the theater commander to have the authority to attack the Chinese troop concentrations without waiting for the invasion to start; and they wanted it understood that if required, the president should approve the use of atomic weapons.[60] Radford feared a revolt in Taiwan and loss of American control over the ROC if the offshore islands fell to China. Taiwan might even turn communist.[61] On the other hand, the loss of face for China resulting from the defeat of their attack on Quemoy with heavy losses through US action would have "far reaching consequences."[62] General Matthew Ridgway, chief of army staff, argued that the military value of the offshore islands did not justify US military intervention in their defense or the war with China that might follow such an intervention.[63] He did not wish to comment on non-military factors such as the political consequences of the loss of the offshore islands.[64] He felt that the Nationalists did not need Quemoy for an invasion of the mainland. Neither did the Chinese need it to invade Taiwan.[65]

At this stage, the faction favoring US intervention, even at the cost of war with China, consisted only of Radford, the chiefs of the naval and air staffs, and Vice President Richard Nixon. Eisenhower had already expressed doubts about the defensibility of the offshore islands. Under Secretary of State Walter Bedell Smith opposed US action, except to rescue Nationalist troops in the offshore islands.[66] Treasury Secretary George Humphrey suggested that if the United States could get a good excuse to get out of the offshore islands, it should take it "and get out."[67] Defense Secretary Wilson recommended that the administration inform Chiang that the United States would not support him in the defense of the offshore islands and, instead, help him remove his forces from the islands. In return, the United States should sign a treaty for the defense of Formosa and the Pescadores.[68] CIA Director Allen Dulles doubted that the loss of the offshore islands would have a long-term effect on morale in the ROC.[69] Robert Cutler, special assistant for national security, also did not favor going to war with China over the offshore islands.

Dulles had expressed ambivalent views in earlier discussions of the issue.[70] In a remarkable talking paper examining different options that he prepared for the next meeting of the NSC, Dulles affirmed that holding Quemoy indefinitely was bound to lead to a general war with China. *"If we want such a war, Quemoy can be made to provide the issue,"* Dulles reasoned (emphasis added). Going to war with China would require congressional approval, but he expected that

Probably . . . Congress and the nation would respond to an all out appeal to the Congress, on the broad issue that we cannot afford to be acquiescent to any more Communist gains in this area.

A war over the offshore islands would also "alienate world opinion and gravely strain" both the European alliance and the Australia–New Zealand–United States alliance (ANZUS). The strain would be greater if the United States resorted to atomic weapons. If the administration wanted to avoid a major war with China, the problem was "to do so on terms that will avoid a serious loss of ChiNat [Chinese Nationalist] morale and US prestige." The Chinese might use the bad weather season to build up their air and land forces, so that "the issue will be formidably and inescapably posed in a few months." A third alternative was a reference to the UN. If the Soviet Union and China opposed UN action, Dulles anticipated, the United States would reap propaganda advantages.[71]

When the National Security Council met on 12 September at Denver, Radford presented the opinion of the majority of the JCS in favor of US intervention. The JCS, he stated, believed that "we should not go into such a war with any arbitrary limitations on our forces." Eisenhower replied that "he could not agree more." He, however, opposed making too many defense commitments around the world and then having to fulfill them. "[B]y making faces and raising hell," the Chinese could tie the United States down. If there had to be a general war, he would "want to go to the head of the snake" and fight Russia, not China. Radford said that Quemoy could not be defended without hitting the mainland. As soon as an air attack from China seemed likely, he recommended, the United States should attack the Chinese airfields. Eisenhower replied that this would require congressional authorization. The NSC members, he emphasized, "must get one thing clear in their heads, and that is that they are talking about war." A war with China would be an all-out one. It would not be limited to Quemoy. The offshore islands, he maintained, "were only important psychologically." It would be difficult to explain to the American people why these islands were so important to US security as to justify a major war.[72]

Probably taking his cue from the president's remarks, Dulles refrained from voicing the more drastic ideas that he had put down in his talking *[handwritten annotations: Dulles gave the NSC 3 options: 1) let commies take over 2) fight commies 3) get UN to bail to Fobo tall Chinese force]*

paper. He began by expressing "the hope that the Council would never have to take a more difficult decision." He admitted that an "overwhelming case" could be made for or against US intervention. Not stopping the Chinese now would be disastrous for the Far East. On the other hand, the rest of the world other than the ROC and the ROK would condemn the United States for war with China over the offshore islands. Possibly very few Americans would support such a war. This "presented a horrible dilemma." As a way out, Dulles produced his third alternative: taking the case to the UN, to forestall Chinese use of force to overturn the status quo. The NSC authorized Dulles to explore the UN option.[73]

Rankin warned that Chiang would violently oppose taking the dispute to the UN. To Chiang, it would look like "another Yalta by which free China . . . is to be sold down [the] river as a result of secret deals made behind Chinese backs."[74] To make the proposal palatable to the ROC, the United States agreed to the long-standing Nationalist demand for a defense treaty. Dulles had earlier refused to proceed with such a treaty until tensions in the area had cooled down. The State Department now conceded the Nationalist demand for signing the treaty before taking the dispute to the UN. The treaty would be purely defensive, so as not to allow the Nationalists to use these islands as privileged sanctuaries from which to attack China, and would cover only Formosa and the Pescadores. The United States looked to the UN to take provisional measures to stop fighting in the Taiwan Strait. The ultimate fate of the offshore islands would be decided peacefully at a later date.[75] The Nationalists applied intense pressure to have the offshore islands also included in the scope of the US commitment. As a compromise, the treaty referred to "such other territories as may be determined by mutual agreement" in addition to Formosa and the Pescadores. Dulles and Nationalist Foreign Minister George Yeh finally initialed the treaty on 23 November.[76]

With grossly misplaced optimism, Dulles informed Eisenhower that the treaty "staked out" American interests in Taiwan and at the same time denied the Nationalists the opportunity to drag the United States into a war with China.[77] In reality, the administration lost the best opportunity it would ever have to make a clean break with the offshore islands. Enough support existed within the administration as well as outside for limiting the US commitment only to Formosa and the Pescadores. Eisenhower had enough prestige to overcome any opposition from the supporters of the Nationalists in the United States. The treaty offered a leverage that the administration could have used to secure Nationalist concurrence.[78] By fudging the American role in the defense of the offshore islands, the treaty left the Nationalists with enough of an opening to manipulate American policy in the future.

Apart from Dulles's own fears of a loss of US prestige in the region in case China made further territorial gains, the stand of the services probably counted heavily in the decision not to formally exclude the offshore islands from the scope of the treaty. The US military opposed any further softening of US policy in the Far East, which, they alleged, had already contributed to the loss of North Korea, North Vietnam, and Tibet to communism. A JCS memorandum charged, "This is not a policy of containment. It is not even a policy of status quo. It is a policy of demonstrable communist victories at the expense of US prestige and strategic position." The memorandum attributed the communist success to "the willingness of the Chinese to take risks to achieve desired objectives," secure in their "belief that the United States would in the last instant back down." The memo warned that if the United States continued to avoid risks in order to avoid war, it would destroy American interests in the region.[79] Radford took strong objection to the State Department's handling of the Taiwan issue. He opposed UN action, unless it had the concurrence of the ROC. The State Department's policy, he argued, would lay "the groundwork for the ultimate loss to Communism of our present allies in Formosa and of course the loss of that island as a link in our present security chain." Limiting the United States's role to material support alone for the defense of the offshore islands amounted "to setting the stage for the loss of the islands."[80]

RENEWED CRISIS

On 22 November, the Chinese sentenced 13 Americans (11 airmen and 2 civilians captured by China during the Korean War) to prison terms on charges of espionage. On 27 November, Senator William Knowland called for a blockade of China in retaliation. In a State Department meeting convened to discuss the "pros and cons of aggravating actions" against the Chinese, "including overflights, mining of harbors, and bombing of railroads," Dulles suggested disrupting Chinese coastal trade. Other officials present opposed such measures on the ground that they violated international law and had not been thought of even during the Korean War.[81] Eisenhower did not think that Americans were ready to go to war over this issue.[82] The United States, therefore, decided to rely on action by the United Nations to secure the release of the prisoners.

After shelling Quemoy, the Chinese did not make any further moves. They even postponed the attack on Yijiangshan.[83] CIA Director Allen Dulles speculated that the Chinese buildup opposite Quemoy might be a diversion for an invasion of the Dachens.[84] On 6 October, he told the NSC that a Chinese attack on Quemoy was "a distinct possibility." American intelligence had observed considerable Chinese military activity off the Matsus also. The Chinese buildup near the Dachens was even greater than near Quemoy. Although an attack did not appear imminent, the Chinese could attack one of these island groups within a matter of days.[85] Secretary of State Dulles painted an aggressive picture of the Chinese in his testimony before Congress in connection with the Formosa resolution. However, he admitted, "There are at present, as far as our intelligence is aware, no formation on the land of landing forces, or any accumulation of ships which would be required for landing operations." The situation in the Quemoy area, in his view, was one of "relative quiet."[86]

The situation quickly changed in January 1955. Mao was not eager to go ahead with the attack on Yijiangshan and desired to postpone the operation. However, he yielded to the entreaties of the military commanders and authorized the attack. Historians Gordon Chang and He Di have argued that it was the ambiguous American policy on defending the offshore islands that emboldened Mao to go ahead with the Yijiangshan operation. A clear enunciation of the American commitment to defend the offshore islands, they argue, would have deterred the Chinese attack. As such, they consider this a case of deterrence failure. This argument, however, contradicts their claim that Mao wanted to postpone the operation and was only persuaded by the military, who stressed military reasons for going ahead with the attack. Further, considering how much opposition the Eisenhower administration faced for its commitment to the defense of Quemoy, it is hardly possible that the administration would have mustered the required support for the defense of the much smaller and harder to defend Dachens.[87]

Chinese aircraft attacked Ha Hsia Dachen on 10 January.[88] On 18 January, 3,000 to 4,000 Chinese troops attacked and captured Yijiangshan, overcoming a force of 1,000 Nationalist guerrillas after two hours of fighting. This brought the Dachen island within Chinese artillery range. A Chinese assault on the island appeared imminent.

THE FORMOSA RESOLUTION

The US response to the new situation took shape on 19 January. Dulles set the process in motion by suggesting to Nationalist Foreign Minister George Yeh that it might be wise to evacuate the Dachens. Holding the Dachens, Dulles tried to persuade Yeh, was not feasible militarily.[89] Dulles then approached Radford and Eisenhower with the suggestion that the United States should encourage the Nationalists to evacuate the island group and assist them in doing so. Further, Washington should indicate its willingness to defend Quemoy and "stimulate UN activity" to bring about peace in the area. Radford offered his support to this compromise, although he preferred holding all of the offshore islands. Eisenhower indicated his "general agreement." They agreed that

Contemporaneously [with the withdrawal from the Dachens], the United States would state that in view of the aggressive actions of the Chinese and their proclaimed intention to seize Formosa, the United States will assist the ChiNats to hold Quemoy Island which, under existing circumstances, is deemed important for the defense of Formosa and the Pescadores.

Dulles would ascertain whether Congress would extend authority to the president broad enough to permit attacks on the mainland in defense of Quemoy.[90]

When he met Yeh later in the day, Dulles offered US help in the evacuation of the Dachens and expressed his willingness to announce that under present conditions and pending appropriate action by the UN, the United States would help defend Quemoy. His "strong advice" to the ROC was to pull out of Matsu. The United States could not extend its guarantee to Matsu, as Washington did not consider the island defensible.[91] In the evening, Dulles confirmed at a meeting at the State Department that the Nationalists "would withdraw from *all* of the offshore islands, except Big and Little Quemoy" (emphasis in original).[92] When the NSC discussed this plan, Humphrey and Wilson supported giving up all of the offshore islands. Wilson thought that "it was foolish to fight a terrible war with Communist China simply in order to hold all these little islands." Dulles did not disagree "over the long period." However, in his view, the time was not appropriate to tell the Nationalists that they should not expect American help to defend the offshore islands. If the Chinese later renounced their intention to take Taiwan, the United States could give them up.[93]

At this stage, the American commitment covered only Quemoy island. When Dulles met with congressional leaders on 20 January, he did not mention Matsu in the list of islands the United States would defend. In the NSC later in the day, however, he suggested that to offset the loss of the Dachens, the United States should defend "Quemoy and possibly the Matsu group." The next day, Dulles told Yeh that the United States would defend Matsu as well as Quemoy. The United States would, however, make no public statement about this commitment. Radford had told congressional leaders that the majority of the JCS favored holding Matsu and the Dog group in addition to Quemoy. Most likely, Matsu came to be included among the islands that the United States agreed to defend at the instance of the JCS.[94]

Having decided to abandon the Dachens, Eisenhower felt that the time had come to draw the line. To impress upon the Chinese as well as foreign governments how far Washington would go and to bolster Nationalist morale, Eisenhower asked Congress on 24 January for authority to use US forces in the confrontation with China over the offshore islands. Congress quickly passed the "Formosa Resolution" with an overwhelming majority. This resolution committed the United States to defend Formosa, the Pescadores, and other "closely related localities" when the president recognized an attack on them as preliminary to an assault on Formosa itself.[95]

The State Department instructed Rankin on 31 January to inform Chiang that "under the present circumstances" the United States would assist in the defense of Quemoy and Matsu if the president judged that an attack on them appeared to be "in aid of and in preparation for an armed attack on Formosa and the Pescadore islands and dangerous to their defense." Rankin was to give Chiang the crucial undertaking that in Washington's view, *"An attack by the Chinese at this time on Quemoy and Matsu which seriously threatened their loss would be deemed by the President to be of this character"* (emphasis added).[96]

The Chinese had charged that the mutual defense treaty was not a treaty of defense but "a treaty of naked aggression."[97] They reacted equally harshly to the Formosa Resolution. In Beijing, a tense meeting on 28 January with the British Charge, Humphrey Trevelyan, Zhou charged that Eisenhower's message to Congress was a "war message." For the UN to discuss the Chinese action to recover the offshore islands amounted, in his view, to interference in China's internal affairs. The Chinese, he asserted, "would not separate the question of the off-shore islands from that of Formosa." They would not enter into any "deal" over the offshore islands; they would "liberate" them. Zhou declared that "The Chinese Government were not afraid of war threats and would resist if war was thrust on them."[98]

The Nationalist evacuation of the Dachens began on 4 February. To help in the evacuation, the United States deployed five aircraft carriers and 12 destroyers.[99] Eisenhower authorized attacks on Chinese airfields in self-defense while assisting in the evacuation, if "this was essential to the success of the operation."[100] Mao, in the meantime, developed second thoughts on the attack on Dachen island. He rejected the local commander's request for permission to attack the withdrawing Nationalists. He decided that the best course was to wait and see. He did not want a clash with the American forces.[101] Shortly after, the Nationalists evacuated Nanchi island after the United States refused to assist in its defense. The Chinese occupied the Dachen and Nanchi islands after the Nationalists withdrew from them.

FAILURE OF UN MEDIATION

The scene of action meanwhile shifted to the UN. The reference to the UN had been delayed not only by Nationalist objections but also by Anglo-American differences. British and American thinking on the reference to the UN differed fundamentally. The British had believed that the UN intervention was only an intermediate step in the eventual hand-ing over of the islands to China, while the State Department looked on the reference to the UN as a means of ensuring continued Nationalist hold on the offshore islands.[102] The British also worried that the United States would allow the Nationalists to use the offshore islands as a sanc-tuary from which to attack the mainland. They strongly objected to any American guarantee of the offshore islands. On 21 January, Dulles in-formed British Ambassador Sir Roger Makins that the United States would make only a private, not a public, commitment to the Nationalists to defend Quemoy and Matsu. Makins, however, misunderstood Dulles and reported to London that the US government had abandoned the idea of a provisional American guarantee of the offshore islands and "will make no additional public or private commitment." The ambassador be-lieved that the British precondition for the reference to the UN had thus been met.[103] Though this misunderstanding was later clarified, it left the British distrustful of Dulles.[104]

Britain and the United States had persuaded New Zealand to act as a front for the reference to the UN. On 28 January, New Zealand intro-duced a resolution in the Security Council calling for a cease-fire in the Taiwan Strait. The Security Council invited China to participate in a discussion on the resolution. China, however, refused to participate in any meeting that would include the ROC on an equal basis. Instead, China proposed direct negotiations with the United States. A few days later, Zhou again wrote to the UN secretary-general expressing interest in negotiations without ROC participation.[105] A *Renmin Ribao* editorial on 7 March stressed that China favored negotiations and announced that

For the sake of relaxing tension and preserving peace, the Chinese people sup-port holding an international conference by China, the United States, Britain, the Soviet Union, India, Burma, Indonesia, Pakistan and Ceylon to discuss the easing of the Taiwan Straits situation.[106]

Zhou told the Swedish representative in Beijing that China would not accept the New Zealand resolution, as it placed the ROC and the PRC on an equal footing. Zhou explained that, in principle, China did not refuse to negotiate but wanted further study of concrete proposals.[107] Nehru told the Commonwealth prime ministers meeting in London that China was ready to participate in a conference from which the ROC would be excluded. China was also agreeable to enter into talks with the UN secretary-general or with the United States direct, Nehru added.[108] Washington, however, ruled out talks on Taiwan without the partici-pation of the ROC.

Despite its refusal to appear before the UN, China made no further threatening move, except continuing work on construction of airfields in the coastal region. To the State Department's Office of Intelligence Research, the Chinese policy "does not appear to presage an imminent invasion of Taiwan or to indicate a deliberate Communist effort to provoke hostilities with the US." China's most important motive seemed to be to prevent the solidification of the US-ROC relationship and to "dramatize" its claim to Taiwan and the offshore islands.[109]

The picture changed dramatically with Dulles's Far East visit later in February. While in the region, Dulles became convinced, for reasons that are not quite clear, of the seriousness of the Chinese threat and the calamitous consequences for Nationalist morale of US failure to defend the offshore islands. He cabled Eisenhower from Manila on 21 February that if the Chinese construction of airfields, artillery emplacements, and roads went on without disruption, it might need a large-scale US intervention, including even the use of atomic weapons, to defend Quemoy and Matsu. He urged permitting the Nationalists to attack the Chinese buildup.[110] Unlike two weeks earlier, Dulles now believed that China intended to attack Taiwan. He found the briefing at Honolulu by Admiral Stump "disturbing." He recalled (probably influenced by the memories of the Korean War) that the Chinese were skilled at camouflaging.[111]

Before his departure for the Far East, Dulles had told the British ambassador in Washington that if the Chinese or British governments or anyone else could provide a "dependable assurance" that a Chinese attack on the offshore islands would not lead to an attack on Taiwan itself, "then the situation would be changed automatically." Otherwise, the United States had no alternative but to take seriously the frequently expressed Chinese threats to take the islands.[112] When Dulles met British Foreign Secretary Anthony Eden at Bangkok during this trip, Eden brought up his plan for a diplomatic solution: he would promise Zhou that if China undertook not to attack Taiwan, he would sound out Washington on a peaceful solution of the dispute. Dulles considered this "vague proposal" "worth exploring." He showed Eden a memo in which he claimed that the United States had gone far enough in making concessions to China. "If the Chinese communists, while retaining their claim to Formosa, would give assurances that they would not seek a verdict by force, then [the] situation might be different." He let Eden take a copy of the memo, thinking that Eden might try to get China to agree not to use force to settle its claim to Taiwan. Dulles hoped that "if he makes the effort and fails, he will then be better able [to] justify our position before British parliament and public. If he succeeds, so much the better."[113]

Eden conveyed to Zhou his proposal that if China agreed not to use force, while maintaining its claim to Taiwan, a peaceful solution could be found. He offered to meet Zhou at Hong Kong to discuss this. Zhou, however, demanded that the United States stop its "aggression" against China, stop interfering in China's internal affairs, and withdraw all of its armed forces from the area. He was prepared to receive Eden in Beijing to discuss these terms. After Zhou's reply, Eden, who was by then already in Southeast Asia, dropped his idea of going to Hong Kong.[114] The gap between what Zhou expected Eden to deliver and what Dulles was prepared to deliver was beyond Eden's ability to bridge. Dulles gave Eden no firm indication of what a Chinese renunciation of force, should he succeed in getting one, would lead to. Dulles was obviously not playing straight with Eden. The American commitment to the Nationalists to defend Quemoy and Matsu was still in force when he hinted to Eden of a much less firm US stand on the islands. Even if Dulles did not mislead Britain in January, he failed to disclose his full hand to Eden in February.

NUCLEAR THREATS

Upon his return to Washington, Dulles recommended to the president that "as things now stood," the United States should help defend Quemoy and Matsu. He claimed that "this would require the use of atomic missiles" [sic]. Eisenhower "thoroughly agreed with this," as the United States did not have sufficient air strength in the area to destroy Chinese airfields and gun emplacements with conventional bombs. He advised Dulles to add to his forthcoming radio and television broadcast a paragraph to the effect that "we should use atomic weapons as interchangeable with the conventional weapons."[115] Accordingly, in a reference to the crisis in his broadcast on March 8, Dulles spoke of "new and powerful weapons of precision which can utterly destroy military targets.[116] The next day, Dulles told Senator Walter George, chairman of the Senate Foreign Relations Committee, that the United States could not "stand by and do nothing" while the Chinese invaded Quemoy and Matsu. The United States might have to use atomic weapons to overcome "Chinese manpower and capacity to replace and rebuild." Dulles assured the senator that "the missiles we had in mind had practically no radioactive fall-out and were entirely local in effect."[117]

Surprisingly, no one questioned on what basis Dulles had concluded that a serious Chinese threat to the offshore islands, not to speak of Taiwan, existed. Chang and He Di have argued that the fall of the Dachens and China's renewed propaganda barrage led Washington to expect another Chinese attack and thus hardened its stand against China. Accordingly, they hold Mao responsible for Dulles's perception of the Chinese threat to Taiwan "and frustrating the diplomatic efforts of the United States."[118]

From the information available to the administration, it is hard to see how a firm conclusion of a Chinese invasion could be drawn. A military estimate on 9 March showed that the Chinese had sufficient troops for an invasion of the Matsus and the smaller islands in the Quemoy group, but not for invading Quemoy island. It might take two days to build up the troop strength for an attack on Quemoy and this could be accomplished without being observed by US intelligence. The Chinese had sufficient shipping in the vicinity for an invasion of any of the islands. Therefore, an attack could be launched against either group "with little or no warning."[119]

But this report took into account only the availability of troops and shipping (mostly junks, which could not transport tanks and other heavy equipment needed for an invasion). The administration already knew that Chinese airfields in the north would not provide adequate air cover to the invading forces. Existing Chinese airfields in the coastal areas "were little more than runways without facilities or discernible ammunition and fuel storage areas." They had no railways or good roads servicing them. Fuel had to be brought in by sea.[120] In order to launch an invasion that would overcome the maximum Nationalist opposition, China would have to build airfields and augment its invasion force. China did not yet have the capability to provide naval and logistic support for an amphibious operation against the heavily defended islands.

Aerial reconnaissance showed little evidence of a serious Chinese air buildup.[121] General Nathan Twining, chief of air staff, judged that the Chinese were not going to attack Taiwan because the Chinese airfields were still inadequate for the purpose.[122] The air force's director of intelligence informed the State Department that even when complete, the Chinese airfields under construction would have only a minor role in an invasion of Formosa. They would not contribute significantly even to an attack on the offshore islands.[123] The Chinese would take several months to complete the airfields under construction. Even when complete, these airfields could not hold more than 50 fighters each. By that time, the Nationalist air force would also be considerably stronger.[124] Vice Admiral Alfred Pride, commander of the Seventh Fleet, felt that the Chinese coastal airfields were so primitive that the likely losses to attacking planes outweighed any possible gain from bombing them.[125] Ridgway felt that

[W]hat the Chinese were doing there did not justify a conclusion that they were planning an attack on Formosa. Their activities could just as well be defensive as offensive in nature. They were building airfields, and rail lines, which could rush troops to the seafront in the event of an invasion *from* Formosa. But there was no indication they were concentrating ground troops there, or organizing an invasion force of their own.[126]

Information from diplomatic sources supplemented the military intelligence. Molotov told the British ambassador in Moscow that American actions would be the sole cause of any breach of peace in the area while the UN attempted to resolve the dispute.[127] On 3 March, Under Secretary of State Herbert Hoover, Jr. told the Canadian ambassador that Chinese propaganda relating to Formosa and the offshore islands had "declined within the last few weeks to the lowest point since last summer." The Chinese appeared to be "adopting a tacit cease-fire."[128] Dulles himself told the New Zealand ambassador on 9 March that despite continued work on Chinese artillery and airfield installations, there was no evidence of preparations for an attack in the next two or three weeks.[129] He told the ambassador on 15 March that the Chinese propaganda about Formosa had slackened considerably.[130] He also told Australian Prime Minister Robert Menzies on 14 March that "there was no great indication of preparations for an immediate invasion."[131] If the Chinese were signaling a cooling off, the United States certainly had picked up the signals.

and the cooling of tensions

Despite these indications of absence of an immediate Chinese threat, the president called his advisers on 11 March to discuss the best way to defend Taiwan.[132] Dulles repeated his opposition to using atomic weapons during the next two months. He urged that the United States should, if possible, "avoid intervention of any kind" in the Taiwan Strait during this period. He warned that "there would be great trouble in Europe if this happened."[133] He suggested that the United States should build up the strength of the Nationalists. If the Nationalists could not hold out on their own, US forces should intervene with conventional weapons to help them. Only as a last resort should the United States go in with full force. Radford suggested that Washington ought "to set the stage so as to defer an effective Chinese attack during the next two months." Eisenhower agreed that if the United States used atomic weapons during this period, it would have an adverse impact on Europe. He summed up that Washington should do whatever it could to help the Nationalists defend themselves. If US intervention was inevitable, it should first use only conventional weapons. He recognized that if the United States restricted itself to conventional weapons, its intervention might not be decisive. It might be forced to intervene with atomic weapons, but should do so only at the end. Before that, Washington would have to consult its allies.[134] The meeting ended with a decision to send a staff officer to the Pacific Command to assess the chances of a Chinese attack on the offshore islands. Eisenhower evidently did not trust the officer from the Pentagon to give him the true picture. He sent his staff secretary, Colonel Andrew Goodpaster, to accompany the staff officer "to observe and develop impressions" on how imminent a Chinese attack was and how long the Nationalist forces could hold out, with or without US logistical assistance.[135]

Upon his return, Goodpaster reported on his discussions with Admiral

Stump. The admiral felt that although China could launch an invasion of Quemoy or Matsu any time, he considered an all-out attack unlikely before four weeks at a minimum, and probably not before 1 June, against Matsu; he thought an attack on Quemoy unlikely for at least eight weeks, and probably not before 1 September.[136] After 25 March it would take "a coordinated amphibious, artillery, air supported" Chinese attack against Quemoy and Matsu to overcome the Nationalist forces alone. During the next 10 days, while the defenses in Matsu were being strengthened, a sudden Chinese amphibious attack might succeed. Unless the Chinese redeployed their air force in the coastal area, the Nationalists alone could probably repel an attack. If the United States supported the Nationalists with conventional forces, "the defense would appear to be assured." However, if the Chinese used significant air power, "the US would have to be prepared to employ atomic weapons."[137] Stump felt that American intelligence on the buildup of the Chinese forces was poor. Analysts had no way of knowing whether the fishing junks in the harbors were concentrated for an invasion or were merely pursuing their regular business.[138] After talking to Goodpaster, Eisenhower's press secretary, James Hagerty, concluded that

[O]ur military do not believe that those islands can be knocked out by any Communist attack. . . . Our military do not believe that any effective threat to the islands off Formosa can materialize until and unless the Chinese build airports closer to the coastline in the area between Quemoy and Matsu.[139]

Surprisingly, this information did not cool off the talk of war in Washington. At a press conference on 15 March, Dulles introduced what the *New York Times* called a doctrine of "less-than-massive retaliation." He said that the availability of tactical nuclear weapons made it unnecessary to attack the enemy's cities with high-yield nuclear weapons.[140] Before the speech, Dulles had cleared it with Eisenhower as well as Lewis Strauss, chairman of the Atomic Energy Commission, who "was all for it" and "wanted to show our enemies that we now deal with A-bombs as conventional weapons." Strauss probably told Dulles about the recent successful tests of low-yield atomic weapons.[141] On 16 March, Eisenhower, asked whether the United States would use tactical nuclear weapons, replied: "[W]here these things are used on strictly military purposes, I see no reason why they shouldn't be used just as exactly as you would use a bullet or anything else."[142] He hoped that this statement "would have some effect in persuading the Chinese of the strength of our determination."[143] The next day, Vice President Richard Nixon said that "tactical atomic explosives are now conventional and will be used against the targets of any aggressive force."[144]

Eisenhower believed that "hostilities are not so imminent as is indicated by the foreboding of a number of my associates." If so, he had hardly any reason for confiding to his diary on 26 March that "the Red Chinese appear to be completely reckless, arrogant, possibly overconfident, and completely indifferent as to human losses." He went on in a philosophical vein that "I have so often been through these periods of strain that I have become accustomed to the fact that most of the calamities that we anticipate never really occur."[145]

The administration, however, continued to act as though the calamity might occur at any time. The service chiefs other than Ridgway suggested informing China, through diplomatic channels, of the American resolve to defend the offshore islands "with all means available" and making public an order to the JCS to defend Taiwan. This, they hoped, would have the desired effect on China. They assumed that US forces would have authorization to use atomic weapons against military targets in case of hostilities with China.[146] On 26 March, the press carried a sensational story attributed to Admiral Robert Carney, Chief of Naval Operations, that war would break out by 15 April and that the military had advised the president to retaliate with nuclear strikes against China.[147] The reports in the American press had unexpected consequences in Taiwan. The press there interpreted American assertions that the offshore islands could be defended only by the use of atomic weapons against China as an indication that the United States would *not* intervene to defend the islands. Some speculated that the United States had information on Chinese war plans and that *Time* magazine was advancing its cover feature on Chiang by a week to coincide with the impending war.[148] A furious Eisenhower told Hagerty to inform reporters:

They're going to look awfully silly when April 15 comes along and there is no incident, because honestly our information is that there is no build-up off those islands as yet to sustain any attack, and believe me, they are not going to take those islands just by wishing for them. They are well-equipped and well-defended and they can only be taken, if at all, by a prolonged all-out attack.[149]

Eisenhower himself made it clear at a press conference on 30 March that the administration had no intelligence pointing to an imminent Chinese attack on the offshore islands.[150]

Even after Eisenhower moved to calm the nation's fears, the administration continued to be driven by war scare. In a meeting with his advisers on 28 March, Dulles remarked that nuclear weapons "would undoubtedly figure" in the JCS plans for war against China. He proposed for consideration the possibility of a blockade of major Chinese ports such as Shanghai and Canton. He suggested that the United States might respond to an attack on Quemoy and Matsu by destroying China's oil dumps, bridges, and rail lines, and "generally engage in a severe punitive action" throughout China. He thought it would deter China if the United States let it be known that its reaction to a Chinese attack would not be a limited one. A "limited defense of the islands was no great deterrent," he argued. It might have to be resorted to several times. The repeated nuclear strikes that such a defense would involve "obviously would entail a great and probably an unacceptable waste of such weapons." The United States could not "splurge our limited supply of atomic weapons without serious danger to the entire international balance of power." Any use of nuclear weapons must be "carefully planned and thought out."[151]

On March 31, Radford briefed the NSC on the contingency war plans in case of war with China. Dulles expressed concern over the "political repercussions" of the atomic strikes on mainland targets. "Precision atomic weapons would be used," Radford replied, and assured Dulles that "except in one or two instances no large cities or concentrations of civilian population were involved in the targets."[152] As we have seen, US forces already had nuclear and non-nuclear components of atomic weapons prepositioned in Japan, Guam, Okinawa, and Hawaii. On 31 March, General Curtis LeMay, commander of the Strategic Air Command, confirmed that plans for B-36 strikes on Chinese targets were ready. One wing of B-36s stood ready in Guam while two more wings stood on alert in the United States. Targets had been selected and assigned to the crews.[153] The JCS even considered deploying Honest John tactical nuclear missile units in Taiwan.[154] Bowie, worried by the talk of atomic bombing, asked the CIA for an estimate of the likely civilian casualties. The CIA came up with a figure of 12 million to 14 million. Bowie promptly showed this to Dulles and assumed that the data had changed the secretary of state's mind.[155]

OPPOSITION MOUNTS

The talk of nuclear war in the corridors of Washington found its echo in the press. James Reston wrote in the *New York Times* of rumors in Washington that the United States was drifting into a war over Quemoy and Matsu. The administration was coming to accept, Reston commented, that

[T]actical atomic weapons are now "conventional weapons" and should be used wherever they were militarily effective. . . . Moreover officials in Washington are now talking about tactical atomic weapons as if they were instruments of mercy that could knock out military targets more neatly and quickly than conventional weapons.[156]

New York Times military correspondent Hanson Baldwin ridiculed the reference to atomic weapons as precision weapons as "wishful thinking." He considered the idea an inherent contradiction. The type of weapons carrier, weather, and the extent of enemy opposition, he pointed out, limited the accuracy of delivery. Military targets such as airfields were often too near civilian areas to avoid large-scale civilian casualties.[157]

British Prime Minister Winston Churchill wrote to Eisenhower that it would not "be right or wise for America to encourage him [Chiang] to keep alive the reconquest of the mainland in order to inspirit his faithful followers. He deserves the protection of your shield but not the use of your sword."[158] American arguments about the importance of Quemoy and Matsu did not convince Churchill, who argued:

It would surely be quite easy for the United States to drown any Chinese would-be invaders of Formosa whether they started from Quemoy or elsewhere. If ever there was an operation which may be deemed impossible it would be the passage of about a hundred miles of sea in the teeth of overwhelming naval and air superiority and without any tank and other special landing-craft.

Churchill recommended the evacuation of Quemoy and Matsu while defending Formosa and the Pescadores.[159] The Commonwealth prime ministers who were meeting in London hoped that the United States would persuade the Nationalists to withdraw from the offshore islands.[160] Robert Menzies, Australian prime minister, made it clear that the Australian public would not support war over the offshore islands.[161] Canadian Foreign Minister Lester Pearson ruled out Canada's support for the United States in the dispute over the offshore islands.[162] The British press was highly critical of the whole US policy. General Alfred Gruenther, Supreme Allied Commander, Europe, wrote Eisenhower that the United States faced a handicap in terms of public relations: "[M]ost Europeans think that Chiang Kai-shek is a palooka."[163] A roundup of international opinion on the issue by the State Department and the United States Information Agency showed that only the ROC, South Korea, and a section of Philippine opinion supported American defense of the offshore islands. The rest of the Far East reacted with "uneasiness to outright condemnation of the US stand."[164] As Eisenhower wrote to Gruenther, "we have a Europe that, speaking generally, is fearful of what some Europeans consider American recklessness, impulsiveness and immaturity in the foreign field."[165]

Public opinion in the United States supported a tough stand against China. A Gallup Poll on 3 April showed that 55 percent of those polled supported the use of atomic weapons in a war with China. Few Americans, however, understood the issues involved in the dispute or cared about them.[166] The Democrats in Congress, who had helped pass the Formosa Resolution in January, had by and large changed their stand by the spring. When Adlai Stevenson queried how American prestige had come to be "staked on some little islands within the shadow of the Chinese coast," Eisenhower had no reply. He contented himself with pouring ridicule on Stevenson in his memoirs.[167] A *New York Times* editorial called for a "new Formosa declaration" confined to the defense of Formosa and the Pescadores only. The editorial argued that

If he [the enemy] learns that he can take the Quemoy and the Matsu Islands without provoking a major war, that fact may be tragic. Nevertheless, there are small tragedies and vast tragedies. A vast tragedy would be the stumbling into war against the intentions and wishes of the majority of our people and our allies. . . . It is time that the firebreathers in Washington, whether in the Pentagon or elsewhere, went into silence."[168]

The paper followed this up with another editorial on 31 March, calling for the abandonment of the offshore islands. Senator Walter George expressed his misgivings about the slide toward war. Democratic congressional leaders Sam Rayburn and Lyndon Johnson condemned the talk of impending war by administration officials. They extracted a statement from Eisenhower deploring such "irresponsible" talk and a promise that the president would ignore the belligerent advice he received and would personally deal with the crisis.[169]

CHANGE IN POLICY

The mounting criticism called for a fresh look at the US policy. Bowie had throughout remained critical of the US commitment to the defense of Quemoy and Matsu. In a memorandum to Dulles on 7 February, he pointed out the flaws in the administration's handling of the issue. Bowie explained that Europeans and Asians did not look on Taiwan and the offshore islands in the same light. An American commitment to the defense of the offshore islands would split the Western alliance and thus play into communist hands. The fear of "a useless war" would lead to pressures for a new international conference to resolve the status of Taiwan. Bowie suggested that the United States disengage itself from the defense of the offshore islands "in a way which will not damage our prestige or leave any doubts as to our will or ability and willingness to defend Formosa and the Pescadores." Washington could use the withdrawal of its commitment to defend the offshore islands to obtain allied support for its policy of defending Formosa. Bowie suggested that the United States should obtain UN and allied condemnation of the use of force to alter the status of Formosa and the

Pescadores, as well as the mainland. Thereafter, it should abandon the offshore islands and help the Nationalists in their evacuation.[170]

Whether prompted by this memo or not, the evacuation idea cropped up in several rather cryptic exchanges between Dulles and Eisenhower. Eisenhower had argued in the NSC as far back as August 1954 that the offshore islands were only "outposts for the defense of Formosa," not worth defending at the cost of "inflaming world opinion against us."[171] However, he preferred to see Chiang taking the initiative for deescalating the conflict.[172] He told Dulles on 16 February 1955 that it was important to develop the thinking of the Nationalists "along somewhat different lines." Dulles replied that he had "broached this matter" with Yeh. Eisenhower suggested that Robertson go to Taipei and talk informally with Chiang.[173] A week later, in a cable to Dulles, who was in Manila, Eisenhower spoke of their mutual "hope" that the Nationalists might come to realize that they could improve their situation by withdrawing from the offshore islands. "As you and I have agreed," the president continued, "any approach to Chiang along this line would have to be so skillfully conducted as to make him ostensibly the originator of the idea."[174] Eisenhower and Dulles "discussed the matter of planting a seed with Chiang out of which might grow in due course the idea of a voluntary withdrawal from Quemoy and Matsu."[175] Eisenhower also talked along similar lines with newspaper publisher Roy Howard, who was about to visit Taiwan.[176]

This idea resurfaced in April. At a White House meeting on 1 April, Eisenhower suggested that "what is needed is an attempt to bring Jiang to withdraw voluntarily—he would offer to deploy US forces up to a division and an air wing on Formosa if Quemoy and Matsu were made outposts rather than strongholds and symbols of prestige."[177] In a memo to Dulles on 5 April, Eisenhower proposed that without abandoning Quemoy and Matsu, the United States and the ROC should declare that they would not engage in the "full-out" defense of the islands but would regard them only as outposts, to be defended as long as possible to inflict the maximum possible losses on the enemy. If the outposts were ultimately lost, the psychological impact of the loss would be negligible compared to the impact of their loss if they were defended to the full. In return for Nationalist concurrence with this plan, the United States would accelerate programs for strengthening the ROC forces and would station additional US air, marine, and anti-aircraft units in Taiwan. The president wanted the process of bringing around Chiang to this line of thinking to begin immediately.[178]

On 17 April, Dulles met the president in Augusta with a memo prepared by State and Defense Department officials. Dulles argued that if the United States would not let the Nationalists attack the Chinese forces before they were ready for an invasion, or help the Nationalists after the

Chinese were fully prepared, it was better to make a "clean break" and abandon the offshore islands. After that, the United States should institute an interdiction of the Chinese coastal traffic. Eisenhower approved the plan after some hesitation. The two finally agreed that if the Nationalists evacuated the islands, the United States would assist in the withdrawal operations. Unless and until China renounced its plan to take Taiwan by force, the United States would join the Nationalists in interdicting Chinese coastal traffic between Swatow and Wenchow to prevent seaborne supplies that might be used in the invasion of Taiwan. The United States would also station atomic, air, and marine units in Taiwan and would declare its intention to veto China's admission to the UN. [179] *Chiang Rejected it fearing . . . .*

Congressman Walter Judd, a prominent supporter of the Nationalists, initially expressed approval of the plan and volunteered to go as the presidential envoy to Taiwan.[180] However, he soon developed second thoughts and backed out. The choice finally fell on Robertson and Radford. The two were chosen because they enjoyed Chiang's trust. Neither of them, however, had their hearts in the assignment. Radford favored holding the islands, even if Chiang was prepared to abandon them. Robertson had been reluctant when Dulles sounded him in February. He had feared that "he may lead the Generalissimo into thinking wrongly."[181] Their presentation of the case to Chiang was, understandably, not very persuasive, and Chiang flatly turned down the proposal. According to Robertson's report of his conversation with Chiang,

Gimo [Chiang] indicated he understood fully details and implications of our proposal. He stated primary consideration was one of confidence and trust, secondly that any proposal must be within reasonable bounds of compliance to each party. He lacked faith in US ability to adhere in face of outside pressures to proposed interdiction of seaborne traffic after having given up islands. The abandonment of his little remaining territory at this time would be completely unacceptable to his people and to overseas Chinese everywhere, shattering their confidence in him as well as [the] United States.[182]

If Nationalist forces withdrew from Quemoy and Matsu, Chiang insisted, "even a child would not believe that his Government would be assisted by [the] US in holding Taiwan itself." Robertson made it clear that the United States would not intervene to defend Quemoy and Matsu.[183] A bitter Chiang told Yeh that he knew that the US commitment to defend Quemoy and Matsu was not permanent, but "never in his darkest moments did he expect [the] US to alter [its] decision as to [the] immediate situation."[184]

In the middle of the 1958 crisis in the Straits, Eisenhower recalled that Robertson and Radford had not carried out his instructions faithfully.

He even implied that they secretly sympathized with Chiang.[185] In retrospect, it is surprising that Eisenhower gave up his idea of treating the offshore islands as outposts—which made sound strategic sense—and accepted Dulles's idea of a blockade of the China coast. Blockade was an act of war, as the administration had itself pointed out when Knowland recommended one in November 1954. China could hardly have been expected to quietly accept an American blockade of its sea lanes. If a peaceful solution was indeed the administration's aim, nothing could have been more counterproductive than the plan Eisenhower and Dulles agreed on in April.

The crisis, however, subsided as suddenly as it had begun, when Zhou dramatically announced his offer of direct talks with the United States in the Bandung Conference on 23 April. Before the conference began, the State Department had made vigorous efforts through friendly governments to persuade China to adopt a less aggressive stance. However, the initial US reaction to Zhou's announcement was tentative and seemed to indicate that Washington was taken by surprise. The State Department insisted on the participation of the ROC in any discussion concerning the Taiwan area and called on China to release the American prisoners held in China, agree to a cease-fire, and accept the Security Council's invitation for discussion, in order "to give evidence before the world of its good intentions."[186] This was somewhat disinguous, as it amounted to calling for prior Chinese compliance on the very issues that would form the agenda for the talks. However, under mounting public and diplomatic pressure, Dulles, on 26 April, dropped the insistence on the ROC's participation and indicated US readiness to negotiate with Beijing. Dulles told Republican Senate leaders that "we had worked very hard" to get US Asian allies at Bandung to restrain the Chinese. Refusal of Zhou's offer would alienate these countries, which had persuaded Zhou to follow "a pacific rather than belligerent course."[187] On 27 April, Eisenhower publicly declared that negotiations with China were "perfectly legitimate," even if the Nationalists were excluded.[188] With Britain acting as the intermediary, the two nations concluded preliminary arrangements for the talks.

The State Department's claim that its own diplomatic efforts had brought about China's moderate stance during the Bandung Conference has obscured the fact that the Chinese offer at Bandung was nothing new. Chang and He Di argue that Mao's judgment that the United States did not want a war with China led to China's refusal to agree to a diplomatic settlement.[189] This argument overlooks China's February offer, made well before the war scare of March, for direct talks with the United States. China had also signaled that from its side it was cooling off tensions by refraining from invading any more islands and drastically cutting down its propaganda on liberating Taiwan. The Chinese objection was to negotiations involving the ROC, not to negotiations per se. The United States had indeed picked up these signals, and had probably correctly assessed their significance. Dulles, however, rejected negotiations with China without involving the ROC.[190] Had Washington then responded to the Chinese offer in the same way it finally responded in April, the talk of nuclear war that dominated much of March and early April would have been avoided. Nor would there have been any need for behind-the-scenes diplomacy before the Bandung Conference.[191]

CONCLUSIONS

The administration hesitated to respond to the initial Chinese overtures because it had surrendered the initiative to the Nationalists. To some extent, this Republican administration was a victim of its party's anti-communist scare tactics adopted to embarrass its Democratic predecessor. The China Lobby in fact exerted very little influence in favor of US intervention for the defense of the offshore islands. The Truman administration had made it clear that the protective umbrella of the Seventh Fleet did not extend to the offshore islands. Far from objecting to this, leading Republicans such as Senators Robert Taft and Knowland had expressed agreement. After Eisenhower announced his decision to unleash Chiang, no one from the China Lobby had interpreted this to mean that the United States would henceforth defend the offshore islands.[192] Senator Alexander Smith, a leading Nationalist supporter, lost interest in the offshore islands when he heard that an invasion of the mainland would not need Quemoy and Matsu.[193] Congressman Judd told Dulles that "he himself has always had reservations as to the defensibility of Quemoy and Matsu islands and has some reservations as to the desirability of attaching either United States or Chinat prestige to holding them."[194] Knowland did call for strong action to compel the release of Americans imprisoned in China, but his most vocal demands for military action to defend the offshore islands came in response to Zhou's Bandung offer. His fear apparently was that negotiating with China would confer legitimacy on the PRC.[195] James Reston commented that Congress took note of the powerful antiwar sentiment in the country, "so much so that, on this issue, Senator Knowland probably heads the smallest bloc any leader ever tried to carry into battle against so popular a President." By Reston's count, Knowland could carry with him only five senators— Bridges, McCarthy, George Malone, William Jenner, and Herman Welker.[196]

Nevertheless, Dulles and Eisenhower acted as though they feared a severe backlash if they were in any way seen as failing the Nationalists. Dulles went to great lengths to conceal the fact that the United States had initiated the move for UN intervention. When Dulles and Eisenhower talked of getting Chiang to withdraw from the offshore islands, their overriding concern was that they themselves should not be seen as pressuring Chiang in that direction. Dulles feared being blamed for the withdrawal from the Dachens so much that he told Robertson to doctor the minutes of his meeting with Yeh in such a way as to show that he had not suggested withdrawal from the islands. The administration came out in acceptance of the Chinese offer to negotiate, only after reports in the media made it clear that the nation by and large would welcome a positive response.

Once the crisis began in the fall of 1954, Dulles felt that the situation in Asia did not permit the United States to retreat further before communism. The United States could not remain a spectator while China gained at the expense of the Nationalists. The Chinese, he claimed, were "dizzy with success" and were on a path of "aggressive fanaticism."[197] He told a meeting of legislators on 30 March that Chinese arrogance sprang from their success in Korea, Dien Bien Phu, and the Dachens. The free world appeared to the Chinese, in Dulles's estimation, as though it were "almost asking for more."[198]

In dealing with China, the administration had reason to believe that it enjoyed freedom from Soviet intervention, unless US military action threatened to destroy the PRC. Historian Shu Guang Zhang has claimed that by the early fall of 1954, "Chinese leaders generally felt that they could count on Soviet support in the Taiwan Strait." This conclusion is backed by very little evidence of Soviet expressions of support for China in the offshore islands crisis. Soviet leader Nikita Khrushchev's presence in China from 29 September to 13 October did not produce any clear declaration of Soviet support for China.[199] Ambassador Charles Bohlen in Moscow believed that the Soviet Union would keep out of the conflict as it did not affect any vital Soviet interest. However, because of the importance of China to Soviet global interests, a Sino-US conflict would pose a serious problem for the Soviet Union. He could not say in advance what the Soviet course of action would be. It appeared that the Soviet Union did not have much influence over China. Bohlen noted the "extreme caution" of the Soviet press, which had avoided reference to any Soviet military commitment in support of China. The Indonesian ambassador, after a meeting with Molotov, told Bohlen that the Soviets wanted to see a cease-fire in the Taiwan Strait, and that Beijing was playing "an independent hand" in the crisis.[200] Neither Eisenhower nor Dulles believed that Russia had a major role in the crisis or wanted war.[201] US intelligence estimated that in case of a Sino-American war, the Chinese might attempt to keep the hostilities from escalating. However, if US action threatened the survival of the PRC, the Soviet Union might intervene but would still try to keep military operations from spreading beyond the Far East.[202]

To see the American nuclear diplomacy in this crisis in perspective, it is essential to see what exactly the American stakes in this crisis were. The territory to be defended involved a few dozen small islands within wading distance of mainland China, which Eisenhower himself acknowledged had always been part of China politically and geographically.[203] The JCS had long held that these islands were not militarily important, as none of the islands had harbors suitable as bases for large amphibious operations.[204] Except Radford, nobody in the Eisenhower administration held these islands to be worth a war with China. No legal or moral reasons called for US intervention on behalf of the Nationalists. In response to Churchill's criticism, Eisenhower had contended that

We must not lose Chiang's army and we must maintain its strength, efficiency, and morale] ... The French are gone [from Indochina] making it clearer than ever that we cannot afford the loss of Chiang unless all of us are to get completely out of that corner of the globe.[205]

It is surprising to see this statement made by Eisenhower, of all people, to Churchill, of all people. The fighting capability of the Nationalist army did not justify such exaggerated expectations. General Chase, who had a good knowledge of the Nationalist forces, estimated the effectiveness of the Nationalist army, in comparison with the standards of the US armed forces, at 15 percent, the Nationalist air force at 25 percent, and the Nationalist navy at 10 percent. Chase thought that "minus 10 percent was an accurate estimate" of the effectiveness of the Nationalists' logistics branch.[206]

The administration argued that what was propping up the Nationalist morale was the hope of one day returning to the mainland, for which the offshore islands were "the stepping stones." If this was indeed so, Bowie had pointed out, morale was bound to suffer as long as the United States did not support an invasion of the mainland, even if the United States helped defend the offshore islands against the Chinese. The morale of the native Taiwanese, Bowie argued, would in fact have improved if they knew that they would not be involved in the risks of fighting over the offshore islands or invasions of the mainland. Few Nationalist leaders would dare to defect to China, even if they were frustrated by the failure to return to the mainland. They would, thus, be hardly in a position to endanger the defense of Taiwan.[207] While Ambassador Rankin favored the United States defending the offshore islands, he did not believe that the loss of the islands meant the end of the ROC. He felt that Yeh had exaggerated the effects of the loss of the islands on Nationalist morale when he briefed Dulles during his February visit to Taiwan.[208]

By the end of March, Eisenhower had come to feel that the United States should not be "even remotely committed to the defense of these

islands."[209] In fact, even while arguing that the loss of the offshore islands would ruin the morale of the Nationalists, Dulles and Eisenhower
were maneuvering to get Chiang to withdraw from the islands voluntarily. Obviously, what worried them was not the effect of the loss of
the islands, but *the blame for being responsible for their loss.* Eisenhower
himself had come to doubt the morale argument, at least by April 1955.
He wrote to Dulles:

Incidentally, there is room to suspect that the sincerity of Chiang's conten-
tion that the retention or loss of the offshore islands would spell the difference
between a strong and a destroyed Nationalist government in Formosa. If this is
so, his own headquarters *should* be on the offshore islands.[210] (emphasis in original)

Eisenhower had told congressional leaders on 1 February that "They
have 60,000 Nationalist troops on Quemoy and if Chiang can't protect
that island with those troops, plus, if necessary, assistance from American air and naval power, then I don't think Quemoy would be worth
holding."[211]

Grossly exaggerated accounts of Eisenhower's leadership in this crisis
occupy a central place in the historiography of Eisenhower revisionism.
From the beginning, Eisenhower was conscious of the poor legal case for
US intervention in the offshore islands dispute. The argument about the
military value of the islands had never impressed him. At least toward
the end of the crisis, he appreciated the falsity of the administration's
long-standing argument that shoring up Nationalist morale required the
defense of the offshore islands. There was nothing in the dispute that
justified global war, as he confided to Gruenther.[212] Still, he failed to take
a firm stand and end the US commitment to the defense of the islands.
Instead, he allowed US policy to be determined by Chiang, whom he
described as "a fellow who hasn't anything to lose."[213]

In his memoirs Eisenhower, attempting to present a picture of a president fully in command of the situation, talked of his administration

threading its way, with watchfulness and determination, through narrow and
dangerous waters between appeasement and global war. For nine months the
administration moved through treacherous cross currents with one channel leading to peace with honor and a hundred channels leading to war or dishonor.[214]

The picture was far from true. Eisenhower set out to "draw the line" on
more than one occasion. The line, however, kept shifting. On 12 September 1954, the NSC decided to seek UN intervention. The administration
then allowed Nationalist resistance to delay the reference to the UN until
the mutual defense treaty was signed. The treaty itself failed to draw a

line and left the US commitment to the defense of the offshore islands open ended. In January 1955, Dulles and Eisenhower agreed to defend Quemoy only, but quickly enlarged the list to include Matsu. Immediately after giving this commitment, Eisenhower started to think of ways to wriggle out of it. Eisenhower's decision in the White House meeting on 11 March 1955 against using nuclear weapons initially against China has been presented as an example of his ability to assert himself in a crisis. However, Eisenhower was only summarizing what Dulles said earlier in the meeting. He proposed a well-conceived plan to convert the offshore islands into outposts rather than strongholds, only to allow Dulles to talk him into the explosive proposal to institute a blockade of the China coast. This was hardly a "hidden hand president" in action. The presidential hand was absent, not simply hidden, on crucial occasions.

A crucial error of the administration—for which much of the blame should go to Eisenhower—was to decide in advance that in case of US intervention in the defense of the offshore islands, it would place no restrictions on the use of weapons, or targets to be hit. Even when Eisenhower decided on 11 March that initial US intervention would be with conventional weapons, he indicated that, if necessary, nuclear weapons would be used. Whatever lessons on limited war had been learned in the Korean War, Eisenhower and his advisers had apparently forgotten them. This refusal to consider using only limited force to achieve a limited goal was largely the result of Eisenhower's ready acceptance of highly questionable military advice from Radford. When Eisenhower wondered whether destroyers "would not have a field day" against the Chinese junks, Radford replied that junks were "extremely difficult to sink." The US Navy, he told the president, had studied ways of destroying junks and "had concluded that they were extremely difficult to dispose of by any method."[215] However, as contemporary press reports indicated, not all Pentagon experts shared Radford's view on the unsinkability of junks. The Nationalist forces had not faced much difficulty in sinking these crafts.[216]

The crucial question remains, why did the American decision to stand firm take the form of nuclear diplomacy? McGeorge Bundy has argued that Eisenhower did not really intend to use nuclear weapons against China.

[The] real sentiment of Eisenhower was that he must do everything he could *not* to have to use nuclear weapons over those small islands, and his one public warning . . . was intended only to encourage Chinese caution while conventional defenses on the two islands were strengthened.[217]

US leaders, however, knew that the Chinese simply did not have the ability to launch a full-scale invasion of Quemoy or Matsu during the period that they feared the islands were vulnerable. Their only serious concern was whether the Chinese junks in the vicinity had assembled for a hostile purpose or were merely there for their normal activity of fishing. Moreover, even after 25 March, by which time Nationalist defenses should have been strong enough to withstand a full-scale Chinese attack, American preparations for nuclear attacks against China continued.

H. W. Brands has argued that the nuclear diplomacy in this crisis was aimed at ensuring the credibility of the administration's strategy of massive retaliation.[218] This argument is not convincing either. The New Look strategy proposed all-out nuclear retaliation only in case of global war. In the case of local conflicts, the administration's policy was not massive retaliation but use of indigenous forces supported by US air and naval forces and, if necessary, tactical nuclear weapons. Massive retaliation in a global war was meant to deter a serious threat to the United States and, as such, constituted a credible threat. Nuclear war in defense of the offshore islands did not carry the same degree of credibility. It is illogical to argue that a threat that lacked credibility would bolster the credibility of an already credible threat. Further, Eisenhower and Dulles had contemplated, but rejected, the wisdom of preparing US and allied opinion for the general use of nuclear weapons in a global war. Dulles had thought that talk of nuclear war tended to produce "peace-at-any-price people," and thus to increase appeasement sentiment. [219]

The key to understanding the American nuclear threats lies in the thinking of Dulles. In the NSC meeting on 10 March, Dulles asserted that "the Chinese were determined to capture Formosa." He thought it "at least an even chance that the United States would have to fight in this area before we were through." The "question of a fight for Formosa" appeared to him "as a question of time rather than a question of fact." The United States, however, could not enter into hostilities with China until the Europeans ratified the agreements on the Western European Union and West Germany's accession to NATO. The American public needed to be informed of the gravity of the situation. Moreover, "urgent steps to create a better public climate for the use of atomic weapons" were needed. He had gathered from the US military that only atomic weapons would be effective against Chinese targets such as airfields, railroad lines, and gun emplacements. The administration, he insisted, "would have to face up to the question whether its military program was or was not in fact designed to permit the use of atomic weapons." He feared that "We might wake up one day and discover that we were inhibited in the use of these weapons by a negative public opinion." If this happened, "our entire military program would have to be drastically revised." The United States would then have to develop separate plans centered on conventional weapons and nuclear weapons.

It was of vital importance, therefore, that we urgently educate our own and world opinion as to the necessity for the tactical use of atomic weapons. . . . *[M]uch more remained to be done if the US were to be able to make use of tactical atomic weapons, perhaps within the next month or two.* (emphasis added)

Radford added:

Indeed our whole military structure had been built around this assumption. . . . We could not handle the military situation in the Far East, particularly as regards aircraft, unless we could employ atomic weapons. We simply did not have the requisite numbers of air bases to permit effective air attacks against Communist China, using conventional as opposed to atomic weapons.[220]

What the administration spokesmen threatened during this crisis was in fact not massive retaliation but limited use of nuclear weapons—the strategy of "less than massive retaliation." The Pentagon did not feel that it could defend Quemoy and Matsu without using tactical nuclear weapons to take out Chinese airfields and artillery positions. It did not have adequate conventional forces in the theater to deal with these installations, nor was it willing to incur the casualties that conventional defense would inflict. The administration did not expect the crisis to become a global war, even if fighting broke out between the United States and China. So it contemplated only a limited war using tactical nuclear weapons. The public calls for the use of atomic weapons were designed to prepare the domestic and international opinion for limited use of such weapons. The administration, in fact, went far beyond mere statements. It moved US nuclear forces into position and selected targets for nuclear strikes against China.[221]

Much more, however, was passing through Dulles's mind in these critical days. During an NSC meeting in June 1954, he had stated that the United States had issued China several warnings not to resort to any overt aggression. If China went on the offensive in South Korea, Japan, Taiwan, or Indochina, despite these warnings, Dulles argued, he "would regard it as throwing down the gauge of battle [sic] to the United States. If we did not pick it up we might just as well get out of the Pacific."[222] As already noted, in September 1954, he had toyed with the idea of using the offshore islands to provoke a war with China. He reverted to this theme in March 1955.

At the height of the public discussion of atomic war against China, Dulles confided his thoughts to a paper, in which he argued: "Because of the Chinese-Communist mentality, *we have a choice of either 'egging them on' to make a plunge that we could exploit not only near Formosa but elsewhere,* or of making deployments of US forces to the area to reinforce the deterrent of our verbal warnings" (emphasis added). He recalled that the

Chinese had "scorned" the possibility of American attacks on mainland targets while deciding to enter the Korean War. He considered a number of "precautionary military deployments for the purpose of either deterring a Communist military assault or, if deterrence fails, placing our forces in a better state of readiness to stop the Communist attack." These included movement of a [nuclear-capable] B-47 wing to the Far East, installation of 280mm guns (which could fire atomic shells) on Quemoy and Matsu, and practice bombing runs in the Far East.[223]

Between Dulles's September 1954 and March 1955 ruminations, there was one significant difference. Evidence now available shows that between December 1954 and February 1955, the United States moved atomic bombs minus their nuclear cores to Japan and complete nuclear bombs to Okinawa. By January 1955, nuclear bombs and their non-nuclear components were also stored aboard five US naval munitions ships in the Pacific.[224] The details surrounding the decision to preposition nuclear weapons close to China are not yet known, including the date of the decision. It is quite possible that the decision was totally unrelated to events in the Far East. It should also be kept in mind that in early 1955, the United States had the capability to quickly transfer complete nuclear weapons to bases within range of Chinese targets in a matter of days. However, the striking change in the tone of administration spokesmen, including those at the highest levels, in their comments on the use of nuclear weapons against China in the days after these weapons were moved to the Far East is noteworthy. We have seen that the nuclear war talk and the nuclear war preparations in Washington took place when the president, the secretary of state, and many senior military officials did not anticipate an imminent Chinese military threat to Taiwan or the offshore islands. Whatever the reasons for transferring atomic weapons to the area at that particular juncture, their presence within striking distance of China could well have been a factor in the administration's handling of the crisis in the spring of 1955.

Since it was Dulles who first started the scare about an impending Chinese threat late in February, the possibility that he was influenced by a desire to "egg on" the Chinese is very strong.[225] The fact that China was not ready in the spring of 1955 for an attack did not offer much comfort to Dulles in the long term in view of the continued Chinese work on constructing airfields in the coastal area. As Admiral Stump helpfully pointed out, the Chinese would not launch a major war until they were fully prepared; by the time they *were* prepared, it would be too late for the United States to stop them.[226] From Dulles's perspective, it made no sense to wait around while the Chinese completed their preparations for an invasion and then attacked Taiwan or the offshore islands. It made perfect sense to strike before a Chinese invasion was actually underway, even if it called for provoking the Chinese into taking the offensive. For someone who had enunciated the policy of striking at the enemy at the time and place of American choosing, and had wanted to launch an offensive in the Korean War to advance the UN line up to the waist of Korea, this was not an uncharacteristic line of thinking.[227] Eisenhower himself was not very far behind Dulles's thinking in this respect. After China turned down the New Zealand resolution, he told Hagerty on 2 February: "You know, they (the Chinese Communists) are certainly doing everything they can to try our patience. It's awfully difficult to remain calm under these situations. Sometimes I think that it would be best all around to go after them right now without letting them pick their time and the place of their own choosing."[228] The plan for blockading the China coast that Dulles persuaded Eisenhower to approve made perfect sense as a move to provoke the Chinese. In fact, the blockade plan made sense in no other context.

NOTES

1. Dwight D. Eisenhower, *The White House Years, Vol. 1: Mandate for Change* (Garden City, NY: Doubleday & Co., 1963), 459. For other works, see H. W. Brands, "Testing Massive Retaliation: Credibility and Crisis Management in the Taiwan Strait," *International Security* (Spring 1988); McGeorge Bundy, *Danger and Survival: Choices About the Bomb in the First Fifty Years* (New York: Vintage Books, 1988); Michael Dockdrill, "Britain and the First Chinese Offshore Islands Crisis, 1954–1955," in Michael Dockdrill and John W. Young (eds.), *British Foreign Policy, 1945–1956* (New York: St. Martin's Press, 1989); J. H. Kalicki, *The Pattern of Sino-American Crises: Political-Military Interactions in the 1950s* (New York: Cambridge University Press, 1975); Shu Guang Zhang, *Deterrence and Strategic Culture: Chinese-American Confrontations, 1949–1958* (Ithaca, NY: Cornell University Press, 1992); Zhai Qiang, *The Dragon, the Lion, and the Eagle: Chinese-British-American Relations, 1949–1958* (Kent, OH: Kent State University Press, 1994); Warren Cohen and Akira Iriye (eds.), *Great Powers in East Asia, 1953–1960* (New York: Columbia University Press, 1990); Harry Harding and Yuan Ming (eds.), *Sino-American Relations, 1945–1955: A Joint Assessment of a Critical Decade* (Wilmington, DE: Scholarly Resources, 1989); Robert Accinelli, *Crisis and Commitment: United States Policy toward Taiwan, 1950–1955* (Chapel Hill: University of North Carolina Press, 1996).

2. Memo of 240th meeting of the NSC, 10 March 1955, *FRUS 1955–57, II*, 346.

3. Memo of the 237 NSC, 17 February 1955, ibid., 280–81.

4. Bowie memo to Dulles, 7 February 1955, ibid., 238.

5. For views in support of this claim, see Bundy, *Danger and Survival*, 273–89; John Lewis Gaddis, *The Long Peace: Enquiries Into the History of the Cold War* (New York: Oxford University Press, 1987), 133–40. H. W. Brands, however, argues that these nuclear threats were meant to bolster the credibility of the administration's strategy of massive retaliation. See Brands, "Testing Massive Retaliation."

6. Zhang, *Deterrence and Strategic Culture*, 67–72.

7. Goncharov et al., *Uncertain Partners: Stalin, Mao, and the Korean War* (Stanford, CA: Stanford University Press, 1993), 148. According to the CIA, the Chinese communists were "estimated to possess the capability of carrying out their frequently expressed intention of seizing Taiwan during 1950, and will probably do so during the period of June–December 1950." Recent improvements in the condition of the Nationalists could delay this outcome only slightly. The American Charge d'Affaires in Taipei speculated that the communists might utilize their improved morale following their success in Hainan to attack Taiwan. A few weeks later, the US Embassy staff in Taipei concluded that the communists would attack "between June 15 and [the] end of July." They recommended the evacuation of American personnel in Taiwan and the removal of cryptographic equipment. A few days later, the State Department authorized the embassy to start reducing American personnel in Taiwan. Officials in Washington reasoned that capture of American personnel in Taiwan by the communists would be a "serious matter" that could damage American prestige. Rusk to Acheson, 17 April 1950, *FRUS 1950, VI*, 330; Taipei to DOS, 27 April and 17 May, ibid., 336–37, 340–41; DOS to Taipei, 26 May 1950, ibid., 345.

8. Goncharov et al., *Uncertain Partners*, 152.

9. Ibid., 158. The CIA had already noted that unlike in the CCP's New Year's message, Mao avoided a firm commitment to the liberation of Taiwan and Tibet in 1950 in his speech to the CCP Central Committee and merely referred to this as a "serious task." This left room for a change in the timetable. By 5 July, US observers concluded that despite air activity in the Zhejiang area, preparations for the Taiwan campaign had ended. CIA memo, 19 June 1950, PSF, Subject, Intelligence, Box 255, "Central Intelligence Memo 1950–52," HSTL; Peake to Carroll, 5 July 1950, 793.51/7–550, RG 59, NA.

10. Doris M. Condit, *History of the Office of the Secretary of Defense, Vol. II: The Test of War, 1950–1953* (Washington, DC: Historical Office, Office of the Secretary of Defense, 1988), 175–79.

11. Second draft of the oral presentation to the NSC by the Secretary of State, 27 April 1951, PPS Papers, Box 14, "China 1950–51," RG 59, NA.

12. Lay memo to the NSC, 17 May 1951, *FRUS 1951, VI*, 57.

13. Condit, *History of the Office of the Secretary of Defense*, 180–82.

14. JCS to Secretary of Defense, 4 March 1952, *FRUS 1952–54, XIV*, 16–17.

15. The new aggressive stance in Washington quickly found public expression. At a press conference in Tokyo on 1 April 1952, Navy Secretary Kimball declared that if the Nationalists invaded China, the Seventh Fleet would "stand on sidelines and cheer"; if the Chinese attacked Taiwan, "we would clobber the hell out of them." On 22 July, about 100 US planes flew "just outside" China's territorial waters in order to "give the Communists something to think about" and demonstrate the navy's ability to bomb major Chinese coastal cities. The next day, Admiral William Fechteler, Chief of Naval Operations (CNO), claimed responsibility for this decision. He claimed that "the Navy could deliver baby atom bombs in Korea if it is ordered to do so," although, he admitted, the navy did not yet have these bombs. Bowles to DOS, 14 April 1942, *FRUS 1952–54, XIV*, 45; memo of telecon, 23 July 1949, ibid., 79; memo of telecon, 24 July 1949, ibid., 81; *New York Times*, 1 April 1952.

16. *FRUS 1952–54, XIV*, 140. A draft of the presidential address contained

the following line: "We have no intention of aggressive action against Communist China, but we certainly have no obligation to protect it." This was omitted from the final message. "Six Draft," 27 January 1953, AWF, Adm. Series, Box 35, "State Department—Top Secret Materials," DEPL.

Long before assuming his new charge, Dulles had disapproved of the Seventh Fleet's mission of neutralizing the Taiwan Strait. "Chiang needs to be restrained," he conceded, but argued that "we have ample means of doing so privately and without public humiliation." Dulles hoped that the end of a public commitment to restrain Chiang might create in the minds of the Chinese "a theoretical risk of attack on the mainland" and thus deter them from increasing their commitments in Korea and Indochina. This might provoke the Chinese to try to take Formosa, but the United States could handle that. He concluded that the Seventh Fleet's orders should be amended, *"after proper private arrangements with Chiang"* (emphasis in original). Dulles Memorandum, 31 March 1952, Dulles Papers, Box 60, "Formosa 1952," Seeley Mudd Library, Princeton University.

17. Memcon, 2 February, *FRUS 1952–54, XIV*, 139.

18. Notes of conversation with Allison, 2 February 1953, Koo Papers, Box 187, "Conversations, 1953," Butler Library, Columbia University.

19. *FRUS 1952–54, XIV*, 144.

20. Memo of State-Defense meeting, 27 March, ibid., 165–66.

21. *FRUS 1952–54, XIV*, 174. Dulles shared the worry of the JCS and some State Department officials that Chiang might use American-supplied F-84 long-range fighter-bombers against China and thus involve the United States in a clash with China. He considered it "of the utmost importance" to secure a formal commitment from Chiang not to use these aircraft without first getting American clearance. He wanted deliveries of the aircraft held up until the Nationalists gave such a commitment. The ROC gave the commitment on 23 April. Taipei to DOS, *FRUS 1952–54, XIV*, 193, 169–70 note 2.

22. Appendix to JCS 2118/65, 8 July 1954, JCS Records, Box 16, CCS 381 Far East (11–28–50) Sec. 21, RG 218, NA; Zhang, *Deterrence and Strategic Culture*, 195–97.

23. The CNO opposed any such extension of the American role. He also opposed offensive operations against the Chinese mainland from these islands supported by forces based on Formosa and the Pescadores. The Chief of Army Staff concurred with this view. The State Department announced that the Seventh Fleet would protect only Formosa and the Pescadores. Ambassador Koo, after a meeting with Rusk and Dulles, confirmed this. Congress did not object to this interpretation, and no member expressed disagreement in Congress. Influential Republican Senators Robert Taft and William Knowland, in fact, expressed agreement with this policy. CNO to the JCS, and memo by Chief of Army Staff, 20 July 1950, CCS 383.21 Korea (3–19–45) Sec. 23; JCS memorandum for Secretary of Defense, 21 July 1950, CCS 383.21. Korea (3–19–45) Sec. 25, RG 218, NA; Memo by Attorney General on Congressional Attitude to Formosa Defense, enclosed to Lay memo to the NSC, 13 September 1954, OSANSA, Special Assistant Series, Presidential Subseries, Box 2, "President's Papers 1954 (7)," DEPL.

24. DOS to Taipei, 9 May 1952, *FRUS 1952–54, XIV*, 49–50.

25. Memo by Attorney General on Congressional Attitude to Formosa Defense, enclosed to Lay memo to the NSC, 13 September, OSANSA, Special Assistant Series, Presidential Subseries, Box 2, "President's Papers 1954 (7)," DEPL.

26. McConnaughy memcon, 30 January 1953, *FRUS 1952–54, XIV*, 134.

27. Bradley pointed out that none of the islands had harbors suitable for the kind of amphibious operation necessary for an invasion of Taiwan. The Chinese would have to rely on their mainland ports for an invasion of Formosa. The JCS also felt that owing to the initial advantages an attacking force would enjoy, the Chinese "could take any of the islands against any defense that could be mustered, if they were willing to commit the requisite forces." Johnson memo, 3 August 1953, ibid., 240–41.

28. Minutes of 211th NSC, 18 August 1954, *FRUS 1952–54, XIV*, 517, 538–39. The policy paper was approved and circulated as NSC 5429/2.

29. NSC 146/2, 6 November 1953, *FRUS 1952–54, XIV*, 308. See also memo for the NSC, 28 September 1954, OSANSA, Policy Papers, Box 4, "NSC 146/2-Formosa and Chinese National Government (1)," DEPL.

30. CIA Report #50318, 8 September 1954, AWF, International, Box 9, "Formosa (1)," DEPL; Special National Intelligence Estimate (SNIE), 4 September, *FRUS 1952–54, XIV*, 563–71; Notes of conversation with Stevenson, 15 February 1953, Wellington Koo Papers, Box 187, "Conversations: 1953," Butler Manuscripts Library, Columbia University.

31. CIA Report #50318, 8 September 1954, AWF, International, Box 9, "Formosa (1)," DEPL.

32. Tamsui to FO, 20 February 1953, FC 1018/60, and BBC monitoring, 20 February 1953, FC 1018/62, FO 371/105197, PRO.

33. Tamsui to FO, 10 February 1953, FO 371/105197/FC 1018/64, PRO.

34. Rankin to DOS, 20 February 1954, *FRUS 1952–54, XIV*, 363–64.

35. Memo of 153rd NSC, 9 July 1953, ibid., 227–28.

36. Taipei to DOS, 15 July 1953, ibid., 228–29.

37. Eisenhower, *The White House Years, Vol. 1: Mandate for Change*, 462.

38. *Newsweek*, 31 May 1954.

39. Zhang, *Deterrence and Strategic Culture*, 190–92. The Chinese took note of Walter Robertson's congressional testimony in early 1954 that "the US will maintain an unrestricted control in the Far East in order to have a continuous threat of attack on Red China." Ibid.

40. Ibid., 193–98; He Di, "The Evolution of the People's Republic of China's Policy Toward the Offshore Islands," in Warren Cohen and Akira Iriye (eds.), *The Great Powers in East Asia 1953–1960* (New York: Columbia University Press, 1990), 223–25; Gordon Chang and He Di, "The Absence of War in the US-Chinese Confrontation Over Jinmen and Mazu in 1954–1955: Contingency, Luck, Deterrence?" *American Historical Review* (December 1993), 1507.

41. Taipei to DOS, 20 May 54, *FRUS 1952–54, XIV*, 425–26.

42. Cutler memcon, 22 May, idid., 428.

43. Memo of 199th NSC meeting, ibid., 433–34.

44. Memcon, 22 May 1954, Dulles Papers, White House Memorandum, Box 1, "Meetings with the President 1954 (3)," DEPL; *FRUS 1952–54, XIV*, 428–30.

45. Dulles memo of telecon, 25 July 1954, *FRUS 1952–54, XIV*, 506–7.

46. *Newsweek*, 2 and 9 August 1954.

47. Zhang, *Deterrence and Strategic Culture*, 197.

48. CIA Report #50318, 8 September 1954, AWF, International, Box 9, "Formosa (1)," DEPL.

49. Excerpts from the memo of NSC discussions, 5 August 1954, *FRUS 1952–54, XIV*, 518–19.

50. Eisenhower, *The White House Years, Vol. 1: Mandate for Change*, 463; *Newsweek*, 30 August 1954.

51. Draper memo of meeting in the State Department, 31 August 1954, ibid., 554.

52. He Di, "Paper or Real Tiger: America's Nuclear Deterrence and Mao Zedong's Response," paper presented at the International Conference on New Evidence on the Cold War in Asia, Hong Kong, 1996; Gordon Chang and He Di, "The Absence of War," 1,507.

53. CIA Report #50318, 8 September 1954, AWF, International, Box 9, "Formosa (1)," DEPL.

54. Acting Secretary of Defense to President, 3 September 1954, *FRUS 1952–54, XIV*, 556.

55. Chang, *Friends and Enemies*, 120.

56. Manila to DOS, 4 September and 5 September 1954, ibid., 560, 572.

57. Smith to Dulles, 6 September 1954, ibid., 574.

58. CIA Report #50318, 8 September 1954, AWF, International, Box 9, "Formosa (1)," DEPL.

59. SNIE, 10 September 1954, *FRUS 1952–54, XIV*, 596–97.

60. Radford memo to Wilson, 11 September 1954, ibid., 598–604.

61. 213th meeting of the NSC, 9 September 1954, ibid., 591.

62. Smith to Dulles (in Philippines), 3 September 1954, ibid., 558.

63. Radford memo for Wilson, 11 September 1954, ibid., 605–9.

64. Anderson to Eisenhower, 3 September 1954, ibid., 557.

65. Matthew Ridgway, *Soldier* (Westport, CT: Greenwood Press, 1974), 278.

66. Smith to Dulles, 3 September 1954, *FRUS 1952–54, XIV*, 558.

67. 216th meeting of the NSC, 6 October 1954, ibid., 696.

68. Ibid., 698.

69. 213th meeting of the NSC, 9 September 1954, *FRUS 1952–54, XIV*, 591.

70. See memo of NSC meeting on 18 August, ibid., 537–38. In October 1954, he admonished the hard-liners: "You can talk all you want of the bad effect on Asia if the United States does not fight to defend these offshore islands, but you say nothing about the bad effect on Europe if we do undertake to fight to hold these islands." He warned that the allies would not back the United States in this fight. "Europe," he warned, "could be written off in such a contingency." 216th meeting of the NSC, 6 October 1954, ibid., 699.

71. Memo by Dulles, 12 September 1954, ibid., 611–12.

72. Memo of 214th NSC, 12 September 1954, ibid., 615–23.

73. Ibid. For details of the reference to the UN, see Rosemary Foot, "The Search for a *Modus Vivendi*: Anglo-American Relations and China Policy in the Eisenhower Era," in Warren Cohen and Akira Iriye (eds.), *Great Powers in East Asia, 1953–1960* (New York: Columbia University Press, 1990).

74. Taipei to DOS, 5 October 1954, ibid., 682.

75. Dulles to the NSC, 28 October 1954, ibid., 811.

76. The treaty was signed on 2 December, sent to the Senate on 6 January 1955, approved by the Senate on 9 February, and became effective on 3 March.

77. Dulles memo for the president, 23 November 1954, AWF, Dulles–Herter Series, Box 4, "Dulles, JF, November 54 (1)," DEPL.

78. During the war scare in March 1955, the *New York Times* editorialized: "If we had been able to persuade our Nationalist Chinese friends to pull out of them [Quemoy and Matsu] when they abandoned the Dachen Islands, we would all be easier in our minds." *New York Times*, 27 March 1955.

79. Gerhart memo for Radford, 28 October 1954, Radford Papers, Box 7, "091 China (Oct.–Dec. 1954)," RG 218, NA.

80. Radford memo, 29 October 1954, *FRUS 1952–54, XIV*, 818–19.

81. Memcon, 7 January 1955, *FRUS 1955–57, II*, 6–8.

82. Memo of conversation with the President, 10 January 1955, ibid., 9.

83. Zhang, *Deterrence and Strategic Culture*, 199.

84. 215 NSC, 24 September 1954, *FRUS 1952–54, XIV*, 659.

85. 216th meeting of NSC, 6 October 1954, ibid., 689.

86. John W. Lewis and Xue Litai, *China Builds the Bomb* (Stanford, CA: Stanford University Press, 1988), 33.

87. Chang and He Di, "The Absence of War," 1512–14.

88. *FRUS 1955–57, II*, 10.

89. Memcon, 19 January 1955, ibid., 38–41.

90. Memcon with the President, 19 January 1955, ibid., 41–43.

91. Memcon, 19 January 1955, ibid., 46–47.

92. Memcon, 19 January 1955, 50–52. Dulles wrote to Robertson on 24 January about his two conversations with Yeh on 19 January: "I am very anxious that the memorandum of the first conversation should show that it was he who first brought up the question of the evacuation of the Dachens and not I. This may be important later on if the Chinats should claim it was we who forced evacuation upon them." Note 1, ibid., 38.

93. 232nd meeting of NSC, 20 January 1955, ibid., 77.

94. Memcons, 20 and 21 January 1955, ibid., 57–62, 100; memo of 232nd meeting of the NSC, ibid., 71.

95. The House passed the resolution by 410 votes to 3 votes on 25 January 1955, and the Senate by 83 to 3 on 28 January 1955. Foster Rhea Dulles, *American Policy Toward Communist China 1949–1969* (New York: Thomas Y. Crowell Co., 1972), 154.

96. DOS to Taipei, #421, 31 January 1955, ibid., 183. Even while making this promise to the Nationalists, Eisenhower and some of his senior advisors were already beginning to have second thoughts. Cutler argued that the United States should not stress that Quemoy was important to the defense of Formosa. The United States might wish to give up Quemoy while retaining Formosa, "because the Quemoys are *not* necessary to the defense of Formosa." Eisenhower desired that US intentions regarding the offshore islands be worded in such a way as not to tie the United States down forever. He did not want to be "hooked" into a defense of Quemoy or Matsu, even if they were attacked by small Chinese forces. Memcon, 19 January and 30 January 1955, ibid., 50–51, 175.

97. Kalicki, *The Pattern of Sino-American Crises*, 140.

98. Beijing to Foreign Office, 28 January 1955, FO371/115028/FC1041/132, PRO, London.

99. 234th meeting of the NSC, 27 January 1955, *FRUS 1955–57*, II, 136.

100. White House memo for the record, 31 January 1955, NND931186.

101. Zhang, *Deterrence and Strategic Culture*, 219. Major General William C. Chase, who had commanded the Military Assistance and Advisory Group (MAAG) in Taiwan, later recalled that "The Red Chinese did not interfere in the least, much to the regret of our naval pilots on the big carriers who were spoiling for a fight." William C. Chase, *Frontline General: The Commands of Maj. Gen. William C. Chase* (Houston: Pacesetter Press, 1975), 193.

102. Washington to FO, 21 January 1955, FO371/115024/FC1041/80, PRO.

103. New York to FO, 20 January 1955, FO371/115024/FC1041/32, Washington to FO, 21 January 1955, ibid., FC 1041/37, and Washington to FO, ibid., FC1041/37, PRO. On Anglo-American differences during this crisis, see Foot, "The Search for a *Modus Vivendi*."

104. Foot, "The Search for a *Modus Vivendi*," 153–55.

105. Lodge to DOS, 6 February 1955, *FRUS 1955–57*, II, 231–33; and Wadsworth to the DOS, 11 February 1955, ibid., 266. Burmese Prime Minister U Nu also conveyed to Dulles Zhou's willingness to negotiate unofficially directly with the United States. Kenneth Young, a State Department official who was present at the occasion, recalled that Dulles "tactfully skirted the proposal." Kenneth Young, *Negotiating with the Communist Chinese: The United States Experience, 1953–1967* (New York: McGraw-Hill, 1968), 43. Hammarksjeold himself did not favor direct Sino-US talks. He wanted it to remain a UN matter. *FRUS 1955–57*, II, 233.

106. Quoted in Jia Q, "Unmaterialized Rapprochement: Sino-American Relations in the Mid-1950s" (Ph.D. dissertation, Cornell University, 1988).

107. New York to FO, 6 February 1955, PREM 11/867, PRO.

108. PREM 11/867, PRO.

109. Intelligence Report #6084, 21 January 1955, PPS Papers, 1955, Lot 66D70, Box 97, "China," RG 59, NA.

110. Dulles to the President, 21 February, *FRUS 1955–57*, II, 300.

111. Dulles to DOS, 25 February, ibid., 308.

112. Washington to FO, 9 February 1955, PREM 11/867, PRO.

113. Dulles telegrams 8, 9, and 10, to DOS, 25 February, *FRUS 1955–57*, II, 309–12.

114. Bangkok to FO, 25 February; Beijing to FO, 28 February; Rangoon to Beijing, 2 March; Beijing to FO, 1 March 1955, all in PREM 11/879, PRO.

115. Memcon with President, 6 March 1955, *FRUS 1955–57*, II, 336–37.

116. *State Department Bulletin*, 21 March, 1955, 459–60.

117. Memcon, 7 March 1955, *FRUS 1955–57*, II, 337.

118. Chang and He Di, "The Absence of War," 1514, 1517.

119. Unsigned report, "Situation on Warning With Regard to Offshore Islands," 9 March 1955, 794a.5/3–955, RG 59, NA.

120. Sebald to the Acting Secretary of State, 21 April 1955, 793.5/4–2155, RG 59, NA.

121. Memo for Record by Adm. Carney, 6 March 1955, *FRUS 1955–57*, II, 334.

122. Cutler memo for record, 11 March 1955, ibid., 357.

123. Samford to Armstrong, 1 April 1955, 793.563/4–155, RG 59, NA.

124. Memo of Rankin's meeting with Chiang, 4 May 1955, Rankin Papers, Box 7, Folder 2, Seeley Mudd Library, Princeton University.

125. Sebald to Acting Secretary, 793.5/4–2155, RG 59, NA.

126. Ridgway, *Soldier*, 278–79.

127. Bohlen to DOS, 10 February 1955, *FRUS 1955–57, II*, 248.

128. Hoover memo for Dulles, 3 March 1955, ibid., 319.

129. Memcon, 9 March 1955, ibid., 342.

130. Editorial note, ibid., 372.

131. Memcon, 14 March 1955, ibid., 371.

132. Cutler memo for record, 11 March 1955, ibid., 357; see also memo for the files, 11 March 1955, AWF, Whitman Diary, Box 4, "March 1955 (6)," DEPL.

133. The administration's principal concern during this period was the fate of the treaty for the Western European Union and the admission of West Germany to NATO, due for ratification by European nations. Dulles feared that a war with China involving nuclear weapons would turn European opinion away from the United States and thus jeopardize ratification of the treaty. See memo of 240th NSC meeting, 10 March 1955, *FRUS 1955–57, II*, 347–48.

134. Cutler memo for the record, 11 March 1955, *FRUS 1955–57, II*, 358–59; Notes of meeting on 11 March 1955, dated 16 March 1955, AWF, International, Box 9, "Formosa—Visit to CINPAC, 1955 (1)," DEPL.

135. Goodpaster memcon, 16 March 1955, *FRUS 1955–57, II*, 360.

136. Goodpaster memo for the record, 18 March 1955, AWF, International, Box 9, "Formosa Visit to CINPAC 1955 (2)," DEPL; Goodpaster memo for the President, 15 March 1955, *FRUS 1955–57, II*, 366–67.

137. Goodpaster memo for the President, 15 March 1955, *FRUS 1955–57, II*, 367.

138. Ibid., 367.

139. James Hagerty, *The Diary of James C. Hagerty: Eisenhower in Mid-Course* (Bloomington: Indiana University Press, 1983), 210.

140. *New York Times*, 16 March 1955.

141. Hagerty, *The Diary of James C. Hagerty*, 211.

142. The *New York Times* headline read: "President Says Atom Bomb Would Be Used Like Bullet." *New York Times*, 17 March 1955. See also Eisenhower, *The White House Years, Vol. 1: Mandate for Change*, 477.

143. Eisenhower, *Mandate for Change*, 477.

144. *New York Times*, 18 March 1955.

145. Eisenhower diary entry, 26 March 1955, *FRUS 1955–57, II*, 405.

146. JCS memo to Secretary of Defense, 27 March 1955, ibid., 406–8.

147. *New York Times*, 26 March 1955.

148. Taipei to DOS, Dispatch # 671, 30 March 1955, White House Central Files, Confidential File, Subject Series, Box 28, "Formosa Question," DEPL. See *Time*, 18 April 1955.

149. Hagerty, *The Diary of James C. Hagerty*, 218–19. See also *New York Times*, 29 March 1955.

150. *New York Times*, 31 March 1955.

151. Hanes memcon, 29 March 1955, Dulles Papers, White House Memo, Box 2, "White House Memoranda, 1955-Formosa Straits (1)," DEPL; *FRUS 1955–57, II*, 409–15. Although Dulles did not think that the thought of nuclear bombing

of Chinese targets would unduly bother Chiang, he thought that the idea might give Chiang pause.

152. Memo of discussions in the 243rd NSC, 31 March 1995, *FRUS 1955–57, II*, 406–8, 432–33. See also ibid., 356–57, Note 6.

153. LeMay to Twining, quoted in Chang, *Friends and Enemies*, 132. The next day the Chinese charged that 18 US planes had overflown Chinese territory in the north and in the south.

154. Ridgway to Radford, undated, AWF, International Series, Box 9, "Formosa Area-US Military Ops—Messages, Directives, etc. (non-presidential), 1," DEPL.

155. Townsend Hoopes, *The Devil and John Foster Dulles* (Boston: Little, Brown & Co., 1973), 278. According to Hoopes, Dulles "possessed a vast technical ignorance of nuclear weapons effects." Ibid., 277. Allen Dulles had told Hagerty that because of the nearness of Quemoy to the mainland, Quemoy itself might receive nuclear fallout from nuclear strikes against the mainland if the winds were wrong. Fallout might also hit the nearby Chinese city of Amoy, with its large population, if the winds were wrong. Hagerty, *The Diary of James C. Hagerty*, 220. It would be surprising if the secretary of state did not receive this information.

156. *New York Times*, 27 March 1955.

157. *New York Times*, 17 March 1955. On 23 March, the AEC tested a small atomic device described as a "satchel" charge with the explosive power of 1 kiloton. One man could carry this weapon in a sneak attack. The same day, US forces conducted a simulated exercise on the use of this weapon. *New York Times*, 24 March 1955.

158. Churchill to Eisenhower, undated, *FRUS 1955–57, II*, 271.

159. Ibid., 271–72.

160. 237th NSC, 17 February 1955, ibid., 280–81.

161. Memcon, 14 March 1955, ibid., 371.

162. *New York Times*, 25 March 1955.

163. Gruenther to Eisenhower, 8 February 1955, AWF, Administration, Box 16, "Gruenther, Gen. Alfred 1955(4)," DEPL.

164. Rockefeller memo for President, 27 June 1955, White House Central File, Confidential File, Subject Series, Box 28, "Formosa Question," DEPL.

165. Eisenhower to Gruenther, 1 February 1955, *FRUS 1955–57, II*, 190.

166. George H. Gallup (ed.), *The Gallup Poll: Public Opinion, 1935–1971, Vol. II* (New York: Random House, 1972), 1319–20, 1322.

167. Eisenhower, *The White House Years, Vol. 1: Mandate for Change*, 481.

168. *New York Times*, 27 March 1955.

169. *New York Times*, 27, 30, 31 March 1955.

170. Bowie memo to Dulles, 7 February 1955, *FRUS 1955–57, II*, 238–40. In any case, the kind of UN resolution that Bowie had in mind did not seem feasible. The British looked on such a course with deep suspicion. They did not wish to be "jockeyed" into the position of having to support the ROC if the Chinese attacked after such a resolution was passed. FO to Washington, 12 March 1955, PREM 11/879, PRO.

171. Memo of 211th NSC meeting, 18 August 1954, *FRUS 1952–54, XIV*, 537.

172. Goodpaster memcon, 19 February 1955, *FRUS 1955–57, II*, 298.

173. Memo of telecon between the president and Dulles, 16 February 1955, ibid., 276–77 note 2.

174. Eisenhower to Dulles, 21 February 1955, ibid., 301–2.

175. Goodpaster memo for the record, 24 March 1955, AWF, International Series, Box 9, "Conferences on Formosa," DEPL.

176. Hagerty diary entry, *FRUS 1955–57, II*, 305.

177. Goodpaster memcon, 4 April 1955, AWF, International Series, Box 9, "Conferences on Formosa," DEPL.

178. Eisenhower to Dulles, 5 April 1955, ibid., 445–50.

179. Dulles memcon, 17 April 1955, ibid., 491–97. Later, in a discussion with Hoover and Carney, Eisenhower suggested avoiding the word "blockade" and using "a more flexible term such as 'maritime zone.' " Goodpaster memo, 25 April 1955, AWF, Whitman Diary, Box 5, "ACW Diary April 1955 (3)," DEPL.

180. Dulles memo for Eisenhower, 6 April 1955, AWF, Dulles–Herter series, Box 5, "Dulles-April 1955 (1)." DEPL. Eisenhower had been rather apprehensive about Judd's reaction and remarked to Dulles that "he's rather emotional and, if the thought is advanced to him, he'll probably see the world going to ruin overnight." Diary Entry, 6 April 1955, AWF, DDE Diary, Box 9, "Phone Calls—January–July 1955 (2)," DEPL.

181. *FRUS 1955–57, II*, 277.

182. Robertson to Dulles, undated, NND 931186.

183. Robertson to Dulles, 25 April, ibid., 510–15.

184. CINPAC to CNO, 28 April 1955, containing Robertson to Dulles, Radford Papers, Box 7, "091 China (April–December 1955)," RG 218, NA.

185. Diary entry for 26 September 1958, AWF, AW Diary, Box 10, "September 1958," DEPL.

186. *FRUS 1955–57, II*, 507–8, Note 3.

187. *FRUS 1955–57, II*, 527.

188. *New York Times*, 28 April 1955.

189. Chang and He Di, "The Absence of War," 1515–17.

190. Dulles statement, USIS press release, 3 March 1955.

191. Part of the blame should go to the Chinese for failing to highlight their offer of talks. They failed to take any diplomatic initiatives to back up their offer, perhaps in the hope that US allies and neutral nations would try on their own to secure a US withdrawal from the Taiwan Strait. They probably overestimated the influence of international opinion on Washington. The Chinese seemed to have misread the significance of the elections of 1954, in which the Democrats regained control of Congress. Perhaps they thought the election results were a reflection of the popular opposition to the administration's policy and to war. Kalicki, *The Pattern of Sino-American Crises*, 124.

192. Memo by Attorney General on Congressional Attitude to Formosa Defense, enclosed to Lay memo to the NSC, 13 September 1954, OSANSA, Special Assistant Series, Presidential Subseries, Box 2, "President's Papers 1954 (7)," DEPL.

193. Smith to Dulles, 7 April 1955, Dulles Papers, Gen. Correspondence and Memo Series, Box 3, "Strictly Confidential, Q-S (3)," DEPL.

194. Dulles memo for the President, 6 April 1955, AWF, Dulles–Herter Series, Box 5, "Dulles April 1955 (1)," DEPL.

195. *New York Times*, 24 April 1955. Probably the only member of Congress to strongly support military action to defend the offshore islands was Congressman James P. Richards, Chairman, House Foreign Affairs Committee. He told Ambassador Koo that he "had clearly understood at the time the Congressional Resolution was first discussed in the House that the Government would help defend Quemoy and Matsu if attacked by the Communists." He "had understood from Adm. Radford who had testified before his committee that Quemoy and Matsu were important for the security of Formosa and the Pescadores because the port of Amoy under Communist control was very close to Quemoy." If the administration declined to defend them, "he would get up in the House and publicly declare his understanding." He believed that other members of Congress who held similar views would act likewise. Memo of conversation, 9 February 1955, Box 195, Koo Papers.

196. *New York Times*, 29 April, 1955.

197. Eisenhower, *The White House Years, Vol. 1: Mandate for Change*, 478.

198. Memcon, 30 March 1955, *FRUS 1955–57, II*, 425. Churchill probably understood how Dulles felt. He said at the Commonwealth prime ministers meeting that "it was essential always to appreciate how this situation was regarded by Americans. Never before had such a great nation been threatened with war by so weak a power. . . . It was contrary to the Russian interest to commit themselves to support of Beijing at this stage; knowing this, the Americans might well feel that they could safely take action against China alone." Minutes of Commonwealth Prime Ministers' Meeting, 4 February 1955, PREM/11/867, PRO.

199. Zhang, *Deterrence and Strategic Culture*, 195.

200. Bohlen to SD, 27 January 1955, *FRUS 1955–57, II*, 147–48.

201. Eisenhower to Gruenther, 1 February 1955, ibid., 192; Hagerty, *The Diary of James C. Hagerty*, 186; Minutes of Cabinet meeting, 11 March 1955, *FRUS 1955–57, II*, 353.

202. NIE, 16 March 1955, ibid., 378.

203. Eisenhower to Gruenther, 1 February 1955, *FRUS 1955–57, II*, 190.

204. *FRUS 1952–54, XIV*, 240–41.

205. Dulles worried that the morale of the Nationalist forces was so bad that the Chinese might win over some of the Nationalist generals through bribery. He told the NSC that "This had happened many times before in the history of China, and indeed one of the reasons for becoming a general in China was to get oneself bought."

206. *FRUS 1952–54, XIV*, 10–11.

207. PPS memo, 28 March 1955, Dulles Papers, White House Memo Series, Box 2, "Position papers on offshore islands, April–May 1955 (2)," DEPL.

208. Rankin to Robertson, 13 March 1955, Rankin Papers, Box 7, Folder 1, Princeton University.

209. Eisenhower memo for Dulles, 5 April 1955, *FRUS 1955–57, II*, 447–48.

210. Ibid., 448. The US Embassy did a "discreet survey" of morale in the ROC. It showed that the mutual security treaty had to a large extent offset the adverse impact of the loss of Dachens. Karl Lott Rankin, *China Assignment* (Seattle: University of Washington Press, 1964), 227.

211. Hagerty, *The Diary of James C. Hagerty*, 183.

212. Eisenhower to Gruenther, 1 February 1955, *FRUS 1955–57, II*, 192.

213. 237th meeting of the NSC, 17 February, ibid., 284.

214. Eisenhower, *The White House Years, Vol. 1: Mandate for Change*, 483.

215. Memo of 183rd meeting of the NSC, 4 February 1954, *FRUS 1952–54, XIV*, 356.

216. *Newsweek* quoted US officials as stating that the junks would be sitting ducks for the Seventh Fleet. The Nationalists claimed destroying more than 100 of these crafts in one day. *Newsweek*, 30 August and 20 September 1954.

217. Bundy, *Danger and Survival*, 526. See also ibid., 273–87. For a similar view, see Gaddis, *The Long Peace*, 136–45.

218. Brands, "Testing Massive Retaliation."

219. Minutes of the 209th NSC, 5 August 1954, AWF, NSC, 5, DEPL.

220. 240th meeting of the NSC, 10 March 1955, *FRUS 1955–57, II*, 346–49.

221. See notes 152–54. See also "Deployment by Country 1951–1977," NSA website; Kalicki, *The Pattern of Sino-American Crises*, 149.

222. Memo of 200th NSC meeting, 3 June 1954, AWF, NSC Series, Box 5, DEPL.

223. Draft by Dulles, 19 March 1955, Dulles Papers, White House Memo Series, Box 2, "White House Memoranda, 1955—Formosa Straits (2)," DEPL. It is not clear why Dulles prepared this paper, or to whom he showed it.

224. "History of the Custody and Deployment of Nuclear Weapons," and "Deployment by Country 1951–1977," NSA website.

225. Nevertheless, there was a softer side to Dulles. Hagerty has recorded that "As we finished our work [going over the message on the Formosa Resolution], Dulles walked to the front door with me and then outside. 'I'm as nervous as a kitten. I feel just the same way I did waiting for my son to be born. It's a ticklish and very delicate question, and of course, none of us knows how the Chinese are going to react.' " Hagerty, *The Diary of James C. Hagerty*, 172.

226. CINPAC to CNO, #2242/2243, 9 April 1955, Sec. 22, CCS 381F (11–8–48), Sec. 21, RG 218, NA.

227. In June 1953, Dulles had argued in the NSC that the United States need not refrain from "doing what it ought to do simply because certain of its actions might serve the Soviets as a pretext for war." *FRUS 1952–54, II*, 375. On the talk of "preventive war" during the Eisenhower administration, see Marc Trachtenberg, *History and Strategy* (Princeton, NJ: Princeton University Press, 1991). See also Russell D. Buhite and William Hamel, "War for Peace: The Question of American Preventive War Against the Soviet Union, 1945–1955," *Diplomatic History* (Summer 1990).

228. Hagerty, *The Diary of James C. Hagerty*, 186.

CHAPTER 5

"Who's Daddy" in the Taiwan Strait? The Offshore Islands Crisis of 1958

The shelling of Quemoy on 23 August 1958 by the PLA found the United States caught in a trap. The shelling, preceded by China's military buildup in its Fujian coast (opposite Taiwan), seemed to many in the United States to herald an invasion of the offshore islands. The strategic importance of the islands did not justify US military intervention in their defense. However, with one-third of the Nationalist army deployed in Quemoy and Matsu, the fall of the islands to communist China would have spelled disaster for the ROC. Therefore, the Eisenhower administration decided to intervene in the defense of the islands. American plans for the defense of the offshore islands called for the use of nuclear weapons against targets in mainland China. However, domestic and international opinion strongly opposed a nuclear war in defense of the tiny islands and forced a change in the US policy. Nevertheless, for a time, the United States found itself in a crisis in which it probably came closer to using nuclear weapons than on any other occasion after the atomic bombing of Nagasaki.

Some accounts of this crisis, written before significant volumes of American documents for the period were declassified, have treated the episode as a case of successful American deterrence of a Chinese attempt to invade the offshore islands.[1] In recent years, several studies based on newly declassified American documents as well as Chinese sources have examined this crisis. Shu Guang Zhang treats the crisis as a case of mutual Sino-American deterrence. Thomas J. Christensen argues that Mao's primary goal in the crisis was to mobilize domestic support for the Great Leap Forward. George Eliades focuses on the role of public opinion in moderating the US policy in the crisis.[2]

This study agrees with the conclusion that public opinion succeeded in bringing about a major shift in the American policy in the crisis. However, it argues that the crisis has far greater significance than has been hitherto understood for the United States's China policy as well as its strategic policy. The initial American war plans and force dispositions and the very real possibility that a Chinese escalation of the crisis would have left the United States no choice but to use atomic weapons made the risk of a nuclear war extremely high. By exposing the disadvantages of the American reliance on nuclear deterrence and emphasizing the need for conventional forces to deal with situations short of total war, this episode highlighted the flaws of the Eisenhower administration's New Look national security policy. The evidence now available suggests that China did not plan an invasion of the offshore islands and that the Chinese decision to deescalate was not in response to US deterrence signals. This episode, therefore, cannot be treated as a case of American deterrence of a Chinese invasion. The crisis highlighted the folly of allowing Nationalist leader Chiang Kai-shek to determine American policy on the basis of Nationalist priorities. As a consequence, the US policy toward East Asia underwent a fundamental change. Behind the cover of their uncompromising rhetoric, China and the United States made a series of parallel concessions that defused the crisis. The United States distanced itself publicly from Chiang's ambitions for a return to the Chinese mainland and clearly signaled its intention to end Nationalist guerrilla attacks on the mainland. This ended the threat to China from its southern flank for the first time since the founding of the PRC. By transforming the US-ROC equation, this crisis ultimately worked to China's advantage.

THE PRELUDE TO THE CRISIS

By the time the first crisis in this area ended in April 1955, the rationale underpinning the US policy in the crisis, and consequently the policy itself, had undergone a significant change. Eisenhower questioned the validity of the ROC's claim that the loss of the offshore islands would destroy the morale of the Nationalists in Taiwan. He realized that the American commitment to the defense of the offshore islands did not enjoy the support of the American public. Doubts also rose about the administration's conviction that the use of tactical nuclear weapons in airbursts would not lead to large-scale civilian casualties.[3] At the very outset of the crisis in the fall of 1958, however, the Eisenhower administration reversed itself on all of these points.

The Sino-American ambassadorial talks in Geneva that began after the first Taiwan Strait crisis ended did not lead to any substantive improvement in Sino-US relations or to a reduction in tension in the area. Zhou

Enlai's offer at Bandung in April 1955 for direct talks between the United States and China had led Dulles to expect a cease-fire agreement and thus an end to the crisis in the Taiwan Strait. Dulles hoped China would not attack the offshore islands while the talks went on in the full glare of worldwide publicity.[4] The talks commenced in Geneva in August 1955, with Ambassador U. Alexis Johnson representing the United States and Ambassador Wang Bingnan representing China.[5] By 10 September, the two sides reached agreement on the repatriation of Americans imprisoned in China on espionage charges since the Korean War and the repatriation of Chinese nationals in the United States, whose return to China Washington was blocking. China made most of the concessions that led to this agreement.[6] Beijing obviously took a conciliatory line in the talks in the expectation that more substantive issues would next be taken up for discussion between Zhou and Dulles.

The United States, however, refused to proceed to substantive issues, such as relaxation of the US trade embargo on China imposed during the Korean War. Washington hoped to stall the discussion of such issues by negotiating in detail the steps for the implementation of the agreement on repatriation of the prisoners.[7] When it appeared that further delay might prompt China to break off the talks, the United States brought in the question of renunciation of force by China in its Taiwan policy. Washington hoped this would sidetrack discussion of the issues proposed by China.[8] Wang presented draft agreements that, without specifically referring to Taiwan, expressed Chinese willingness to settle disputes with the United States by peaceful means. To Johnson, some of these drafts appeared to go a long way toward meeting American demands. The tenor of Washington's instructions to Johnson, however, indicated that in case China accepted the US terms, he must stall further progress in the talks. The State Department considered that a Chinese agreement on renunciation of force would not "constitute much if any greater deterrent than their [China's] continued participation in negotiations along present lines."[9] China's hopes for relaxation of the American trade embargo met no better fate.[10] On 28 June 1957, Dulles said in a speech in San Francisco,

Internationally, the Chinese Communist regime does not conform to the practices of civilized nations; does not live up to its international obligations; has not been peaceful in the past and gives no evidence of being peaceful in the future. Its foreign policies are hostile to us and our Asian allies. Under these circumstances, it would be folly for us to establish relations with the Chinese Communists which would enhance their ability to hurt us and our friends.[11]

Dulles's speech firmly shut the door to progress in the talks with China. To China, US moves appeared headed toward a "two-China policy."[12]

By the end of 1957, the two countries required only a pretext for breaking off the talks. In December, Washington transferred Johnson and announced that his deputy would henceforth represent the United States.[13] Objecting to the downgrading of the talks, China refused to continue the meetings at the lower level. Robertson recommended naming a new ambassador to succeed Johnson. Dulles, however, was concerned that "the only things left to talk about are those subjects which the Communists insist upon." He thought that the Chinese refusal to continue the talks below the level of ambassadors gave the United States "a plausible opportunity to break off the talks" and that "if we do not take advantage of this opportunity, we may be in for trouble."[14] The United States understandably dragged its feet over designating a successor to Johnson. On 30 June, China demanded that Washington nominate an ambassador within 15 days to resume the talks. A US spokesman responded that although the question of Johnson's successor was under consideration, Washington would not abide by any Chinese ultimatum. The State Department waited until 17 July before informing China that it had designated Jacob Beam, the US ambassador in Warsaw, to represent the United States in the talks.[15]

CHINA'S MOTIVES

Even before the ambassadorial talks had first begun in August 1955, the Nationalists had initiated a step that was to have a profound influence on the 1958 crisis. In July 1955 (less than three months after the abortive Robertson–Radford mission to Taiwan), the ROC began moving an army division from Taiwan to Quemoy, despite objections by the chief of the MAAG in Taiwan. The JCS assured a worried Robertson that the movement of one division from Taiwan did not "substantially diminish the defensibility of Taiwan and the Pescadores." Nor, in their view, did the deployment of an additional division to Quemoy substantially increase that island's defensibility. However, they did not consider this matter worth pursuing.[16]

Chiang, however, did not stop with one division. The reinforcement of the offshore islands continued until the forces there reached about 110,000 (85,000 of them on Quemoy alone), representing one-third of the total Nationalist strength. The United States was then confronted with the prospect that the loss of these heavily defended islands to China might endanger the survival of the ROC. Most likely, Chiang intended to use the presence of the troops there to trap the United States into defending the islands, on the plea that their fall to China now would be catastrophic for the ROC. Indeed, Dulles used this argument to persuade Eisenhower to commit the United States to the defense of Quemoy and Matsu when the crisis began in August 1958. The Nationalist reinforcement of these islands thus proved to be an important factor in determining whether the United States would intervene in this crisis.[17]

After the crisis began, there was much hand-wringing in Washington over Chiang's making his soldiers "hostages" on the islands with the aim of gaining leverage over American policy and then "whining" to the United States.[18] However, it does not appear that anyone—the State Department, the Pentagon, or the CIA—informed Eisenhower of the reinforcement of the offshore islands, undertaken in direct opposition to his wishes, or strongly opposed the Nationalist action. Nor does it appear that the significance of this development was discussed at the highest levels of the administration at this early stage.[19]

The immediate origins of the crisis coincided with the end of the talks in Geneva in the last weeks of 1957. On 9 December, the PLA's deputy chief of staff informed the Chinese government that Nationalist planes had frequently intruded into Chinese air space and dropped propaganda material over coastal cities. Chinese aircraft were unable to intercept these intruders from their bases in the interior of China. On 18 December, Mao ordered the PLA Air Force to consider moving its planes to the air bases in the Fujian province.[20] Soon after the air force began preparations for moving fighters into these airfields, the CMC ordered the Fujian Military Command (FMC) to prepare plans for an artillery attack on the offshore islands. The FMC completed the plans in April 1958. Beijing, however, decided to wait for an opportune moment to begin the shelling.[21]

In July, a crisis in the Middle East offered Mao an opportunity to implement his plan. On 15 July, Anglo-American troops landed in Lebanon and Jordan. On 17 July, Chiang placed the ROC forces on alert. That same day, the CCP Central Committee made the decision to shell Quemoy.[22] On 18 July, the CMC received Mao's orders for air units to move to the coastal bases on 27 July. Despite the typhoon that hit the area on 19 July, causing massive floods, support personnel moved into the Fujian airfields on 24 July and set up a command post. After the PLA set up 21 radar sites and anti-aircraft batteries, 48 MiG-17 fighters moved to the Liancheng and Shantou air bases in the Fujian and Guangdong provinces on 27 July. By the middle of August, a total of 520 aircraft had moved into these and other coastal airfields. The rules of engagement prohibited the PLA Air Force from operations over the high seas, bombing Quemoy and Matsu unless the Nationalists bombed the mainland, or attacking US aircraft except in self-defense. Mao also decided to start the shelling of Quemoy on 25 July. However, he postponed the shelling at the last minute. After spending a sleepless night pondering over the matter, he decided to wait for a better opportunity. Mao hoped Chiang would order an attack on the mainland, to which China could respond with a counterattack. He wrote Defense Minister Peng Dehui: "We must

persist in the principle of fighting no battle we are not sure of winning."
With uncharacteristic candor, Mao added: "To make a plan too quickly
usually results in an unthoughtful consideration. I did such things quite
often and sometimes had unavoidable miscalculations."[23]

It is not easy to pin down Mao's exact motives for starting the shelling
of Quemoy. Several considerations, such as dealing with the security
threat to China from the Nationalists and the United States, supporting
the Arabs, intra-bloc rivalry, probing the American resolve to support
the Nationalists, and domestic considerations, have been cited to explain
Mao's decision.[24] Christensen, whose study is the most comprehensive
and analytical treatment of Mao's motives in initiating this crisis, concludes that "if Mao had motives other than mobilization of the public
around the Great Leap, they were secondary."[25] A detailed examination
of Mao's motive in embarking on a confrontation with the United States
is beyond the scope of this study. In the absence of the kind of documentary evidence required for making a definitive judgment on Mao's
thinking, one can only speculate. No single factor—domestic political
considerations, security considerations, and intra-bloc considerations—
was perhaps sufficient by itself to persuade Mao to start on a course that
might well have sparked off a direct clash with US forces that he did
not want. The very first military step—ordering the air force to the Fujian
bases—certainly seems to have had its origin in security considerations,
and by itself, served to set off a crisis. It is quite possible that Mao first
conceived of the idea of shelling Quemoy as a military response to the
aggressive Nationalist actions, and later, thought of using the shelling to
probe American intentions, and still later decided to take advantage of
the resulting crisis for domestic propaganda purposes.

An examination of the events in the Taiwan Strait in the period between the two crises shows that Mao did indeed have adequate security
grounds for the very limited and circumscribed military moves he initiated. In September 1954, Eisenhower had ordered the end of Nationalist
commando raids against the mainland. In January 1955, however, he
agreed to permit "small scale" raids by the Nationalists for intelligence
gathering. The government in Taipei interpreted this directive rather
loosely and resumed guerrilla attacks against China from their bases in
Quemoy and Matsu. Nationalist forces conducted training exercises under the observation of the Chinese in order to advertise their ability to
launch larger raids. In 1957, these acts began to assume a more serious
turn.[26] In February 1958, the Nationalists proposed training paratroops
for covert operations in the mainland. Chiang wanted to raise a force of
30,000 trained in parachute landings and special operations to infiltrate
the mainland and instigate uprisings against the PRC. Washington advised Taipei to economize in other areas so the ROC could train even
more than the 3,000 paratroops funded by the fiscal year 1958 aid pro-

gram.[27] In Taipei, US Ambassador Everett Drumwright, MAAG Chief Vice Admiral A. K. Doyle, and his subordinates all favored encouraging and supporting the Nationalists "to resume infiltration activities ... which would have as their basic purpose the creation of bases of resistance on the mainland."[28]

Early in January 1957, in their largest overflight of the mainland and their first ever over Beijing since they withdrew to Taiwan, Nationalist planes dropped propaganda leaflets over the Chinese capital and several other major Chinese cities, calling on the Chinese people to revolt against communist rule. Around this time, the United States began construction of a large air base in Taiwan that could handle even B-52 bombers. On 6 May, the United States announced its plan to station medium-range nuclear-capable Matador missiles in Taiwan. Press reports stated that although these missiles could fire conventional or atomic warheads, "For practical purposes the missile's usefulness as a weapon would be largely as a carrier of atomic warheads." The reports did not disclose whether atomic warheads were being sent to Taiwan but speculated that they "could be stationed with US personnel in Taiwan or kept at naval or air bases nearby to be flown there in the event of war." The Chinese charged the United States with converting Taiwan into a second Okinawa. Atomic weapons, they declared, would not frighten them.[29]

Throughout the period between the two crises, Washington faced a dilemma that Ambassador Karl Rankin summed up succinctly:

the basic decision was, whether Formosa should be considered simply a strategically important island which should be denied to the Communists, or an important factor which could be helped to play a significant part in the eventual liberation of mainland China from Communist rule.

The trend of the US policy seemed to him to indicate the former alternative.[30] The Nationalists, however, found this unacceptable. They did not abandon their talk of returning to the mainland. Nor did the United States disassociate itself publicly from such Nationalist aspirations. Chiang nourished the hope that Eisenhower would prove more amenable to Nationalist designs in his second term. Soon after Eisenhower's reelection, Chiang wrote to him of his hope for initiating military steps to return to the mainland. The Hungarian uprisings and reports of unrest in China revived the aging Nationalist supremo's hopes. In his reply, Eisenhower, while paying lip service to the UN principles, agreed that, "We must be prepared to take advantage of any such developments [unrest in China] in an appropriate manner when the time comes." In the National Security Council, Dulles strongly opposed any change in the (offensive) mission of the ROC armed forces and deletion of reference to the possibility of a return to the mainland in the new US policy toward the ROC under formulation in Washington. Eisenhower defended the need to let Chiang believe that he could return to China. NSC 5723, the new policy statement approved on 4 October 1957, retained the policy of continuing covert activities against China. US policy in this period seemed to display a noticeable shift toward Rankin's second alternative.

US and Nationalist actions began to take on a more ominous turn from the Chinese point of view in the beginning of 1958. In January 1958, Admiral Doyle informed the Taipei press that the Matador missiles would be used in retaliation for Chinese attacks. "Observers" speculated that nuclear warheads were stored in Taiwan or Okinawa. Information now available shows that the nuclear warheads were in fact stored in Taiwan, along with other US bases in the area, and on US warships in the Pacific. In March, the Pentagon announced the consolidation of the various US military groups in Taiwan into the Headquarters, US Taiwan Defense Command and Military Assistance and Advisory Group. In April and May, US, Taiwanese, and South Korean forces conducted joint exercises involving the firing of Matador missiles. These developments and the pronouncements of American officials on the need for nuclear forces for limited war led Chinese analysts to conclude by early 1958 that China might face American nuclear strikes in any future confrontation with the United States.[31]

The Chinese had good reasons to resent what they perceived to be an ominous turn of events. Their behavior had been fairly restrained while talks went on in Geneva. They had built airfields close to Taiwan in 1955 itself but had refrained from deploying combat aircraft on them. After 20 July 1955, they had initiated very little shelling of the offshore islands and had even refrained from responding to Nationalist shelling. In the Geneva talks, they had gone quite far to secure an accommodation with the United States.[32]

The provocative Nationalist activities, Dulles's uncompromising stance on accommodation with China, the reinforcement of the offshore islands far beyond the requirements for its defense, and the arrival of the Matador missiles gave China grounds for concern. Mao might well have been speaking what was really on his mind when he argued that the best way to deal with the threat to China was to "demonstrate our boldness" by embroiling the United States in a localized crisis of China's choice as part of a strategy of "active defense." This was in keeping with China's experience in the first Taiwan Strait crisis. A policy of controlled crisis then had enabled China to acquire the Dachens and secured American agreement to enter into direct bilateral negotiations.

THE CRISIS BEGINS

Once the Chinese Air Force moved to its bases near the coast, Nationalist reconnaissance flights over the mainland began to meet with increasing opposition and the rate of interception of these flights increased. In an encounter with four Nationalist F-84s on 29 July, Chinese MiG-17 fighters shot down two of the Nationalist fighters and damaged another without sustaining any losses themselves. To retaliate against possible Nationalist bombing of the mainland, the PLA moved two Il-28 bomber regiments and a Tu-4 bomber regiment to the coastal area.[33]

China, however, did not undertake the kind of buildup of ground and naval forces required for launching an invasion of the offshore islands. In fact, Chinese troop strength opposite Taiwan remained unchanged. The US Embassy in Taiwan felt that Chinese threats to liberate Taiwan did not constitute a threat of direct attack against the island but might be aimed at gaining air superiority over the Taiwan Strait and interdiction of the offshore islands. Chinese actions could also be reactions to the Nationalist overflights and covert operations against China. In the embassy's view, "We can hardly expect Commies to remain wholly passive while GRC [the ROC] carries out [the] type of anti-mainland operations" that Chiang had proposed for US concurrence.[34] "It is highly possible," Robertson wrote Dulles, "that . . . Peiping's [Beijing's] move represents the first of a series of probing actions designed to test GRC and, more importantly, United States reactions."[35]

When the National Security Council met on August 7 in the absence of Secretary of State Dulles, CIA Director Allen Dulles reported that although the situation was "heating up," the Chinese buildup did not yet point to an immediate invasion. However, Chinese control of the air over the Taiwan Strait raised the possibility of a Chinese aerial and naval blockade of the offshore islands. The CIA chief observed that the Nationalist attacks on Chinese shipping had offered China a precedent for attacks on Nationalist shipping. Eisenhower asserted that under the Formosa Resolution, the Chinese air activity did not justify US intervention unless it was a prelude to an attack on Taiwan.[36]

When the president and the secretary of state met on August 12, however, Dulles argued that in view of the integration of Quemoy and Matsu with the rest of the ROC, he "doubted whether there could be an amputation without fatal consequences to Formosa itself." When Eisenhower objected that "this was not true from a military standpoint," Dulles responded that "the connection from a political and psychological angle" had become so strong that the United States could no longer allow China to take these islands. He felt that "the Communist bloc might now be pushing all around the perimeter" to see whether the Soviet possession of nuclear missiles had weakened American resolution. China, he insisted, needed to be given a further warning.[37]

Washington had recognized the possibility of a Chinese interdiction of the resupply of the offshore islands at least as early as January 1956. However, US forces had not prepared plans to meet this contingency. Plans for the defense of Quemoy and Matsu, formulated in the midst of the earlier crisis in the Strait, called for nuclear strikes on targets deep inside China. If necessary, atomic strikes using low-yield weapons would include targets in the densely populated Canton, Nanjing, and Shanghai areas. Intelligence estimates anticipated that if US forces carried out this plan, the Soviet Union and China might well respond with nuclear attacks on Taiwan and the Seventh Fleet. Under the US strategic doctrine, "this would be the signal for general nuclear war" between the Soviet Union and the United States. Gerard Smith, director of the Policy Planning Staff in the State Department, therefore urged the development of an alternative military plan that would limit hostilities to the Taiwan Strait. Until such a capability was created, he recommended delaying a public declaration of a US commitment to the defense of Quemoy and Matsu. The JCS, however, did not believe that the United States could defend these islands with only conventional forces, even if the Chinese threat was limited to these islands and not to Taiwan proper. They advised State Department planners that although it was possible, it would be difficult even to keep open the supply lines to the offshore islands with conventional weapons only.[38]

Senior State and Defense Department officials, including the Joint Chiefs of Staff, considered the problem in a meeting called by Secretary of State Dulles on 22 August. The participants agreed that the president should publicly announce that the ties between Taiwan and the offshore islands had now grown so close that the United States could not treat the offshore islands as separate from Taiwan. An attack on them now would not be considered a limited attack. If China attacked these islands, the United States would support a Nationalist military response.[39]

The Strategic Air Command meanwhile placed five B-47 bombers (which had been configured to carry only nuclear bombs) on alert in Guam. Washington also ordered other air and naval reinforcements to the area. As a deterrent to China as well as to reassure Chiang, the administration made public on August 23 a letter from Dulles to the chairman of the House Foreign Affairs Committee, in which Dulles asserted that the ties between Formosa and the offshore islands had increased in the last four years. The letter warned that "It would be highly hazardous for anyone to assume" that if the Chinese invaded the islands, "this act could be considered or held to a 'limited operation.'"[40]

Some of the US responses to the Chinese buildup had begun even earlier. On 3 August, the air force deployed F-100 fighters in Taiwan to offset the superiority of the Chinese MiG-17 fighters over the Nationalists' F-86s. On 5 August, the CNO ordered an attack carrier group to remain in the Taiwan area and for two destroyers to maintain a continuous patrol in the Taiwan Strait. On 6 August, the US Pacific Air Force went on alert. The ROC forces and the Seventh Fleet had already been placed on alert on 17 July, "in view of the present explosive situation in the Middle East" caused by the Lebanon crisis.[41]

After waiting fruitlessly for three weeks for the Nationalists to either attack the mainland or pull out of the offshore islands, on 20 August, Mao decided to go ahead with the shelling of Quemoy. He hoped that "After being hit by us for a period of time, the enemy might consider either evacuating from Jinmen/Mazu [Quemoy/Matsu] or putting up a last-ditch defense there. Whether we attack these islands will depend on how the military situation changes. One step at a time."[42]

On 22 August, Mao ordered that shelling would start at noon the next day. Before he made this decision, Mao summoned General Ye Fei, head of the FMC, to Beidaihe to satisfy himself that Chinese shelling would not inflict needless American casualties. To avoid confrontations with US air power, Mao ordered the PLA not to pursue intruding Nationalist aircraft into the air space over the offshore islands.[43] Later that day, Mao placed his goals before the Politburo: the United States should withdraw its forces from Taiwan and the Nationalist forces should withdraw from the offshore islands. On 25 August he explained to the Politburo that "The main purpose of our bombardment was not to reconnoitre Jiang's [Chiang's] defenses on these islands, but to probe the attitude of the Americans in Washington, testing their determination." Mao told the Supreme State Conference that "We, however, do not intend to launch an immediate landing on Jinmen-Mazu [Quemoy-Matsu]. [Our bombardment] was merely aimed at testing and scaring the Americans, but we would land if the circumstances allowed."[44]

The crisis entered a new phase on August 23, with the Chinese firing 20,000 artillery rounds on Quemoy. The next day, they attempted to capture Tungting, a small island near Quemoy. The Nationalists easily repelled this attempt. After this, China did not attempt an invasion of any of the offshore islands. Although sporadic shelling continued, the majority of the shells fired on the islands carried propaganda material rather than explosives. Chinese forces did not bombard airfield and port installations in Quemoy despite having the air and artillery capability to do so, leading US naval officials to believe that they had no desire to destroy these facilities. Chinese PT boats sank a Nationalist landing craft and damaged a second one on 24 August. However, despite the limited nature of China's action and the realization that communist propaganda "had left the way open for breaking off" the operation, China now appeared to the CIA to be "prepared to do more than merely prevent Chinese Nationalist operations over the mainland."[45]

THE US RESPONSE

The United States quickly responded to the Chinese shelling. On the first day of the intensified crisis, US forces mobilized to support the Nationalists. In a meeting with senior advisers on 25 August, held in the absence of the vacationing secretary of state, Eisenhower confirmed that unlike in 1954, the United States was now "concerned also with the larger offshore islands." Intelligence estimates showed that China had not yet built up adequate ground and amphibious forces to the level required for an invasion of the offshore islands. It thus did not appear that they intended to invade these islands. Nevertheless, the president "thought it desirable to make a show of force, with a few calculated leaks" of US actions. He ordered the reinforcement of the Seventh Fleet and air defense forces in Taiwan and US naval escort of Nationalist re-supply operations within international waters. The Seventh Fleet's strength quickly increased to 5 aircraft carriers, 3 cruisers, 41 destroyers and destroyer escorts, and 7 attack submarines. CINPAC doubted that the islands could be defended against a major Chinese attack using conventional weapons only but began urgent planning to determine US capabilities and force requirements in case the president did not authorize use of nuclear weapons.[46]

As Eisenhower recalled later, his dilemma was that he could not spell out in advance exactly what he would do. He could not say that the United States would defend "every protruding rock that was claimed by the Nationalists as an 'offshore island.'" If, however, he specified what islands the United States *would* defend, the Chinese would be free to attack the remaining ones. He did not wish to put the United States "on the line with a full commitment" to the Nationalists. "The Orientals," he warned, "can be very devious; they would then call the tune."[47]

A high-level meeting on 29 August, with Dulles again absent, considered three distinct phases of possible Chinese action: (1) harassment of the offshore islands and interdiction of their supply; (2) invasion of one or more of the islands; and (3) extension of operations against Taiwan itself. Pentagon representatives suggested that in case of phase one, the United States should support the Nationalists, but should itself stay out of the fighting. In case of phase two, US forces should intervene without using atomic weapons or extending operations beyond the immediate tactical area. In case of phase three, the US commander should seek instructions from Washington. The president wondered whether US forces should not use tactical atomic weapons in case of phase two itself. However, he agreed to keep them in reserve, so as not to "outrage world opinion." Since the Chinese action so far did not appear to go beyond phase one, for the moment he ordered US forces to escort Nationalist convoys engaged in the resupply of Quemoy. However, US forces would stay within international waters.[48]

The JCS now ordered US forces in the area to prepare to assist the Nationalists in case a major Chinese attack endangered the principal offshore islands. If necessary, they could attack Chinese coastal air bases. Only conventional weapons would be used initially. Preparations for the eventual use of atomic weapons, however, were authorized. If the president approved the use of atomic weapons, bombing would extend to targets deep inside China. A nuclear-configured Strategic Air Command (SAC) B-47 squadron stood ready on Guam. A wing-strength reinforcement of the SAC would be ready for first strike 30 hours after authorization.[49]

The presidential directive to proceed on the basis that only conventional weapons would be used initially, and that nuclear weapons would only be used as a last resort with specific approval of the president, caught naval and air force commanders unprepared. It caused "much anxiety" for Admiral Harry D. Felt, commander in chief, Pacific Fleet. His forces, he feared, were inadequate to overcome the numerically larger Chinese forces in a protracted conventional operation. Reinforcing his command required a massive airlift. US forces did not initially have operational plans for assisting the Nationalist resupply of Quemoy. They began planning for convoy escort only in late August, when it became clear that the Nationalists alone could not resupply Quemoy. They completed the plans by 3 September, and the first convoy sailed three days later.[50]

AMERICAN THINKING

When the administration chose to explain its intention to defend the offshore islands, it put forth two somewhat contradictory explanations. Eisenhower claimed that he was concerned that the capture of the offshore islands might lead to the loss of Taiwan. This would endanger the security of Japan, the Philippines, Thailand, Vietnam, and Okinawa. As he explained in his memoirs, "This modern possibility that 'for want of a nail, a shoe was lost' [sic] had led to reaffirmation of the conclusion that Quemoy and Matsu were essential to America's security." The second explanation argued that the United States itself did not look upon the offshore islands as very important for the defense of Taiwan, but had no way of getting the Nationalists to budge from there. Chiang adamantly refused to accept any suggestion that detracted from his claim to be the head of the legitimate government of all of China, or the loss of any territory still under his control.[51]

The administration's problem was that the stakes involved in this crisis did not appear to anyone, except a few die-hard supporters of the Nationalists, to be worth the risks involved. The arguments about the offshore islands' strategic importance and the linkage between these islands and morale in Taiwan were by now several years old and sounded less and less convincing. CINPAC believed that, "From a pure military point of view, they are not worth the risk of getting involved" in even a limited war.[52] As Admiral Arleigh Burke, CNO, told Eisenhower,

They [the offshore islands] don't mean anything, it is a purely symbolic thing, they don't mean anything except, who's daddy? Who runs that part of the world, the Red Chinese or Nationalist Chinese? . . . It is like the virtue of a man's wife. . . . you don't let anybody attack her. You just don't do it.[53]

Raising the question of American credibility, the Basic National Security Policy that the administration approved in the spring of 1958 commented that "uncertainty is growing whether US massive nuclear capabilities would be used to defend Free World interests." The "disastrous character of general nuclear war, the danger of local conflicts developing into general war, and the serious effect of further Communist aggression" necessitated a policy of deterrence. It was necessary to convince the communists "that aggression will not serve their interests: that it will not pay."[54] The question was, what level of costs could the United States incur in a fight for such symbolic goals? Fighting China with conventional weapons for purely symbolic gains carried great risk. The administration would stand to gain politically only if it could win this encounter with the communists without too high a cost.

Here the advent of tactical nuclear weapons came in handy. The idea of using tactical nuclear weapons made the unthinkable fairly feasible. *New York Times* military correspondent Hanson Baldwin estimated that it would take only seven sorties to "take out" the Chinese airfields with tactical nuclear weapons, while the same job would take about 7,000 sorties with conventional bombs.[55] The US decision to intervene explicitly took into account the possibility of escalation beyond Chinese shelling of Quemoy and interdiction of the Nationalist supply lines. Without the backing of its nuclear capability, it would have been very difficult for the United States to make such a decision. If the Nationalist reinforcement of the offshore islands made it imperative for the United States to defend the islands, the feasibility of using tactical nuclear weapons made it possible for such a decision to be made.

DULLES TAKES CHARGE

The decision taken on 29 August to keep in abeyance plans for the use of nuclear weapons did not meet with the approval of Dulles. On the morning of 2 September he protested to General Nathan Twining, chairman of the JCS, that "There was no use of having a lot of stuff and never being able to use it." Twining agreed that conventional weapons would take too long to destroy Chinese air and artillery installations and that nuclear weapons were indeed usable against them.[56] Later that day, Dulles reviewed the situation with senior State Department officials and the JCS. Burke confirmed that there appeared to be no "unusual concentration of junks," although the Chinese had several thousand of these boats in the vicinity. However, Dulles extracted from General Maxwell Taylor, chief of army staff, an admission that the Chinese were fully capable of quickly assembling a large concentration of junks and launching a surprise attack just as they had done in the Korean War. Dulles summed up that "the Communists could conceivably stage a major assault at any time with a combination of heavy shelling, air bombing, and amphibious landing operations." Twining said that if the United States intervened, "we would strike at Communist air fields and shore batteries with small atomic weapons." Initially, US forces would attack five coastal airfields with one 7- to 10-kiloton airburst bomb each. These bombs, Twining claimed, had a "lethal area" of three to four miles and had "virtually no fallout." Taylor explained that if the Chinese launched an amphibious operation, the Nationalists could defend themselves with only conventional assistance by US forces. Conventional forces could certainly delay an invasion long enough to offer time for a reference to Washington for authorization to use nuclear weapons. If the Chinese determinedly pressed the attack, the need for nuclear weapons would arise; if they engaged in a prolonged and intense shelling of the islands, or launched a sustained and heavy aerial bombardment, US forces would need to use nuclear weapons to destroy artillery and air installations. Dulles warned that "if we shrink from using nuclear weapons when military circumstances so require, then we will have to reconsider our whole defense posture."[57]

In a meeting with Dulles and other State Department officials, Taylor and Burke agreed that the Nationalists, assisted by US forces with conventional weapons, stood a good chance of handling an amphibious assault on Quemoy backed by artillery and air support. The hostilities might escalate, however, since neither the United States nor China would back down. The Chinese might extend areas and bases of operation, and might even use atomic weapons. The Soviet Union also might intervene. The question was

whether we can use our best weapons in "limited war." . . . are we to risk loss of US prestige and influence in the world, through loss of the Offshore Islands occasioned by failure to exert a maximum defense; or are we to risk loss of prestige and influence, through limited use of nuclear weapons to hold the Islands.

The participants agreed that the United States should take the latter risk. If not, "we would have to recast our whole philosophy of defense planning. . . . [E]ach succeeding crisis and its concomitant decisions will become increasingly difficult for us."[58]

On the basis of these deliberations, Dulles prepared a draft summary paper for use in briefing the president. He proposed that to minimize the impact among allies of atomic strikes against mainland targets, only low-yield warheads should be used initially in airbursts. Dulles went on to argue: "It is not certain, however, that this would do the job and a risk of a possibility of extensive use of nuclear weapons and a risk of general war would have to be accepted." Gerard Smith protested that this sentence seemed "too light a treatment of this most serious aspect of the matter." A special intelligence report, NIE 100-7-58, had pointed to the danger of communist retaliation with atomic bombs in case the United States used nuclear weapons against China. Smith warned Dulles that JCS plans included possible use of atomic weapons on targets as far as 500 miles from the offshore islands and "enemy strike bases wherever located in China." He argued that "extended nuclear strikes beyond the immediate locale of the hostilities cannot be justified in the defense of the Offshore Islands."[59]

On 3 September, State and Defense Department representatives met to revise the summary paper. Admiral Roland Smoot, commander of the US Taiwan Defense Command, had reported that China did not yet have sufficient forces in position for an invasion of Quemoy. The four Chinese field armies in the area did not exceed the Nationalist strength in the offshore islands. However, the navy felt that the Chinese could assemble a large force quickly. Dulles summed up that the United States could not rule out an invasion of the offshore islands within three or four days.[60]

NUCLEAR SIGNALS

With the JCS once again behind him, Dulles turned to Eisenhower. When he met the vacationing president at Newport, Rhode Island, on 4 September, he told him that "we had acknowledged the risk of the political and psychological dangers of the use of these weapons when we decided to include them in our arsenal." If "we will not use them when the chips are down because of world opinion, we must revise our defense setup." The president raised the possibility that "Communist retaliation with nuclear weapons might well be against Taiwan itself and beyond rather than directed simply at Quemoy." However, he apparently allowed himself to be persuaded by Dulles. The record of the Eisenhower–Dulles conversation available does not help explain how Eisenhower gave up so tamely.[61]

Eisenhower and Dulles "studied, edited, and agreed on" the summary paper that Dulles had brought along. The revised memorandum affirmed that unless China gave up its attempt on the offshore islands in the face of a US intervention using only conventional weapons, the United States could not limit itself to conventional weapons. Use of atomic weapons would arouse "a strong popular revulsion against the US" worldwide.

If a quick victory could be achieved, and civilian casualties could be limited by employing only airbursts of small atomic weapons, however, the consequences of the use of atomic weapons would be less damaging than the political disaster that failure to stand up to China would cause. Eisenhower and Dulles explicitly accepted "the risk of a more extensive use of nuclear weapons, and even a risk of general war" that limited intervention with nuclear weapons might lead to. Clearly, military, political, or moral considerations would not prevent the United States from using nuclear weapons if China did not back off. "Self-deterrence," which, historian John L. Gaddis has argued, had restrained the Eisenhower administration from using nuclear weapons, was nowhere in evidence.[62]

With the president's approval, Dulles issued a statement later that day, in which he declared that

the securing and protecting of Quemoy and Matsu have increasingly become related to the defense of Taiwan. . . . Military dispositions have been made by the United States so that a Presidential determination [that a threat to Taiwan existed], if made, would be followed by action both timely and effective.

In a background briefing to the press, Dulles clarified that if the Nationalists were unable to defend the islands unaided, US forces would intervene. He added that "If I were on the Chinese Communist side, I would certainly think very hard before I went ahead in the face of this statement." The statement, however, kept the door open for a peaceful settlement by hinting that negotiations on renunciation of force could resume without the Chinese giving up their claim to Taiwan.[63]

Dulles also wrote to British Prime Minister Harold Macmillan the same day that if the United States did intervene to oppose the Chinese, it was doubtful whether US efforts would succeed without the use of atomic weapons. He hoped that "no more than small airbursts without fallout" would suffice. "That is of course an unpleasant prospect," he admitted, "but one I think we must face up to, because our entire military establishment assumes more and more that the use of nuclear weapons will become normal in the event of hostilities."[64]

On 4 September, General Curtis LeMay, Vice Chief of Air Staff (formerly Commander in Chief of the Strategic Air Command and the best-known proponent of nuclear bombing), left for Taiwan amidst considerable publicity. The day after Dulles's Newport statement, a New York Times headline read: "US DECIDES TO USE FORCE IF REDS INVADE QUEMOY." Coming out of a meeting with Dulles on 5 September, Senator Alexander Smith told reporters that the administration had "definitely" decided to intervene militarily to defend the offshore islands. On

12 September, Secretary of Defense Neil H. McElroy refused to rule out neutralizing the Chinese coastal batteries engaged in attacking the off- shore islands. As if the Matador missiles did not convey a strong enough message, on 17 September, the US Navy landed on Quemoy three 8-inch nuclear-capable howitzers. On 27 September, Air Force Secretary James Douglas announced that US forces stood ready to use nuclear weapons against China.[65]

Chinese actions, however, ruled out any immediate need for the United States to make good on its nuclear threats. On 6 September, Zhou Enlai announced China's acceptance of the US offer to resume the sus- pended ambassadorial talks at the new venue of Warsaw. A White House press release on the same day welcomed the Chinese offer and stated that "The United States ambassador at Warsaw stands ready promptly to meet with the Chinese Communist Ambassador there." Prodded by Eisenhower, who thought that "a concrete and definite ac- ceptance" of Zhou's offer to negotiate would help the United States seize the diplomatic initiative, the talks started on 15 September.[66]

Despite the Chinese offer to resume negotiations, the JCS sought from Eisenhower advance authority for air operations against Chinese forces, including targets on the mainland, in case China launched a major am- phibious attack on the offshore islands. Eisenhower, however, refused to grant any such prior authority to the JCS and directed that any US air operation against Chinese targets would require his authorization.[67]

THE RESUPPLY CRISIS

Chinese shelling had caused only negligible casualties and hardly any damage to the Nationalist gun positions in Quemoy. Since Chinese forces did not concentrate their fire, they failed to knock out a single Nationalist gun position. The resupply of Quemoy, however, emerged as a critical issue. From 23 August to 7 September, the Chinese prevented any sup- plies from reaching Quemoy. Against Quemoy's average daily require- ment of 300 tons of supplies, total landings from the beginning of the crisis through 18 September did not amount to even a single day's con- sumption. The defenders had only a 10-day supply of ammunition if they were to effectively engage the Chinese gunners. On 4 September, the Nationalists admitted that resupplying Quemoy was beyond their capability.[68]

The Nationalist failure to press forward with supply operations pro- duced consternation in Washington. Eisenhower was annoyed that a Na- tionalist convoy that reached Quemoy had backed off as soon as it came under fire. He was furious at what he felt was Chiang's pressure tactics to get the United States involved. He wondered whether the determi- nation the Nationalists displayed justified the risk the United States was taking. The JCS in Washington and Admiral Smoot in Taiwan suspected that the Nationalists were being "deliberately inept" in order to build a case for direct US intervention. In a private meeting with Chiang, Smoot minced no words. He promised that the United States would help but insisted that the Nationalists had to do the job themselves, something the ROC's navy "has made no effort to even try." Smoot told Chiang that "GRC authorities [were] so involved in what [the] US is not doing for them they have overlooked their own ineffective planning and have not exploited the things they can do with what they have." Dulles alone challenged the notion that the Nationalists were engaged in a "pretty complicated plot" to get the United States involved. It was more likely, he thought, that they needed experience in amphibious resupply operations under fire. Nationalist failure seemed to him to be ineptness rather than deliberate.[69]

Keeping Chiang under control so that the United States would not find itself in the position of supporting an aggressor proved difficult throughout the crisis. Chiang felt that he appeared to his people as an American puppet who could do nothing without clearance from Washington. Yeh told Drumwright that the "Generalissimo feels his honor is being impugned and his prestige lowered among his own officials and public." Continuous subjection to American directives damaged his standing among his people and subordinates. Chiang worried that unless he recovered his prestige, he risked his survival in power.[70]

The resupply crisis had more ominous implications than Chiang's wounded pride. The US Taiwan Defense Command feared that the American air strength in the theater was insufficient to neutralize the Chinese gun positions without atomic weapons. Its analysis showed that the Nationalists, with their own air cover, could successfully run a convoy on the first day. The Chinese, by reinforcing their air force, could prevent subsequent convoys, unless Chinese airfields were first rendered inoperable. Resupply under the continuous threat of air and artillery attacks over prolonged periods was not feasible. It would be justifiable only as a short-term tactic to demonstrate US determination to maintain Quemoy at any cost.[71] If the Chinese tightened their blockade by using their air power or increasing the intensity of their artillery bombardment, the United States would have faced the clear-cut choice of either abandoning Quemoy or intervening with nuclear weapons. An intelligence estimate concluded that if the United States attacked targets in the mainland beyond the coastal areas, "there would be a better than even chance" that the Soviet Union would give China atomic weapons for use against US forces. Further, if US nuclear attacks threatened the survival of the PRC, the Soviet Union might accept the risk of general war and attack US forces and their bases of operations against China.[72]

As it turned out, the United States did not have to face this hard choice. The Chinese refrained from using their air power to bomb Nationalist supply operations or from intensifying their shelling, even though they had the capability to do so. By the end of September, the Nationalist air force's Sabre jets, armed with newly supplied Sidewinder missiles, wrested air superiority from the Chinese MiG fighters. This spared US forces the need to intervene more deeply. By 30 September, the crucial problem of resupplying the offshore islands was, as Twining informed Eisenhower, "broken."[73]

PUBLIC AND INTERNATIONAL OPINION PREVAILS

Domestic and international opinion now came to exercise a decisive role in American decision making. Chiang's efforts to get the United States involved in a shooting war with China had by now entered public debate. Columnist Walter Lippmann wrote that "it has become brutally clear that Chiang thinks he has the opportunity, and is determined to seize it, to embroil the United States in a war with the Chinese mainland." Dean Acheson, former secretary of state, launched a scathing attack on the Eisenhower administration's policy in the crisis, in particular, Dulles's Newport statement. Chiang, Acheson scoffed, "was unleashed just enough to permit the incredible folly of transporting about a third of his forces to the untenable Quemoy. . . . The fact of the matter is that our government has most unwisely maneuvered itself, with the help of Chiang Kai-shek, into a situation of which it has lost control." Acheson did not think that the stakes in this crisis were worth a single American life.[74]

American public opinion had by now clearly swung away from the administration's policy. Out of 640 letters on the crisis received by the White House until 9 September, 470 supported the United States staying out of a war, 89 supported taking the issue to the UN, and only 39 supported the administration's policy of defending the offshore islands. A Gallup Poll showed that 80 percent of Americans followed the news about the crisis, of whom 62 percent opposed US intervention to hold the offshore islands if it meant serious hostilities and the use of atomic weapons. Only 28 percent supported US intervention, even if it led to a major war and atomic bombing. As many as 82 percent favored the United States seeking a solution through the UN before resorting to force. The editorial opinion of leading papers such as the *Christian Science Monitor* and the *Wall Street Journal* criticized the administration's decision to defend the islands. The *New York Times*, which had strongly supported the tough US line against China so far, suddenly changed its tone. The paper now found the domino theory "too naive" and dismissed as irrelevant the administration's argument that the communists had never exercised authority over the offshore islands. Senator Theodore F. Green, chairman of the Senate Foreign Relations Committee, did not feel that Quemoy was vital to the defense of either Taiwan or the United States. In a letter to Eisenhower, he opposed "military involvement at the wrong time, in the wrong place, and on issues not of vital concern to our own security, and all this without allies." Senators Mike Mansfield and John F. Kennedy opposed the administration's policy in the crisis. Democratic congressional leaders Sam Rayburn and Lyndon Johnson, who had organized bipartisan support for the US intervention in Lebanon only weeks earlier, refused to support Eisenhower this time.[75]

In a perceptive analysis of the change in American public opinion, the British Embassy reported to London that dissatisfaction with the administration's China policy was not a new phenomenon. Americans were, however, expressing their opposition to this policy more openly now. The embassy noted an unprecedented tendency in the country to question the foundations of this policy. Americans no longer feared to express disapproval of Chiang and his wife, or to say that Chiang was bent on dragging the United States into a war with China.[76]

The United States Information Agency's analysis of the international reaction to the crisis showed that the governments of only the ROC, South Korea, South Vietnam, Thailand, and the Philippines might approve of US intervention with nuclear weapons. Even in these countries, the people had "mixed feelings." Many influential people in the Philippines openly expressed criticism. "The governments and the peoples of *every other country* in the world would condemn and oppose in varying degrees of intensity" (emphasis added). While most Latin American and other allied governments might extend some approval for US intervention with conventional weapons, the public in most of these countries would disapprove. Except in Latin America, Taiwan, South Vietnam, Korea, and the Philippines, virtually all other governments would be relieved by a US decision not to intervene militarily. Public opinion throughout the world would support such a decision.[77]

A German official made it clear that Germany "would not understand" if the United States intervened to defend the offshore islands. The German government believed that if China gained control of these islands, rather than weakening the Western position, it would stabilize the situation in the area. The CIA reported that the British press did not accept the president's comparison, in a 11 September broadcast, of the Chinese action with the Axis powers' aggressions. They felt that the islands "were patently a part of mainland China and certainly not worth fighting for at the risk of sparking off a nuclear war." Japan wanted a revision of its mutual defense treaty with the United States to provide for Japanese concurrence in the deployment of US forces elsewhere from their bases in Japan. Ambassador Charles Bohlen in Manila worried that the Philippine government might formally declare its "noninvolvement" or neutrality in the crisis. Although Dulles assured Senator Green that the Philippines supported a "strong policy" in the crisis, the Philippine foreign minister pointed out that Manila had no commitment to enter the conflict even if the United States were involved. Australian Prime Minister Robert Menzies publicly stated that Australia had no commitment to help defend the offshore islands.[78]

US POLICY SHIFTS

The JCS began to worry that US forces were spread "dangerously thin." Uncertainty about the use of nuclear weapons worsened this problem. They wanted the situation in the Taiwan Strait to be normalized quickly, as major involvement in prolonged operations there would seriously diminish US capability elsewhere. Over 15,000 troops (taken from divisions in Germany), three marine landing battalions, and the Sixth Fleet were tied down in the Middle East. If fighting broke out there, the United States would find it difficult to mobilize the forces required to deal with the Chinese in the Taiwan Strait. Reversing their stand on the importance of the offshore islands, the JCS argued that the offshore islands were not essential for the defense of Taiwan and that from a purely military point of view, the islands should be vacated.[79]

Eisenhower agreed, and admitted that while he would not yield the offshore islands under attack, he would support an arrangement by which Chiang could pull his forces out of the islands without losing face. He told Dulles that the opinion poll data "shook" him. He was prepared to abandon the offshore islands, but could not yet say so publicly. The "financial burden of the Formosa operation" weighed on the president's mind. He worried about the "rapidly and immensely increasing cost of the military establishment" and of the "fiscal dangers ahead." He had had enough of "what Chiang Kai-shek wanted us to do" and "was just about ready to tell Chiang Kai-shek where he (Chiang) got off."[80]

The pressure of domestic and international opinion forced a change in Dulles's thinking also. Even while talking tough, Dulles had foreseen that a lasting solution to the problem would involve removal of the Nationalist threat to China from the offshore islands. Echoing what other countries, especially Britain, had argued in 1954, Dulles had conceded as early as 23 August:

I do not feel that we have a case which is altogether defensible. It is one thing to contend that the Chicoms should keep their hands off the present territorial and political status of Taiwan, the Ponghus [sic], Quemoy and Matsu and not to attempt to change this by violence which might precipitate general war in the area.

It is another thing to contend that they should be quiescent while this area is used by the Chinats as an active base for attempting to foment civil strife and to carry out widespread propaganda through leaflets, etc. against the Chicom regime. We are, in effect, demanding that the islands be a "privileged sanctuary" from which the Chinats can wage at least political and subversive warfare against the Chicoms but against which the Chicoms cannot retaliate.[81]

He came to appreciate that the crisis "had strained our relations with Congress and foreign governments almost to the breaking point." As he later pointed out to Drumwright, "the overwhelming majority of corre-spondents in Washington dealing with this problem are strongly hostile" to the US policy. "Our whole China policy" stood in danger of "being swept overboard." He had begun to "wonder whether there is not the basis for some peaceful modus vivendi." He was now prepared to accept "some form of demilitarization of the offshore islands" with the Nation-alists in control.[82] He thought that Washington had "quite a little" lev-erage over Taipei to use in securing an easing of tension in the area.[83]

PARALLEL CONCESSIONS

Dulles's search for a way out offers the key to understanding the way the resumed ambassadorial talks in Warsaw progressed. Until the State Department papers for the period were declassified, the key role these talks played in ending the crisis was not appreciated. The conventional view of the talks was reflected in Richard Stebbins's colorful contem-porary account: " 'Conclude a ceasefire,' said Ambassador Beam. 'Get out of Taiwan,' Wang Bingnan retorted.' "[84] With the documentation now available, the critical role that the talks played in communicating the American desire to stop provoking China, thus ending the cycle of crises in the Taiwan Strait area, has now emerged.

When China offered to revive the ambassadorial talks, the US Navy argued:

The fact that Red China has made overtures for cessation of hostilities should encourage us to proceed along somewhat the same lines as if we had gained a military victory and are now in a position to dictate the terms on which hostilities will be ceased. . . . For purposes of stabilizing a potentially troublesome area, we should enter into the negotiations with the objective of demilitarization of the whole of a coastal zone of Mainland China from Macao to Foochow, declaring that all of the ports should be open ports and that armed forces located in the demilitarized zone should be only such as are necessary for the purpose of law enforcement and regulation of peaceful pursuits.[85]

However, realizing that neither the UN nor any third party could do enough to mediate between China and the United States, Dulles decided to utilize the ambassadorial talks for this purpose. Once China agreed to resume direct contacts, Dulles quickly saw the need to break new ground in the talks if the United States was not to lose the propaganda war. He argued that if the American policy was to "merely replay an old record, asking the Chinese Communists to accept the formula of renunciation of force" in the resumed talks in Warsaw, it would not impress the rest of the world. Accordingly, Dulles decided to use the talks for the "purpose of providing cover under which there conceivably might be some de facto easing of war tensions."[86] In this endeavor, the talks offered the means to explore with China how to stop actions by *both sides* considered provocative by the other. Recognizing that "we shouldn't really expect the Communists to refrain from attacking the islands if they were being used as bases for hostile activities against the mainland," Dulles sought information on Nationalist activities carried out from the offshore islands that the Chinese might regard "with justification" as "provocative."[87]

Eisenhower and Dulles agreed that covert activities conducted by the Nationalists from the offshore islands should be stopped gradually. Dulles suggested that US forces stop operations in China's newly defined territorial waters (12 miles), at least for a few days. Eisenhower agreed.[88] Dulles desired that if the Chinese cut down their military operations, "we should ease off our own operations where feasible, and certainly should be careful not to increase provocation under such circumstances." He also suggested keeping Chinese activity under close monitoring, "to see if there is any relationship between this activity and the positions taken at Warsaw." Twining concurred.[89] Even when the US Embassy in Taiwan objected to US insistence on restricting its convoy escort to outside the three-mile limit, Washington did not change its orders.[90]

At the talks in Warsaw, Ambassador Beam proposed a cease-fire, following which, he suggested, under State Department instructions, that "there should be reduction of forces and halting of actions by *either side* which could be considered provocative" (emphasis added).[91] Wang Bingnan, once again representing China, "categorically and absolutely" rejected Beam's cease-fire offer as "absurd and absolutely unacceptable."[92] In Chinese thinking, probably the proposals Beam made in the secrecy of the talks were inadequate compensation for letting their enemies off the hook. China, however, was equally alive to the utility of the Warsaw talks. The British Embassy in Beijing learned from Indian diplomats that China was keen on keeping the talks alive.[93]

Washington finally realized that the key to ending the crisis lay in persuading the Nationalists to end their aggressive policies against China. Eisenhower worried that the United States was not doing enough "to convert Chiang to flexibility." He felt that "we have to do something; we have to sell someone something or we shall be accused of desertion of an ally or bringing war."[94] In a public speech, Dulles admitted that the United States was willing to accept "any arrangement which . . . eliminated from the situation features that could reasonably be regarded as provocative."[95]

Realizing that tension would recur as long as China perceived a threat from the offshore islands, attention in Washington turned to reducing the Nationalist forces in the offshore islands. Finally succumbing to US pressure, Chiang conceded on 29 September that he would no longer use the offshore islands as a springboard for the invasion of the mainland. In what the *New York Times* called "an effort to break the deadlock in the Warsaw talks," Dulles, at a news conference on 30 September, distanced the United States a long way from the Nationalists. He declared that Washington had "no commitment of any kind" to assist the Nationalists to return to power in the mainland. He admitted that the United States would consider a "de facto cease-fire" acceptable. He hinted that if a such a cease-fire could be obtained, Washington would favor reducing the Nationalist forces on Quemoy. He then proceeded to stun the Nationalists: "If there were a cease-fire in the area which seemed to be reasonably dependable, I think it would be foolish to keep these forces on these islands. We thought that it was rather foolish to put them there."[96]

When the Nationalists objected to this statement, Dulles minced no words in his reply that Drumwright conveyed to Chiang personally: the administration had to contend with the belief among large numbers of the American public, members of Congress (including many Republicans), and American allies, that

President Chiang was dragging the United States into a world war, that the destiny of the American people had been placed at his (President Chiang's) disposal, that because he (President Chiang) was stubborn and would not agree to a cease-fire, and because he (President Chiang) believed that the only fruitful way would be to start a world war, the American government had no flexibility in its position.[97]

The far-reaching change in US and Nationalist policy signaled in the statements by Dulles and Chiang produced their result. On 6 October, China's Defense Minister Peng Dehui announced a unilateral Chinese cease-fire for one week, on the condition that the United States would end convoying. The Chinese ambassador in Moscow told his Norwegian counterpart that he "had reason to believe" that the seven-day cease-fire would be extended if US forces kept off the 12-mile limit set by Beijing.[98] Washington promptly responded by suspending its convoy escorts to avoid giving China an excuse for charging the United States with deliberate acts of hostility and continuing to escort Nationalist convoys when the Chinese cease-fire had made it unnecessary for the United States to participate in convoying.[99] The State Department instructed Beam to inform Wang that the United States had stopped escorting Nationalist convoys and would not resume convoy escorts as long as China did not attack. The Department directed Beam to specifically ask what the Chinese considered "sabotage" and "harassment," to ensure "reciprocal cessation" of such activities.[100] The State Department was also willing to negotiate "reciprocal reduction of forces and armaments" in the area.[101] Wang refused to discuss a cease-fire with the United States, claiming that China and the United States were not fighting. However, he demanded that the "US cease convoying GRC ships, halt intrusions and war threats."[102] The United States moved quickly to comply. Washington ordered US forces to avoid any possibility of Chinese charges of American provocations. The US Taiwan Defense Command ordered that *"For the time being we must lean over backwards even in international waters to avoid any move which Chicom [Chinese communist] propaganda could exploit"* (emphasis added).[103]

The desire to avoid provoking China continued even after the crisis calmed down. Admiral Smoot protested when Nationalist planes flew close to Quemoy in large numbers on 26 December and 28 December, since the flights, which had not been cleared with him, "could be regarded as provocative." Although the Nationalists repeatedly argued for the resumption of commando raids on the mainland in subsequent years, the United States stood firm.[104] Eisenhower directed that only US aircraft would henceforth fly reconnaissance flights over the mainland, for which permission "must be secured *on a mission-by-mission basis*" from him (emphasis in original).[105]

The easing of tension following the Chinese cease-fire still left the need for a longer term solution in the Taiwan Strait. Twining suggested the reduction of Nationalist troop strength in the offshore islands by two-thirds.[106] Eisenhower wrote Dulles that

Chiang might be sold on the proposition that he would be in a better position to realize his purpose of retaining a capacity to return to the mainland in the event of internal disorder, if he should acquire from the United States a strong amphibious lift and simultaneously remove all or nearly all his garrison from the offshore islands.

This would make the Nationalist forces mobile enough to take advantage of any chance to reoccupy the mainland and lessen the importance of the offshore islands. Ever mindful of the political implications of being seen to pressure the Nationalists into unwelcome actions, the president added, "Of course this would have to be a plan voluntarily adopted by him, during a period when there was no hostile action. Otherwise he would be acting under duress and this would be, of course, unacceptable."[107]

Chiang showed little inclination to comply with US desire for him to pull out some of his troops from Quemoy. He considered his 29 September statement the limit of his concessions. Eisenhower, therefore, dispatched Dulles to reason with him.[108] When he met Chiang on 22 October, Dulles, speaking from a prepared statement, spoke of "the feeling shared by most of the free world countries that the relationship between the GRC [ROC] and CPR [PRC] not only endangers the peace but that the GRC *wants* it to endanger the peace and involve the US as the only means of returning to the mainland" (emphasis in original). He suggested that the ROC rely on "the minds and souls of the 600 million Chinese people on the mainland," rather than on its armed forces or its occupation of the offshore island, for its counterattack against the PRC. To transform the Nationalists' "militaristic image" abroad, Dulles urged that Nationalist China should: conduct itself on a reciprocal basis as though an armistice existed in the Taiwan Strait; reiterate that it would not initiate a military campaign to return to the mainland; avoid commando raids, overflights, and similar provocations; accept any dependable solution to ensure that the offshore islands would not be handed over to China; and review the "character and size" of its forces on the offshore islands in order to make them more mobile. As positive measures, he wanted Chiang to cast himself in the role of the "custodian of China's real greatness."[109] The Nationalists did not look kindly at Dulles's suggestion. Their "initial reaction" was that it was "of such a nature as almost to shake the foundation of the Republic of China." Nevertheless, they had no choice but to go along with the new American line. The joint communique issued at the end of Dulles's visit formally committed the Nationalists to renounce force in their plans for returning to the mainland.

During their meeting, Dulles asked Chiang whether the latter wanted the United States to use nuclear weapons against Chinese gun positions. Chiang replied that he "believed that it would not be necessary to use nuclear weapons." However, he "believed that the use of tactical atomic weapons might be advisable." Dulles, whose views on the effects of nuclear weapons seemed to have undergone a dramatic transformation in the last two months, replied:

[T]here is no tactical atomic weapon in existence which could be used at Kinmen [Quemoy] to knock out enemy gun placements that would not have the power of the Hiroshima or Nagasaki bombs. The use of such weapons at Kinmen [Quemoy] could kill millions of people. There would be a heavy fissionable fall-out if bombs exploded in or on the ground. The danger lies not in the size of the bomb but in how it is exploded. If an atomic bomb is exploded on or in the ground, then there would inevitably be a heavy loss of human life. On the other hand if an atomic bomb was exploded in the air, the explosion would have no effect on gun positions.[110]

Worried that this conversation "demonstrated alarming ignorance of Gimo [Chiang] on capabilities and limitations of nuclear weapons," Dulles asked that Chiang be given a briefing on the subject.[111]

Washington used various channels to communicate to Beijing the implications of the change in the Nationalist position. The US ambassador in New Delhi impressed upon Indian officials the importance of the shift in the ROC's position contained in the joint communique.[112] The State Department sent a circular to all embassies outside of the communist bloc with instructions to impress upon their host governments the "significance" of this shift.[113] Obviously, Dulles hoped that someone would suitably brief Chinese diplomats.

On 13 October, China extended the cease-fire. This Chinese cease-fire continued until 25 October, when they resumed shelling, but only on odd-numbered days. In defiance of orders from Washington, the US Navy escorted three Nationalist landing operations on Quemoy during the Chinese cease-fire. China used the last convoy as an excuse to resume shelling during Dulles's Taiwan visit. US officials thought the Chinese decision to resume shelling during Dulles's trip to Taiwan was motivated, since they had overlooked the first two landing operations.[114] After Dulles left Taiwan, the Chinese reverted to their odd-day shelling.[115]

The United States responded to the Chinese deescalation with alacrity. Dulles, Twining, and the president conferred and decided that the United States would not escort Nationalist convoys unless China conducted air or naval action to block resupply on what the United States regarded as international waters on even days. Further, US forces would refrain from conducting air or naval patrols within the 12-mile limit claimed by China. Although Admiral Felt wanted to conduct periodic patrols within this limit to express American refusal to accept the Chinese 12-mile claim, Dulles suggested, and Eisenhower agreed, that the United States had made its position on the Chinese territorial waters perfectly clear at the Warsaw talks and did not need a more overt demonstration of its stand.[116] With the resupply of Quemoy proceeding unimpeded on even-numbered days, the crisis came to an end.

Soon after the Chinese announced their cease-fire, Dulles had told British Ambassador Harold Caccia that:

It was possible that each side might move further in more or less parallel lines without any expressed agreement and that progress would be made in this way.

The Chinese Communists said they wished us to stop convoys. We did so and publicized it, whereupon they took some credit for obtaining this result. If the shooting continues to be suspended, there might be more.[117]

The crisis ultimately ended very much the way Dulles had anticipated.

CONCLUSIONS

The proximity of the Chinese offer to negotiate to Dulles's Newport statement probably caused some scholars to count this episode as a case of successful American deterrence of Chinese aggression. The NSC staff also came to this conclusion.[118] US documents leave no doubt that the United States signaled its intention to intervene, with nuclear weapons if necessary, if China launched an attack on Quemoy or Matsu. Further, the United States was prepared to back up this threat with action. However, on the basis of Chinese actions and whatever information has come out of China, one can say with a great deal of certainty that China was not about to launch an invasion of the offshore islands, let alone Taiwan. To believe that a Chinese invasion of the offshore islands was imminent, one must assume that the Chinese gave the United States two months' notice of their intention to invade, then planned to assemble the forces required to overcome the 85,000 defending troops in the full view of the defenders and send the invading forces over in thousands of small wooden boats in rough weather against the powerful naval force that confronted them.

Chinese sources indicate that it is equally doubtful that the Chinese deescalation was in response to the Newport statement and US nuclear signals. Mao had decided as early as 21 August to limit the shelling to three days. On the late evening of 3 September (i.e., the day before Dulles's Newport statement), Mao ordered the PLA to stop shelling altogether for three days and assess the US response. When Eisenhower and Dulles discussed the Newport statement, they noted that China's latest statement on the extent of its coastal waters "seemed to soften the Chinese Communist threat against Taiwan." At the expiry of the three days, the Chinese resumed bombarding Quemoy. The Chinese decision to return to the ambassadorial talks also predated the Newport statement. In late August, Mao had recalled Ambassador Wang to discuss the resumption of the talks with the United States. After a briefing by Wang on 2 September, the CCP Politburo decided that China should try to reopen the talks.[119]

This is not to say that nuclear deterrence did not take place in the Taiwan Strait. Nuclear deterrence did occur, but not in September 1958. Here one must ask why China did not plan a full-scale invasion of Quemoy. Once the Chinese built air bases in the Fujian province and stationed aircraft on them, they stood a very good chance of succeeding in an invasion of the offshore islands if the United States refrained from using nuclear weapons against them. The reinforced Seventh Fleet was certainly capable of stopping a Chinese invasion of the offshore islands by conventional means alone. Against China's full power, however, this would have been a costly operation and would, in all probability, have been ruled out as unjustified by the strategic importance of the offshore islands. Hence, not wishing to surrender these islands to China, the United States clearly signaled its intention, starting in late 1957, to defend them with nuclear weapons. The stationing of Matador missiles on Quemoy was part of this deterrence strategy. This deterrence should be counted as a definite success.

Once the American response to the crisis in the Taiwan Strait crystallized, Mao signaled a thorough reexamination of his policy of "confrontation with the US." He told the Fifteenth Meeting of the Supreme State Council on 5 September and 8 September that the United States had shifted to a defensive policy toward China and the Soviet Union while it attempted to gain dominance over the Third World. Therefore, the US-Taiwan mutual defense treaty did not pose as grave or as immediate a threat to China as it had done earlier. The treaty was now defensive, restraining rather than unleashing Chiang. Mao asserted that both China and the United States were afraid of war, but "they" were "more afraid than we are." War was, therefore, unlikely to break out.[120] Mao concluded that Chiang wanted to drag the United States into a war with China that Washington did not want. He speculated that the United States had three options: (1) seek a cease-fire that would leave the islands with Chiang; (2) pressure Chiang to withdraw from them; and (3) if either of the two failed, forcibly dislodge the Nationalists from them, thus creating a de facto two-China situation.[121]

Mao examined military steps to liberate the offshore islands, but probably concluded that the costs outweighed the benefits, even if the operation met with success.[122] If the Nationalists left these islands, Mao reasoned, it would sever the last Taiwanese link to the mainland. This would let the United States "off the hook," leaving them to pursue their goal of dividing China. Therefore, Mao apparently decided to postpone the plan to invade Quemoy and Matsu and to leave them temporarily in Nationalist hands. He thus linked the future of the offshore islands to the Taiwan question. The Politburo decided that all future negotiations would have to be on the basis of "one lump sum," as there was no point in talking about other issues without resolving the Taiwan issue.[123]

In the Politburo meeting on 3 and 4 October, Zhou argued that Dulles's speech of 30 September exposed the American plan to create two Chinas. Mao pointed out that China was unable to liberate Taiwan in the near future; neither were the Nationalists capable of returning to the mainland. The question was what to do about the offshore islands. Since "Jiang [Chiang] is unwilling to withdraw from Jinmen-Mazu [Quemoy-Matsu] and we do not need to land on Jinmen-Mazu," Mao suggested, "Let us make a proposal of leaving Jinmen and Mazu in the hands of Jiang Jieshi." Whenever China needed to raise tensions, it could shell the Nationalists and thus tighten the noose around the United States. If China occupied the offshore islands, it would make two Chinas a reality and deprive China of a means of applying pressure on Washington. Other Politburo members agreed with Mao's analysis and his proposal to allow the Nationalists to remain in the offshore islands.[124] On 1 November, and again on 16 December, Chinese Foreign Minister Chen Yi declared that China would aim to liberate Taiwan and the offshore islands together. Defense Minister Peng declared that "To recover Taiwan, Penghu, Jinmen and Mazu as a whole and complete the unification of our motherland is the sacred task of our 650 million people."[125]

As farfetched as the idea that China actually wanted the offshore islands to remain in Nationalist hands might appear, evidence to substantiate such a policy did appear. The CIA tracked Chinese diplomatic moves to stop an Afro-Asian resolution in the UN calling for a cease-fire in the Taiwan Strait and to prevent UN debate on the crisis.[126] In an article in a Moscow weekly, which the State Department read with much interest, communist writer Anna Louise Strong analyzed Chinese policy on exactly the lines Mao presented to his colleagues.[127] Such evidence led the NSC staff to conclude that "Strong Chinese opposition to the two-China concept undoubtedly played a role in bringing about the cease-fire."[128] Smith thought that the status quo suited China. By keeping the situation tense and "shaken up" periodically, China could split the United States from its allies. British Ambassador Sir Harold Caccia "wondered if the Chinese Communists really wanted the Chinese Nationalists to get off of the islands. . . . [I]f the Chinese Nationalists would evacuate the offshore islands it would deny the Communists the pleasure of playing this game."[129] Dulles, however, disagreed. He was sure that China would consider securing the offshore islands a "great victory."[130] He thought the Chinese "line was rather curious." They claimed

to encourage the Chinese Nationalists to do something which the Communists had been unable to prevent them from doing. The only thing which the Communists insisted upon stopping was United States convoying, which they knew we would stop anyway. The Communists had been unable to stop resupply of Quemoy so they pretend they are glad to have it resupplied.[131]

Many scholars have accepted Mao's claims, but Dulles was probably closer to the truth.[132] China simply had no hope of recovering the offshore islands in the face of US opposition. Two crises in the area in the brief period of four years should have convinced the Chinese leadership that the United States was not about to let the islands go. A debate in the UN—if the issue ever came to a debate—would have raised the question of renunciation of force, which the Chinese would not have accepted (as they regarded the dispute as their internal matter). Mao was probably merely putting a theoretical gloss over a situation that was beyond his control, while appearing to his comrades to be fully in charge.

Newly available documentation also challenges conventional views about the Soviet policy in this crisis. As Eisenhower claimed in his memoirs, Soviet leader Nikita Khrushchev's visit to China in early August had fueled US suspicions of Soviet complicity in the origins of the crisis. However, the very subdued Soviet comments on the crisis seemed to indicate their lack of interest in getting involved. The Soviet press displayed a notable lack of enthusiasm for supporting China in its comments on the crisis. Khrushchev waited until Zhou's offer of negotiations removed serious risk of war before he wrote to Eisenhower on 7 September that "an attack on the Chinese People's Republic . . . is an attack on the Soviet Union."[133] The risks were even lower by the time Khrushchev wrote again, on 15 September, to say that neither Beijing nor Moscow was intimidated by the US "atomic blackmail" and "may no one doubt that we shall completely honor our commitments" to China.[134] Based on such evidence, Gordon Chang argues that Moscow had taken a dim view of Mao's policy in the Taiwan Strait. For the Soviets, according to this view, the strategic dialogue with the United States carried stakes too great to be endangered by involvement in Chinese irredentism. Throughout the crisis, US-Soviet contacts went on without a hitch. On 21 August, Eisenhower invited the Soviets to a meeting to negotiate a comprehensive nuclear test ban. On 29 August, Khrushchev announced his acceptance of the invitation.[135] A few days after Khrushchev's belligerent message of 7 September, Washington confirmed the details of the test ban conference. On 15 September, the Soviet Union accepted a US invitation to a conference on the prevention of surprise attacks. During this time American delegations concluded major cultural exchanges with the Soviets in Moscow. On 1 October, the Soviet Union proposed a meeting of the US secretary of state and the Soviet foreign minister to discuss the test ban issue.[136]

At his press briefing at Newport on 4 September, Dulles was ambivalent about whether he expected the Soviet Union to intervene on behalf of China. He did not think the Soviet Union would support China simply because of its treaty commitments, and he was unsure whether the Soviet Union would consider it in its interest to aid China in the current crisis.[137] He told reporters on 17 September that he expected the Soviets to come to China's aid in the event of a war, but he expressed himself unable to "guess intelligently" about what took place between Khrushchev and Mao. He could not "explain the vagaries and the apparent inconsistencies of Soviet policy."[138] However, if either Dulles or Eisenhower seriously thought that the Soviets might actively support China in this crisis, such fears were notably absent in the administration's internal debates. US discussions on the use of atomic weapons were singularly free of references to the possibility of a Soviet nuclear retaliation, although review papers prepared earlier (which figured in some of the discussions) did mention such a possibility.

That the Soviet Union and China looked on the nuclear dimension from totally different perspectives became clear from the subsequent Soviet version of what transpired during Soviet Foreign Minister Andrei Gromyko's Beijing visit on 5 September. Mao, Gromyko wrote in his memoirs, proposed that

If the USA attacks China with nuclear weapons, the Chinese armies must retreat from the border regions into the depths of the country. They must draw the enemy in deep so as to grip US forces in a pincer inside China. . . . [T]he Soviet Union should not take any military measures against the Americans in the first stage. Instead, you should let them penetrate deep inside the territory of the Chinese giant. Only when the Americans are right in the central provinces should you give them everything you've got.

Gromyko claimed that he was "flabbergasted" by Mao's proposal and firmly scotched the idea.[139] Gordon Chang doubts the veracity of this account, on the ground that "it seems doubtful that Mao really expected the United States to land troops on the mainland."[140] Gromyko, however, did not say that Mao told him that he (Mao) "expected" an American landing in China, but only that Mao mentioned it as a possibility that China must reckon with. On hearing Gromyko's account, George Kennan expressed the view that although he was surprised that Mao made such a proposal, Gromyko was unlikely to make up such a tale.[141]

Even with the limited availability of Soviet documents, it is clear that Soviet backing for China was far stronger than anyone had realized until now. Mao failed to take Khrushchev fully into confidence before starting military operations. However, Khrushchev offered Soviet backing for the effort. In August, the Soviet Union sent China long-range artillery, anti-aircraft missiles, amphibious equipment, and aircrafts, as well as Soviet military advisers, so China could undertake "a decisive move" against Taiwan.[142] The day after Dulles's Newport statement, *Pravda* announced that the Soviet Union would not "stand idly by" if the United States attacked China. The next day, *Pravda* declared that Soviet retaliation for an American attack on China would not be confined to the Taiwan Strait area.[143] One week after his 7 September warning to the United States, Khrushchev told Chinese Ambassador Liu Xiao that he was still looking forward to China's "decisive" operations against Taiwan. Khrushchev felt let down when Mao decided to deescalate the crisis.[144] Khrushchev's concern was not that China would precipitate a war with the United States but over Mao's insistence that the Soviet Union stay out while a Sino-US confrontation took place. Khrushchev wrote to Mao that "We cannot allow the illusion to be created among our enemies that if an attack will be launched against the PRC by the USA or Japan . . . that the Soviet Union will stand on the sidelines as a passive observer." Such a departure from the solidarity of the communist bloc, he asserted, "would be a retreat from the holy of holies of the Communists—from the teaching of Marxism-Leninism." He reiterated: "It is necessary that neither our friends nor our enemies have any doubts that an attack on the Chinese People's Republic is a war with the entire Socialist Camp. . . . [A]n attack on China is an attack on the Soviet Union."[145] Soon after this, Zhou told the Indian ambassador in Beijing, in a conversation relayed to Washington through London, that if the United States attacked mainland China or used tactical nuclear weapons, "general war" would follow.[146]

Apart from intra-bloc issues, the Lebanon crisis (during which Eisenhower had ordered a nuclear alert), might well have influenced the Kremlin's thinking. The Soviet leadership could not have ignored the implications of backing down a second time before American atomic diplomacy in the space of less than two months. Before the Eisenhower administration decided to intervene in Lebanon, Dulles had argued that "If we do not accept risk now, they [the Soviet Union] will probably decide that we will never accept risk and will push harder than ever." Khrushchev could hardly have overlooked a similar consideration.[147]

During the crisis, the NSC had never seriously expected China to invade Quemoy. When the crisis ended, however, the NSC staff concluded that "it was the show of strength on the part of the United States" that had deterred China from attacking Quemoy. In their view, the recent crisis demonstrated the soundness of a policy of firmness backed by force. They noted that within two days of Dulles's Newport statement, China agreed to return to the negotiating table.[148]

The US plans for the defense of the offshore islands that existed when the crisis began assumed that atomic weapons would be used against China.[149] The administration also took into account the possibility of Soviet intervention in case US forces attacked China. Had China invaded Quemoy in late August (when the US forces did not have plans even for escorting Nationalist convoys, but had plans for nuclear attacks on Chinese air installations and staging areas), the United States would not have been in a position to institute a conventional defense of the island. The invasion would have been over before US forces could even finalize plans for conventional defense of the islands. Having threatened to use nuclear weapons to defend Quemoy, the United States could not have backed down and surrendered the island to China without shattering allied confidence in its nuclear umbrella and its doctrine of massive retaliation for the defense of its vital interests. When convoying ran into problems in the middle of September, again, escalation by China would have placed the United States in the position of choosing between surrender and nuclear war. In the international climate of the 1950s, it is difficult to visualize the United States choosing retreat. The possibility of nuclear diplomacy changing into nuclear war was very real indeed.

The experience of the US armed forces in this crisis highlighted serious deficiencies in the US force posture. The Pacific Fleet's report on the naval operations in the crisis faulted the navy's plans for their excessive reliance on nuclear weapons. Because of "the assumption in existing military plans that nuclear weapons would be used" and a lack of detailed plans for the defense of the offshore islands (possibly due to confidence that US nuclear deterrence would forestall a Chinese threat), considerable delay occurred before decisions, plans, and procedures were sufficiently developed. Only "emergency, on-demand delivery of critical personnel, material, and nuclear weapons" saved the day. The report criticized the majority of operational plans for assuming that atomic weapons would be used and for not taking into account the possibility of relying only on conventional weapons. It stressed that "for the past few years, money and materials have been directed toward the nuclear capability to the detriment of the conventional weapon capability." US aircraft designed for high speed and atomic bombing were not ideal for conventional operations. The report recommended that "capabilities of, and plans for the use of conventional weapons systems, should be reviewed to provide for greater flexibility of action under various contingencies short of nuclear war."[150] The NSC staff also came to similar conclusions. In their view, the communists would provoke crises in such a manner that the risks for the United States would appear disproportionately high compared to the stakes in question. Handling such crises called for greater conventional capabilities for the US forces.[151] The US experience in this crisis thus powerfully reinforced the doubts that had already begun to crop up about the doctrine of massive retaliation. Plans for increasing US capability for limited war gained support as a result. This crisis put an end to the Eisenhower administration's glib talk that nuclear weapons were no different from conventional weapons.

Secretary of State Dulles clearly emerges as the driving force behind the US nuclear diplomacy in this crisis. To appreciate Dulles's dominance of American decision making during this period, one only needs to compare the outcomes of meetings that Dulles attended with those he did not attend. Dulles did not attend the NSC meeting of 7 August, at which

Eisenhower decided that there was no reason for the United States to intervene in the crisis. On 12 August, Dulles talked Eisenhower into agreeing that because of all the Nationalist troops in Quemoy, the United States had no choice but to defend it. Again, the meetings of 29 August, in Dulles's absence, had decided against the use of nuclear weapons, at least until Chinese actions became more threatening. By 4 September, Dulles succeeded in reopening the nuclear debate. Eisenhower in fact indicated on more than one occasion that he had differences of opinion with his secretary of state.[152]

The way the crisis ended was also very much Dulles's own handiwork. Dulles's pro-Nationalist leanings were founded not on any great liking for Chiang but on his anti-communist inclinations. In his opinion, formed long before he became secretary of state, "Chiang is bitter, arrogant and difficult for us and his Chinese associates to deal with. He distrusts the British, the Communists and the Americans, in that order. He has a vested interest in World War III, which alone, he feels, might restore his mainland rule."[153] Halfway through the latest crisis, Dulles learned that the risks of continuing to pander to Chiang's whims were far too high, and he deftly moved to defuse the main reason for tension in the Taiwan Strait.

This crisis marked a watershed in the US China policy. Right from the day the PRC came into existence, it had to live with the fear of a threat to its southern flank from the Nationalists, aided by the United States. From the end of the Korean War until the beginning of the crisis of 1954–1955, the United States had pursued an aggressive policy in this region consisting of support for Nationalist raids on the mainland and on Chinese and foreign shipping destined for Chinese ports, covert activities on the mainland, and provocative air and naval movements. The crisis of 1954–1955 focused attention on these activities. The United States had a hard time justifying its pursuit of these policies even while it castigated the Chinese for their aggressive line. As a result, these operations markedly declined after September 1954. After a few months, however, these activities resumed. In October 1957, NSC 5723 explicitly incorporated covert activities against China in US policy.[154]

The US nuclear diplomacy in this crisis drew adverse domestic and international attention to the American Far East policy, thus calling for a major revision of this policy in a way not foreseen by US policy makers. As a result, the United States changed over to a totally defensive posture in the region. Washington now not only publicly committed itself not to support a Nationalist invasion of the mainland, it even extracted a declaration by the ROC to abjure the use of force in its plan for returning to the mainland. The order to US forces to bend over backwards to avoid provoking the Chinese would have been unthinkable (if not politically suicidal) as late as when the crisis began. The United States also worked hard to end the Nationalist use of the offshore islands as bases for acts that provoked or threatened China. The outcome of the US nuclear diplomacy in the long term thus turned out to be in China's favor.

NOTES

1. See Alexander George and Richard Smoke, *Deterrence in American Foreign Policy: Theory and Practice* (New York: Columbia University Press, 1974); McGeorge Bundy, *Danger and Survival*. For other accounts of this crisis written before declassified documents became available, see J. H. Kalicki, *The Pattern of Sino-American Crises*; Melvin Gurtov and Byong-Moo Hwang, *China Under Threat: The Politics of Strategy and Diplomacy* (Baltimore, MD: Johns Hopkins University Press, 1980); Leonard H. Gordon, "United States' Opposition to Use of Force in the Taiwan Strait 1954–1962," *Journal of American History* (December 1985); Gordon Chang, *Friends and Enemies*; Richard Betts, *Nuclear Blackmail and Nuclear Balance*; Allen Whiting, "Jinmen 1958: Mao's Miscalculations," *China Quarterly* (June 1975).

2. Shu Guang Zhang, *Deterrence and Strategic Culture*; Thomas J. Christensen, *Useful Adversaries: Grand Strategy, Domestic Mobilization, and Sino-American Conflict, 1947–1958* (Princeton: Princeton University Press, 1996); George Eliades, "Once More unto the Breach: Eisenhower, Dulles, and Public Opinion During the Offshore Islands Crisis of 1958," *Journal of American–East Asian Relations* (Winter 1993). See also He Di, "The Evolution of the People's Republic of China's Policy Toward the Offshore Islands," in Warren Cohen and Akira Iriye (eds.), *The Great Powers in East Asia, 1953–1960* (New York: Columbia University Press, 1990); Zhai Qiang, *The Dragon, the Lion, and the Eagle: Chinese-British-American Relations, 1949–1958* (Kent, OH: Kent State University Press, 1994).

3. See Chapter 4.

4. Dulles told ROC Foreign Minister Dr. George Yeh that "we are trying by diplomacy to create a situation where you can keep the islands." Memcon, 4 October 1955, *FRUS 1955–57, III*, 111–12.

5. For documentation on these talks, see *FRUS 1955–57, III*.

6. Text of Agreed Announcement, 10 September 1955, ibid., 85–86. This agreement, insignificant when seen in the perspective of the foreign relations of two such large powers as the United States and China, was the only bilateral agreement reached between the United States and the PRC until the Shanghai Communique, signed by President Nixon and Zhou Enlai in 1972.

7. DOS to Johnson, 2 September and 13 September 1955, ibid., 75, 87.

8. Ibid., 102–5.

9. *FRUS 1955–57, III*, 193ff.

10. Dulles conceded that "the negotiating value of controls on trade with Communist China had just about reached the zero point" and was willing to consider relaxing them. The JCS, led by Radford, however, argued that if Washington relaxed controls on its trade with China, "we would be 'finished' in the Far East." In the end, the JCS views prevailed. Memo of 269th meeting of the NSC, *FRUS 1955–57, III*, 211.

11. *FRUS 1955–57, III*, 565.

12. On the reports of Chinese opposition to a "two-China" policy, see Meeker memo, 10 July 1956, Records of the Policy Planning Staff, "China," Lot 66D487, Box 18, RG 59, NA; Edwin Martin to Ralph Clough, 22 November 1957, and Clough to Robertson, 27 November 1957, "306.2 US Policy," Office of Chinese Affairs Files, Lot 60D648, Box 4, RG 59, NA; memo from Hugh S. Cumming (INR) to the Under Secretary, 29 November and unsigned memo, 22 November 1957, Box 5, ibid; CIA memo for Robert Cutler, 5 March 1958, OSANSA Files, Special Assistant Series, Subject Subseries, Box 11, "Basic National Security Policy," (DEPL).

13. *FRUS 1955–57, III*, 657–59.

14. Editorial note, *FRUS 1958–60, XIX*, 1.

15. Editorial note, *FRUS 1958–60, XIX*, 29; DOS to embassy in UK, 17 July 1958, 31–32.

16. Davis to Robertson, 3 August 1955, *FRUS 1955–57, III*, 13–14.

17. Chiang could not have used the strengthened forces on Quemoy to invade China, as Quemoy did not have adequate harbor facilities for launching a seaborne invasion. He might have felt that in the absence of an American guarantee of their defense, he needed increased forces on the islands to defend them. But he would have known that the forces in the islands would be at the mercy of a Chinese blockade that he could overcome only with strong American assistance. The significance of the large Nationalist presence in Quemoy and Matsu did not escape Mao. In his speech at the Supreme State Council meeting on 8 September, he said, "The problem lies in the 110,000 Guomindang troops, 95,000 men on Quemoy and 15,000 on Matsu. America has to pay attention to them as long as these two large garrisons are on the islands." *CWIHP Bulletin* (Winter 1995/1996), 219.

18. Summary of White House meeting, 29 August 1958, *FRUS 1958–60, XIX*, 98.

19. A State Department memo prepared in October 1958 for use by the White House Staff for public purposes glossed over the Nationalist reinforcement of the offshore islands as well as US acquiescence in it. The memo argued that the Nationalists had not increased the number of divisions in Quemoy, but only filled out their table of organization. "The United States," it maintained, "has allies, not satellites, and cannot force compliance with its ideas." State Department memo for Goodpaster, 13 October 1958, Staff Secretaries File, Subject Series, State Department Subseries, Box 3, "State Department—September 1958 to January 1959 (2)," DEPL; Green to Robertson, 6 October 1958, PPS Files (Declassified document, NND93301).

MAAG's information showed that Nationalist troop strength on the offshore islands increased from 68,000 in August 1954 to 79,000 in September 1954; from 79,000 in September 1955, it increased to 87,000 in September 1957 and decreased by 1,000 over the next year. The number of divisions declined from six in 1951 (when the troop strength was only 60,000) to five in August 1954, increased to six in September 1954, and stayed at six thereafter. Troops in Matsu totaled 23,000 in 1957. See Green to Robertson, 6 October 1958, PPS Records, NND 933301, RG 59, NA. As the numbers were supplied by the ROC in the midst of the controversy over the large Nationalist presence in the islands, they should be treated with some skepticism. US officials had reported in 1955 that a new division was moved to Quemoy in August 1955 (see note 16 above). Even the

ROC's figures showed that they had 109,000 troops in Quemoy and Matsu in August 1958.

20. Li Xiaobing, Chen Jian, and David Wilson, "Mao Zedong's Handling of the Taiwan Straits Crisis of 1958: Chinese Recollections and Documents," *CWIHP Bulletin* (Winter 1995/1996), 224, Note 22; ibid., 215.

21. Zhang, *Deterrence and Strategic Culture*, 234. China also indulged in a little nuclear diplomacy of its own. In the 23 May 1958 issue of the *Liberation Army Daily*, a Chinese Air Force general wrote that "The working class and scientists of China in the not too distant future will definitely be able to produce the most modern aircraft and atomic bombs." Chinese Foreign Minister Chen Yi told German reporters on 10 May that "at present China does not have atomic weapons, but in the future we will have them." Hong Kong to DOS, 793.5/11–2558, RG 59, NA.

22. Zhang, *Deterrence*, 235.

23. Li Xiaobing, "The Second Taiwan Straits Crisis Revisited," paper presented at the International Conference on New Findings on the Cold War in Asia at Hong Kong, 1996; Li Xiaobing et al., "Mao Zedong's Handling of the Taiwan Straits Crisis of 1958," 224, Note 5; Mao to Peng, ibid., 215–16; Kenneth Allen et al., *China's Air Force*, 62–64.

US aerial reconnaissance detected 36 aircraft at Chenghai airfield near Swato and 29 aircraft at Lungchi airfield, situated only 40 miles off of Quemoy. Robertson to Dulles, 8 August 1958, *FRUS 1958–60, XIX*, 44.

24. For a discussion of these factors, see Christensen, *Useful Adversaries*, Chapter 6.

25. Ibid., 240.

26. Lay memo, 28 September 1954, OSANSA Files, Policy Papers Series, Box 4, "NSC 146/2-Formosa and Chinese National Government (1)," DEPL; NSC Action No. 1302, *FRUS 1955–57, II*, 25, Footnote 23; ibid., *Vol. III*, 51; dispatch 357, Taipei to DOS, 10 September 1958, AWF, International, Box 10, "Formosa 1958 (1)," DEPL.

27. Herter to Chiang, 11 February 1958, *FRUS 1958–60, Vol. XIX*, 4–5; Robertson to Drumwright, 29 April 1958, 20. The United States, however, insisted on continued adherence to existing understandings regarding prior US-ROC consultation before undertaking any operations on the mainland.

28. Taipei to DOS, 3 April 1958, ibid., 12–15.

29. Record of NSC meeting on 13 January 1955, *FRUS 1955–57, II*, 25, Footnote 23; ibid., *Vol. III*, 51; dispatch 357, Taipei to DOS, 10 September 1958, AWF, International, Box 10, "Formosa 1958 (1)," DEPL; *New York Times*, 4 January and 7 May 1957; Thomas E. Stolper, *China, Taiwan, and the Offshore Islands* (Armonk, NJ: M. E. Sharpe, 1985), 115; NCNA editorials, 10 May and 11 May 1957, quoted in Clough to Robertson, 13 May 1957, Office of Chinese Affairs Files, Lot 60D648, Box 8, "430.1a Matador," RG 59, NA.

30. Rankin to DOS, 21 October 1955, *FRUS 1955–57, III*, 139–40.

31. Melvin Gurtov and Byong-Moo Hwang, *China Under Threat*, 82; Kalicki, *The Pattern of Sino-American Crises*, 180; Zhang, *Deterrence*, 225–27; "History of the Custody and Deployment of Nuclear Weapons" and "Deployment by Country 1951–1977," NSA website. On 2 May, Chiang, accompanied by US officials, witnessed the firing of Matadors. *New York Times*, 3 May 1958.

32. Bowie to Dulles, 19 August 1955, *FRUS 1955–57, III*, 51.

33. Allen et al., *China's Air Force*, 65; Robertson to Dulles, 8 August 1958, *FRUS 1958–60, XIX*, 44.

34. Taipei to DOS, 7 August 1958, *FRUS 1958–60, XIX*, 40–41; Dispatch No. 65, Taipei to DOS, 793.5/8–1358, RG 59, NA.

35. Robertson to Dulles, 8 August 1958, *FRUS 1958–60, XIX*, 44.

36. Memo of discussions at the 375th meeting of the NSC on 7 August 1958, AWF, NSC Series, Box 10, DEPL. The Formosa Resolution passed by Congress in January 1955 authorized the president to use US forces to defend Formosa and the Pescadores, as well as the offshore islands if, in his opinion, a Chinese attack on them was a prelude to an attack on Formosa and the Pescadores. See Chapter 4.

37. Memcon, 12 August 1958, Dulles Papers, White House Memo Series, Box 7, "White House—Meetings with the President, July 1, 1958–December 31, 1958 (8)," DEPL.

38. Goodpaster memcon, meeting with Eden, 31 January 1956, *FRUS 1955–57, III*, 294, Note 2; memo of Radford meeting with Nationalist Defense Minister, 24 February 1956, ibid, 315–16; PPS memo, 793.5/8–1358, RG 59, NA; Commander, Pacific Fleet, to CINPAC, 2 December 1958, CCS 381 Formosa (11–8–48) Sec. 42, JCS Records, RG 218, NA; Green to Parsons, 793.5/8–1858, RG 59, NA; Joseph F. Bouchard, *Command in Crisis* (New York: Columbia University Press, 1991), 65. See also Herter's account of the State-JCS meeting on 15 August in which the JCS explained their plans for atomic bombing of targets deep in China to stop a Chinese blockade of the offshore islands. Herter memo for Dulles, 15 August 1958, *FRUS 1958–60, XIX*, 56. The "low yield" atomic weapons in the JCS plans included 20-kiloton bombs—more powerful than those dropped on Japan in 1945.

39. Memo from General Cloves E. Byers, US Army, to Sprague, 22 August 1958, Envelope #2, Box 7, Radford Papers, RG 218, NA. Eisenhower later told a press conference that the offshore islands were now strategically more significant than they were during the last crisis. *New York Times*, 28 August 1958.

40. Bouchard, *Command in Crisis*, 68; Dwight D. Eisenhower, *The White House Years. Vol. 2: Waging Peace, 1956–1961* (Garden City, NY: Doubleday & Co., 1965), 296.

41. Bouchard, *Command in Crisis*, 68; Kalicki, *The Pattern of Sino-American Crises*, 173.

42. Zhang, *Deterrence and Strategic Culture*, 237.

43. Li, "The Second Taiwan Straits Crisis Revisited."

44. Ibid.

45. Bouchard, *Command in Crisis*, 60, 69, 71; Rear Admiral Robert J. Stroh (USN) to Green, 793.5/8–2558, RG 59, NA; memo of 378th NSC, 27 August 1958, AWF, NSC Series, Box 10, DEPL.

46. Goodpaster memo of conference on August 25, 1958, AWF, International, Box 10, "Formosa 1958 (3)," DEPL; Special Watch Report of the Intelligence Advisory Committee, August 29, 1958, ibid; JCS 947298, August 29, 1958, ibid; Bouchard, *Command in Crisis*, 69–70; CINPAC to JCS, 793.5/8–2658, RG 59, NA. Some have characterized this armada as the most powerful naval force ever assembled. See Bundy, *Danger and Survival*, 280.

47. Eisenhower, *Waging Peace*, 296; Goodpaster memcon, 25 August 1958, AWF, International Series, Box 10, "Formosa 1958 (3)," DEPL.

48. Goodpaster memcon, 29 August 1958, ibid.

49. JCS 947298, 29 August 1958, ibid; JCS 947414 to CINPAC, 2 September 1958, AWF, International, Box 10, "Formosa 1958 (1)," ibid.

50. COMTAIWANDEFCOM to CNO 9209, 3 September 1958, 793.5/9–358; Bouchard, *Command in Crisis*, 64–65; Chang, *Friends and Enemies*, 189.

51. Eisenhower, *Waging Peace*, 294; Dulles to Macmillan, 4 September 1958, AWF, International, Box 10, "Formosa 1958 (2)," DEPL; Eisenhower to Macmillan, 6 September 1958, AWF, International, Box 21, "Macmillan-President 6-1-58 to 9-30-58 (4)," ibid. In February 1958, Foreign Minister George Yeh had warned that the ROC might end its mutual defense treaty with the United States if the latter prevented it from invading the mainland. Radio Taipei broadcast of 5 February 1958, quoted in Kalicki, *The Pattern of Sino-American Crises*, 170.

52. CINPAC to JCS, 6481/6483, 26 August 1958, 793.5/8–2658, RG 59, NA.

53. Arleigh Burke Oral History, DEPL.

54. NSC 5810/1, 5 May 1958, NND 933301.

55. *Atlantic* (May 1959), 42.

56. Memo of telephone call to General Twining, 2 September 1958, Dulles Papers, Telephone Calls, Box 9, "Memo of Telecons—Gen. August 1, 1958, to October 31, 1958 (4)," DEPL.

57. Memcon 2 September 1958, *FRUS 1958–60, XIX*, 115–22.

58. "Taiwan Straits: Issues Developed in Discussions with the JCS," 2 September, 1958, AWF, International, Box 10, "Formosa 1958 (2)," and White House Staff Secretary File, Subject Series, State Department Subseries, Box 3, "State Department, September 1958–January 1959 (1)," DEPL.

59. "Summary," 3 September 1958, Dulles Papers, General Correspondence and Memo Series, Box 1, "Memcon-Gen-E through I (1)," DEPL; Smith to Dulles, 3 September 1958, *FRUS 1958–60, XIX*, 122–24. Although Smith participated in a meeting on 3 September at which the summary was redrafted, not much seems to have been changed. Memcon, 3 September 1958, *FRUS 1958–60, XIX*, 125–27.

60. Memo of conference in the office of the Secretary of State, 3 September 1958, AWF, International, Box 10, "Formosa 1958 (2)," DEPL; Memcon, 3 September 1958, *FRUS 1958–60, XIX*, 125–27.

61. Memcon, 4 September 1958, Dulles Papers, White House Memo Series, Box 7, "White House—Meetings with the President, 1 July, 1958–December 31, 1958 (7)," DEPL; Goodpaster memo, 4 September, AWF, International, Box 10, "Formosa (China) 1958–61 (3)," ibid. Marc Trachtenberg has argued that Dulles's statement "perhaps should be interpreted as an argument for revising 'our defense setup' and for moving away from such a great reliance on nuclear forces, or at the very least that it reflected a certain ambivalence about the nuclear question." Trachtenberg bases this argument on several statements by Dulles expressing ambivalence about the massive retaliation doctrine. However, in the context in which this particular statement was made, such a construction on it is simply not plausible. Trachtenberg, *History and Strategy*, 266–67.

62. Memcon, 4 September 1958, Dulles Papers, White House Memo Series, Box 7, "White House—Meetings with the President, 1 July, 1958–December 31,

1958 (7)," DEPL; Goodpaster memo, 4 September AWF, International, Box 10, "Formosa (China) 1958–61 (3)," ibid; Eisenhower, *Waging Peace*, 295, 299, 691–93. On "self-deterrence," see John L. Gaddis, "The Origins of Self-Deterrence: The United States and the Non-Use of Nuclear Weapons, 1945–1958," in Gaddis, *The Long Peace*. See also Gaddis, "The Unexpected John Foster Dulles: Nuclear Weapons, Communism, and the Russians," in Richard H. Immerman (ed.), *John Foster Dulles and the Diplomacy of the Cold War* (Princeton, NJ: Princeton University Press, 1990).

    63. Eisenhower, *Waging Peace*, 299; Transcript of news conference, Dulles Papers, White House Memo Series, Box 7, 'White House—Meetings with the President, July 1, 1958–December 31, 1958 (8)," DEPL.

    64. Dulles to Macmillan, 4 September 1958, AWF, International, Box 10, "Formosa 1958 (2)," DEPL.

    65. *New York Times*, 4, 5, 6 September 1958; UPI Bulletin, 3 September 1958, AWF, International Series, Box 10, "Formosa 1958 (3)," DEPL; Telephone call to Greene from Cumming, 17 September 1958, Dulles Papers, Telephone Series, Box 9, "Memos of tel cons.—Gen. August 1, 1958, to October 31, 1958," ibid.; *New York Times*, September 13 and 28, 1958.

    66. Press release, dated 6 September 1958, AWF, DEPL; Goodpaster memo, 8 September AWF, International, Box 10, "Formosa 1958 (2)," ibid.

    67. Ibid.

    68. Green memo, 18 September 1958, *FRUS 1958–60, XIX*, 221; Bouchard, *Command in Crisis*, 71–72. See also *New York Times*, 14 September 1958.

    69. COMUSTDC to JCS, 793.5/9–1458, RG 59, NA; Bouchard, *Command in Crisis*, 71–72; dispatch No. 65, Taipei to DOS, 793.5/8–1358, RG 59, NA; JCS 947931, AWF, International, Box 10, "Formosa 1958 (1)," ibid.; COMTAIWAN-DEFCOM (US) to CINPAC, 2 September 1958, ibid; Memo of conference in the office of the Secretary of State, 3 September 1958, AWF, International, Box 10, "Formosa 1958 (2)," DEPL; Memo of telephone conversation with the President, September 1, 1958, Dulles Papers, Telephone Calls Series, Box 13, "Memos of Telecons—White House—August 1, 1958–December 5, 1958, (3)," DEPL; Telegram from Smoot to CINPAC, 2 September 1958, *FRUS 1958–60, XIX*, 114; COMTAIWANDEFCOM to CINPAC, 793.5/9–2758, RG 59, NA; Memcon 793.5/9–1258; Memcon, 793.5/9–1558, RG 59, NA; Robertson memo to Dulles, 793.5/9–1258, ibid. Dulles was being more charitable than the situation warranted. The Nationalists had been conducting raids on the mainland for years using the kind of landing crafts used in resupplying Quemoy.

Despite his sympathy for the Nationalists, Dulles was critical of Nationalist naval tactics. When he heard that two landing crafts of the last convoy simply turned tail and returned to base after their first attempt to land failed, without waiting to try again, Dulles wondered why they had not waited beyond range of the Chinese guns and suddenly dashed in at an opportune moment.

    70. COMTAIWANDEFCOM (US) to JCS, 31 August 1958, AWF, International, Box 10, "Formosa 1958 (1)"; Dispatch No. 352 from Taipei to DOS, 793.5/9–1058, RG 59, NA.

    71. Message #3705 from COMUSTDC, 793.5/9–1458, RG 59, NA.

    72. SNIE 100–11–58, 16 September 1958, *FRUS 1958–60, XIX*, 205–6.

    73. "381st meeting of the NSC, 2 October 1958," AWF, NSC Series, Box 10,

DEPL; *New York Times*, 25 and 29 September 1958; Memcon, 30 September 1958, AWF, DDE Diary, Box 36, "Staff Notes—September 1958." DEPL; Goodpaster memcon, 29 September 1958, *FRUS 1958–60, XIX*, 296; COMUSTADC to CIN-PAC, 8 October 1958, ibid., 348–49.

74. Kalicki, *The Pattern of Sino-American Crises*, 193; *New York Times*, 5 and 7 September 1958. Columnist James Reston also wrote in the *Times* on 4 September that Chiang had deployed his forces in Quemoy in order to force the US hand.

75. Letters and telegrams regarding Formosa and the Offshore Islands as of 9/9/58, AWF, International, Box 10, "Formosa 1958 (1)," DEPL; Washburn to Eisenhower, 9 September 1958, AWF, Adm. Series, Box 29, "Quemoy and Matsu—Washburn, Abbott," ibid; Green to Eisenhower, 29 September 1958, Dulles Papers, White House Memo Series, Box 7, "White House—Meetings with the President, July 1, 1958–December 31, 1950 (5)," DEPL; *New York Times*, 26 and 13 September 1958.

76. AJ de la Mare to Dalton, September 26, 1958, FO 371/133535/ FCN 1193/ 339, PRO.

77. Enclosure to Washburn to Eisenhower, 9 September AWF, Adm. Series, Box 29, "Quemoy and Matsu-Washburn, Abbott," DEPL; Staff Notes No. 414, 3 September AWF, DDE Diary, Box 36, "Toner Notes—September 1958," ibid.

78. Dispatch 551 from Bonn to Sec. of State, 793.5/9–558, RG 59, NA; CIA Summary of World Reaction to the President's Speech of September 11 on the Far East Crisis, Staff Secretary Papers, Subject Series, Alphabetical Subseries, Box 7, "CIA, Vol. 1, (9) August–September 1958," DEPL; *New York Times*, 2, 11 September 1958; Dispatch 782, Manila to DOS, 1 September 1958, 793.5/9–158, RG 59, NA; Macomber memcon, 12 October 1958, Dulles Papers, General Correspondence and Memo Series, Box 1, "Memos of Conversations, E through I, (1)," DEPL.

79. JCS memo (undated, but probably dated September 3, 1958) to Secretary of Defense, AWF, International, Box 10, "Formosa 1958 (2)," DEPL; "The Taiwan Strait Situation," 3 September 1958, Appendix to ibid; Boster memo, 12 September 1958, 793.5/9–1258, RG 59, NA; Howe, *Multicrises*, 164; Eisenhower, *Waging Peace*, 300.

80. Telephone call from the President, 10 September 1958, Dulles Papers, Telephone Calls Series, Box 13, "Memos of Tel Cons—White House—August 1, 1958–December 31, 1958 (3)," DEPL; Memcon with the President, 11 and 29 September 1958, Dulles Papers, White House Memo Series, Box 7, "White House—Meetings with the President, July 1, 1958, to December 31, 1958 (5)," ibid.; Gray Memo for the record, 12 September 1958, NSC Series, Subject Subseries, Box 1, "Atomic Weapons, Corr. & Background for Presidential Approval, Policy re Use(2)," ibid.; Memcon, 21 September 1958, AWF, DDE Diary, Box 36, "Staff Notes—September 1958," ibid. McElroy suggested that if Chiang could not be persuaded "to get off the islands without losing control in Formosa," the United States should look for someone else who could do so. Eisenhower's response to this suggestion was not recorded. Goodpaster memo, 15 September 1958, AWF, DDE Diary, Box 36, "Staff Notes—September 1958," ibid; Herter to Dulles, 6 October 1958, *FRUS 1958–60*, XIX, 335.

81. Dulles memo to Herter and Robertson, 23 August 1958, *FRUS 1958–60, XIX*, 69.

82. Green to Robertson, 7 September 1958, 793.5/9–758, RG 59, NA; Memcon, 793.5/9–1258, ibid.; State Department to Taipei, 1 October 1958, ibid; memcon, 19 September 1958 (with Lloyd), PPS Files, NND 933301, ibid.; Chang, *Friends and Enemies*, 198; Dulles memo of telephone call from Vice President, 25 September 1958, Dulles Papers, Telephone Calls Series, Box 9, "Memos of Tel. Conversations—Gen., August 1, 1958, to October 31, 1958 (3)," DEPL; memcon, 8 September 1958, ibid.

83. Record of State Department meeting, 8 October 1958, *FRUS 1958–60, XIX*, 351.

84. Richard Stebbins, *The United States in World Affairs, 1958* (New York: Simon and Schuster, 1959), 322.

85. Navy memo for the JCS, 8 September 1958, JCS Records, Radford Papers, Box 7, "091 China 1959," RG 218, NA.

86. DOS to Taipei, 25 September 1958, *FRUS 1958–60, XIX*, 274; Memo of Dulles conversation with French Foreign Minister Couve de Murville, 26 September 1958, PPS Files, NND 933301; memo of Dulles conversation with Selwyn Lloyd, 25 September 1958, ibid.

87. Memo of conversation in the State Department, 8 September 1958, *FRUS 1958–60, XIX*, 157.

88. Memcon, 11 September 1958, Dulles Papers, White House Memo Series, Box 7, "WH—Meetings with the President, July 1–31 December 1958 (6)," DEPL.

89. Memcon, 20 September 1958, ibid., 242; Whisenand Memo for Twining, 22 September 1958, Radford Papers, Box 7, "O91 China 1957" (Envelope), RG 218, NA.

90. Since the base point for the three-mile limit was given as the shores of Quemoy, it seemed to the embassy to be a tacit admission of Chinese claims to the islands. Dispatch 485, Taipei to DOS, 793.5/9–2658; Dispatch 291, dated 1 October 1958, DOS to Taipei, 793.5/9–2658, RG 59, NA.

91. Beam to DOS, 18 September 1958, *FRUS 1958–60, XIX*, 209–10.

92. Beam to DOS, 22 September 1958, ibid., 258.

93. Memo of Dulles meeting with Selwyn Lloyd, 25 September 1958, PPS Records, NND 933301, RG 59, NA.

94. Dulles memo of telephone call to the President, 22 September, Dulles Papers, Telephone Calls Series, Box 13, "Memos of Tel. Con.—White House—August 1, 1958–December, 31, 1958 (2)," DEPL; Dulles memo of telephone call from President, 16 September 1958, Folder (3), ibid.; Memcon, 30 September AWF, DDE Diary, "Staff Notes—September 1958," DEPL.

95. *New York Times*, 26 September 1958.

96. *New York Times*, 29 September, 1 October 1958; Kalicki, *The Pattern of Sino-American Crises*, 197. Dulles told Italian Prime Minister Fanfani that Beam had "in a very gingerly fashion" "attempted to ascertain whether, if Taiwan in fact abandoned the offshore island positions, they would give a meaningful guarantee of the status quo in the Pacific at large." Memo of Dulles conversation with Fanfani, 18 October 1958, PPS Files, NND 933301.

97. Taipei to DOS, 6 October 1958, 793.00/10–658.

98. USUN to DOS, 7 October 1958, *FRUS 1958–60, XIX*, 347.

99. CNO to CINPAC, No. 25002, 6 October 1958, AWF, International, Box 10, "Formosa 1958 (1)," DEPL; CNO to CINPAC, No. 25022, October 6, 1958, ibid.

100. DOS to Beam, 8 October 1958, *FRUS 1958–60, XIX*, 355–56; Beam to DOS, 10 October 1958, ibid., 373.

101. DOS to Beam, 13 October 1958, ibid., 398.

102. Beam to DOS, 10 October 1958, ibid., 373. See also Beam to DOS, 16 September 1958, PPS Records, NND 933301.

103. COMUSTDC MAAG to Taiwan Patrol Force, 21 October 1958, Staff Secretary Papers, Subject Series, State Dept. Subseries, Box 3, "State Dept.—September 1958–January 1959 (2)," DEPL.

104. Dispatch 828, Taipei to DOS, 793.5/12–3058, RG 59, NA. Only minor incidents such as stray firing on foreign vessels calling at Chinese ports took place in the next couple of years. OCB Report, 18 May 1960, OSANSA Files, NSC Series, Policy Papers Subseries, Box 22, "NSC 5723-Policy toward Taiwan and ROC," DEPL; Martin to Parsons, 10 July 1959, 793.5/7–1059, RG 59, NA.

105. John S. D. Eisenhower memo for the record, 30 October 1958, *FRUS 1958–60, XIX*, 475.

106. Smith memo for Dulles, 15 October 1958, PPS Files, NND 933301.

107. Eisenhower to Dulles, 7 October 1958, *FRUS 1958–60, XIX*, 346. British Admiral Lord Louis Mountbatten's advice, based on his personal experience with Chiang, was that "if one took a strong line with Chiang and at the same time gave him a face-saving means of retreat, he would back down." He thought that if Washington handled the Generalissimo firmly and gave him some sops, such as equipment for amphibious operations, Chiang could be persuaded to withdraw from the offshore islands. Memo of Mountbatten's meeting with Dulles, 17 October 1958, *FRUS 1958–60, XIX*, 410–11.

108. Dulles thought of sending John J. McCloy to deal with Chiang. McCloy, however, refused. McCloy to Dulles, 27 September 1958, Staff Secretary Files, Subject Series, State Department Subseries, Box 3, "State Department—September 1958–January 1959 (1)," DEPL.

109. Dispatch DULTE 4, 22 October 1958, Staff Secretary Papers, Subject Series, State Department Subseries, Box 3, "State Dept.—September 1958 to January 1959 (2)," DEPL; Memcon, 22 October 1958, *FRUS 1958–60, XIX*, 428–29. This idea was first raised by Gerard Smith. Smith memo for Dulles, 17 October 1958, PPS Files, NND 933301.

110. Memo of Dulles conversation with Chiang, 22 October, 7:00 P.M., PPS Files, NND 933301. On 7 November 1958, by which time the second crisis had wound down, Dulles asked the JCS for information on the effects of atomic strikes against Chinese artillery installations. After considerable debate, the JCS informed him that airbursts that could destroy artillery emplacements would have "no significant radioactive fallout implications." The JCS's views were probably based on the conclusions of a new staff study. This study, however, did not consider the effects of radiation. PPS officials felt that the Nationalist forces in the offshore islands as well the civilian population there should undergo drills for sheltering themselves from radiation. The Chinese would notice the drills and draw appropriate conclusions. Mathews to Green, 31 January 1958, 793.5/1–3159; Betts, *Nuclear Blackmail and Nuclear Balance*, 69–70.

111. COMTAIWANDEFCOM (US) TO CINPAC, 25 October 1958, 793.5/10–2558, RG 59, NA.

112. Dulles to Lloyd, 19 November 1958, PPS Files, NND933301.

113. Ibid., 216–17.

114. Green to Parsons, 22 October 1958, PPS Files, NND 933301.

115. Between 24 August and 29 August, Chinese shelling of Quemoy averaged 10,000 shells a day. From 30 August to 4 September, it fell to less than 1,000 a day. The only Chinese aerial bombardment of Quemoy took place on 24 August, when they dropped eight bombs. The Chinese stopped shelling from 5 September to 7 September and resumed on 8 September in protest against American escort of Nationalist shipping. Shelling increased to more than 11,000 a day until 6 October, when the Chinese declared a cease-fire. Stolper, *China, Taiwan, and the Offshore Islands*, 118–19. The Chinese shelling on odd-numbered days continued for the next 20 years.

116. Memcon, 30 October 1958, Staff Secretary Papers, Subject Series, State Dept. Subseries, Box 3, "State Department—September 1958 to January 1959 (2)," DEPL; memo of conversation with the President, 30 October 1958, Dulles Papers, White House Memo Series, Box 7, "White House Meetings with the President, July 1, 1956–December 31, 1958 (3)," DEPL. On China's extension of its territorial waters to 12 miles, see the *New York Times*, 5 September 1958.

117. Memcon, 9 October 1958, ibid., 357.

118. See Note 1. On the NSC staff's views, see "Ten Principal Conclusions and Lessons Deriving from the Taiwan Crisis," 27 February 1959, OSANSA Records, NSC Series, Briefing Notes Subseries, Box 8, "Foreign Policy Matters," DEPL.

119. Zhang, *Deterrence and Strategic Culture*, 250–52; He Di, "Paper or Real Tiger"; Li Xiaobing et al., "Mao Zedong's Handling of the Taiwan Straits Crisis of 1958"; Memo of Dulles's conference with Eisenhower, 4 September 1958, *FRUS 1958–60, XIX*, 131. Beijing radio reported on 6 September that China had stopped shelling two days before. *New York Times*, 7 September 1958.

120. He Di, "Evolution of the People's Republic of China's Policy toward the Offshore Islands," 236; Li Xiaobing et al., "Mao Zedong's Handling of the Taiwan Straits Crisis of 1958," 216–21.

121. Ibid., 240.

122. He Di, "Evolution of the People's Republic of China's Policy toward the Offshore Islands," 240.

123. Ibid., 240–41; Li Xiaobing et al., "Mao Zedong's Handling of the Taiwan Straits Crisis of 1958," *CWIHP Bulletin* (Winter 1995/1996), 221–23.

124. Li Xiaobing, "Second Taiwan Strait Crisis Revisited."

125. Stolper, *China, Taiwan, and the Offshore Islands*, 131.

126. Memo of proceedings, AWF, NSC Series, Box 10, 382nd meeting of NSC, 13 October 1958, DEPL.

127. Undated Cuming memo to Acting Secretary, PPS Files, NND 933301.

128. "Ten Principal Conclusions and Lessons Deriving from the Taiwan Crisis," 27 February 1959, OSANSA Records, NSC Series, Briefing Notes Subseries, Box 8, "Foreign Policy Matters," DEPL.

129. Memcon, 25 October 1958, PPS Files, NND933301.

130. Memo of State Department meeting, 8 October 1958, *FRUS 1958–60, XIX*, 350.

131. Memo of Dulles conversation with Yeh, 13 October 1958, *FRUS 1958–60, XIX*, 383.

132. Zhang, *Deterrence and Strategic Culture*, 261; Christensen, *Useful Adversar-*

ies, 230–33. See also Zhai Qiang, *The Dragon, The Lion and the Eagle*; He Di, "Evolution of the People's Republic of China's Policy toward the Offshore Islands."

133. *New York Times*, 9 September 1958.

134. He later told a TASS correspondent that "the USSR will come to the help of the CPR if the latter is attacked from without; speaking more concretely, if the United States attacks the CPR." Ibid., 195.

135. Chang, *Friends and Enemies*, 191–92.

136. Ibid., 193–94.

137. Transcript of news conference, Dulles Papers, White House Memo Series, Box 7, "White House—Meetings with the President, July 1, 1958–December 31, 1958," DEPL.

138. Chang, *Friends and Enemies*, 195–96.

139. Andrei Gromyko, *Memories* (London: Hutchinson, 1989), 251.

140. Chang, *Friends and Enemies*, 190.

141. *New York Times*, 22 February 1988. For Mao to mention this plan to Gromyko, he really did not need to believe in an American invasion of China. Mao was hardly the person from whom to expect a standard of rectitude seldom applied to political leaders.

142. Mark Kramer, "The USSR Foreign Ministry's Appraisal of Sino-Soviet Relations on the Eve of the Split, September 1959," in *CWIHP Bulletin* (Winter 1995/1996), 174.

143. *New York Times*, 5, 6 September 1958.

144. Ibid. Wu Lengxi also claimed that Khrushchev "did not have any idea about our intentions in shelling Jinmen [Quemoy]." Wu Lengxi, "Inside Story of the Decision Making during the Shelling of Jinmen," *CWIHP Bulletin* (Winter 1995/1996), 211.

145. Text of Khrushchev letter, ibid., 226–27.

146. British Embassy, Washington, to DOS, 2 October 1958, *FRUS 1958–60, XIX*, 322.

147. Memo of White House conversation, 14 July 1958, *FRUS 1958–60, XI*, 212.

148. "Ten Principal Conclusions and Lessons Deriving from the Taiwan Crisis," 27 February 1959, OSANSA Records, NSC Series, Briefing Notes Subseries, Box 8, "Foreign Policy Matters," DEPL.

149. C-in-C, Pacific Fleet, to CINPAC, 20 December 1958, CCS 381 Formosa (11–8–48) Sec. 42, Box 147, Records of the JCS, RG 218, NA.

150. C-in-C, Pacific Fleet, to CINPAC, 20 December 1958, CCS 381 Formosa (11–8–48) Sec. 42, Box 147, Records of the JCS, RG 218, NA.

151. "Ten Principal Conclusions and Lessons Deriving from the Taiwan Crisis," 27 February 1959, OSANSA Records, NSC Series, Briefing Notes Subseries, Box 8, "Foreign Policy Matters," DEPL.

152. Gray Memcon, 12 September 1958, NSC Series, Subject Subseries, Box 1, "Atomic Weapons, Corr. & Background for Presidential Approval, Policy re Use(2)," DEPL; Goodpaster memo, 15 September 1958, AWF, DDE Diary, Box 36, "Staff Notes—September 1958," DEPL.

153. Dulles memo, 31 March 1952, Dulles Papers, Box 60, "Formosa 1952," Princeton University.

154. NSC 5723, 4 October 1957, *FRUS 1955–57, III*, 621.

CHAPTER 6

Conclusions

NUCLEAR DIPLOMACY AND THE US CHINA POLICY

American nuclear diplomacy toward China in the 1950s offers a practical lesson on the merits of what Eisenhower, as the US Chief of Army Staff, had argued in 1946:

The atomic bomb is not an all-purpose weapon. One would not use a pile-driver for driving tacks when a tack hammer would do a better and a cheaper job. . . . The atomic bomb cannot stand alone in the nation's arsenal. To put all our reliance on that one powerful weapon is to court disaster.[1]

Sino-American relations had stood at a crossroads in the beginning of 1950. Despite Washington's decision to disengage itself from the Chinese civil war, the United States continued to recognize the ROC as the legitimate government of the whole of China. Some American assistance to the Nationalists had continued, although in vastly reduced quantities than earlier. Nevertheless, the possibility had remained of the United States arriving at some form of working relationship with the PRC. By the spring of 1950, the chances of a Sino-American rapprochement receded and the Truman administration began to move in the direction of denying Taiwan to communist China. The Korean War then turned Sino-American relations into active hostility. As the war dragged on, the American commitment to the defense of Taiwan solidified. The United States began first to tolerate and then to encourage Nationalist raids on China. Since the Truman administration left office before the end of the war, one can only speculate as to what its postwar policy toward China might have been. Even during the war, Acheson had not given up hopes of eventually splitting communist China from the Soviet bloc.[2] The Democratic Party and its administration did not have many ardent supporters of the Nationalists within their ranks. It is, therefore, unlikely that Sino-American relations would have become as hostile under a Democratic administration as they became during the Eisenhower administration. A Democratic administration might not also have been as eager to rebuff Chinese overtures for a rapprochement as the Republican administration was in the period between the two Taiwan Strait crises.

Strategically, the beginning of 1950 found the United States heavily dependent on the deterrent power of its nuclear arsenal. However, when the Korean War seemed to confirm the exaggerated fears of communist expansionism contained in NSC 68, the Truman administration quickly embarked on a massive rearmament program aimed at providing the United States with the conventional forces required to give it "preponderant power" on a global scale. The Truman administration consistently held atomic weapons to be in a wholly separate category from conventional weapons, despite its strategic reliance on atomic weapons throughout the late 1940s and its willingness to resort to nuclear diplomacy in the Korean War.

The incoming Eisenhower administration did not relax American hostility toward China even after the Korean War ended. It actively assisted in maintaining a threat to China's southern flank by building up the Nationalist forces to levels far beyond what the ROC's defense required, encouraging the Nationalists to carry out raids on China, and keeping alive Chiang's dreams of one day returning to the mainland. After repeated crises with China, the Eisenhower administration found this policy no longer tenable. By the end of the second crisis in the Taiwan Strait in 1958, the United States effectively "re-leashed" Chiang. Moreover, Dulles went on record with statements one would never have thought him capable of making if one did not see them in cold print. If peace in the Taiwan Strait meant giving up much of the administration's policies of the preceding six years, Dulles was prepared to oblige. US policy toward communist China reverted to more or less its status just before the Korean War started, with the difference that the United States now had a formal commitment to defend the ROC. After eight years of confrontation and war, Sino-American relations had come full circle.

The Eisenhower administration also began by totally breaking with the Truman administration's policy on nuclear weapons. It decided to drastically scale back outlays for conventional forces and proposed to treat nuclear weapons just like any other weapon, to be used against *any* adversary's military targets. By the end of 1958, the Eisenhower administration's nuclear policy also had come full circle. The administration learned that nuclear weapons were indeed different from conventional weapons. Nuclear diplomacy would no longer play the central role in the American strategy for containing communist China. In its approach to nuclear diplomacy, just as much as in its China policy, the Eisenhower administration thus spent the greater part of its time reinventing the wheel.

In the eight years covered by this study, American presidents found themselves on several occasions in situations where nuclear weapons placed them in invincible positions as they faced critical decisions that, in the absence of nuclear weapons, they would have been hard pressed to take. The first occurred when the Korean War started and Truman faced the choice of intervening or not intervening in defense of South Korea. Under current US strategic planning, Korea was not important enough for the United States to fight a full-scale land war in that theater; nor did the United States possess the conventional forces required for fighting a major war in Korea if, at the same time, it had to deal with a serious conflict in the strategically more important European theater. As the situation appeared to American leaders in Washington, the North Korean invasion might well have been part of a wider Soviet decision to challenge the West. The second occasion was when China entered the Korean War and confronted the United States with a choice between a forced evacuation from Korea or staying on and fighting a war in which, if the communist side resorted to further escalation, US forces would have met with disaster. If the Soviet Union intervened in Korea or raised tensions in Europe on either of these occasions, the US presence in Korea would have been untenable. US global war plans specifically called for the evacuation of Korea in the event of a war with the Soviet Union. In June 1950, as well as when China entered the war in November 1950, Truman had to take into account the possibility that both the Soviet Union and China could, if they employed the full power at their disposal, drive the US forces out of Korea.

The third and fourth occasions were in the two Taiwan Strait crises, when Dulles convinced himself and others in the administration that the United States faced a war with China over Quemoy and Matsu. The Eisenhower administration did not consider these islands vital to the survival of Taiwan and, hence, of little strategic importance to the United States. The American stakes in these crises did not justify significant American costs. On both occasions, the Pentagon considered the losses to US forces from a conventional intervention unacceptable. In the two crises, the United States had a clear choice whether or not to intervene.

Although not critical for US national interests, the stakes in these situations were vital for American presidents from a political standpoint. The "loss of China" debate, the personal attacks on Acheson, and the need to sustain domestic support for the administration's overall national security strategy made it impossible for Truman to stand by and let South Korea fall to communism. A withdrawal from Korea in the face of Chinese intervention would have been equally, or more, disastrous politically. The extent of domestic support for American intervention in defense of Quemoy and Matsu was questionable. However, what is important is that Eisenhower and Dulles believed that the political fallout of the loss of these islands to communist China was unacceptable. The decisions that dependence on conventional forces alone would have forced on the Truman and Eisenhower administrations were, on political grounds, unacceptable to the two administrations.

If Truman did not flinch during the critical moments of the Korean War, it was, to a considerable extent, because in the last resort he could use atomic weapons to save US forces from disaster. Truman could also be confident that the threat of strategic atomic bombing would deter the Soviet Union from using the American preoccupation in Asia to threaten American interests in Europe. In the judgment of this author, it is unlikely that just when the Korean War seemed to vindicate the fears of Soviet expansionism that NSC 68 had spelled out in such graphic detail, Truman would have risked considerable American forces in a theater from which they would have been evacuated in the event of global war, if he did not have something up his sleeve to prevent that eventuality. American atomic superiority over the Soviet Union gave Truman a trump card he could use to deter Soviet intervention. Atomic weapons also gave Truman the confidence that in case US troops found themselves in an untenable situation after China entered the war, he could extricate them from a total disaster. In the ultimate analysis, atomic weapons made the US intervention in the Korean War possible; they also made it easy for the United States to continue fighting and to follow a tough stand in the armistice negotiations.

Nuclear weapons gave the Eisenhower administration a similar hedge against failure in the Taiwan Strait crises as well as a guarantee that China would not escalate the military situation in both the conflicts. Tactical nuclear weapons ensured that in material and human terms, the cost of defending the offshore islands would have been negligible for the United States. The Eisenhower administration would never have thought of fighting a purely conventional war on the Chinese mainland so soon after the end of the Korean War, nor would Dulles have thought of provoking a war with China, if he was sure that such a war would be a conventional one.

Reliance on nuclear weapons influenced the course of American policies in these confrontations in other ways besides facilitating decisions to intervene in situations from which the United States might well have kept out absent its nuclear capability. In the Taiwan Strait crises, conventional forces could have easily repulsed any invasion of the offshore islands that China was capable of launching in the 1950s. It was the desire to limit American casualties that led to the talk of using nuclear weapons. Once it was decided in principle to use nuclear weapons, the military became even more ambitious and developed plans to bomb targets deep in China far beyond the coastal artillery positions and airfields China might have used in any operation against the offshore islands. The Eisenhower administration, principally the JCS and the secretary of state, also tended to gloss over the high levels of civilian casualties that nuclear bombing in the vicinity of China's large cities might inflict. While the United States sought to avoid the political costs of high American casualties in a conventional defense of the offshore islands, the rest of the world considered the preferred American military plans far exceeding the level of commensurate force to meet the objective that they were willing to support.

There are two aspects to the question of linking means and ends. One is to look at it from the angle of cost-effectiveness. When the JCS or Dulles discussed the use of nuclear weapons against China, they merely noted that nuclear weapons were indeed usable against Chinese artillery installations and that they would do the job very quickly and cheaply. From their point of view, that was all there was to it. But the rest of the world and large segments of American opinion looked at the matter from a different perspective. They refused to accept that a nuclear war was an appropriate means to gain the ends involved—defending the Nationalist possession of a few tiny, barren islands that most people believed rightly belonged to China, which possessed no strategic value from the US point of view, and the Nationalist possession of which was the major destabilizing factor in the region.

The question whether resort to nuclear diplomacy would eventually have led to actual use of nuclear weapons is debatable. Given the state of the documentation available, it is difficult to say definitively whether Truman would have authorized the use of atomic weapons in the Korean War if suitable targets had been available. As this study has shown, in contrast to the verbal nuclear diplomacy directed at China, all of the movements of atomic bombers that Truman made targeted the Soviet Union. However, the way Pentagon planning proceeded, and from available evidence that a plan that involved the use of nuclear weapons with prior presidential authorization *was* approved, one must conclude that if a Chinese offensive had reached a point where it threatened the Eighth Army, Truman would have authorized the use of atomic weapons to secure its withdrawal. In such an operation, targets for atomic strikes might well have been found when the Chinese forces massed for an attack. Truman might have initially suffered moral doubts about using atomic weapons against the Chinese or the North Koreans. If so, he seems to have overcome them fairly quickly. The *New York Times* had editorialized during the war:

The atom bomb has impressed the imagination and the emotions of the world in a way unparalleled in history. Therefore its use raises great moral, psychological and political as well as military issues. . . . The duty of the President, of all statesmen and all citizens of the free world, is to recognize that the use of the atom bomb would be an earth-shaking development but that the time may come when the fate of the Western World is at stake. If that time comes we will have all free people with us, but we must be sure that we are not alone in the world in believing the moment has come, or that even our great allies like Britain and France disapprove.[3]

Truman's record in following this advice is, at best, spotty.[4]

Moral scruples, based on the disproportion between the insignificant stakes in these crises and nuclear war in their defense, played no part in preventing the Eisenhower administration from actually using nuclear weapons against China either. The moral issue certainly troubled large segments of American public opinion. The Eisenhower administration, however, deserves no credit for this. Its primary concern was how to overcome the public's qualms about the use of nuclear weapons for offensive purposes. From the administration's own point of view, atomic weapons were perfectly appropriate for use in these crises. As late as June 1958, the NSC was discussing a "public education and information program to show the relative efficiency of nuclear weapons."[5]

What prevented the Eisenhower administration from using atomic weapons against China might have been a combination of several factors. First, China did not have definite plans for an invasion of the offshore islands in either of the two crises. Confronted by the possibility of US intervention with nuclear weapons, they backed down from even their limited attempts to raise the level of tension in the Taiwan Strait area. Second, the administration did not have adequate domestic support for using atomic weapons to defend the offshore islands. This became a serious concern, especially during the crisis in 1958. Third, the administration realized that using atomic weapons against China to defend the offshore islands would have serious consequences for overall US strategic interests. Washington feared that the threat of global nuclear war might tempt key allies such as the Europeans and the Japanese to opt for neutralism, with disastrous consequences for the US capability to deal with the Soviet Union. This more than anything else was the chief worry of the Eisenhower administration. At no point is there any evidence of the American leaders' own moral scruples influencing any decision by the Eisenhower administration on the use of atomic weapons.

Some historians have tried to paint the Eisenhower administration's policy toward China as an ingenious policy—the so-called "wedge strategy"—designed to split China from the Soviet Union by applying pressure on China. Faced with unrelenting American pressure, the wedge strategy holds, China would make demands on the Soviet Union for aid on a scale that the latter would be unable to meet, leading China, in frustration, to leave the Soviet camp.[6] But while the idea of applying pressure on China indeed influenced all of these decisions, the idea of applying such pressure *as a deliberate policy in order to drive a wedge between the Soviet Union and China* never figured in the administration's considerations in any of these decisions, in the administration's statements of basic US policy toward China, or in its discussions on responses to various crises. Moreover, Dulles had no intention of relaxing the pressure on communist China even if China broke with the Soviet Union. The Eisenhower administration maintained that a communist China, even if it was not aligned with the Soviet Union, would still be an enemy. In fact, the US policy toward China was harsher than its policy toward the Soviet Union, with which it had trade and diplomatic relations. China could not afford two enemies. If the Chinese could get some assurance that the breaking of their alliance with the Soviet Union would lead to normal relations with the United States, the situation might have been different. But Washington held out no such prospect. Even in late 1958, Dulles was positive that "as long as he is Secretary of State there will be no change in US policy toward the Chinese Communists so far as US recognition or their admission to the UN are concerned." He was "emphatic" that "the basic concept of US policy toward Communist China as set forth in it [his San Francisco speech] should remain unchanged."[7] As Robertson wrote to Under Secretary of State Christian Herter in August 1958, "in the absence of any real evidence that Moscow and Peiping are drifting apart, it would be dangerous, even fatal, to base our policies or actions on the shifting sands of hopes and speculations."[8] If the wedge strategy was indeed the Eisenhower administration's approach to relations with China, the administration was, in the words of Louis Halle, a member of the State Department's Policy Planning Staff, "in the position of a man who gets his adversary to surrender by threatening to shoot him if he doesn't, but who also allows him to believe that he will also shoot him if he does."[9]

If it was not the wedge strategy, what then drove the US policy toward China? The Republican Party's ideology, Dulles's own predilections, the continuing hold of McCarthyism, the aggressive communist propaganda, and the efforts of the China Lobby were enough to ensure that the Eisenhower administration followed an uncompromising line against communist China. Nuclear weapons provided the administration with the means to carry out such a policy. Reliance on nuclear diplomacy to sustain an anticommunist policy chosen largely for domestic political reasons, not the wedge strategy, was the bedrock of the US China policy under president Eisenhower. Over and above their deterrent capability, nuclear weapons had a major proactive role in the US policy toward

China. Even their presence in the theater seems to have taken the policy debate in Washington in directions unthinkable in their absence.

THE UTILITY CONUNDRUM

Although nuclear diplomacy enabled American presidents to follow their preferred policies against China without having to worry too much about the political costs of their decisions, the outcomes of nuclear diplomacy for US national security interests turned out to be quite different from what American policy makers had anticipated. The United States emerged from eight years of confrontation with communist China without losing any further territory to communism except for a handful of the smaller offshore islands. It did so without deploying anywhere near the level of conventional forces required to overcome the full strength of communist China. In the later stages of this confrontation, Washington did not have to think of deploying forces for even a limited land war. At the same time, until 1958, the United States kept the PRC under tremendous pressure by posing a constant threat to its southern flank. Nuclear diplomacy made this policy of pressure on China possible.

Prior to 1949, the offshore islands had always been under mainland Chinese rule, and their possession by the Nationalists caused communist China a great deal of trouble. China would undoubtedly have gone to great lengths to recover them. Yet after 1950, the Chinese made a serious attempt to take only the Dachens. It is not easy to definitively answer the question why China did not attempt to take Quemoy and Matsu. American leaders had repeatedly stated in public that they accepted no restrictions on the use of atomic weapons against military targets. Chinese leaders would not have had much difficulty understanding that one small atomic bomb would have wiped out an entire Chinese invasion force at its assembly point even before it ventured into the Taiwan Strait. Although detailed documentary evidence on the Chinese thinking is lacking, one can safely conclude that the threat posed by American nuclear weapons was definitely in the minds of Chinese leaders when they contemplated "liberating" the offshore islands.

Even if the United States did not openly threaten China with nuclear war, would Chinese leaders have taken the decision to invade Quemoy and Matsu? They could never have overlooked what American nuclear weapons would do to their troops, industries, and cities if they ever set out in earnest to gain control of Taiwan and the offshore islands. In both the Taiwan Strait crises, Chinese leaders would have been grossly ill advised if they did not anticipate American use of atomic weapons against their forces in case they attempted to invade the offshore islands.

The Chinese hopes of capturing the offshore islands withered in the face of what McGeorge Bundy calls "existential deterrence"—the uncertainty that a state has to take into account about what could happen when its adversary possessed atomic weapons. Existential deterrence, says Bundy, needs no provocative threats to support it. "It makes full and impartial use of one of the great realities of nuclear weapons: that they are far more terrifying to adversaries than they are comforting to their possessors."[10] Eisenhower fully appreciated this. He believed that "The power of the bomb is not of itself a threat to us or to others. The danger arises from its existence."[11]

Although nuclear diplomacy in the first Taiwan Strait crisis prevented the loss of the offshore islands to the communists, it had far-reaching consequences for Sino-US relations. Being on the receiving end of years of American nuclear diplomacy brought home to the Chinese the importance of possessing their own atomic weapons. On 15 January 1955, in the midst of a campaign in the Chinese press against American nuclear diplomacy during the first offshore islands crisis, the CCP politburo made the decision to start a Chinese atomic weapons program. On 17 January, Moscow declared its willingness to aid China and its European satellites in nuclear technology.[12] American nuclear diplomacy against China thus had strategic consequences far beyond the immediate issues involved in the dispute.

In terms of outcomes, the balance sheet of the eight years when nuclear diplomacy dominated America's China policy is, thus, heavily lopsided. On the credit side from the American point of view, there is the success of atomic diplomacy in preventing the loss of the offshore islands to China, keeping up pressure along the Fujian coast, and pinning down large Chinese forces. On the debit side, we have China's decision to become a nuclear power, the relaxation of the principal security threat that China faced, and the total failure of deterrence and compellence in the Korean War. When measured against the long-term cost of driving China on the path to becoming a nuclear power, the success of American nuclear diplomacy in preserving the strategically insignificant offshore islands for the Nationalists appears meager indeed.

As we have seen in Chapter 5, the immediate impact of American nuclear diplomacy on the security scenario in the Taiwan Strait was far removed from the calculations of American leaders. As the Nationalist defense minister explained to Robertson, by consolidating its hold over the border regions from Manchuria to Tibet and entering into an alliance with the Soviet Union, the PRC had achieved greater security along its land frontier than any previous regime in Chinese history. The Nationalist threat along the coast now remained the main security threat to China.[13] The actions the United States took, in order to extricate itself from the untenable position in which it had landed itself by its nuclear diplomacy in support of its aggressive policy toward China, had the effect of lifting the principal security threat China faced. The main instrument of the policy of pressure—nuclear diplomacy—thus ended up devouring the very policy it was meant to advance. China came out of eight years of confrontation with the United States with greater security than at the beginning of the crisis period in Sino-American relations.

Whatever inconvenience the Nationalist possession of the offshore islands caused, China obviously did not consider the capture of these islands important enough to risk nuclear bombing. In the Korean War, however, the outcome was entirely different. American nuclear weapons did not deter China from intervening in the war, in the face of the Chinese conviction that failure to intervene to stop an American advance to their frontier, no matter what intervention might cost, would be calamitous for their national security. Nor did explicit nuclear diplomacy compel China to accept the armistice terms that the United States sought. Where salience was high, thus, nuclear diplomacy was a total failure.

THE NUCLEAR PRESIDENCY

The Sino-American nuclear confrontations illustrate one of the interesting political effects of nuclear weapons—what Michael Mandelbaum calls the "nuclear presidency."[14] Mandelbaum suggests that the concentration of authority in the United States over decision making on all matters relating to nuclear policy in the president's hands makes the US president "an extraordinarily powerful person," reminiscent of the ancient practice of "imputation to the ruler of divine power."[15] Mandelbaum, however, does not credit the nuclear presidency with having created the "imperial presidency."[16] "Insofar as the President has taken greater command of American foreign policy since 1945," he asserts, "this has not been wholly—perhaps not even mainly—due to his nuclear authority." Against the "proposition that the nuclear presidency has fed the imperial presidency," Mandelbaum argues that although both Truman and Johnson started wars *without* congressional authority, neither president acted *against* the wishes of Congress. Moreover, Mandelbaum points out, "Congress has often opposed and sometimes overruled the President" on nuclear matters.[17]

It is, however, rather disingenuous to expect that the concentration of authority in the hands of the president—a concentration so enormous as to endow him with divine-like powers—would not affect the office of the presidency. Congress has never opposed presidents over plans and policies relating to the use of nuclear weapons. Unquestioned authority over nuclear weapons confers on American presidents the means to choose policy options that would otherwise have been ruled out. The "divine" power gives the president the power to wreak enormous destruction and to use the threat of this destruction to impose his will on other states that do not possess corresponding means to resist or retaliate. Nuclear brinkmanship against non-nuclear adversaries was appealing because the walk to the brink guaranteed favorable outcomes. Although foreign policy issues rarely enthuse American voters, popularity ratings of presidents shoot up after successful confrontations with foreign adversaries. Nuclear weapons enable American presidents to be seen as they like to be seen—staring down an adversary from a position of invincibility.

THE PERILS OF NUCLEAR BRINKMANSHIP

In the 1950s, the belief that the American nuclear capability gave the leadership a cost-free means of reaping domestic political advantage underpinned the brinkmanship of the Eisenhower administration. Nuclear diplomacy repeatedly landed the United States in "horrible dilemmas." The Eisenhower administration's learning curve in its nuclear strategy and China policy coincided with the rise and fall of nuclear brinkmanship. According to Thomas Schelling,

The creation of risk—usually a shared risk—is the technique of compellence that probably best deserves the name of "brinkmanship." It is a competition in risk-taking. It involves setting afoot an activity that may get out of hand, initiating a process that carries some risk of unintended disaster. One cannot initiate *certain* disaster as a profitable way of putting compellent pressure on someone, but one can initiate a moderate *risk* of mutual disaster if the other party's compliance is feasible within a short enough period to keep the cumulative risk within tolerable bounds.[18] (emphases in original)

In nuclear diplomacy toward a non-nuclear adversary, the dynamics of brinkmanship are fundamentally altered. From a military point of view, in nuclear brinkmanship (brinkmanship backed by nuclear weapons) with a non-nuclear adversary, there is no "shared risk" and no competitive risk taking. It is the adversary who faces *certain disaster*. As a Rand Corporation briefing for US policy makers in 1952 stressed, "the political objectives of war cannot be consonant with national suicide."[19] For any non-nuclear state confronting a nuclear adversary, escalation amounts to choosing national suicide. For the nuclear-armed initiator, there is *no* risk. That knowledge had a great deal to do with Dulles's strong predilection to walk to the nuclear brink with communist China.

Dulles's brinkmanship began not with the threat allegedly issued to China through Nehru to compromise on the armistice, but in his strong push for an advance to the waist of Korea. As he argued then, the US military superiority made it possible to try for a far more ambitious peace settlement in Korea than the one the Truman administration had tried for. Fortuitous circumstances saved him and his administration from the consequences of this line. Although the lessons of brinkmanship in the first Taiwan Strait crisis were far from satisfactory, Dulles persisted with the same policy in the second crisis too.

When the idea of nuclear diplomacy toward the Soviet Union was discussed in the National Security Council in the spring of 1951, Acheson had opposed it vehemently. It seemed to him that "the threat represented by our stockpile of atomic bombs was not a political advantage or asset, but, rather, a political liability." The threat to use them would "frighten our allies to death," but would not worry America's enemies.[20] By the end of the second Taiwan Strait crisis, Dulles would have heartily agreed with his predecessor.

THE REVIVAL OF NUCLEAR DIPLOMACY

The dramatic revival of nuclear diplomacy toward non-nuclear states by the United States in recent years belies hopes of a decline in the role of nuclear weapons in the post–Cold War era. It will be decades before scholars can lay their hands on the relevant contemporary documents and study the US policy in these cases. But there is enough information available to establish that the United States conveyed threats of nuclear strikes to Iraq, Libya, and North Korea in the 1990s in exactly the same way that such threats were conveyed to China in the 1950s. As James Baker III, secretary of state under president George Bush, recalled his conversation with his Iraqi counterpart Tariq Aziz in Geneva just before the allied forces began their military action in the Gulf War,

"If the conflict involves use of chemical or biological weapons against our forces," I warned, "the American people will demand vengeance. We have the means to exact it. With regard to this part of my presentation, this is not a threat, it is a promise." . . . Bush had also decided US forces would not retaliate with chemical or nuclear weapons if the Iraqis attacked with chemical munitions. There was obviously no reason to inform the Iraqis of this. In hopes of persuading them to consider more soberly the folly of war, I purposely left the impression that the use of chemical or biological agents by Iraq could invite tactical nuclear retaliation. (We do not really know whether this was the reason there appears to have been no confirmed use by Iraq of chemical weapons during the war. My own view is that the calculated ambiguity regarding how we might respond has to be part of the reason.)[21]

The Clinton administration inherited the crisis over the North Korean nuclear weapons from the Bush administration. In 1989, US aerial and satellite reconnaissance picked up what was suspected to be evidence of a clandestine North Korean nuclear weapons program.[22] The US intelligence community expressed divergent conclusions on the extent of North Korea's nuclear weapon capability and intent.[23] However, widespread talk of a North Korean nuclear threat and how the United States should respond to this threat dominated the American media.[24] Bush had suspended the annual joint US-South Korean military exercises close to the demilitarized zone (DMZ) known as Team Spirit for 1992, but he decided to conduct them in 1993. In January 1993, Clinton confirmed Bush's decision.[25] On 8 March, Team Spirit began, in which F-117 and B-1B bombers took part for the first time. In retaliation, North Korea withdrew from the Non-Proliferation Treaty (NPT) on 12 March. On 15 March, North Korea offered to discuss rejoining the NPT in return for, inter alia, removal of the US nuclear threat and cessation of Team Spirit exercises. After several rounds of talks between the United States and North Korea, the latter suspended its withdrawal from the NPT on 11 June, one day before the withdrawal was to take effect.[26]

Negotiations on a final settlement and resumption of International Atomic Energy Agency (IAEA) inspections of the North Korean nuclear facilities made no progress. During a visit to the DMZ on 11 July 1993, Clinton warned that if North Korea ever used a nuclear weapon, "we would quickly and overwhelmingly retaliate. . . . It would mean the end of their country."[27] On 7 November 1993, Clinton said in a television interview that "any attack on South Korea is an attack on the US."[28] In May 1994, North Korea shut down its nuclear reactor and withdrew fuel rods from it. The suspicion that North Korea would extract plutonium from the fuel rods and use it to make nuclear bombs once again led to heightened tensions, accompanied by the usual war talk in South Korea and Washington. Mediation by former President Jimmy Carter achieved a dramatic breakthrough. Further negotiations culminated in the signing of the Framework Agreement, under which North Korea would get light water reactors (with much less potential for use in a nuclear weapon program) in return for the closure of the existing North Korean reactor and interim fuel oil supplies by the United States.[29]

The Libyan episode ended without becoming a full-blown crisis. On 28 March 1996, Secretary of Defense William Perry testified before a Senate Foreign Relations Committee session on ratification of the Chemical Weapons Convention that the United States possessed a variety of conventional weapons to deal with chemical weapons threats. He went on to add, "and then we have nuclear weapons. If any country were foolish enough to use chemical weapons against the United States, the response would be absolutely overwhelming and devastating." On 3 April 1996, Perry said that the United States would not allow the Tarhunah chemical plant (where the United States suspected Libya to be constructing an underground chemical weapons plant) to become operational, hinting at the use of force.[30] On 23 April, Harold Smith, the assistant to the secretary of defense for nuclear, chemical, and biological programs, told reporters that only a nuclear weapon could destroy the

Tarhunah plant. Conventional weapons capable of deep ground penetration would not be available for another two years. The newly designed B61–11 nuclear bomb, capable of penetrating deeply underground before exploding, he said, "would be the nuclear weapon of choice" in any plan to attack the plant.[31] Pentagon spokesman Kenneth Bacon said, "[w]e believe that [the] threat to respond with devastating force was something that may have deterred Iraq from using chemical weapons during Desert Storm." On 7 May, Bacon clarified that "we are not talking about using nuclear weapons against the Tarhunah plant." However, he refused to rule out the use of nuclear weapons in retaliation for an attack on the United States or an attack on US forces using chemical or biological weapons.[32] A few weeks later, US sources disclosed that Libya had stopped construction at the Tarhunah plant. Officials speculated that American threats to bomb the plant before its completion was a contributing factor.[33]

The veiled nuclear threats against Iraq early in 1998[34] followed the disclosure of Clinton's November 1997 presidential directive, PDD 60, which, according to a *Washington Post* story, "contains language that would permit US nuclear strikes after enemy attacks using chemical or biological weapons." Senior NSC official Robert Bell clarified that "It's not difficult to define a scenario in which a rogue state would use chemical weapons or biological weapons and not be afforded protection under our negative security assurances."[35]

The shift in attention to potential Third World targets for US nuclear weapons began even as the Cold War was winding down. In March 1990, the JCS pointed to the "increasingly capable Third World threats" as a reason for maintaining US nuclear weapons. In June 1990, Secretary of Defense Dick Cheney projected weapons of mass destruction (WMD) in the hands of unfriendly states as a justification for retaining US nuclear weapons. In January 1993, General Lee Butler, commander of the newly created Strategic Command (StratCom), told a *New York Times* reporter that "our focus now is not just the former Soviet Union but any potentially hostile country that has or is seeking weapons of mass destruction." Soon after, StratCom began programming its computers to aim its nuclear weapons at Third World targets. Butler told a reporter, "Deterrence may not work in the old Soviet-American terms, but I am convinced that having nuclear weapons still matters." Single Integrated Operational Plan (SIOP)-94, under which US nuclear weapons would be retargeted on states possessing or developing WMD, went into effect in the spring of 1993.[36]

However, a 1992 StratCom study found that US nuclear hardware and data processing capabilities, both configured for strikes against targets in the northern hemisphere, were unsuitable for easy retargeting of Third World enemies. The report called for the creation of a new nuclear war planning system with a "global capability" that could meet the requirements for rapid target data updating. This led to the development of "adaptive planning," which provides for executing limited nuclear attacks against targets outside the SIOP using weapons earmarked for the SIOP. In December 1992, StratCom set up a task force "to develop a flexible, globally-focused, war-planning process known as the Strategic War Planning System (SWPS). The task force developed a "living SIOP," described as a "real time" plan for nuclear war, capable of "instantaneous war fighting commands and upgrades." The SWPS would achieve initial operational capability in 1998 and be fully in place by 2003. According to Kristensen's study, "Work currently underway at the Air Force's Rome laboratory aims to provide planners with the capability to plan 'critical nuclear options' in the SIOP 'within days rather than months' and limited SIOP re-planning options 'in less than 30 minutes.' "[37]

In April 1995, the Strategic Advisory Group at StratCom prepared a review of deterrence against WMD proliferation. It criticized offering negative security assurances and called for nuclear deterrence of WMD proliferators. The United States should threaten these states not simply with military defeat, "but the threat of even worse consequences," the fear of "national extinction." In December 1995, just months after the United States joined other nuclear weapons states in negative security assurances during the negotiations on extending the NPT, the JCS approved this concept.[38] The nuclear threat against Libya followed in the next few months.

To provide the hardware for implementing the new policy, the navy began working on a new retargeting system for submarine-launched ballistic missiles to enable Trident nuclear submarines "to quickly, accurately, and reliably retarget missiles to targets" and "to allow timely and reliable processing of an increased number of targets." The air force is equipping Minuteman II intercontinental ballistic missiles (ICBMs) with a system for "rapid message processing [and] rapid re-targeting." The B-2 stealth bomber will carry the new ground-penetrating B61-11 nuclear bomb. This bomb has already entered US stockpiles, providing US nuclear forces with a capability sought since the Korean War to attack underground targets. Work also continues on a variety of other exotic designs for nuclear weapons to more effectively implement the new policy.[39]

Paralleling the official planning for the post–Cold War use of US nuclear weapons, experts have debated the role of nuclear weapons in the post–Cold War era in recent years. "Maximalists" favor continued reliance on nuclear weapons, including for the deterrence of regional adversaries. They also support the development of low-yield nuclear weapons for use against local conventional forces. "Minimalists" favor reliance on nuclear weapons only for deterrence of a nuclear attack on the United States and oppose threatening non-nuclear states with nuclear weapons as counterproductive and likely to tempt these states into acquiring nuclear weapons.[40] An example of the minimalist position was contained in a 1993 study by McGeorge Bundy, Admiral William Crowe, and Sidney Drell, which urged on the United States a "doctrine of defensive last resort."[41] The Clinton administration, however, seems to have opted for the maximalist position.

Some reasons for the revival of nuclear diplomacy toward non-nuclear opponents by the United States are fairly obvious. Many of the restraints on American nuclear diplomacy in the 1950s either no longer exist or are no longer strong enough to constrain the United States. During the Korean War and both of the Taiwan Strait crises, there was a possibility, however slim, of Soviet retaliation for American use of atomic bombs against China. Unlike the 1950s, now there is no threat, not even a remote one, of a Russian retaliation for American nuclear attacks on any other state. It is only close American allies who now have extended nuclear deterrence to shield them. The nuclear balance also is moving in a reverse direction. From a US monopoly, the nuclear balance reached parity in the late 1960s after passing through a period of unquestioned American superiority. The collapse of the Soviet Union, the inability of Russia to maintain and upgrade its nuclear forces on a par with similar US efforts, international arrangements banning nuclear testing (which will retard Russian efforts to improve warhead designs more than they will affect similar US efforts), and the possible development of a US missile defense system are working toward a gradual return to American strategic nuclear superiority.

In the 1950s, the fear that use of nuclear weapons against China could lead to a weakening of the American alliance system and thus harm US global interests acted as a check on American plans. There is no such fear now, especially in the context of the possible use of nuclear weapons in the Middle East. In the case of North Korea, the fear is just the opposite: failure to stop the North Korean nuclear weapons program could lead to South Korea and Japan developing their own nuclear weapons and thus freeing themselves from the US umbrella. Even in the 1950s, there was always a faction in the Eisenhower administration that argued that, with time, the adverse diplomatic consequences of atomic war against China would be overcome and the alliance system would return to its original state. Eisenhower and Dulles, however, were reluctant to take that risk. Here again, the position is the reverse now. The dominant argument in the American establishment now is that the alliance system would break apart if the United States is not seen to be tough enough.

Although advances in weapons technology have not made "the unthinkable" an acceptable option, they have considerably lowered the threshold for the use of nuclear weapons in recent years. Despite years of efforts, the Eisenhower administration never succeeded in its endeavor to gain acceptance of its stand that nuclear weapons were on a par with conventional weapons. Even the low-yield tactical nuclear weapons available those days were unsuitable for precision strikes. The kind of low-yield kiloton-range nuclear weapons now available to US forces or under development allow for nuclear strikes against certain kinds of military targets without significant collateral damage. At the same time, the United States has had considerable success in recent years in projecting Third World weapons of mass destruction as the world's latest evil. Consequently, the United States has been able to get away with practically no objections, either from the American public or foreign governments, to its recent nuclear diplomacy toward non-nuclear states.

As this study has shown, nuclear weapons enabled American presidents to follow choices that gave them domestic political advantage in the 1950s. But, as Halperin points out, these crises helped create a "myth" about the diplomatic utility of nuclear weapons among US policy makers. That myth is now being revived. US officials seem to have concluded that against both Libya and Iraq in 1991, nuclear threats were successful. Evidence now available shows that Chinese plans for invading the offshore islands, which US officials believed American nuclear threats had deterred, never existed. Only detailed studies based on archival evidence would show whether Iraq was planning to use chemical and biological weapons against the coalition in 1991, or whether Libya was indeed constructing a chemical weapons plant at Tarhunah. But the absence of chemical attacks by Iraq and the reported stoppage of work on the Tarhunah plant by Libya seem to have been credited to American nuclear diplomacy.

As a result of the new myth, the downside of nuclear diplomacy is not getting adequate attention. As we have seen, American presidents relied on nuclear capability to follow aggressive policies toward China that they would otherwise have found too risky to adopt. From the end of the Korean War through the early 1990s, the United States followed a similarly aggressive policy toward North Korea, backed by tactical nuclear weapons stationed in South Korea in violation of the Korean War armistice agreement. Although the policy toward Iraq did not rely on the US atomic arsenal, as the Gulf War had left the Iraqi conventional forces in ruin, nuclear weapons were not entirely out of the picture. By proclaiming the intention to use disproportionately high levels of force in pursuit of objectives that fall short in terms of both internationally accepted standards of legitimacy and American strategic interests, American presidents have courted repeated diplomatic failures. The tough US policy toward China in the 1950s did not survive the international attention drawn to it by the repeated crises in the Taiwan Strait. After the recent nuclear confrontation with North Korea, the US North Korea policy underwent a similar transformation. If reports as of this moment are any indication, the Iraq policy would not remain unchanged either.[42]

The trouble with calculated ambiguity is that it is a game that two sides can play. As Bruce Cumings points out, North Korea has been successful in extracting concessions from the United States through its own version of calculated ambiguity. After milking the nuclear issue in 1999, North Korea turned to missiles. In June 1999, US satellites observed signs of a possible North Korean test-launch of a missile capable of reaching the continental United States. After a series of negotiations between US and North Korean officials, North Korea agreed to suspend missile test flights in return for the Clinton administration's undertaking to exempt North Korea from the provisions of the Trading With the Enemy Act of 1950.[43] Considering how weak North Korea is and that, unlike in the 1950s, it stands on its own, the North Korean success is amazing.[44]

But it has been China that, during the 1995–1996 crisis in the Taiwan Strait, startled the world with its own brand of nuclear diplomacy. The years following the Sino-US normalization of relations had seen the progressive isolation of the ROC, China's emergence as a major military and economic power, and a reversal of Taiwan's position on its international status. The ROC's long-standing claim to be the sole government of the whole of China and its opposition to a "two-China policy" gave way to President Lee Teng-hui's declaration in an interview in June 1994 that "Taiwan must belong to the people of Taiwan."[45] The post–Chiang dynasty leadership in Taiwan initiated "pragmatic diplomacy," aimed at achieving "sovereign independence" and membership in international organizations for Taiwan. In May 1995, the Clinton administration, succumbing to congressional pressure, overruled Chinese objections and decided to issue a visa for Lee to visit the United States. Coming on the heels of a plethora of Sino-US differences over human rights, trade relations, non-proliferation, US arms sales to Taiwan, and what China sees as Taiwanese intransigence over unification, China viewed the US action as interference in China's internal affairs.

In July 1995, the PLA conducted missile tests involving the firing of nuclear-capable M-9 and DF-21 missiles into the sea 80 miles northeast of Taiwan. Following this, Chinese Defense Minister Chi Haotian declared that China "will not sit idle if foreign forces interfere in China's reunification and get involved in Taiwan's independence." Another round of Chinese missile and live-fire exercises followed in August, slightly to the north of the July test area.[46] In October, China conducted large naval exercises, including amphibious landings, in the Yellow Sea north of Taiwan. On 15 November, the PLA began another amphibious exercise, involving the simulated invasion of Dongshan Island.[47] On 19

December, the US aircraft carrier USS *Nimitz* passed through the Taiwan Strait, after being diverted, a press report stated, by bad weather. This was the first passage through these waters by a US aircraft carrier since the 1958 crisis in the area. Washington announced this six weeks later, in the wake of reports of Chinese plans of military action against Taiwan.[48]

In February 1996, China began preparations for a massive exercise. The PLA assembled 150,000 troops supported by large air and naval forces for a simulated amphibious invasion. On 5 March, China announced that it would hold missile exercises from 8 March to 15 March, during the campaign for the 23 March presidential elections in Taiwan. The Chinese foreign ministry once again warned that China "will not sit by watching with folded arms" if foreign powers intervened. On 8 March and 13 March, China fired M-9 missiles close to Taiwan. On 7 March, Perry told Liu Huaqua, a senior Chinese national security official, who was on a US visit, that "grave consequences" would follow any Chinese attack on Taiwan. The next day, Perry announced the deployment of a carrier battle group led by the USS *Independence* to the area. Undeterred by the tough US response, China announced the very next day another nine-day tri-service exercise in a 17,000 square kilometer area in the Taiwan Strait to start on 12 March. On 10 March, Secretary of State Warren Christopher disclosed in a television interview that "We've made it quite clear to the Chinese that if they try to resolve this problem through force rather than through peace, that will be a grave matter with us. We've made it as clear as we possibly can to them, because we don't want any miscalculation on their part." The next day, another battle group led by the *Nimitz* was ordered to the area. From 18 March to 25 March, China held yet another combined service exercise, involving the simulation of an amphibious assault around Haitan Island.[49]

There were, however, no clashes between US and Chinese forces. Both US carrier groups kept out of the Taiwan Strait. It was also obvious that China had not mobilized the forces required for an invasion. Overall, the 1996 crisis resembled the pattern of earlier crises in the Taiwan Strait: Taiwanese actions against perceived Chinese interests, followed by Chinese military action well short of a serious military threat to the ROC but enough to focus international attention to the area.

In one significant aspect, however, the crisis was profoundly different from past Sino-American crises: China is now a nuclear power. Although minuscule in comparison to the US nuclear stockpiles, the Chinese nuclear arsenal includes ICBMs, a handful of which can reach the continental United States.[50]

The impact of the crisis on the Clinton administration was sobering.

James Sasser, the US ambassador to China, saw the episode as a turning point in Sino-US relations. "I think it forced both sides to draw back and look at the relationship anew.... All of a sudden, senators and congressmen were looking around and seeing aircraft carriers speeding down there to Taiwan, and they were thinking, 'How far do we really want this thing to go?'"[51] The reassessment of US policy toward China that followed this crisis culminated in President Clinton's "three noes" statement in June 1998. As historian Waldo Heinrichs points out, the United States had used force against China on several occasions in the nineteenth century and the early part of the twentieth century. "Yet the militarized relationship of 1950–71 was profoundly different from previous encounters because the United States now respected China's will and capacity to fight."[52] The Sino-American relationship of the future promises to be equally profoundly different from everything until now.

Recent American arms sales to Taiwan have made a conventional Chinese invasion of Taiwan impossible in the foreseeable future, despite China's own significant acquisition of modern conventional weapons. China has no alternative but to play the nuclear card in any future crisis over Taiwan. The tough anti-China rhetoric in the United States, at the official as well as the media level, takes place in the absence of a serious Chinese military threat to Taiwan. Actions now do not need to match words. It remains to be seen how the American public, Congress, and the administration will respond to a genuine Chinese threat to Taiwan backed by a Chinese nuclear threat against any intervening external power.

China did not give up its claim to Taiwan throughout the era of overwhelming American superiority, nuclear as well as conventional. Already there exists Chinese nuclear deterrent capability. In the next decades, China can reach parity with the United States, and eventually even achieve superiority. It is, therefore, unlikely that China will give up its claim to Taiwan or abandon its hopes of eventually completing the unification of China. Just before a meeting with Christopher in November 1996, Chinese Foreign Minister Qian Qichen told reporters that the Taiwan issue was China's principal concern and the way the issue was dealt with would shape Sino-US relations in the future. Taking a page from the American book, China has begun to publicize its nuclear capability.[53] The basis of the Cold War was ideological. It involved no direct vital interests of the United States or the Soviet Union. Failure to resolve the Taiwan issue could lead to a Sino-US Cold War, in which the United States would be standing in the way of China's hopes of advancing its vital interests. Existential deterrence preserved the offshore islands under the ROC's control. The question for the future is, will existential deterrence now deliver Taiwan to China?

NOTES

1. JCS 1477/6, 21 January 1946, CCS 471.6 (8–15–45) Sec. 2, RG 218, NA.
2. John Lewis Gaddis, *The Long Peace*, 169–73.
3. *New York Times*, 2 December 1950.
4. When Churchill met Truman for dinner during his visit to Washington in January 1953, he asked Truman whether the latter "would have his answer ready when they both stood before St. Peter to account for their part in dropping the atomic bomb on Japan." Before Truman could reply, Lovett, displaying a presence of mind that won him Dean Acheson's admiration, but should surely earn him the strong disapproval of historians, diverted the conversation. Dean Acheson, *Present at the Creation*, 715–16.
5. Memo of 370th meeting of NSC, *FRUS 1958–60, III*, 121.
6. See Gaddis, *The Long Peace*; David Allan Mayers, *Cracking the Monolith: US Policy Against the Sino-Soviet Alliance, 1949–1955* (Baton Rouge: Louisiana State University Press, 1986) Chapters 1–4; Gordon Chang, *Friends and Enemies*.
7. Smith memo, 29 October 1958, PPS Files, NND 933301. Dulles added that "he believed we had made a serious mistake in recognizing the USSR and that he would be much happier about a UN without Soviet membership."
8. Robertson memo for Herter, 1 August 1958, *FRUS 1958–60, Vol. XIX*, 37.
9. Halle to Nitze, 4 February 1953, PPS Papers, Box 14, "China 1952–1953," RG 59, NA.
10. McGeorge Bundy, "The Bishops and the Bomb," *New York Review of Books* (16 June 1983). Bundy raises this concept in the context of superpower nuclear deterrence. But the concept is equally, if not more, valid when a nuclear power confronts a non-nuclear adversary.
11. Eisenhower's handwritten remark, 13 April 1954, AWF, Ann Whitman Diary Series, Box 2, "ACW Diary April 1954 (3)," DEPL.
12. John W. Lewis and Xue Litai, *China Builds the Bomb*, 36–41. Long before this, however, reports had surfaced about China's nuclear program. In November 1952, *Le Monde* reported the visit of a Chinese scientific team to Moscow to study Sino-Soviet atomic research. The paper reported that British official circles had discounted the possibility of the Soviet Union sharing weapons know-how with China and speculated that the visit was in connection with the export of atomic minerals from Sinkiang to the Soviet Union. A report in September 1953, however, spoke of persistent rumors in China that China was planning to make the bomb. Although the Chinese leadership announced its decision to develop nuclear weapons only in 1955, the possibility that it made the decision during the Korean War cannot be ruled out. Paris to Washington, 21 November 1952, 793.5611/11–2152, RG 59, NA; Paris to Washington, 1 September 1953, 793.5611/11–9–153, ibid.
13. Memcon, 3 September 1954, CJCS-091 China, NND 931186, NA.
14. Michael Mandelbaum, *The Nuclear Revolution*, 177ff. See also Frank Klatz Jr., "The President and the Control of Nuclear Weapons," in David C. Kozak and Kenneth N. Ciboski (eds.), *The American Presidency: A Policy Perspective from Readings and Documents* (Chicago: Nelson-Hall, 1985).
15. Ibid., 182–83.

16. On the imperial presidency, see Arthur M. Schlesinger Jr., *The Imperial Presidency* (Boston: Houghton Mifflin Co., 1973).

17. Mandelbaum, *The Nuclear Revolution*, 187.

18. Schelling, *Arms and Influence*, 91.

19. Enclosure to Henderson to Arneson, 16 April 1952, PPS Records 1947–1953, Box 6, "Atomic Energy Armaments 1952–1953," RG 59, NA.

20. Memo for the president, 25 January 1951, PSF, NSC Meetings, Box 220, "NSC Meetings-Memos for President-Meeting Discussion, 1951," HSTL.

21. James A. Baker III, *The Politics of Diplomacy: Revolution, War, and Peace, 1989–1992* (New York: G. P. Putnam's Sons, 1995), 358.

22. Bruce Cumings, *Korea's Place in the Sun: A Modern History* (New York: W. W. Norton & Co., 1997), 466. This part closely follows Cumings's account of the episode. For a book-length study of the US-North Korean nuclear confrontation in the 1990s, see Leon V. Sigal, *Disarming Strangers: Nuclear Diplomacy With North Korea* (Princeton, NJ: Princeton University Press, 1998). See also Don Oberdorfer, *The Two Koreas: A Contemporary History* (Reading, MA: Addison-Wesley, 1997).

23. Ibid., 467.

24. Ibid., 468–73.

25. Ibid., 474.

26. *New York Times*, 12 March, 16 March, and 12 June 1993.

27. *Washington Times*, 13 July 1993.

28. Cumings, *Korea's Place in the Sun*, 471.

29. Ibid., 484–85.

30. *Washington Post*, 4 April 1996.

31. *Washington Times*, 24 April 1996; *Jane's Defense Week*, 1 May 1996.

32. *Washington Post*, 8 May 1996.

33. *Washington Times*, 24 June 1996.

34. See Chapter 1.

35. Hans Kristensen, *Nuclear Futures*, 7. Negative security assurances are pledges made in the context of the NPT by nuclear weapons powers not to use nuclear weapons against non-nuclear states.

36. Ibid., 11; *New York Times*, 25 February 1993.

37. Kristensen, *Nuclear Futures*, 11–12.

38. Ibid.

39. Ibid.

40. Michael Mazaar, "Nuclear Weapons After the Cold War," *Washington Quarterly* (Summer 1992). For an insightful discussion of the future of nuclear diplomacy, see Richard Betts, *Nuclear Blackmail and Nuclear Balance*, Chapter 6.

41. McGeorge Bundy, Admiral William Crowe, and Sidney Drell, *Reducing Nuclear Danger: The Road Away from the Brink* (New York: Council on Foreign Relations Press, 1993), 81.

42. The quantity of oil that Iraq has been permitted to export has increased with each successive crisis in the Persian Gulf. The Security Council is soon likely to further relax its sanctions against Iraq.

43. See *Washington Times*, 17 June 1999; *New York Times*, 14 September 1999. The missile issue generated press coverage almost on a daily basis throughout the summer of 1999.

44. Cumings, *Korea's Place in the Sun*, 477, 485.

45. John W. Garver, *Face Off: China, the United States, and Taiwan's Democratization* (Seattle: University of Washington Press, 1997), 24.

46. Garver, *Face Off*, 74.

47. Ibid., 92–93.

48. *New York Times*, 27 and 31 January 1996. For questions on who had authorized the passage, see Garver, *Face Off*, 96–97.

49. Ibid., 96–110; *Washington Post*, 22 June 1998.

50. After the crisis, reports of China's increasing capability in the area of ICBMs surfaced periodically in the American media, fed by leaks of classified intelligence information. See *Washington Times*, 10 July 1997, 1 April 1998, and 1 May 1998.

51. *Los Angeles Times*, 9 January 1997.

52. Waldo Heinrichs Jr., "The Use and Threat of Force in Sino-American Relations," in Michel Oksenberg and Robert Oxnan (eds.), *Dragon and Eagle: United States–China Relations: Past and Future* (New York: Basic Books, 1978), 173.

53. *New York Times*, 21 November 1996. On China's new-found willingness to publicize news of its nuclear weapons advances, see the *New York Times*, 16 July and 3 August 1999.

Bibliography

PRIMARY SOURCES

Manuscripts

Acheson, Dean. Papers. Harry S. Truman Library.
Clifford, Clark. Papers. Harry S. Truman Library.
Dulles, John Foster. Papers. Dwight D. Eisenhower Library.
————. Papers. Seeley Mudd Library, Princeton University.
Eisenhower, Dwight D. Papers. Dwight D. Eisenhower Library.
Great Britain. Cabinet Records. Public Records Office, London.
————. Foreign Office Records. Public Records Office, London.
Hagerty, James C. Papers. Dwight D. Eisenhower Library.
Herter, Christian. Papers. Dwight D. Eisenhower Library.
Judd, Walter J. Papers. Hoover Institution on War, Revolution, and Peace, Stanford University.
Koo, Wellington. Papers. Columbia University Library.
LeMay, Curtis. Papers. Library of Congress.
Smith, Alexander H. Papers. Seeley Mudd Library, Princeton University.
Truman, Harry S. Papers. Harry S. Truman Library.
US Army. Staff Records. Modern Military Branch, National Archives.
US Department of State. Decimal Files. Diplomatic Branch, National Archives.
————. Office of Intelligence and Research. Records. Diplomatic Branch, National Archives.
————. Policy Planning Staff. Records. Diplomatic Branch, National Archives.
US Joint Chiefs of Staff. Records. Modern Military Branch, National Archives.
US National Security Council. Records. Modern Military Branch, National Archives.
Vandenberg, Hoyt S. Papers. Library of Congress.

Diaries, Memoirs, and Other Published Primary Sources

Acheson, Dean. *Present at the Creation: My Years in the State Department*. New York: W. W. Norton & Co., 1969.

Adams, Sherman. *First Hand Report: The Story of the Eisenhower Administration*. New York: Harper & Brothers, 1961.

Anders, Roger M. (ed.). *Forging the Atomic Shield: Excerpts from the Office Diary of Gordon E. Dean*. Chapel Hill: University of North Carolina Press, 1987.

Baker, James A., III. *The Politics of Diplomacy: Revolution, War, and Peace, 1989–1992*. New York: G. P. Putnam's Sons, 1995.

Bohlen, Charles E. *Witness to History, 1929–1969*. New York: W. W. Norton & Co., 1973.

Bowles, Chester. *Ambassador's Report*. New York: Harper & Brothers, 1954.

Bradley, Omar, and Clay Blair. *A General's Life: An Autobiography*. New York: Simon and Schuster, 1983.

Chandler, Alfred D. et al., (eds). *The Papers of Dwight D. Eisenhower*. 13 vols. Baltimore, MD: Johns Hopkins University Press, 1970–1984.

Chase, William C. *Frontline General: The Commands of Maj. Gen. William C. Chase*. Houston: Pacesetter Press, 1975.

Clark, Mark. *From the Danube to the Yalu*. New York: Harper & Brothers, 1954.

Condit, Doris M. *History of the Office of the Secretary of Defense, Vol. II: The Test of War, 1950–1953*. Washington, DC: Historical Office, Office of the Secretary of Defense, 1988.

Condit, Kenneth W. *The History of the Joint Chiefs of Staff: The Joint Chiefs of Staff and National Policy, Vol. II, 1947–1949*. Wilmington, DE.: Michael Glazier, 1979.

———. *History of the Joint Chiefs of Staff, Vol. VI: The Joint Chiefs of Staff and National Policy, 1955–1956*. Washington, DC: Historical Office, Joint Staff, 1992.

Congressional Quarterly. *China: US Policy Since 1945*. Washington, DC: CQ, 1979.

Eisenhower, Dwight D. *Crusade in Europe*. Garden City, NY: Doubleday & Co., 1949.

———. *The White House Years. Vol. 1: Mandate for Change, 1953–1956*. Garden City, NY: Doubleday & Co., 1963.

———. *The White House Years. Vol 2: Waging Peace, 1956–1961*. Garden City, NY: Doubleday & Co., 1965.

Ferrell, Robert H. (ed.). *The Diary of James C. Hagerty: Eisenhower in Mid-Course, 1954–1955*. Bloomington: Indiana University Press, 1983.

———. *The Eisenhower Diaries*. New York: W. W. Norton & Co., 1981.

Gallup, George H. (ed.). *The Gallup Poll: Public Opinion, 1935–1971*. 3 vols. New York: Random House, 1972.

Gavin, James A. *War and Peace in the Space Age*. New York: Harper & Brothers, 1958.

Gopal, Sarvepalli. *Jawaharlal Nehru: A Biography, Vol. II, 1947–1956*. Cambridge, MA: Harvard University Press, 1979.

Gromyko, Andrei. *Memories*. London: Hutchinson, 1989.

Hagerty, James. *The Diary of James C. Hagerty: Eisenhower in Mid-Course*. Bloomington: Indiana University Press, 1983.

Heinrichs, Waldo Jr. "The Use and Threat of Force in Sino-American Relations." In Michel Oksenberg and Robert Oxnam, (eds.), *Dragon and Eagle: United States-China Relations: Past and Future*. New York: Basic Books, 1978.

Hughes, Emmet John. *The Ordeal of Power: A Political Memoir of the Eisenhower Years*. New York: Atheneum, 1963.

Johnson, U. Alexis. *The Right Hand of Power*. Englewood Cliffs, NJ: Prentice-Hall, 1984.

Kennan, George. *Memoirs: 1 & 2*. Boston: Little, Brown & Co., 1967 and 1972.

LeMay, Curtis E., and MacKinlay Kantor. *Mission with LeMay: My Story*. Garden City, NY: Doubleday and Co., 1965.

Lilienthal, David. *The Journals of David E. Lilienthal: The Atomic Years, 1945–1950*. New York: Harper and Row, 1964.

MacArthur, Douglas. *Reminiscences*. New York: McGraw-Hill, 1964.

Millis, Walter (ed.). *The Forrestal Diaries*. New York: Viking Press, 1951.

Murphy, Robert. *Diplomat Among Warriors*. Garden City, NY: Doubleday & Co., 1964.

Nitze, Paul H. *From Hiroshima to Glasnost: At the Center of Decision: A Memoir*. New York: Weidenfeld & Nicholson, 1989.

Nixon, Richard. *The Memoirs of Richard Nixon*. New York: Grossett & Dunlap, 1978.

Panikkar, K. M. *In Two Chinas: Memoirs of a Diplomat*. London: Allen and Unwin, 1955.

Peng Dehui. *Memoirs of a Chinese Marshall: The Autobiographical Notes of Peng Dehui (1898–1974)*, translated by Zhang Long. Beijing: Foreign Language Press, 1984.

Poole, Walter S. *The History of the Joint Chiefs of Staff: The Joint Chiefs of Staff and National Policy, 1950–1952, Vol. IV*. Wilmington, DE: Michael Glazier, 1980.

Rankin, Karl Lott. *China Assignment*. Seattle: University of Washington Press, 1964.

Rearden, Steven. *History of the Office of the Secretary of Defense*. Washington, DC: Historical Office, Office of the Secretary of Defense, 1984.

Reid, Escott. *Envoy to Nehru*. New Delhi: Oxford University Press, 1981.

Reston, James. *Deadline: A Memoir*. New York: Random House, 1991.

Ridgway, Matthew. *Soldier*. Westport, CT: Greenwood Press, 1974.

Rusk, Dean. *As I Saw It: As Told to Richard Rusk*. Edited by Daniel S. Papp. New York: W. W. Norton & Co., 1990.

Schnabel, James F., and Robert J. Watson. *The History of the Joint Chiefs of Staff: The Joint Chiefs of Staff and National Policy, Vol. 3: The Korean War*, Part 1 and Part 2. Wilmington, DE: Michael Glazier, 1979.

Stimson, Henry L., and McGeorge Bundy. *On Active Service in Peace And War*. New York: Harper and Row, 1948.

Talbot, Strobe, (ed. and trans.) *Khrushchev Remembers: The Last Testament*. Boston: Little, Brown & Co., 1974.

Taylor, Maxwell D. *Uncertain Trumpet*. New York: Harper & Brothers, 1960.

Truman, Harry S. *Memoirs, Vol. 1: Year of Decisions.* Garden City, NY: Doubleday & Co., 1956.

Truman, Harry S. *Memoirs, Vol. 2: Years of Trial and Hope.* New York: Doubleday & Co., 1956.

US Department of State. *Foreign Relations of the United States*, 1948 to 1963, selected volumes. Washington DC: US Government Printing Office, 1973–.

Van Slyke, Lyman (ed.). *The China White Paper, 1949.* Stanford, CA: Stanford University Press, 1967.

SECONDARY SOURCES

Books

Accinelli, Robert. *Crisis and Commitment: United States Policy toward Taiwan, 1950–1955.* Chapel Hill: University of North Carolina Press, 1996.

Allen, Kenneth W. et al. *China's Air Force Enters the 21st Century.* Santa Monica, CA: The Rand Corporation, 1995.

Alperowitz, Gar. *Atomic Diplomacy: Hiroshima and Potsdam.* New York: Simon and Schuster, 1965.

———. *The Decision to Use the Atomic Bomb and the Architecture of an American Myth.* New York: Alfred A. Knopf, 1995.

Ambrose, Stephen E. *Eisenhower: The President.* New York: Simon and Schuster, 1984.

Bachrack, Stanley. *The Committee of One Million: "China Lobby" Politics, 1953–1971.* New York: Columbia University Press, 1976.

Bernstein, Barton (ed.). *The Atomic Bomb: The Critical Issues.* Boston: Little, Brown & Co., 1976.

Betts, Richard. *Nuclear Blackmail and Nuclear Balance.* Washington, DC: The Brookings Institution, 1987.

Blacket, P. M. S. *Fear, War, and the Bomb: Military and Political Consequences of Atomic Energy.* New York: Whittlesey House, 1948.

Blair, Clay. *The Forgotten War: America in Korea, 1950–1953.* New York: Time Books, 1987.

Blum, Robert M. *Drawing the Line: The Origins of the American Containment Policy in East Asia.* New York: W. W. Norton & Co., 1982.

Borg, Dorothy, and Waldo Heinrichs (eds.). *Uncertain Years: Chinese-American Relations, 1947–1950.* New York: Columbia University Press, 1980.

Borowski, Harry A. *A Hollow Threat: Strategic Air Power and Containment Before Korea.* Westport, CT.: Greenwood Press, 1982.

Bouchard, Joseph F. *Command in Crisis.* New York: Columbia University Press, 1991.

Bowie, Robert. "Eisenhower, Atomic Weapons, and Atoms for Peace." In Joseph F. Pilat et al. (eds.), *Atoms for Peace: An Analysis After Thirty Years.* Boulder, CO: Westview Press, 1985.

Bowie, Robert R., and Richard H. Immerman. *Waging Peace: How Eisenhower Shaped an Enduring Cold War Strategy.* New York: Oxford University Press, 1998.

Brodie, Bernard (ed.). *The Absolute Weapon: Atomic Power and World Order*. New York: Harcourt, Brace and Company, 1946.

———. *Strategy in the Missile Age*. Princeton, NJ: Princeton University Press, 1959.

Bundy, McGeorge. *Danger and Survival: Choices About the Bomb in the First Fifty Years*. New York: Vintage Books, 1988.

———. The Unimpressive Record of Nuclear Diplomacy." In Gwyn Prins (ed.), *The Choice: Nuclear Weapons versus Stability*. London: Chatto Windus, 1984.

Bundy, McGeorge, Admiral William Crowe, and Sidney Drell. *Reducing Nuclear Danger: The Road Away from the Brink*. New York: Council on Foreign Relations Press, 1993.

Chang, Gordon. *Friends and Enemies: The United States, China, and the Soviet Union, 1948–1972*. Stanford, CA: Stanford University Press, 1990.

Chen Jian. *China's Road to the Korean War: The Making of the Sino-American Confrontation*. New York: Columbia University Press, paperback edition, 1994.

Christensen, Thomas J. *Useful Adversaries: Grand Strategy, Domestic Mobilization, and Sino-American Conflict, 1947–1958*. Princeton, NJ: Princeton University Press, 1996.

Coale, Ansley J. *The Problem of Reducing Vulnerability to Atomic Bombs*. Princeton, NJ: Princeton University Press, 1947.

Cochran, Bert. *Harry Truman and the Crisis Presidency*. New York: Funk & Wagnalls, 1973.

Cochran, Thomas B. et al. *Nuclear Weapons Databook*, vols. 1 & 2. Cambridge, MA: Ballinger Publishing Company, 1984 and 1987.

Cochran, Thomas B., Robert S. Norris, and Oleg Bukharin. *The Making of the Russian Bomb: From Stalin to Yeltsin*. Boulder, CO: Westview Press, 1995.

Cohen, Warren. *American's Response to China*. New York: Columbia University Press, 1990.

Cohen, Warren, and Akira Iriye (eds.). *Great Powers in East Asia, 1953–1960*. New York: Columbia University Press, 1990.

Crabb, Cecil V., and Kelvin Mulcahy. *Presidents and Foreign Policy Making: From FDR to Reagan*. Baton Rouge: Louisiana State University Press, 1986.

Cumings, Bruce. *Origins of the Korean War, Vol. II*. Princeton, NJ: Princeton University Press, 1990.

———. *Korea's Place in the Sun: A Modern History*. New York: W. W. Norton & Co., 1997.

Dean, Gordon E. *Forging the Atomic Shield: Excerpts from the Office Diary of Gordon E. Dean*, ed. Roger M. Anders. Chapel Hill: University of North Carolina Press, 1987.

Divine, Robert. *Foreign Policy and U.S. Presidential Elections, 1952–1960*. New York: New Viewpoints, 1974.

Dockdrill, Michael. "Britain and the First Chinese Offshore Islands Crisis, 1954–55." In Michael Dockdrill and John W. Young (eds.). *British Foreign Policy, 1945–1956*. New York: St. Martin's Press, 1989.

Dockrill, Saki. *Eisenhower's New Look National Security Policy, 1953–61*. London: Macmillan Press, 1996.

Donovan, Robert J. *Tumultuous Years: The Presidency of Harry S. Truman, 1949–1953*. New York: W. W. Norton & Co., 1982.

Dulles, Foster Rhea. *American Policy Toward Communist China 1949–1969*. New York: Thomas Y. Crowell Co., 1972.

Ellsberg, Daniel. "Introduction: Call to Mutiny." In E. P. Thompson and Dan Smith (eds.), *Survive and Protest*. New York: Monthly Review Press, 1981.

Etzold, Thomas H., and John L. Gaddis. *Containment: Documents on American Policy and Strategy, 1945–1950*. New York: Columbia University Press, 1978.

Evangelista, Matthew. *Innovation and the Arms Race: How the United States and the Soviet Union Develop New Military Technologies*. Ithaca, NY: Cornell University Press, 1988.

Ferrell, Herbert. *Harry S. Truman: A Life*. Columbia: University of Missouri Press, 1994.

Foot, Rosemary. *The Wrong War: American Policy and the Dimensions of the Korean Conflict, 1950–1953*. Ithaca, NY: Cornell University Press, 1985.

———. *A Substitute for Victory: The Politics of Peacemaking at the Korean Armistice Talks*. Ithaca, NY: Cornell University Press, 1990.

Freedman, Lawrence. *The Evolution of Nuclear Strategy*. New York: St. Martin's Press, 1981.

Freedman, Lawrence et al. (eds.). *The Evolution of Nuclear Strategy: A Reader*. New York: New York University Press, 1989.

Futrell, Robert F. *The United States Air Force in Korea, 1950–53*. New York: Duell, Sloan and Pierce, 1961.

Gaddis, John Lewis. *Strategies of Containment: A Critical Appraisal of Postwar American National Security Policy*. New York: Oxford University Press, 1982.

———. *The Long Peace: Enquiries Into the History of the Cold War*. New York: Oxford University Press, 1987.

Garver, John W. *Face Off: China, the United States, and Taiwan's Democratization*. Seattle: University of Washington Press, 1997.

George, Alexander, and Richard Smoke. *Deterrence in American Foreign Policy: Theory and Practice*. New York: Columbia University Press, 1974.

Gittings, John. *Survey of the Sino-Soviet Dispute*. London: Oxford University Press, 1968.

Glasstone, Samuel, and Philip Dolan (eds.). *The Effects of Nuclear Weapons*. 3d ed. Washington, DC: US Government Printing Office, 1977.

Goldhamer, H. *Communist Reaction in Korea to American Possession of the A-Bomb and Its Significance for US Political and Psychological Warfare*. Rand Research Memorandum #RM-903. Santa Monica, CA: The Rand Corporation, 1952.

Goncharov, Sergei N., John W. Lewis, and Xue Litai. *Uncertain Partners: Stalin, Mao, and the Korean War*. Stanford, CA: Stanford University Press, 1993.

Goulden, Joseph. *Korea: The Untold Story of the War*. New York: Time Books, 1982.

Grasso, June. *Truman's Two-China Policy, 1948–1950*. Armonk, NY: M. E. Sharpe, 1987.

Greenstein, Fred I. *The Hidden Hand Presidency: Eisenhower as Leader*. New York: Basic Books, 1982.

Gurtov, Melvin, and Byong-Moo Hwang. *China Under Threat: The Politics of Strategy and Diplomacy*. Baltimore, MD: Johns Hopkins University Press, 1980.

Halliday, Jon, and Bruce Cummings. *Korea: The Unknown War*. London: Viking, 1988.

Halperin, Morton. *Nuclear Fallacy: Dispelling the Myth of Nuclear Strategy*. Cambridge, MA: Ballinger Publishing Company, 1987.

Halperin, Morton, and Tang Tsou. "The 1958 Quemoy Crisis." In Morton Halperin (ed.), *Sino-Soviet Relations and Arms Control*. Cambridge, MA: MIT Press, 1967.

Hamby, Alonzo L. *Man of the People: A Life of Harry S. Truman*. New York: Oxford University Press, 1995.

Hansen, Chuck. *US Nuclear Weapons: The Secret History*. Arlington, TX: Aerofax, 1988.

Harding, Harry, and Yuan Ming (eds) *Sino-American Relations, 1945-1955: A Joint Assessment of a Critical Decade*. Wilmington, DE: Scholarly Resources, 1989.

He Di. "The Evolution of the People's Republic of China's Policy Toward the Offshore Islands." In Warren Cohen and Akira Iriye (eds.), *The Great Powers in East Asia, 1953-1960*. New York: Columbia University Press, 1990.

Heinrichs, Waldo Jr. "The Use of Threat of Force in Sino-American Relations." In Michel Oksenberg and Robert Oxnan, eds., *Dragon and Eagle: United States-China Relations: Past and Future*. New York: Basic Books, 1978.

Herken, Gregg. *The Winning Weapon: The Atomic Bomb in the Cold War, 1945-1950*. New York: Alfred A. Knopf, 1980.

Holloway, David. *Stalin and the Bomb: The Soviet Union and Atomic Energy, 1939-1956*. New Haven, CT: Yale University Press, 1994.

Hoopes, Townsend. *The Devil and John Foster Dulles*. Boston: Little, Brown & Co., 1973.

Howe, Jonathan. *Multicrises: Sea Power and Global Politics in the Missile Age*. Cambridge, MA: MIT Press, 1971.

Hunt, Michael H. *Crises in US Foreign Policy*. New Haven, CT : Yale University Press, 1996.

Immerman, Richard H. (ed.). *John Foster Dulles and the Diplomacy of the Cold War*. Princeton, NJ: Princeton University Press, 1990.

James, D. Clayton, with Anne Sharp Wells. *Refighting the Last War: Command and Crisis in Korea, 1950-1953*. New York: The Free Press, 1993.

Jervis, Robert. *The Meaning of the Nuclear Revolution: Statecraft and the Prospect of Armageddon*. Ithaca, NY: Cornell University Press, 1989.

———. *The Illogic of American Nuclear Strategy*. Ithaca, NY: Cornell University Press, 1984.

Kalicki, J. H. *The Pattern of Sino-American Crises: Political-Military Interactions in the 1950s*. New York: Cambridge University Press, 1975.

Kaplan, Fred. *The Wizards of Armageddon*. Stanford, CA: Stanford University Press, 1991.

Kaufman, Burton. *The Korean War: Challenges in Crisis, Credibility, and Command*. Philadelphia: Temple University Press, 1986.

Kaufman, William. "The Requirements of Deterrence." In William Kaufman (ed.), *Military Policy and National Security*. Princeton, NJ: Princeton University Press, 1956.

Kissinger, Henry. *Nuclear Weapons and Foreign Policy*. New York: Harper & Brothers, 1957.

Klatz, Frank Jr. "The President and the Control of Nuclear Weapons." In David

C. Kozak and Kenneth N. Ciboski (eds.), *The American Presidency: A Policy Perspective from Reading and Documents*. Chicago: Nelson-Hall, 1985.

Knaack, Marcelle Size. *Encyclopedia of US Air Force Aircraft and Missile Systems, Vol. I: Post World War II Fighters, 1945–1973*. Washington, DC: Office of Air Force History, 1978.

Koen, Ross Y. *The China Lobby in American Politics*. New York: Octagon Books, 1974.

Lauren, Paul G. (ed.). *The China Hands' Legacy: Ethics and Diplomacy*. Boulder, CO: Westview Press, 1987.

Leffler, Melvyn. *A Preponderance of Power: National Security, the Truman Administration, and the Cold War*. Stanford, CA: Stanford University Press, 1992.

Levering, Ralph B. *The Public and American Foreign Policy, 1918–1978*. New York: William Morrow & Co., 1978.

Lewis, John W., and Xue Litai. *China Builds the Bomb*. Stanford, CA: Stanford University Press, 1988.

Li Xiaobing. "The Second Taiwan Straits Crisis Revisited." Paper presented at the International Conference on New Findings on the Cold War in Asia at Hong Kong, 1996.

Mandelbaum, Michael. "International Stability and Nuclear Order: The First Nuclear Regime." In David C. Gompert et al. (eds.), *Nuclear Weapons and World Politics: Alternatives for the Future*. New York: McGraw-Hill, 1977.

———. *The Nuclear Revolution: International Politics before and after Hiroshima*. Cambridge: Cambridge University Press, 1981.

May, Ernest R. "Eisenhower and After." In May (ed.). *The Ultimate Decision: The President as Commander in Chief*. New York: George Braziller, 1960.

———. *American Cold War Strategy: Interpreting NSC 68*. Boston: Bedford Books, 1993.

Mayers, David Allan. *Cracking the Monolith: US Policy Against the Sino-Soviet Alliance, 1949–1955*. Baton Rouge: Louisiana State University Press, 1986.

Meilinger, Philip S. *Hoyt S. Vandenberg: The Life of a General*. Bloomington: Indiana University Press, 1989.

Messer, Robert L. *The End of an Alliance: James F. Byrnes, Roosevelt, Truman, and the Origins of the Cold War*. Chapel Hill: University of North Carolina Press, 1982.

Midgley, John J. Jr. *Deadly Illusions: Army Policy for the Nuclear Battlefield*. Boulder, CO: Westview Press, 1986.

Miller, Richard L. *Under the Cloud: Three Decades of Nuclear Testing*. New York: The Free Press, 1986.

Morgan, Patrick. *Deterrence: A Conceptual Analysis*. Beverly Hills, CA: Sage Library of Social Science, 1977.

Newhouse, John. *War and Peace in the Nuclear Age*. New York: Alfred A. Knopf, 1989.

Newman, Robert. *Truman and the Hiroshima Cult*. East Lansing: Michigan State University Press, 1995.

Nichols, K. D. *The Road to Trinity: A Personal Account of How America's Nuclear Policies Were Made*. New York: William Morrow & Company, 1987.

Nuclear America: A Historical Biography. Santa Barbara, CA: ABC-Clio Information Service, 1984.

Oberdorfer, Don. *The Two Koreas: A Contemporary History.* Reading, MA: Addison-Wesley, 1997.

Porter, David L. "The Ten Best Secretaries of State and the Five Worst." In William D. Pederson and Ann M. MacLaurin (eds.), *The Rating Game in American Politics: An Interdisciplinary Approach.* New York: Irvington Publishers, 1987.

Prados, John. *The Sky Would Fall: Operation Vulture: The US Bombing Mission in Indochina, 1954.* New York: The Dial Press, 1983.

Quester, George. *Nuclear Diplomacy: The First Twenty-five Years.* 2d ed. New York: Dunellen, 1973.

Qiang Zhai. *The Dragon, the Lion, and the Eagle: Chinese-British-American Relations, 1949–1958.* Kent, OH: Kent State University Press, 1994.

Rearden, Steven, and Samuel R. Williamson Jr. *The Origins of US Nuclear Strategy, 1945–1953.* New York: St. Martin's Press, 1993.

Rearden, Steven, and Kenneth W. Thompson (eds.). *Paul H. Nitze on National Security and Arms Control.* Lanham, MD: University Press of America, 1990.

Rose, John P. *The Evolution of US Army Nuclear Doctrine, 1945–1980.* Boulder, CO: Westview Press, 1980.

Rosenberg, David Alan. "The Origins of Overkill: Nuclear Weapons and American Strategy." In Norman Graebner (ed.), *The National Security: Its Theory and Practice, 1945–1960.* New York: Oxford University Press, 1986.

Ryan, Mark. *Chinese Attitudes Toward Nuclear Weapons: China and the United States During the Korean War.* Armonk, NY: M. E. Sharpe, 1989.

Schaller, Michael. *The United States and China in the Twentieth Century.* New York: Oxford University Press, 1979.

———. *The American Occupation of Japan: Origins of the Cold War in Asia.* New York: Oxford University Press, 1985.

———. *Douglas MacArthur: The Far Eastern General.* New York: Oxford University Press, 1989.

Schelling, Thomas C. *The Strategy of Conflict.* Cambridge, MA: Harvard University Press, 1963.

———. *Arms and Influence.* New Haven, CT: Yale University Press, 1966.

Schlesinger, Arthur M. Jr. *The Imperial Presidency.* Boston: Houghton Mifflin Co., 1973.

Sherwin, Martin. "The Atomic Bomb and the Origins of the Cold War." In Melvyn Leffler and David Painter (eds.), *Origins of the Cold War: An International History.* New York: Routledge, 1994.

Sherwin, Martin J. *A World Destroyed: The Atomic Bomb and the Grand Alliance.* New York: Alfred A. Knopf, 1975.

Shlaim, Avi. *The United States and the Berlin Blockade, 1948–1949: A Study in Crisis Decision-Making.* Berkeley: University of California Press, 1983.

Sigal, Leon V. *Disarming Strangers: Nuclear Diplomacy With North Korea.* Princeton, NJ: Princeton University Press, 1998.

Spurr, Russell. *Enter the Dragon: China's Undeclared War Against the United States in Korea, 1950–51.* New York: New Market Press, 1988.

Stebbins, Richard. *The United States in World Affairs, 1958.* New York: Simon and Schuster, 1959.

Stolper, Thomas E. *China, Taiwan, and the Offshore Islands.* Armonk, NY: M. E. Sharpe, 1985.

Stueck, William. *The Road to Confrontation: American Policy Toward China and Korea, 1947–1950.* Chapel Hill: University of North Carolina Press, 1987.

———. *The Korean War: An International History.* Princeton, NJ: Princeton University Press, 1995.

Takaki, Ronald T. *Hiroshima: Why America Dropped the Atomic Bomb.* Boston: Little, Brown & Co., 1995.

Trachtenberg, Marc. *History and Strategy.* Princeton, NJ: Princeton University Press, 1991.

Tsou, Tang. *America's Failure in China.* Chicago: University of Chicago Press, 1963.

Tucker, Nancy Bernkoff. *Patterns in the Dust: Chinese-American Relations and the Recognition Controversy, 1949–1950.* New York: Columbia University Press, 1983.

Wainstock, Dennis. *The Decision to Drop the Atomic Bomb.* Westport, CT: Praeger, 1996.

Walker, J. Samuel. *Prompt and Utter Destruction: Truman and the Use of Atomic Bombs Against Japan.* Chapel Hill: University of North Carolina Press, 1997.

Westerfield, Bradford. *Foreign Policy and Party Politics: Pearl Harbor to Korea.* New Haven, CT: Yale University Press, 1955.

Whiting, Allen S. *China Crosses the Yalu: The Decision to Enter the Korean War.* New York: The Macmillan Co., 1960.

Young, Kenneth. *Negotiating With the Communist Chinese: The United States Experience, 1953–1967.* New York: McGraw-Hill, 1968.

Zagoria, Donald S. *The Sino-Soviet Conflict, 1956–1961.* Princeton, NJ: Princeton University Press, 1962.

Zhai Qiang. *The Dragon, the Lion, and the Eagle: Chinese-British-American Relations, 1949–1958.* Kent, OH: Kent State University Press, 1994.

Zhang, Shu Guang. *Deterrence and Strategic Culture: Chinese-American Confrontations, 1949–1958.* Ithaca, NY: Cornell University Press, 1992.

———. *Mao's Military Romanticism: China and the Korean War, 1950–1953.* Lawrence: University Press of Kansas, 1995.

Zubok, Vladislav, and Constantine Pleshakov. *Inside the Kremlin's Cold War: From Stalin to Khrushchev.* Cambridge, MA: Harvard University Press, 1996.

Articles

Alperowitz, Gar, and Robert Messer. "Marshall, Truman, and the Decision to Drop the Bomb." *International Security* (Winter 1991/1992).

Bernstein, Barton. "The Perils and Politics of Surrender: Ending the War With Japan and Avoiding the Third Atomic Bomb." *Pacific Historical Review* (February 1977).

———. "A Postwar Myth: 500,000 US Lives Saved." *Bulletin of the Atomic Scientists* (June/July1986).

———. "Crossing the Rubicon: A Missed Opportunity to Stop the H. Bomb." *International Security* (Fall 1989).

———. "Eclipsed by Hiroshima and Nagasaki: Early Thinking About Tactical Nuclear Weapons." *International Security* (Spring 1991).

————. "Seizing the Contested Terrain of Early Nuclear History: Stimson, Conant, and Their Allies Explain the Decision to Use the Atomic Bomb." *Diplomatic History* (Winter 1993).

Blechman, Barry M., and Douglas M. Hart. "The Political Utility of Atomic Weapons." *International Security* (Summer 1982).

Blechman, Barry M., and Robert Powell. "What in the Name of God Is Strategic Superiority?" *Political Science Quarterly* (Winter 1982–1983).

Brands, H. W. "Testing Massive Retaliation: Credibility and Crisis Management in the Taiwan Strait." *International Security* (Spring 1988).

————. "The Age of Vulnerability: Eisenhower and the National Insecurity State." *American Historical Review* (October 1989).

Buhite, Russell D., and William Hamel. "War for Peace: The Question of American Preventive War Against the Soviet Union, 1945–1955." *Diplomatic History* (Summer 1990).

Bundy, McGeorge. "The Bishops and the Bomb." *New York Review of Books* (16 June 1983).

Calingaert, Daniel. "Nuclear Weapons and the Korean War." *Journal of Strategic Studies* (June 1988).

Chang, Gordon, and He Di. "The Absence of War in the US-Chinese Confrontation Over Quemoy and Matsu in 1954–1955: Contingency, Luck, Deterrence?" *American Historical Review* (December 1993).

Christensen, Thomas J. "Threats, Assurances, and the Last Chance for Peace: The Lessons of Mao's Korean War Telegrams." *International Security* (Summer 1992).

————. "A 'Last Chance' for What? Rethinking the Origins of US-PRC Confrontation." *Journal of American-East Asian Relations* (Fall 1995).

Cohen, Warren. "Conversations with Chinese Friends: Zhou Enlai's Associates Reflect on Chinese-American Relations in the Late 1940s and the Korean War." *Diplomatic History* (Summer 1987).

Dingman, Roger. "Atomic Diplomacy During the Korean War." *International Security* (Winter 1988/1989).

Dulles, John Foster. "A Policy for Security and Peace." *Foreign Affairs* (April 1954).

Eliades, George. "Once More unto the Breach: Eisenhower, Dulles, and Public Opinion During the Offshore Islands Crisis of 1958." *Journal of American–East Asian Relations* (Winter 1993).

Evangelista, Matthew. "Stalin's Postwar Army Reappraised." *International Security.* (Winter 1982/1983).

Farrar Hockley, Anthony. "A Reminiscence of the Chinese People's Volunteers in the Korean War." *The China Quarterly* (June 1984).

Foot, Rosemary. "Nuclear Coercion and the Ending of the Korean Conflict," *International Security* (Winter 1988/1989).

————. "Making Known the Unknown War: Policy Analysis of the Korean Conflict in the Last Decade." *Diplomatic History* (Summer 1991).

Freedman, Lawrence. "I Exist; Therefore I Deter." *International Security* (Summer 1988).

Gerson, Joseph. "Nuclear Blackmail." *The Bulletin of the Atomic Scientists* (May 1984).

Gordon, Leonard H. "United States' Opposition to Use of Force in the Taiwan Strait 1954–1962." *Journal of American History* (December 1985).

Hao Yufan and Zhai Zhihai. "China's Decision to Enter the Korean War: History Revisited." *China Quarterly* (March 1990).

He Di. "Paper or Real Tiger: America's Nuclear Deterrence and Mao Zedong's Response." Paper presented at the International Conference on New Evidence on the Cold War in Asia, Hong Kong, 1996.

Heinzig, Dieter. "Stalin, Mao, Kim, and Korean War Origins, 1950: A Russian Documentary Discrepancy." *CWIHP Bulletin* (Winter 1996/1997).

Hunt, Michael. "Korea and Vietnam: State-of-the-Art Surveys of our Asian Wars." *Reviews in American History* (June 1987).

———. "Beijing and the Korean Crisis, June 1950–June 1951." *Political Science Quarterly* (Fall 1992).

Jervis, Robert. "The Political Effects of Nuclear Weapons: A Comment." *International Security* (Fall 1988).

Keefer, Edward C. "President Dwight Eisenhower and the End of the Korean War." *Diplomatic History* (Summer 1986).

Kissinger, Henry. "Force and Diplomacy in the Nuclear Age." *Foreign Affairs* (April 1956).

Kristensen, Hans M. "Nuclear Futures: Proliferation of Weapons of Mass Destruction and US Nuclear Strategy." BASIC Research Report 98.2. British American Security Information Council (March 1998).

Li Xiaobing. "The Second Taiwan Straits Crisis Revisited." Paper presented at the International Conference on New Evidence on the Cold War in Asia, Hong Kong, 1996.

Li Xiaobing, Chen Jian, and David Wilson. "Mao Zedong's Handling of the Taiwan Straits Crisis of 1958: Chinese Recollections and Documents." *CWIHP Bulletin* (Winter 1995/1996).

Mansourov, Alexandre Y. "Stalin, Mao, Kim, and China's Decision to Enter the Korean War, September 16–October 15, 1950: New Evidence From the Russian Archives." *CWIHP Bulletin* (Winter 1995/1996).

Mazaar, Michael. "Nuclear Weapons After the Cold War." *Washington Quarterly* (Summer 1992).

Mueller, John. "The Essential Irrelevance of Nuclear Weapons." *International Security* (Fall 1988).

Rabe, Stephen G. "Eisenhower Revisionism: A Decade of Scholarship." *Diplomatic History* (Winter 1993).

Rosenberg, David Alan. "American Atomic Strategy and the Hydrogen Bomb Decision." *Journal of American History* (June 1979).

———. "US Nuclear Stockpile, 1945 to 1950." *The Bulletin of the Atomic Scientists* (May 1982).

———. "Reality and Responsibility: Power and Process in the Making of United States Nuclear Strategy, 1945–68." *Journal of Strategic Studies* (March 1986).

Shen Zhihua. "The Discrepancy Between the Russian and Chinese Versions of Mao's 2 October 1950 Message to Stalin on Chinese Entry into the Korean War: A Chinese Scholar's Reply." *CWIHP Bulletin* (Winter 1996/1997).

Walker, J. Samuel. "The Decision to Drop the Bomb: A Historiographical Update." *Diplomatic History* (Winter 1990).

Weathersby, Kathryn. "New Findings on the Korean War." *Bulletin of the Cold War International History Project* (Fall 1993).

Wells, Samuel F. Jr. "The Origins of Massive Retaliation." *Political Science Quarterly* (Spring 1981).

Whiting, Allen. "Quemoy 1958: Mao's Miscalculations." *China Quarterly* (June 1975).

Xiao Jingguang. "Chinese Generals Recall the Korean War." *Chinese Historians* (Spring and Fall 1994)

Ph.D. Dissertations

Jia Q. "Unmaterialized Rapprochement: Sino-American Relations in the Mid-1950s." Cornell University, 1988.

Su Ge. "The Horrible Dilemma-the Making of the US-Taiwan Mutual Defense Treaty, 1948–1955." Brigham Young University, 1987.

Magazines/Newspapers

Life
Newsweek
New York Times
Time
Washington Post

Index

About the Author

APPU K. SOMAN is currently affiliated with the Institute for Defense and Disarmament Studies. In addition to the history of American foreign relations, his research interests are international security, nuclear history, and arms control affairs.

ISBN 0-275-96623-2

9 780275 966232

EAN

90000>

HARDCOVER BAR CODE